Joana Julia Greswell

Grammatical Analysis of the Hebrew Psalter

Joana Julia Greswell
Grammatical Analysis of the Hebrew Psalter
ISBN/EAN: 9783744661270
Printed in Europe, USA, Canada, Australia, Japan
Cover: Foto ©Thomas Meinert / pixelio.de

More available books at **www.hansebooks.com**

GRAMMATICAL ANALYSIS

OF THE

HEBREW PSALTER.

BY

JOANA JULIA GRESWELL.

'In all his works he praised the Holy One most high with words of glory; with his whole heart he sung songs, and loved Him that made him.'—Ecclus. xlvii. 8.
'Whatsoever thy hand findeth to do, do it with thy might.'—Eccles. ix. 10.

OXFORD,
AND 377, STRAND, LONDON;
JAMES PARKER AND CO.
MDCCCLXXIII.

OXFORD:
By T. Combe, M.A., E. B. Gardner, E. Pickard Hall, and J. H. Stacy,
PRINTERS TO THE UNIVERSITY.

ADVERTISEMENT.

I fear that it will be thought presumptuous in a Lady to undertake to write a work, the professed intention of which is to afford assistance to Beginners in the Study of Hebrew. It is, therefore, in the way of self-defence against any such charge of presumption, that I am induced to prefix to my volume the accompanying Letters, which have been received by my Father, the Rev. Richard Greswell, from two very distinguished Hebrew Scholars, who have been pleased to express their opinion concerning the probable usefulness of my 'Grammatical Analysis of the Hebrew Psalter.'

JOANA JULIA GRESWELL.

Copy of a Letter addressed by the Very Reverend the Dean of Canterbury to the Rev. Richard Greswell.

DEANERY, CANTERBURY,
April 16th, 1873.

MY DEAR SIR,

WHEN I saw you in Oxford I told you that I had been favourably impressed by Miss Greswell's work, but had not had time to examine it very carefully.

I have since done so, and think that she has produced a most useful work, which must have cost her great labour, and which seems to me executed everywhere with great carefulness and accuracy.

It will prove a great boon to Students preparing for the Divinity Schools at Oxford, and generally to those who wish to learn Hebrew.

Usually one does not much approve of works intended to save trouble; but it is different in Hebrew, which generally is begun late in life, and for the sake of the knowledge itself, and not of the habits gained in acquiring it.

I think that our Students and the younger Clergy generally have reason to be very grateful to Miss Greswell for producing a work which will make the acquisition of Hebrew so much more easy; and I trust that it may aid in inducing a larger proportion of them to study that language in which so large a part of the Scriptures is written.

Believe me to be,
My dear Sir,
Very faithfully yours,
R. PAYNE SMITH.

REV. RICHARD GRESWELL.

Copy of a Letter received by the Rev. Richard Greswell from the Rev. Dr. Perowne, Canon of Llandaff.

TRINITY COLLEGE, CAMBRIDGE,
29th April, 1873.

MY DEAR MR. GRESWELL,

I AM very glad that your Daughter has printed her 'Grammatical Analysis of the Hebrew Psalter.'

After an examination of the work, I can bear testimony to the conscientious care and pains which have been bestowed upon it, and the thorough way in which it has been done.

It seems to me likely to be useful to the class of persons for whom it is intended—Beginners in Hebrew—who are often perplexed and discouraged for want of that kind of assistance which Miss Greswell's book will give them.

There are, I believe, very few books of the kind. Bythner's *Lyra* is antiquated; Bishop Ollivant's *Analysis of the History of Joseph* is out of print; so, too, is Robertson's *Clavis Pentateuchi;* and yet I know of nothing to take the place of these works.

I sincerely hope that Miss Greswell will meet with all the encouragement which she deserves in her praiseworthy efforts to promote and extend the Study of Hebrew in our Colleges.

Theology in England will grow stronger and richer in proportion as the Old Testament, as well as the New, is studied in the Original.

Believe me,
Yours very truly,
J. J. STEWART PEROWNE.

REV. RICHARD GRESWELL.

PREFACE.

THE idea of the present elementary work is taken from the Hebrew Reading Lessons, (consisting of the first four chapters of the Book of Genesis, and the eighth chapter of Proverbs, with a Grammatical Praxis, and an Interlineary Translation,) by S. P. Tregelles, LL.D.

Its object is to give an exact grammatical analysis of every word in the Book of Psalms, in accordance with the principles laid down in the most recent Hebrew grammars. To this are added (as far as I have been able to discover them) the cognate words in various languages, i.e. Sanskrit, Greek, Latin, German, Anglo-Saxon, and English. I have in several places noticed the various renderings of the LXX., Vulgate, Chaldee, Arabic, Syriac, and Æthiopic Versions, taken principally from Rogers' Work on the Psalms.

At the commencement of each Psalm is a short introduction, containing a very brief statement of its subject and of the circumstances under which it was probably composed. In many of the later Psalms I have noticed the Chaldaisms which point to a somewhat late era in the history of the Chosen People.

I have also been careful to mention anything which has appeared to me particularly interesting in some of the Psalms, as, for instance, that Psalms xviii and lxviii contain an unusually large number of ἅπαξ λεγόμενα; that the word *sabachthani*, used by Our Blessed Lord at His Crucifixion, is not *the actual* word which occurs in Ps. xxii, but the equivalent of it in the Aramæan dialect then in use among the Jews; that Ps. li contains a verse of only *seven* words in the original, but which cannot be rendered in English by less than *one and twenty* or *two and twenty* words, &c., &c.

The works which have been most useful to me, and from which I have most largely borrowed, are those of Perowne[1], Phillips[2], Jebb[3], Bishop Horsley[4], Kay[5], Rogers[6], Coleman[7], Hengstenberg[8], Delitzsch[9], and Bythner[10]. The Lexicons

---

[1] The Book of Psalms; with Introductions and Notes explanatory and critical, by J. J. Stewart Perowne, B. D. 1871.

[2] A Commentary on the Psalms, by George Phillips, D. D., President of Queen's College, Cambridge. 1872.

[3] A Literal Translation of the Book of Psalms, by the Rev. John Jebb, A. M. 1846.

[4] The Book of Psalms; translated from the Hebrew; with Notes explanatory and critical, by Bishop Horsley. 1816.

[5] The Psalms translated from the Hebrew, with Notes chiefly exegetical, by William Kay, D. D. 1871.

[6] The Book of Psalms in Hebrew, by J. Rogers, M. A., Canon Residentiary of Exeter Cathedral. 1848.

[7] Revision of the Authorized English Versions of the Book of Psalms, by the Rev. John Noble Coleman, M. A. 1863.

[8] Commentary on the Psalms, by E. W. Hengstenberg, Professor of Theology in Berlin. (English Translation, Clark's Series, 1846.)

[9] Biblical Commentary on the Psalms, by Franz Delitzsch, D. D. (English Translation, Clark's Series, 1871.)

[10] Bythneri Lyra Prophetica. Londini, MDCL.

I have consulted are those of Gesenius and Fürst; I may, however, remark that I have usually given the preference to the former in explaining the derivation of a word.

At the end of the volume is an Index of all the words contained in the Hebrew Psalter, with a reference to the Psalm and verse in which each occurs for the first time, and where it will be found analysed; but no further explanation of any word is given unless there should be something peculiar in the form. It is to be observed that the verses are numbered according to the reckoning in the Hebrew Bible, which differs in most of the Psalms from that of the English and other Versions.

I am bound, in conclusion, to express my sense of the great obligations I am under to the Rev. Dr. Perowne, Canon of Llandaff, for the very valuable assistance which, in various ways, he has been kind enough to afford to me.

J. J. G.

39, St. Giles's, Oxford,
    April, 1873.

INTRODUCTORY REMARKS.

The whole of the Psalter is generally divided into Five Books: the First containing Pss. i–xli; the Second, xlii–lxxii; the Third, lxxiii–lxxxix; the Fourth, xc–cvi; the Fifth, cvii–cl.

There are seventy-three Psalms which bear the Inscription לְדָוִד, viz. thirty-seven in Book I, which consists entirely of Psalms attributed to David, with the exception of four, which in the Hebrew text are without any name, viz. Pss. i, ii, x, and xxxiii, although in the LXX. Ps. xxxiii is called a Psalm of David; eighteen in Book II, li–lxv, lxviii–lxx; only one in Book III, Ps. lxxxvi; two in Book IV, ci, ciii; and fifteen in Book V, cviii–cx, cxxii, cxxiv, cxxxi, cxxxiii, cxxxviii–cxlv.

The Asaphic and Korahitic Psalms are found exclusively in the Second and Third Books. The name of Asaph is connected with altogether twelve Psalms, (l, lxxiii–lxxxiii,) which were composed either by David's Chief Musician himself, or else belong to later times, and proceeded from the family of singers which had Asaph for its founder.

The name of the sons of Korah is attached to twelve Psalms, xlii–xlix, lxxxiv, lxxxv, lxxxvii, and lxxxviii. Of these, six belong probably to the time of David and Solomon; xliv was composed on occasion of the invasion of the Edomites; xlii, xliii, and lxxxiv at the period of Absalom's rebellion; xlix is without any historical reference, though the general character of the theme shews it to belong to an early period; xlv belongs to the age of Solomon. The other six are of later date; xlvii and xlviii perhaps belong to the time of Jehoshaphat; xlvi and lxxxvii appear, from the lively expressions of joy contained in them, to have been called forth by the events of Hezekiah's (or possibly of Jehoshaphat's) reign; lxxxv and lxxxviii are undetermined, the former was probably written *after* and the latter *during* the time of the Babylonish Captivity, although in the latter half of the Inscription it is ascribed to Heman the Ezrahite. In the genealogies (1 Chron. vi. 16 sqq.) the family of Heman, who is named along with Asaph and Ethan as a chief musician to David, is traced back to Korah.

Ethan the Ezrahite is named as the author of Ps. lxxxix.

Ps. xc is attributed to Moses, and Pss. lxxii and cxxvii to Solomon, unless we are to consider them as written by David *for* or *concerning* Solomon.

There are thirty-four Psalms which have no Titles prefixed to them in the Hebrew. The LXX. translators have added Titles to twenty-one of these thirty-four Psalms: of the remaining hundred and sixteen Psalms, the Titles of twenty-two and upwards are added to or altered in the LXX. Version.

The LXX. and the translations which follow it—in particular the Vulgate—connect together Pss. ix and x, then cxiv and cxv, but separate Ps. xcvi. 1–9 from ver. 10–19, and Ps. cxlvii. 1–11 from ver. 12–20; the last division especially was made on purpose to secure the number one hundred and fifty, which must therefore, at the time of the LXX., have been regarded as indispensable. In more than forty ancient versions Pss. xlii and xliii are joined together into one.

The ancient Syriac Version combines Pss. cxiv and cxv as one, but reckons a hundred and fifty by dividing Ps. cxlvii.

The Second Book of the Psalms differs from the First by one distinguishing characteristic—its use of the Divine Name. In the First, God is spoken of and addressed as Jehovah; in the Second as Elohim, the latter name being that which, in our Version, is rendered God.

According to the computation given by Delitzsch, the word יהוה occurs 272 times in the First Book, and אלהים but 15 times; whereas in the Second, אלהים occurs 164 times, and יהוה only 30 times. In the whole of the Fourth Book the word אלהים does not occur once, in the Fifth only 7 times; while יהוה, according to the reckoning of Delitzsch, occurs 236 times. In all these seven cases אלהים is found only in the Psalms of David; in Ps. cviii six times, and once in Ps. cxliv.

LIST OF ABBREVIATIONS.

abs. = absolute.
acc. = accusative.
act. = active.
adj. = adjective.
adv. = adverb.
Æth. = Æthiopic.
aff. = affix.
ant. = antecedent.
apoc. = apocopated.
Arab. = Arabic.
Aram. = Aramaic.
Armen. = Armenian.
art. = article.
A. Sax. = Anglo-Saxon.
causat. = causatively.
Chal. = Chaldee.
charact. = characteristic.
collect. = collective.
com. = common.
comp. = compare.
conj. = conjunction.
constr. = construct state.
contr. = contracted.
convers. = conversive.
cop. = copulative.
demonstr. = demonstrative.
denom. = denominative.
dimin. = diminutive.
Eng. = English.
epenth. = epenthetic.
epic. = epicene.
f. or fem. = feminine.
fig. = figuratively.
gen. = gender.
Ger. = German.
Goth. = Gothic.
Gr. = Greek.
Heb. = Hebrew.
Hiph. = Hiphil.
Hithp. = Hithpael.
Hithpo. = Hithpoel.
Hoph. = Hophal.
imp. = imperative.
indecl. = indeclinable.
indef. = indefinite.
inf. = infinitive.
interrog. = interrogative.
intrans. = intransitive.

irreg. = irregular.
Ital. = Italian.
Lat. = Latin.
m. or masc. = masculine.
metaph. = metaphorically.
MS. = manuscript.
n. = noun.
neut. = neuter.
Niph. = Niphal.
num. = numeral.
obs. = obsolete.
ord. = ordinal.
parag. = paragogic.
part. = participle.
pass. = passive.
penult. = penultimate.
perf. = perfect.
Pers. = Persian.
Pi. = Piel.
Pilp. = Pilpel.
pl. or plur. = plural.
poet. = poetical.
pr. = prefix.
prep. = preposition.
pres. = present.
pret. = preterite.
prob. = probably.
pron. = pronoun.
prop. = proper, properly.
prosth. = prosthetic.
Ps. = Psalm.
Pu. = Pual.
quadril. = quadriliteral.
R. = root.
rad. = radical.
reflex. = reflexive.
relat. = relative.
s. or sing. = singular.
Sans. = Sanskrit.
sc. = scilicet.
Slav. = Slavonic.
subst. = substantive.
suff. = suffix.
Syr. = Syriac.
trans. = transitive.
v. or ver. = verse.
verb. = verbal.
Vulg. = Vulgate.

GRAMMATICAL ANALYSIS

OF THE

HEBREW PSALTER.

BOOK I, Psalms I—XVI.

PSALM I.

This Psalm, which forms an introduction to the whole series, shews us two characters, *the righteous*, who strives to follow God's Law, and *the wicked*, who rejects it.

Verse 1. אַשְׁרֵי Blessed (is), lit. the happiness of, pl. constr. of the unused sing. אֶשֶׁר subst. m.; the word occurs twenty-six times in the Psalms, and once with the suff. 2 m. s., Ps. cxxviii. 2. R. אָשַׁר to be straight, to go straight on, and generally to go; Pi. to pronounce happy, to bless.

הָאִישׁ the-man, subst. m. irreg. with the art.; א not admitting Dagesh, (ַ) of the art. is lengthened into (ָ); pl. אִישִׁים only found three times, Ps. cxli. 4, Prov. viii. 4, and Is. liii. 3, but instead of it is commonly used אֲנָשִׁים from the obsolete sing. אֱנָשׁ. The same word is also used of things without life.

אֲשֶׁר that, relat. pron. indecl., sometimes used as a conj., that, because that, when, if.

לֹא not, adv. of negation.

הָלַךְ walketh, Kal 3 m. s. pret.; Hiph. to cause to walk, to lead; Hithp. to walk up and down.

בַּעֲצַת in-(the)counsel-of, constr. of עֵצָה subst. f. with prefixed prep. בּ (excluding the art.), originally denoting tarryance in a place, hence used as a prep., in, at, by, near. The בּ is pointed with (ַ) because the following letter has the homogeneous compound Sh'va. R. יָעַץ to advise, to take counsel, to resolve; Niph. and Hithp. to take counsel together, to deliberate. In Hebrew, as well as in Welsh, the noun which serves as genitive to limit the other remains unchanged, and is only uttered in more close connection with the preceding noun. Comp. the Welsh '*Gair Duw*,' Word of God, lit. Word God, and the Heb. דְּבַר אֱלֹהִים, without any change in either noun.

רְשָׁעִים (the)ungodly, pl. of רָשָׁע verb. adj. m. from רָשַׁע, prop. to make a noise or tumult, to be wicked; Hiph. to pronounce wicked, to condemn.

וּבְדֶרֶךְ and-in-(the)way-of, subst. com. gen. (pl. דְּרָכִים, constr. דַּרְכֵי), with pr. בּ, and ו cop. pointed thus because the following letter is a labial. R. דָּרַךְ to tread; Hiph. to cause to tread=to lead.

חַטָּאִים sinners, pl. of חַטָּא verb. n. m. from חָטָא, prop. to miss, to err from the mark, to fall, to sin; Pi. to bear the blame of sin, to expiate, to cleanse (by a sacred ceremony); Hiph. to lead into sin=to seduce.

עָמָד standeth, Kal 3 m. s. pret., to stand, to endure; Hiph. to cause to stand=to set, to establish. The pause lengthens (ַ) in the last syllable into (ָ).

וּבְמוֹשַׁב and-in-(the)seat-of, verb. n. m. from יָשַׁב to dwell, with ו cop. and pr. בּ.

לֵצִים (the)scornful, Kal pres. part. m. pl. from לִיץ, prop. to stammer, to speak barbarously, i.e. in a foreign tongue; also to mock, to scorn; Hiph. to act as interpreter; Hithp. to act foolishly. This word occurs nowhere else in the whole Psalter, but is frequently found in the earlier chapters of the Book of Proverbs.

יָשַׁב sitteth, Kal 3 m. s. pret.

PSALM I. vv. 2, 3.

Verse 2. כִּי אִם But, כִּי conj.; אִם a demonstr. interrog. and conditional particle; these two together=but, sometimes that since, unless, except.

בְּתוֹרַת in-(the) Law-of, constr. of תּוֹרָה subst. f. with pr. בְּ. R. יָרָה to throw, to cast (an arrow), to shoot; Hiph. to sprinkle, to water, to throw out the hand; hence to shew, to indicate, to instruct, to teach.

יְהֹוָה the-Lord, subst. m., prop. name of the supreme God amongst the Hebrews. The later Hebrews regarded it as so very holy that it might not even be pronounced; they therefore substituted for it the word אֲדֹנָי, and wrote it with the same vowels. R. הָיָה or הָוָה to be, to exist, hence implying self-existence; this name is not applied in any sense to a created being.

חֶפְצוֹ his-delight, verb. n. m. with suff. 3 m. s. from חָפֵץ to bend, to incline; intrans. and fig. to be favourably inclined to any one, to take delight in him.

יֶהְגֶּה doth-he-meditate, Kal 3 m. s. fut. from הָגָה to murmur, to meditate, poetically to speak. Future used to express repeated action. Instead of *meditating*, Luther has *speaking*, redet.

יוֹמָם day, prop. daily, adv. from יוֹם subst. com. gen. (rarely f.), dual יוֹמַיִם, pl. יָמִים (as if from the sing. יָם), constr. יְמֵי, twice יְמוֹת Deut. xxxii. 7 and Ps. xc. 15. R. prob. יוֹם, unused in Heb., apparently signifying heat.

וָלַיְלָה and-night, subst. m. (abs. form לַיִל), with וְ cop. (pointed with (ָ) instead of (ְ) because of the accent on the next syllable), and ה parag., which may be distinguished from the f. termination הָ by the latter taking the accent.

Verse 3. וְהָיָה And-he-shall-be, Kal 3 m. s. pret. with וְ convers. giving it the force of the aorist=so he is.

כְּעֵץ like-a-tree, subst. m. (with כְּ as, according to, a prefix prep.), a tree, wood. Comp. Gr. ὄζος, a branch; ὀστέον, a bone, (Sans. *asthi*); Lat. *hasta*, a spear. R. עָצָה to be firm.

שָׁתוּל planted, Kal pass. part. m. s. from שָׁתַל a poetic word.

עַל by, prop. a subst. height, but used as a prep.; pl. constr. עֲלֵי, used only in poetry. R. עָלָה to be high, to ascend, metaph.

to increase; Niph. to be exalted; Hiph. to cause to ascend=to bring up, specially to put a sacrifice on the altar; Hithp. to pour oneself forth (in wrath), i.e. to pour forth wrath, to be wroth.

פַּלְגֵי־ rivers-of, pl. constr. of פֶּלֶג subst. m. R. פָּלַג to cleave, to divide, not used in Kal. Comp. Gr. πέλαγος; Lat. *pelagus*.

מָיִם water, subst. m. pl. (constr. מֵי and less frequently מֵימֵי), from the unused sing. מַי. (Pl. forms are often used in Heb. in the names of objects in which *extension* or *parts* form a prominent idea.) R. מוֹא, unused in Heb., to flow. (ָ) of the penult. is lengthened into (ָ) because of the pause accent.

פִּרְיוֹ his-fruit, subst. m. with suff. 3 m. s. R. פָּרָה to bear, to be fruitful. Comp. Sans. *bhṛi*, to bear; Gr. φέρω; Lat. *fero*, *porto*; Goth. *baíran*; Old Ger. baren; Eng. *to bear*.

יִתֵּן bringeth-forth, Kal 3 m. s. fut. from נָתַן.

בְּעִתּוֹ in-his-season, subst. com. gen. with pr. ב i. 1 and suff. 3 m. s.; pl. עִתִּים and עִתּוֹת. R. prob. עָדָה to pass by; Hiph. to remove, to make to pass over, i.e. to put on (ornaments); Ger. überziehen, anziehen, to adorn oneself with anything.

וְעָלֵהוּ his-leaf-also, subst. m. with suff. 3 m. s. R. עָלָה to go up, in the sense of growing and sprouting forth.

יִבּוֹל shall-wither, or fade, Kal 3 m. s. fut. from נָבֵל to wither, to be exhausted, also to act foolishly, wickedly; Pi. to esteem lightly, to reject.

וְכֹל אֲשֶׁר־ and-whatsoever, lit. and all that, כֹּל prop. a subst. m. the whole, totality. R. כָּלַל to complete, to perfect, found only in Ezek. xxvii. 4, 11; אֲשֶׁר Ps. i. 1.

יַצְלִיחַ shall-prosper, Hiph. 3 m. s. fut. from צָלַח to go over or through, to succeed; Hiph. to make successful, to prosper.

Verse 4. כֵן so, adv. R. כּוּן, unused in Kal, to stand upright; Pilel and Hiph. to set up, to establish, to appoint, to make ready.

הָרְשָׁעִים the-ungodly, i. 1, with the art. pointed with (ָ) instead of (ַ) because ר cannot take Dagesh.

כַּמֹּץ like-chaff, subst. m. (only found in the sing.) with pr. כ i. 3. R. מוּץ to press, to separate.

תִּדְּפֶנּוּ driveth-away, Kal 3 m. s. fut. with suff. 3 m. s. from נָדַף.

רוּחַ (the) wind, subst. com. gen. (generally f.); pl. רוּחוֹת. R. רוּחַ, unused in Kal, to breathe, to blow; Hiph. to smell. Comp. Ger. riechen.

Verse 5. עַל־כֵּן Therefore, i. 3 and i. 4; these two together = therefore.

יָקֻמוּ shall-stand, Kal 3 m. pl. fut. from קוּם to arise, to stand up, (of a purchase) to be confirmed; Pi. to make valid, to confirm; Hiph. to cause to arise, to raise up, to establish. The Chal. has 'shall not be acquitted.'

בַּמִּשְׁפָּט in-(the) judgment, verb. n. m. with pr. בּ i. 1, from שָׁפַט to judge. The Chal. has 'in the Great Day.'

בַּעֲדַת in-(the) congregation-of, constr. of עֵדָה subst. f. with pr. בּ i. 1. R. יָעַד to fix, to appoint (a time or place); Niph. to come together at the appointed time or place.

צַדִּיקִים (the) righteous, pl. of צַדִּיק verb. adj. m. from צָדַק to be right, straight, hence to be upright, righteous; Pi. and Hiph. to justify; Hithp. to purge oneself from suspicion.

Verse 6. יוֹדֵעַ knoweth, Kal pres. part. m. s. from יָדַע to know, to perceive (obviously corresponding to the Gr. οἶδα, to see; Sans. *vid;* Lat. *video;* Goth. *vitan*); Hiph. to make to know, to shew, to teach. In Scripture, *to know* often signifies to regard with interest, approbation, or affection.

תֹּאבֵד shall-perish, Kal 3 f. s. fut. from אָבַד to fail, to perish; Pi. and Hiph. to destroy.

PSALM II.

This Psalm, which is of the nature of a prophecy, is in some MSS. found joined to Ps. i. It describes the Kingdom of Christ, and concludes with an exhortation to the kings of the earth to accept it; it is one of the appointed Psalms for Easter Day.

Although not entitled a Psalm of David, we are assured in Acts iv. 25 that it is his.

Verse 1. לָמָּה Why, pron. interrog. with pr. לְ, prob. an abbreviation of אֶל, prop. a subst. indicative of motion, direction to any place, used as a prep.

רָגְשׁוּ do-rage, or tumultuously assemble, Kal 3 pl. pret. from רָגַשׁ to rage, also to come together in heaps or masses. This word occurs in Chal., Dan. vi. 7, in the sense of consulting or taking counsel.

גוֹיִם (the) heathen, pl. of גוֹי subst. m., a people, nation in the widest sense, especially foreign nations, nations not Hebrew. R. perhaps גָּוָה, which appears to have had the sense of flowing together.

וּלְאֻמִּים and-(the) people, pl. of לְאֹם subst. m. (with ו cop. i. 1), from the unused root לָאַם, prob. meaning to join together.

רִיק a-vain-thing, verb. adj. m. used abstractly or as a neut., an empty or vain thing, vanity. R. רִיק or רוּק, not used in Kal, to empty, to pour out, to draw or make bare (the sword). Comp. Lat. *ructo, eructo,* and Gr. ἐρεύγομαι, used of rivers emptying themselves. This and the next verse are quoted Acts iv. 25, 26.

Verse 2. יִתְיַצְּבוּ set-themselves, Hithp. 3 m. pl. fut. from יָצַב (i. q. נָצַב), not used in Kal, to place; Hithp. to place or present oneself. From נָצַב are formed the conjugations Niph. and Hiph., from יָצַב the conjugation Hithp.

מַלְכֵי־ (the) kings-of, constr. of מְלָכִים, pl. of מֶלֶךְ verb. n. m. from מָלַךְ to reign.

אֶרֶץ (the) earth, subst. com. gen., always f. except in a few cases where it stands for *the inhabitants* of the earth. This word without the art. is אֶרֶץ, but when definite it takes the form הָאָרֶץ. Comp. Sans. *dharâ;* Welsh *daear;* Lat. *terra;* Goth. *airtha;* Ger. Erde; Eng. *earth.*

וְרוֹזְנִים and-(the) rulers, Kal pres. part. m. pl. from רָזַן to be weighty, to be respected or honoured, found only in the part. pl.

נוֹסְדוּ־ take-counsel, Niph. 3 pl. pret. from יָסַד to found, to establish; Niph. to take counsel, to consult, to plot. Comp. Sans. *sad*, to sit; Lat. *sedere;* Goth. *satjan*, to place; A. Sax. *sattan;* Eng. *to sit;* Ger. ſitzen.

יַחַד together, subst. m., lit. union, hence as an adv. together. R. יָחַד to be united.

מְשִׁיחוֹ His-Anointed, verb. adj. pass. with suff. 3 m. s. from מָשַׁח, prop. to stroke, to draw the hand over (anything), to spread over, to anoint.

Verse 3. נְנַתְּקָה Let-us-break-asunder, Pi. 1 pl. fut. with ה parag. from נָתַק to tear away; Hiph. to separate. To connect this verse with the preceding, the word לֵאמֹר must be understood.

אֶת־—used to mark the definite object, prop. a demonstr. pron. self, this same, but by degrees the word lost much of its primitive force, so that as set before nouns and pronouns already definite, it scarcely increases the demonstr. power. אֶת not אֵת because of the following Makkeph.

מוֹסְרוֹתֵימוֹ their-bands, subst. m. pl. from the unused sing. מוֹסֵר with (poetic) suff. 3 m. pl. R. אָסַר to bind. The ים. form of the pl. is found only in Ps. cxvi. 16, Is. xxviii. 22 and lii. 2.

וְנַשְׁלִיכָה and-cast-away, Hiph. 1 pl. fut. with ה parag. from שָׁלַךְ, not used in Kal.

מִמֶּנּוּ from-us, suff. 1 pl. with pr. מ, contracted from מִן prop. construct state of the noun מֵן, a part of anything, hence used as *a partitive* (sometimes, as in Job xi. 15, Gen. xxvii. 1, 39, Ps. lxxxiii. 5, &c., as *a privative*) prep., denoting a part taken out of a whole. R. מָנַן, unused in Heb., to divide, to allot. Comp. Sans. *man*, to reckon, to think. The same form may also be 3 m. s.

עֲבֹתֵימוֹ their-cords, pl. of עֲבֹת verb. n. com. gen. (generally m.), with (poetic) suff. 3 m. pl. from עָבַת to be twisted or woven, not used in Kal; Pi. to perplex, to pervert.

Verse 4. בַּשָּׁמַיִם in-(the) heavens, subst. m. dual or pl. with pr. ב i. 1; constr. שְׁמֵי from the unused sing. שָׁמַי; see i. 3. The word occurs only once with the art., Ps. xxxvi. 6. R. שָׁמָה, unused in Heb., to be high.

יִשְׂחָק shall-laugh, Kal 3 m. s. fut. from שָׂחַק i. q. צָחַק but more frequent.

אֲדֹנָי the-Lord, subst. m. for אֲדֹנִים, pl. excellentiae, s. אָדוֹן. R. prob. דּוּן to judge, which idea in the Eastern languages is closely connected with that of ruling. The word אֲדֹנָי with the prefixes בּ, לְ, and וּ rejects the (ֲ) and becomes לַאדֹנָי, בַּאדֹנָי, and וַאדֹנָי.

יִלְעַג־ shall-have-in-derision, Kal 3 m. s. fut. from לָעַג, prop. to stammer, to speak in a foreign or barbarous tongue, to deride.

לָמוֹ them, poetic form for לָהֶם, suff. 3 m. pl. with pr. לְ ii. 1, pointed with (ָ) instead of (ֶ) because of the accent on the next syllable.

Verse 5. אָז Then, adv. of time, lit. a subst., time, from the unused root אָזָה, prob. meaning to pass by or away.

יְדַבֵּר shall-He-speak, Pi. 3 m. s. fut. from דָּבַר to put in order, arrange, connect, hence to connect words, to speak, also to lead, to guide, specially to lead flocks or herds to pasture, in Kal found only in the part. act. דֹּבֵר, pass. דָּבָר, and inf. with suff. דָּבְרְךָ; Pi. to speak, sometimes to destroy; Hiph. to subdue.

אֲלֵימוֹ unto-them, poetic form for אֲלֵיהֶם, prep. אֶל ii. 1, with suff. 3 m. pl. The Syr. seems to read עליון for אלימו 'Then shall *the Highest* speak,' &c.

בְאַפּוֹ in-His-wrath, subst. m. with pr. בּ i. 1 and suff. 3 m. s.; abs. form אַף the nose (also sometimes signifying anger), contraction of אֲנַף, dual אַפַּיִם. R. אָנַף to breathe, also to be angry.

וּבַחֲרוֹנוֹ and-in-His-sore-displeasure, subst. m. (with וּ cop., pr. בּ, and suff. 3 m. s.), heat, burning anger, only found in the pl. in Ps. lxxxviii. 17. R. חָרָה to burn, to be kindled, spoken only of anger.

יְבַהֲלֵמוֹ vex-them, or trouble them, Pi. 3 m. s. fut. with (poetic) suff. 3 m. pl. from בָּהַל, not used in Kal, prop. to tremble; Niph. to be confounded, to perish suddenly; Pi. and Hiph. to terrify.

PSALM II. vv. 6, 7.

Verse 6. וַאֲנִי Yet-I, pron. 1 s. (i. q. אָנֹכִי) emphat., with ו cop. pointed with (ָ) because of the (ֲ) which follows.

נָסַכְתִּי have-set, or anointed or constituted, Kal 1 s. pret. from נָסַךְ to pour out (libations), also to anoint.

צִיּוֹן Zion, the proper name of a part of Jerusalem, consisting of the more elevated southernmost mountain and the upper part of the city. In the Prophets and Poets (as here) it is often used for Jerusalem itself.

הַר־ hill-of, subst. m. Comp. Gr. ὄρος; Slav. *gora*.

קָדְשִׁי my-holy, lit. mount of my holiness, or my sanctuary, subst. m. with suff. 1 s. R. קָדַשׁ to be sacred; Pi. to declare holy, to sanctify; Hithp. to purify oneself. The second of two nouns in regimen very often performs the office of an adj. The LXX., followed by the Vulg. and Arab., reads 'But I have been constituted King by Him upon Zion His holy mountain.' The Chal. has 'I have magnified my King, and have appointed Him on' &c.

Verse 7. אֲסַפְּרָה I-will-declare, (a change of speakers here takes place), Pi. 1 s. fut. with ה parag. from סָפַר, prop. to scratch, to scrape, specially to scribble letters on stone, hence to write, also to number, in Kal found generally in the part. סֹפֵר a scribe; Pi. to narrate, to recount, to celebrate. Comp. Eng. *cypher*.

חֹק (the) decree, subst. m., prop. that which is established or definite, an appointed law, a statute; pl. חֻקִּים. R. חָקַק to engrave, to establish, to decree. For אֶל־חֹק Bp. Horsley would read אֵל חַק and understand אֲשֶׁר as the acc. after the v. חַק = 'I will declare what God has decreed.' Bishops Hare and Lowth propose to read אֶת for אֶל.

אָמַר hath-said, Kal 3 m. s. pret.; the primary meaning of the word is to bear forth; hence to bring to light, to say; Hithp. to boast oneself, only found in Ps. xciv. 4.

בְּנִי my-Son, subst. m. with suff. 1 s.; pl. בָּנִים. R. בָּנָה to build.

אַתָּה Thou (art), pron. 2 m. s. Comp. Sans. *tvam*; Pers. *tu*;

Gr. τύ, σύ; Lat. *tu;* Goth. *thu;* Germ., Dan., and Swed. Du; and Eng. *thou.*

יְלִדְתִּיךָ have-begotten-Thee, for יְלִדְתִּיךָ Kal 1 s. pret. from יָלַד with suff. 2 m. s.

Verse 8. שְׁאַל Ask, Kal 2 m. s. imp. from שָׁאַל to ask, to demand, to borrow; Hiph. to lend.

נַחֲלָתֶךָ (for)Thine-inheritance, verb. n. f. with suff. 2 m. s. from נָחַל to inherit.

וַאֲחֻזָּתְךָ and-(for)Thy-possession, subst. f. with ו cop. ii. 6 and suff. 2 m. s.; abs. form אֲחֻזָּה. R. אָחַז to seize, to hold; Niph. to make oneself possessor of anything.

אַפְסֵי (the)uttermost-parts-of, pl. constr. of אֶפֶס verb. n. m. from אָפַס to fail, have an end, only found in the 3 pret.

אָרֶץ (the)earth, ii. 2; (ַ) is lengthened into (ָ) because of the pause.

Verse 9. תְּרֹעֵם Thou-shalt-break-them, Kal 2 m. s. fut. with suff. 3 m. pl. from רָעַע to make a loud noise, to break, to be evil; Hiph. to do evil. The Syr., LXX., Arab., and Vulg. have 'Thou wilt *shepherd* or *pasture* them,' deriving the word from רָעָה to feed.

בְּשֵׁבֶט with-a-rod-of, subst. m. (once f., Ezek. xxi. 15), with pr. בְּ i. 1, from the unused root שָׁבַט, prob. meaning to prop, to support. Comp. Gr. σκῆπτω.

בַּרְזֶל iron, subst. m.; quadril. from the Chal. בְּרַז, (unused in Heb.), to transfix, to pierce through, with the addition of ל.

כִּכְלִי like-vessel, subst. m. (with pr. כְּ i. 3, pointed with (.) instead of (.) because two (.) cannot stand at the beginning of a word), prop. whatsoever is made or completed, used sometimes for arms, weapons. R. כָּלָה to be completed, to be consumed, to perish, to faint; Pi. to finish, to consume, to destroy.

תְּנַפְּצֵם thou-shalt-dash-them-in-pieces, Pi. 2 m. s. fut. with suff. 3 m. pl. from נָפַץ i. q. פּוּץ, Kal and Pi. to break, to scatter, reflex. to spread abroad.

PSALM II. vv. 10–12.

Verse 10. וְעַתָּה Now-therefore, adv. of time, from עֵת i. 3 with ה parag.

הַשְׂכִּילוּ be-wise, Hiph. 2 m. pl. imp. from שָׂכַל, only found once in Kal, 1 Sam. xviii. 30, prop. to look at, to behold; fig. to be prudent; Pi. to interweave, to cross; Hiph. to consider, to look at, to be successful, to make prudent, to teach.

הִוָּסְרוּ be-instructed, Niph. 2 m. pl. imp. from יָסַר, in Kal found only in the fut. אֶפֳּרֵם Hos. x. 10, and part. יֹסֵר Prov. ix. 7, Ps. xciv. 10; Pi. to instruct, to admonish.

Verse 11. בְּיִרְאָה with-fear, verb. n. f. with pr. בּ i. 1, from יָרֵא to fear.

וְגִילוּ and-rejoice, Kal 2 m. pl. imp. from גִיל or גּוּל, prop. to go in a circle, to dance, to leap for joy, to rejoice.

בִּרְעָדָה with-trembling, subst. f. with pr. בּ i. 1; (ִ) under the בּ is changed into (ְ) because two (ְ) cannot stand at the beginning of a word. R. רָעַד to quake, to tremble.

Verse 12. נַשְּׁקוּ Kiss, Pi. 2 m. pl. imp. from נָשַׁק to join, to arrange, to join mouth to mouth, to kiss, also to put on (armour).

בַר (the) Son, i. e. 'do Him homage as your Sovereign,' a kiss being an ancient mode of expressing veneration, see 1 Sam. x. 1, 1 Kings xix. 18, Hos. xiii. 2; subst. m. only found here and in Prov. xxxi. 2, for בֵּן. R. בָּרָא (always used of the Almighty and never of any created being), originally signifying to cut, to carve out, to form by cutting, to make smooth, hence to fashion, to create, also to beget. The interpretation of this word has always been a difficulty. The Chal. has קבילו אלפנא 'receive instruction,' the LXX. δράξασθε παιδείας, Vulg. *apprehendite disciplinam*. Of the older Versions only the Syr. has 'kiss the Son.' The word בַּר, which occurs frequently in Chal., is probably used here instead of בֵּן to avoid the similarity of sound with the following word פֶּן.

פֶּן־ lest, prop. constr. state of the noun פֵּן, removing, taking away, but in use only as a conj. R. פָּנָה to turn oneself, also sometimes to shine, to appear, to be visible; Pi. to cause to turn away, hence to remove, to take out of the way, to put a house in order.

יֶאֱנַף He-be-angry, Kal 3 m. s. fut. from אָנַף ii. 5.

The LXX. and Syr. read מִדַּרְךְּ.

יִבְעַר is-kindled, Kal 3 m. s. fut. from בָּעַר to eat, to consume, to kindle, also to be brutish; Pi. to take away, to exterminate.

כִּמְעַט but-a-little, strictly a subst., a scraping (with pr. כ ii. 9), used as an adv. a little while, presently, as an adj. small, few. R. מָעַט, prob. to scrape, to be polished, to be little, few; Hiph. to diminish.

כָּל־ all, i. 3; כֹּל is shortened into כָּל because of the following Makkeph.

חוֹסֵי that-put-their-trust, constr. of חוֹסִים Kal pres. part. m. pl. from חָסָה, prop. to flee, to take refuge, to trust in.

PSALM III.

Psalms III and IV form a pair, and express the joy of the Psalmist at the reflection that, notwithstanding the multitude of his enemies, God was on his side. This is the first of the Psalms which has a title.

Verse 1. מִזְמוֹר A-Psalm, subst. m. only found in the headings of several Psalms. R. זָמַר to pluck, to prune; Pi. to play on a musical instrument, to dance, to sing.

לְדָוִד of-David, prop. name m., prob. 'beloved,' from the unused root דּוּד to love, i. q. יָדַד, with pr. ל ii. 1.

בְּבָרְחוֹ when-he-fled, Kal inf. constr. with pr. ב i. 1 and suff. 3 m. s. from בָּרַח to pass through, to reach across, also to flee away; Hiph. to put to flight, to chase.

מִפְּנֵי from, lit. from the face of, constr. of פָּנִים (with pr. מ ii. 3) subst. m. pl. from the unused sing. פָּנֶה the face, the surface, the forepart of anything, sometimes used for the wall of a house opposite the door. R. פָּנָה ii. 12.

PSALM III. vv. 2, 3.

אַבְשָׁלוֹם Absalom, 'Father of peace,' prop. name m. (the third son of David by Maacah), compounded of אָב father, subst. m. (constr. אֲבִי, pl. אָבוֹת, constr. אֲבוֹת), and שָׁלוֹם peace, health, sometimes friend; as an adj. whole, healthy. R. שָׁלַם to be whole, sound, completed, to prosper; Pi. to restore, to requite, to recompense.

Verse 2. מָה־ How, interrog. and indef. pron. applied to things in the same manner as מִי is to persons, pointed with Pathach before the letters ה, ח, ע, or before Makkeph and Dagesh euphonic, with Seghol before ה, ע, and ח with Kamets, with Kamets before א and ר with or without Makkeph. The pron. מָה has the force of exclaiming, and of increasing the emphasis of the word with which it is connected.

רַבּוּ are-increased, Kal 3 pl. pret. from רָבַב to become many or numerous, only found in pret. and inf., the other tenses being formed from the cognate רָבָה. Pu. (denom. from רְבָבָה) part. to be multiplied into myriads.

צָרָי they-that-trouble-me, lit. my enemies, pl. of צַר subst. m. (with suff. 1 s.) an enemy, also distress, affliction, used only in poetry except in Numb. x. 9. R. צָרַר to press, to persecute, also to be hostile, to be in distress.

Verse 3. לְנַפְשִׁי of-my-soul, or to my soul, subst. com. gen., more frequently f., (with pr. ל ii. 1 and suff. 1 s.) soul, desire, will; abs. form נֶפֶשׁ, pl. נְפָשׁוֹת. R. נָפַשׁ, not used in Kal, to breathe strongly, to pant.

אֵין (there is) no, constr. of אַיִן, strictly a subst., nothingness, non-existence, but more frequently used as an adv. of negation, from the unused root אִין or אוּן, which has the signification of nothing, and negation; sometimes applied to *ease, ability* of doing anything.

יְשׁוּעָתָה help, verb. n. f. with ה parag. poet. from יָשַׁע, not used in Kal, to be wide, extended, enlarged; Hiph. to help, succour.

בֵּאלֹהִים in-God, subst. m. pl. with pr. ב i. 1; sing. אֱלוֹהַּ, only used in poetry and in the later Hebrew. The word אֱלֹהִים is generally construed with a sing. verb, but in a few cases it takes a pl. verb, adj. or part., as Gen. xx. 13, Ex. xxxii. 1, Ps. lviii. 12, &c.

As two Sh'vas, simple or compound, cannot stand together at the beginning of a word, the בּ should take (ָ), the vowel homogeneous to the compound (ֱ), and then (ְֱ) are contracted into (ֱ). The LXX., Vulg., and Arab. have בֵּאלֹהָיו, the Syr. בֵּאלֹהֶיךָ.

סֶלָה Selah. A musical term very frequent in the Psalms, only found elsewhere in Hab. iii. 3, 9, 13, usually occurring at the end of a period or strophe, perhaps used as a sign for changing the key or repeating the tune some notes higher. R. prob. סָלָה to rest, to be silent. Delitzsch says the word סֶלָה is found in the Psalter, as Bruno has correctly calculated, 71 times: Bk. I, 17 times (iii. 3, 5, and 9, iv. 3, 5, vii. 6, ix. 17, 21, xx. 4, xxi. 3, xxiv. 6, 10, xxxii. 4, 5, 7, xxxix. 6, 12); Bk. II, 30 times (xliv. 9, xlvi. 4, 8, 12, xlvii. 5, xlviii. 9, xlix. 14, 16, l. 6, lii. 5, 7, liv. 5, lv. 8, 20, lvii. 4, 7, lix. 6, 14, lx. 6, lxi. 5, lxii. 5, 9, lxvi. 4, 7, 15, lxvii. 2, 5, lxviii. 8, 20, 33); Bk. III, 20 times (lxxv. 4, lxxvi. 4, 10, lxxvii. 4, 10, 16, lxxxi. 8, lxxxii. 2, lxxxiii. 9, lxxxiv. 5, 9, lxxxv. 3, lxxxvii. 3, 6, lxxxviii. 8, 11, lxxxix. 5, 38, 46, 49); Bk. V, 4 times (cxl. 4, 6, 9, cxliii. 6). Kay says the word occurs in 39 of the Psalms, viz. *once* in vii, xx, xxi, xliv, xlvii, xlviii, l, liv, lx, lxi, lxxv, lxxxi, lxxxii, lxxxiii, lxxxv, cxliii; *twice* in iv, ix, xxiv, xxxix, xlix, lii, lv, lvii, lix, lxii, lxvii, lxxvi, lxxxiv, lxxxvii, lxxxviii; *three times* in iii, xxxii, xlvi, lxvi, lxviii, lxxvii, cxl; *four times* in lxxxix. Of these Psalms 9 are in Bk. I, 17 in Bk. II, 11 in Bk. III, 2 in Bk. V. סֶלָה does not occur in Bk. IV.

Verse 4. מָגֵן a-shield, subst. m., pl. מָגִנִּים, strictly Hiph. part. from גָּנַן to cover, to protect.

בַּעֲדִי over-me, lit. round about me, strictly a subst. (with suff. 1 s.), but used only as a prep. to denote any kind of nearness.

כְּבוֹדִי my-glory, verb. n. m. (once f., Gen. xlix. 6) with suff. 1 s.

from כָּבֵד or כָּבַד to be heavy, to be honoured; Pi. and Hiph. to honour; Hithp. to boast oneself.

וּמֵרִים and-(the) lifter-up-of, Hiph. pres. part. m. s. with ו cop. i. 1, from רוּם to lift up oneself, to be exalted; Hiph. to raise up, to elevate.

רֹאשִׁי mine-head, subst. m. with suff. 1 s. R. רֹאשׁ, unused in Heb., perhaps i. q. רָעַשׁ to be removed, to tremble. Comp. Gen. xl. 20.

Verse 5. קוֹלִי (with) my-voice, subst. m. (pl. קוֹלוֹת) with suff. 1 s. We must understand the pr. ב before קוֹלִי. R. קוֹל, unused in Heb., to call. Comp. Sans. *kal*, to sound; Gr. καλέω; Lat. *calo;* and Eng. *to call.*

אֶקְרָא I-cried, Kal 1 s. fut. from קָרָא. Comp. Gr. κράζω; Fr. *crier;* Eng. *to cry.*

וַיַּעֲנֵנִי and-He-heard-me, lit. answered me, Kal 3 m. s. fut. with ו convers. and suff. 1 s. from עָנָה.

מֵהַר קָדְשׁוֹ out-of-His-holy-hill, lit. out of the mount of His holiness, ii. 6 with pr. מ ii. 3, pointed with (..) instead of (.) because the following letter (being a guttural) cannot take Dagesh, and ii. 6 with suff. 3 m. s.

Verse 6. וָאִישָׁנָה and-slept, Kal 1 s. fut. from יָשֵׁן or יָשַׁן, with ו cop. and convers. pointed with (ָ) because the next letter does not take Dagesh.

הֱקִיצוֹתִי I-awaked, Kal 1 s. pret. from קוץ, found only in Hiph.

Verse 7. מֵרִבְבוֹת of-ten-thousands-of, constr. of רְבָבוֹת, pl. of רְבָבָה verb. n. f. from רָבַב iii. 2, with pr. מ ii. 3 pointed with (..) instead of (.) because the following letter does not take Dagesh.

עַם people, subst. com. gen. (rarely f.) R. עָמַם to gather together, to collect.

סָבִיב round-about, strictly verb. n. m., circuit, circumference, from סָבַב to surround, to encompass, to turn oneself; as an adv. round about.

שָׁתוּ have-set-themselves, Kal 3 pl. pret. from שִׁית, see ii. 2.

Verse 8. הִכִּיתָ Thou-hast-smitten, Hiph. 2 m. s. pret. from נָכָה to strike, to smite; not used in Kal.

אֹיְבַי mine-enemies, lit. those hating me, Kal pres. part. m. pl. with suff. 1 s. from אָיַב to hate.

לֶחִי (upon the) cheek-bone, subst. f. in pause for לְחִי; dual לְחָיַיִם. R. לָחַח, unused in Heb., to be moist. We must understand בְּ before לְחִי.

שִׁנֵּי (the) teeth-of, constr. of שִׁנַּיִם, dual of שֵׁן, subst. com. gen.; pl. not used.

שִׁבַּרְתָּ Thou-hast-broken, Pi. 2 m. s. pret. from שָׁבַר.

Verse 9. The Chal. and some MSS. have וְעַל.

בִּרְכָתֶךָ Thy-blessing (is), (the Syr. here reads 'for ever'), subst. f. with suff. 2 m. s.; abs. form בְּרָכָה; pl. בְּרָכוֹת, constr. בִּרְכוֹת. R. בָּרַךְ to kneel down; Pi. to bless.

PSALM IV.

Verse 1. לַמְנַצֵּחַ To-(the) chief-Musician or to the Precentor, lit. to him that is over; Pi. pres. part. m. s. with pr. לְ ii. 1, from נָצַח to shine, to be bright; not used in Kal; Pi. to be placed over anything, to have the oversight of it, used in reference to music, prob. meaning to preside over the singing. Delitzsch says that the word occurs in Hab. iii. 19, and in the titles of 55 Psalms, viz. Bk. I, 19 times (iv—vi, viii, ix, xi—xiv, xviii—xxii, xxxi, xxxvi, xxxix—xli); Bk. II, 25 times (xlii, xliv—xlvii, xlix, li—lxii, lxiv—lxx); Bk. III, 8 times (lxxv—lxxvii, lxxx, lxxxi, lxxxiv, lxxxv, lxxxviii); Bk. V, 3 times (cix, cxxxix, and cxl).

בִּנְגִינוֹת on-Neginoth, pl. of נְגִינָה subst. f. with pr. בְּ ii. 11, a stringed instrument of music; also used to signify a song or music for a stringed instrument. R. נָגַן, only found once in Kal, Ps. lxviii. 26; Pi. to play on a stringed instrument.

PSALM IV. vv. 2–4.

Verse 2. בְּקָרְאִי when-I-call, lit. in my calling, Kal inf. constr. from קָרָא iii. 5 with pr. בְּ and suff. 1 s.

צִדְקִי my-righteousness, subst. m. with suff. 1 s.; abs. form צֶדֶק. R. צָדַק i. 5.

הִרְחַבְתָּ Thou-hast-enlarged, Hiph. 2 m. s. pret. from רָחַב to be or become wide; Hiph. to enlarge.

חָנֵּנִי have-mercy-upon-me, Kal 2 m. s. imp. with suff. 1 s. from חָנַן to be gracious to, to pity, to be inclined towards; Hithp. to entreat for mercy.

תְּפִלָּתִי my-prayer, subst. f. a prayer, a hymn, with suff. 1 s. R. פָּלַל, not used in Kal; Pi. to judge, to execute judgment (in punishing), to suppose; Hithp. to pray, to intercede for.

Verse 3. בְּנֵי־אִישׁ O-ye-sons-of-men, pl. constr. of ii. 7 and i. 1, 'men of high degree,' 'nobles,' opposed to בְּנֵי אָדָם 'men of low degree.'

עַד־מֶה how-long (will ye turn), עַד prop. a subst. m. signifying perpetuity of time, eternity; used as a prep., till, until, during. R. עָדָה i. 3. מֶה see iii. 2.

לִכְלִמָּה into-shame, subst. f., with pr. לְ pointed with (.) instead of (.) because two (.) cannot stand at the beginning of a word. R. כָּלַם, not used in Kal, prop. to wound; Niph. to be ashamed; Hiph. to put to shame, to reproach.

תֶּאֱהָבוּן (how long) will-ye-love, Kal 2 m. pl. fut. from אָהַב with ן parag.

תְּבַקְשׁוּ (and) seek-after, Pi. 2 m. pl. fut. from בָּקַשׁ, not used in Kal. (Dagesh in 2nd rad. omitted, as often in ק.)

כָזָב leasing, verb. n. m. from כָּזַב to deceive, to lie to any one; in Kal found only in the part. כֹּזֵב.

Verse 4. וּדְעוּ But-know, Kal 2 m. pl. imp. from יָדַע i. 6 with ו cop. i. 1.

הִפְלָה hath-set-apart, Hiph. 3 m. s. pret. from פָּלָה to separate, to distinguish; not used in Kal. Luther has wunderlich führet.

חָסִיד him-that-is-godly, verb. adj. m. from חָסַד to be good, kind; not used in Kal; Pi. to put to shame; Hithp. to shew oneself gracious, only found in Ps. xviii. 26, and in the parallel passage 2 Sam. xxii. According to the LXX., Vulg., Jerome, Luther, &c., 'that God shews special regard to His saint.'

Verse 5. רִגְזוּ Stand-in-awe, Kal 2 m. pl. imp. from רָגַז to be moved, to quake, to tremble; Hiph. to disturb, to provoke to anger. Comp. Gr. ὀργή, anger, grief, and Ger. regen, to move, to stir.

וְאַל־ and-not, from obs. אָלַל, strictly a subst. nothingness, but by usage only a particle of negation, followed always by a fut.= Gr. μή, Lat. *ne*, and so differing from לֹא=οὐ, *non*.

תֶּחֱטָאוּ sin, Kal 2 m. pl. fut. from חָטָא i. 1. (The fut. and not the imp. is used in prohibitions.) These last three words are rendered in the LXX. 'Be ye angry and sin not,' and are so quoted by St. Paul, Eph. iv. 26. According as this translation or that of the text is adopted, the words seem to have been addressed either to David's comrades, exhorting them to restrain their just indignation, or to his enemies, altogether condemning their rage. Luther has Zürnet ihr, so sündiget nicht, whilst the Welsh *Ofnwch, ac na phechwch* agrees with the Eng. version.

בִּלְבַבְכֶם with-your-own-heart, subst. m. with pr. בְּ i. 1 and suff. 2 m. pl.; abs. form לֵבָב i. q. לֵב, the heart, the seat of the affections of the mind. R. לָבַב to be hollow; not used in Kal.

מִשְׁכַּבְכֶם your-bed, verb. n. m. with suff. 2 m. pl. from שָׁכַב to lie down.

וְדֹמּוּ and-be-still, Kal 2 m. pl. imp. from דָּמַם to be confounded, to be dumb. Comp. Lat. *stupor, stupidus*, Ger. staunen, Eng. *to stun*, and Fr. *étonner*.

Verse 6. זִבְחוּ Offer, lit. sacrifice, Kal 2 m. pl. imp. from זָבַח to slay, specially to slay for sacrifice.

זִבְחֵי־ sacrifices-of, constr. of זְבָחִים, pl. of זֶבַח verb. n. m. from זָבַח.

Verse 7. מִי־ Who, pron. interrog. used of persons as מָה is of things.

יַרְאֵנוּ will-shew-us, lit. make us to see, Hiph. 3 m. s. fut. with suff. 1 pl. from רָאָה to see, to choose, to provide; Niph. to be seen, to appear; Hiph. to cause to see=to shew; Hithp. to look upon one another. Comp. Gr. ὁράω.

טוֹב (any) good, verb. adj. (used substantively) from טוֹב to be good, to be beautiful; Hiph. to do good.

נְסָה־ lift-Thou-up, for נְשָׂא, Kal 2 m. s. imp. from נָשָׂא.

אוֹר (the) light-of, verb. n. m. (once f., Job xxxvi. 32), from אוֹר to be, or become light; Hiph. to enlighten, to kindle.

Verse 8. נָתַתָּה Thou-hast-put, Kal 2 m. s. pret. from נָתַן with ה parag. The final ן is here excluded, and Dagesh inserted to compensate.

שִׂמְחָה gladness, verb. n. f. from שָׂמַח or שָׂמֵחַ to be glad, to rejoice.

בְלִבִּי in-my-heart, subst. m., i.q. לֵב iv. 5, with suff. 1 sing.

דְּגָנָם their-corn, subst. m. with suff. 3 m. pl.

וְתִירוֹשָׁם and-their-wine, or perhaps 'their possession,' subst. m. with suff. 3 m. pl. R. יָרַשׁ to possess, to inherit; Niph. to make poor. The LXX. and Syr. add the word 'oil.'

Verse 9. לְבָדָד only, strictly a subst. from the root בָּדַד to separate (with pr. ל ii. 1), but used as an adv. apart, separately.

לָבֶטַח in-safety, subst. m. (with pr. ל ii. 4), confidence, security, used as an adv. confidently, with confident mind, boldly. R. בָּטַח to confide in any one.

PSALM V.

This is a morning prayer, and represents the Psalmist not fleeing from open enemies, but in peril from the machinations of those who are secretly lying in wait for him.

Verse 1. הַנְּחִילוֹת Nehiloth, pl. of נְחִילָה subst. f., the name of a musical instrument perforated with holes, perhaps a flute. R. חָלַל to perforate, to pierce through, also as a denom. from חָלִיל to play on a flute or pipe; Pi. to lay open, to profane;

Hiph. to open, to begin, construed for the most part with an infin. either with or without לְ. The word occurs nowhere else. The LXX. has ὑπὲρ τῆς κληρονομούσης, the Vulg. *Super ea quae haereditatem consequitur*, and Luther für das Erbe.

Verse 2. אֲמָרַי my-words, pl. of אֵמֶר verb. n. m. from אָמַר ii. 7 with suff. 1 s., used only in poetry, except Josh. xxiv. 27. (In the Book of Joshua, as well as in Deuteronomy, there occur several words used elsewhere only in poetry.)

הַאֲזִינָה Give-ear-to, Hiph. 2 m. s. imp. with ה parag. from אָזַן, not used in Kal, denom. from אֹזֶן ear; Hiph. to prick up the ears, to listen.

בִּינָה consider, Kal 2 m. s. imp. with ה parag. from בִּין to separate, also to discern, to understand; Niph. to be intelligent, prudent; Hiph. to declare, to explain; Hithpalel to shew oneself attentive, to consider.

הֲגִיגִי my-meditation, lit. my mourning, my sighing, verb. n. m. with suff. 1 s. from obs. הָגַג, prob. i. q. הָגָה to meditate, also to mourn, to lament; the word occurs only here and in Ps. xxxix. 4.

Verse 3. הַקְשִׁיבָה Hearken, Hiph. 2 m. s. imp. with ה parag. from קָשַׁב to give attention, to hearken, in Kal only found in Is. xxxii. 3.

שַׁוְעִי my-crying, verb. n. m. from שָׁוַע to cry (only found in Pi.), with suff. 1 s. The word occurs nowhere else.

אֶתְפַּלָּל will-I-pray, Hithp. 1 s. fut. from פָּלַל iv. 2 (see i. 1).

Verse 4. בֹּקֶר in-(the) morning, (the acc. of time), subst. m., pl. בְּקָרִים. R. בָּקַר, not used in Kal, to cleave, to open, applied to the breaking forth and arising of light; only used in Pi. to look at, to contemplate, to enquire after.

אֶעֱרָךְ will-I-direct (my prayer), (as wood was set in order for sacrifice), Kal 1 s. fut. from עָרַךְ to arrange, to direct, to set over against, to compare with (a person or thing), to set an equal value upon, also to make long, to extend, joined with מִלְחָמָה to prepare for battle.

וַאֲצַפֶּה and-will-look-out, Pi. 1 s. fut. with ו cop. ii. 6, from

צָפָה to shine, to be bright, to look out, to view, to observe narrowly.

Verse 5. כִּי For (art), conj., the verb 'to be' is here understood.

אֵל a-God, subst. m. with participial form, from the root אוּל, not used as a verb, but of wide extent in the derivatives; applied to strength, power, pre-eminence.

חָפֵץ that-hath-pleasure (in), verb. adj. m. from חָפֵץ i. 2.

רֶשַׁע wickedness, verb. n. m. from רָשַׁע i. 1.

יְגֻרְךָ shall-dwell-with-Thee, Kal 3 m. s. fut. with suff. 2 m. s. from גּוּר, prop. to turn aside from the way, hence to turn aside to any one, to tarry, to sojourn. Like other verbs of dwelling, it takes an acc. not only of the place but of the person.

רָע evil, verb. adj. m., used as a subst., from רָעַע ii. 9.

Verse 6. יִתְיַצְּבוּ shall-stand, lit. set themselves, ii. 2.

הוֹלְלִים (the) foolish, Kal pres. part. m. pl. from הָלַל to shine, to be clear, also to be mad, foolish; it sometimes means to be haughty, arrogant; Pi. prop. to sing, especially any one's praises, hence to praise, to celebrate, intrans. to glory, to boast; Hithp. to glory, to boast oneself. Comp. Ger. hell sein, to be clear, and hallen, to sound.

לְנֶגֶד עֵינֶיךָ in-Thy-sight, lit. before Thine eyes, נֶגֶד strictly a subst., what is before or in front, with pr. לְ ii. 1, hence as an adv. over against, corresponding to, meet for. R. נָגַד, unused in Kal, to be before or in front, hence to be manifest; Hiph. to bring to light, to shew, to tell. עֵינֶיךָ subst. com. gen. (more frequently f.) dual, with suff. 2 m. s.; abs. form s. עַיִן (dual עֵינַיִם, constr. עֵינֵי; pl. עֲיָנוֹת, constr. עֵינוֹת) an eye, also a fountain, the spring in an Eastern country being the eye of the landscape, and thus used for a natural burst of living water, as distinguished from בְּאֵר water arrived at by digging. R. עִי, not used in Heb., to flow.

שָׂנֵאתָ Thou-hatest, Kal 2 m. s. pret. from שָׂנֵא, in Pi. found only in the part.

פֹּעֲלֵי workers-of, Kal pres. part. m. pl. constr. from פָּעַל i. q. עָשָׂה, but used only in poetry.

אָוֶן iniquity, subst. m. emptiness, vanity, wickedness, sorrow. R. אִן iii. 3. Comp. St. Matt. vii. 23.

Verse 7. דָמִים bloody, lit. of blood, pl. of דָּם verb. n. m. from דָּמַם to be red. The pl. form of this word always refers to effusion of blood, and generally implies violence.

וּמִרְמָה and-deceitful, lit. of deceit, subst. f. with ו cop. i. 1. R. רָמָה to cast, to throw; Pi. to beguile, to deceive.

יְתָעֵב will-abhor, Pi. 3 m. s. fut. from תָּעַב, not used in Kal.

Verse 8. בְּרֹב in-(the) multitude-of, verb. n. m. (strictly Kal inf. constr.) from רָבַב iii. 2 with pr. ב i. 1.

חַסְדְּךָ Thy-mercy, verb. n. m. (pl. חֲסָדִים, constr. חַסְדֵי) with suff. 2 m. s. from חֶסֶד iv. 4.

אָבוֹא I-will-come, Kal 1 s. fut. from בּוֹא to go, or come in; Hiph. to cause to come=to bring. Comp. Sans. *vâ*, to go; Gr. βάω, whence βαίνω; Lat. *vado*.

בֵיתֶךָ (into) Thy-house, subst. m. with suff. 2 m. s., abs. form בַּיִת, constr. בֵּית, pl. בָּתִּים from the unused sing. בֹּתֶת. R. perhaps בּוּת to pass the night, or else בָּנָה to build. Comp. Gr. δόμος from δέμω.

אֶשְׁתַּחֲוֶה will-I-worship, Hithp. 1 s. fut. from שָׁחָה to bow down; Hithp. to prostrate oneself.

הֵיכַל־ Temple, constr. of הֵיכָל subst. com. gen. usually m. (but f. in Is. xliv. 28), a great building, a palace, a temple. R. הָכַל, unused in Heb., in Arab. signifying to be great, lofty.

Verse 9. נְחֵנִי Lead-me, Kal 2 m. s. imp. with suff. 1 s. from נָחָה, pret. and imp. Kal, fut. and inf. Hiph.

לְמַעַן because-of, lit. a subst. (with pr. ל ii. 1) for מַעֲנֶה, intent, purpose, verb. n. m. from the root עָנָה to answer; before verbs it means, that, so that; before substantives, on account of.

שׁוֹרְרָי mine-enemies, Kal pres. part. m. pl. with suff. 1 s. from שָׁרַר to twist, to twine, to be hard, firm, to oppress. Some consider it as=מְשׁוֹרֵר, Pi. pres. part. from שׁוּר to see, to observe, hence those who observe me, my watchers (for evil).

הַיְשַׁר make-straight, (to be read הוֹשֵׁר), Hiph. 2 m. s. imp. from יָשַׁר to be straight, to be right, to be level. The K'ri has הַיְשַׁר, which is found in several MSS. The LXX. has '*my way* ... before *Thy* face.'

Verse 10. בְּפִיהוּ in-their-mouth, lit. in his mouth, i. e. in the mouth of any one of them, subst. m. with pr. בּ i. 1 and suff. 3 m. s.; abs. form פֶּה. R. prob. פָּיָה, unused in Heb., prop. to blow out, hence to speak.

נְכוֹנָה faithfulness, Niph. pres. part. f. s. from כּוּן i. 4, used substantively.

קִרְבָּם their-inward-part, subst. m. with suff. 3 m. pl.; abs. form קֶרֶב; used sometimes as a prep. with pr. בּ, in the midst of, amongst.

הַוּוֹת very-wickedness, pl. of הַוָּה subst. f., a poetical word occurring only in the Psalms, Proverbs, Job, and Micah vii. 3, generally used in the pl. R. הָוָה to breathe, to yawn.

קֶבֶר sepulchre, verb. n. m. from קָבַר to bury; pl. קְבָרִים constr. קִבְרֵי, and קְבָרוֹת constr. קִבְרוֹת.

פָּתִיחַ an-open, Kal pass. part. m. s. from פָּתַח to open, to spread out; Pi. to loosen, also to engrave, to sculpture. Comp. Gr. πετάω and Lat. *pateo*.

גְּרוֹנָם their-throat, subst. m. (with suff. 3 m. pl.), so called from its being rough. R. גָּרָה, unused in Kal, prop. to be rough; Pi. to stir up (strife); Hithp. to be angry.

לְשׁוֹנָם their-tongue, subst. com. gen. (more frequently f.) with suff. 3 m. pl.; abs. form לָשׁוֹן. R. לָשַׁן, unused in Kal, prob. to lap, to lick; Pi. denom. from לָשׁוֹן to make tongue, to use the tongue boldly, to slander, only found in Ps. ci. 5, Hiph. in Prov. xxx. 10. Comp. Sans. *rasanâ*, a tongue; Armen. *liezu;* Welsh *llais*, a voice; and even Gr. γλῶσσα, in which γ is an addition.

יַחֲלִיקוּן they-flatter(with), Hiph. 3 m. pl. fut. with ן parag. from חָלַק to be smooth, also to divide. Many words in the

Western languages beginning with *gl* and *glc* have the signification of smoothness, as χαλκός, χάλιξ; *calculus;* κόλαξ, a smooth man, a flatterer.

Verse 11. הַאֲשִׁימֵם Punish-Thou-them, or make them guilty, Hiph. 2 m. s. imp. with suff. 3 m. pl. from אָשַׁם to be guilty, to suffer, to be punished for sin; Hiph. to cause to suffer, to punish.

יִפְּלוּ let-them-fall, Kal 3 m. pl. fut. from נָפַל to fall; Hiph. to cause to fall=to fell; Hithp. followed by עַל to rush upon, to attack. Comp. Ger. *fallen;* Eng. *to fall;* Gr. σφάλλω; Lat. *fallo.*

מִמֹּעֲצוֹתֵיהֶם by-their-own-counsels, subst. f. pl. from the unused sing. מוֹעֵצָה i. q. עֵצָה counsel, plan, device, with pr. מ ii. 3 and suff. 3 m. pl. R. יָעַץ i. 1.

פִּשְׁעֵיהֶם their-transgressions, pl. of פֶּשַׁע verb. n. m. with suff. 3 m. pl. from פָּשַׁע to fall away, to sin.

הַדִּיחֵמוֹ thrust-them-down, Hiph. 2 m. s. imp. with (poetic) suff. 3 m. pl. from נָדַח to thrust, to push.

מָרוּ they-have-rebelled, Kal 3 pl. pret. from מָרָה to rebel, to murmur. Comp. Lat. *murmur* and *murmuro.*

Verse 12. לְעוֹלָם for-ever, subst. m. with pr. לְ ii. 1; pl. עוֹלָמִים, found only in Ps. lxi. 5 and cxlv. 13; prop. what is hidden, specially hidden time, the beginning or end of which is either uncertain or else not defined, eternity, perpetuity. R. עָלַם to hide, to conceal; in Kal found only in the part. pass. עֲלֻמִים concealed or secret (sins), Ps. xc. 8.

יְרַנְּנוּ let-them-shout-for-joy, Pi. 3 m. pl. fut. from רָנַן Kal and Pi. to cry aloud, to rejoice.

וְתָסֵךְ and-Thou-wilt-put-a-defence, Hiph. 2 m. s. fut. from סָכַךְ to weave, to interweave, especially boughs, to make a hedge, to cover; Hiph. to cover, to protect.

עָלֵימוֹ over-them, poetic form for עֲלֵיהֶם, prep. עַל i. 3, with suff. 3 m. pl.

וְיַעְלְצוּ let-also-be-joyful, Kal 3 m. pl. fut. from עָלַץ i. q. עָלַז and עָלַם.

אֹהֲבֵי (the) lovers-of, constr. of אֹהֲבִים Kal pres. part. m. pl. from אָהַב. The LXX., Vulg., Syr., and Arab. insert כֹּל before אהבי.

שְׁמֶךָ Thy-name, subst. m. (pl. שֵׁמוֹת) with suff. 2 m. s. Comp. Gr. σῆμα, a sign.

Verse 13. כַּצִּנָּה as-(with)a-shield, subst. f. with pr. כ i. 3, *a large shield* covering the whole person, larger than מָגֵן which is *a buckler*. R. צָנַן, unused in Heb., prob. to protect.

רָצוֹן (with) favour, verb. n. m. from רָצָה to be well pleased with, to be gracious. The noun is in the acc. of the instrument.

תַּעְטְרֶנּוּ wilt-Thou-encompass-him, or crown him, Kal 2 m. s. fut. with suff. 3 m. s. from עָטַר to surround; Pi. to crown.

PSALM VI.

This is the first of the penitential Psalms which were used in the special services appointed for the season of Lent. The other penitential Psalms are xxxii, xxxviii, li, cii, cxxx, and cxliii. It is one of the special Psalms for Ash-Wednesday.

Verse 1. הַשְּׁמִינִית Sheminith, or the Octave, ord. adj. f., m. שְׁמִינִי, from שְׁמֹנֶה eight, a musical term denoting the lowest and gravest note sung by men's voices (basso), opposed to עֲלָמוֹת (soprano).

Verse 2. תּוֹכִיחֵנִי rebuke-me, Hiph. 2 m. s. fut. with suff. 1 s. from יָכַח, not used in Kal, prop. i. q. נָכַח to be in the front, hence fig. to be clear, but in Hiph. signifying to confute, to convict, to rebuke, to judge, to decide, followed by ל to appoint or destine for any one; Niph. to be convicted.

בַּחֲמָתְךָ in-Thy-hot-displeasure, subst. f. heat, anger, poison, with pr. ב i. 1 and suff. 2 m. s.; abs. form חֵמָה. R. יָחַם i. q. חָמַם to be hot, to conceive, not used in pret.

תְּיַסְּרֵנִי chasten-me, Pi. 2 m. s. fut. with suff. 1 s. from יָסַר ii. 10.

Verse 3. אֻמְלַל weak, for מְאֻמְלָל, only used in poetry, Pulal pres. part. m. s. from אָמַל to languish, to droop; in Kal found only in the part. pass., Ezek. xvi. 30.

רְפָאֵנִי heal-me, Kal 2 m. s. imp. with suff. 1 s. from רָפָא, prop. to sew together, to mend, to heal.

עֲצָמָי my-bones, subst. f. pl. with suff. 1 s., abs. form sing. עֶצֶם, pl. עֲצָמִים and עֲצָמוֹת. R. עָצַם to be strong.

Verse 4. מְאֹד sore, or greatly, much, prop. a subst. m. strength, force, used as an adv. very, exceedingly, from the unused root אוד to be strong.

וְאַתָּ but-Thou, only found here and in 1 Sam. xxiv. 19, Eccles. vii. 22, Job i. 10, and Neh. ix. 6, for וְאַתָּה ii. 7, which is the reading of several MSS. and of the K'ri.

עַד־מָתָי how-long, lit. until when, עַד iv. 3, מָתַי prop. a subst. extension, space of time, used as an interrog. adv. of time, when? R. מָתָה, unused in Heb., to stretch out. This *Domine quousque* was Calvin's motto. It is an elliptical phrase, which occurs in full in Ps. lxxix. 5.

Verse 5. שׁוּבָה Return, Kal 2 m. s. imp. with ה parag. from שׁוּב to return; Hiph. to bring back, to restore, to convert, to recompense.

חַלְּצָה deliver, Pi. 2 m. s. imp. with ה parag. from חָלַץ to draw out, to loosen; Pi. to set free, to deliver.

Verse 6. בַּמָּוֶת in-death, verb. n. m. with pr. בּ i. 1, from מוּת to die; Hiph. to cause to die=to slay. Comp. Sans. *mri*, to die; *mrita*, dead, death; Malay *mita*, to slay and to die; Zend *mare-tan*, mortal, man; Gr. μορτός; Lat. *mors;* and Eng. *mortal.*

בִּשְׁאוֹל in-Hades, subst. com. gen. (more frequently f.) with pr. בּ ii. 11, the lower world, the region of ghosts, the Hades of the Hebrews.

יוֹדֶה־ will-give-thanks, Hiph. 3 m. s. fut. from יָדָה to throw, to cast; not used in Kal; Hiph. to profess, to confess (perhaps prop. to shew or point out with the hand extended, from the idea of the hand being cast forth), to praise.

PSALM VI. vv. 7–10.

Verse 7. בְּאַנְחָתִי with-my-groaning, verb. n. f. with pr. בְּ i. 1 and suff. 1 s. from אָנַח to groan, only found in Niph. Comp. Gr. ἀνάγκη; Lat. *angere, angustus;* Ger. enge and Angst.

אַשְׂחֶה make-I-to-swim, Hiph. 1 s. fut. from שָׂחָה to swim; Hiph. to inundate.

מִטָּתִי my-bed, verb. n. f. with suff. 1 s. from נָטָה to stretch out, to extend, to turn in; Hiph. to incline downwards, to let down.

בְּדִמְעָתִי with-my-tear(s), verb. n. f. with pr. בְּ i. 1 and suff. 1 s. from דָּמַע to weep.

עַרְשִׂי my-couch, subst. f. with suff. 1 s.; abs. form עֶרֶשׂ, pl. עֲרָשׂוֹת.

אַמְסֶה I-water, lit. make to melt, Hiph. 1 s. fut. from מָסָה to melt, to flow down; Hiph. to dissolve.

Verse 8. עָשְׁשָׁה is-consumed, Kal 3 f. s. pret. from עָשֵׁשׁ to be consumed, to waste away; found only here and in Ps. xxxi. 10 and 11.

מִכַּעַס because-of-grief, verb. n. f. with pr. מִ ii. 3, from כַּעַס to be rocked to and fro, fig. to be disturbed, to rage, to be indignant; Pi. and Hiph. to provoke. Comp. Job xvii. 7.

עָתְקָה it-waxeth-old, Kal 3 f. s. pret. from עָתַק to grow old, also to be removed, transported, to be set free.

בְּכָל־ because-of-all, ii. 12, with pr. בְּ, which has here the force of בַּעֲבוּר on account of.

צוֹרְרָי mine-enemies, Kal pres. part. m. pl. from צָרַר iii. 2 with suff. 1 s.

Verse 9. סוּרוּ Depart, Kal 2 m. pl. imp. from סוּר to turn aside, to depart; Hiph. to cause to depart = to remove.

בִּכְיִי my-weeping, subst. m. with suff. 1 s.; abs. form בְּכִי. R. בָּכָה to weep.

Verse 10. תְּחִנָּתִי my-supplication, verb. n. f. with suff. 1 s. from חָנַן iv. 2.

יִקָּח will-receive, Kal 3 m. s. fut. from לָקַח, which is the only verb beginning with ל which rejects the ל in the course of flexion, and forms its tenses like a verb פ״ן.

Verse 11. יֵבֹשׁוּ Let-be-ashamed, Kal 3 m. pl. fut. from בּוֹשׁ to be pale, to change colour, to be ashamed; Hiph. to put to shame, in perf. found only in Ps. xliv. 8 and liii. 6.

רָגַע suddenly, subst. m.; abs. form רֶגַע (see ii. 8), perhaps lit. a moving, stirring; used as an adv. in a moment, suddenly. R. רָגַע to stir up, also sometimes to terrify, to restrain; intrans. to be afraid, to be quiet, to tremble.

Observe the play upon the words יָשֻׁבוּ, יֵבֹשׁוּ.

PSALM VII.

In full reliance on the righteousness of God, the Psalmist appeals to Him to judge his cause. 'Cush the Benjamite' is by some thought to be an enigmatical designation of Saul, whilst others suppose that it refers to Shimei, or possibly he may have been one of Saul's adherents who took an active part against David.

Verse 1. שִׁגָּיוֹן Shiggaion, subst. m. (pl. שִׁגְיוֹנוֹת), only found here and Hab. iii. 1, a poem in irregular metre comprising a variety of emotions rapidly succeeding each other, a song, an ode, Dithyramb. R. שָׁגָה to wander, to go astray, in Syr. signifying 'to sing.'

שָׁר he-sang, Kal 3 m. s. pret. from שִׁיר i.q. שׁוּר, not used in the other Phœnicio-Shemitic languages.

דִּבְרֵי (the) words-of, constr. of דְּבָרִים, pl. of דָּבָר, word, matter, cause, thing; verb. n. m. from דָּבַר ii. 5.

כּוּשׁ Cush, prop. name m.; Luther has 'the Moor.'

בֶּן־יְמִינִי the-Benjamite, patronymic from בִּנְיָמִין 'son of the right hand,' compounded of בֵּן ii. 7 and יָמִין subst. com. gen., mostly f.

PSALM VII. vv. 2–5.

Verse 2. וְהַצִּילֵנִי and-deliver-me, Hiph. 2 m. s. imp. with suff. 1 s. from נָצַל to draw out, to deliver; not used in Kal.

Verse 3. There is here a change of number from the preceding verse.

כְּאַרְיֵה like-a-lion, subst. m., i. q. אֲרִי, with pr. כ i. 3 and ה parag., only found in the sing. R. אָרָה to pluck, to eat down by plucking, only found in Ps. lxxx. 13 and Cant. v. 1.

פֹּרֵק rending-(it)in-pieces, Kal pres. part. m. s. from פָּרַק to break or tear off, sometimes fig. to tear away (from danger), to deliver.

מַצִּיל to-deliver, lit. delivering, Hiph. pres. part. m. s. from נָצַל vii. 2.

The LXX., Vulg., Syr., Æth., and Arab. have ואין פרק ומציל.

Verse 4. יֵשׁ־ there-be, prop. a subst., being, existence, whence that which is present, ready, wealth; used for the verb substantive without distinction of number or tense. R. יָשָׁה, unused in Heb., prop. to stand, to stand upright, hence to be. Comp. Sans. *as;* Lat. *esse.*

עָוֶל iniquity, verb. n. m. from עָוַל, not used in Kal, prop. to turn away, to distort, hence to be wicked; Pi. to act wickedly.

בְּכַפַּי in-my-hands, dual of כַּף, subst. f. with pr. ב i. 1 and suff. 1 s., lit. something crooked or hollowed out, used of the hollow of the hand, the palm; joined with רֶגֶל the sole of the foot. R. כָּפַף to bend, to bow down. Comp. Gr. κάμπτω and κύπτω; Lat. *cubo,* also *cavus;* and Ger. fippen and umfippen in the sense of folding.

Verse 5. גָּמַלְתִּי I-have-rewarded, Kal 1 s. pret. from גָּמַל to shew or bring on any one (good or evil), specially to shew good, to recompense.

שׁוֹלְמִי him-that-was-at-peace-with-me, Kal pres. part. m. s. with suff. 1 s. from שָׁלַם iii. 1. The LXX., Vulg., and Syr. appear to take the word as equivalent to משלמי 'one who recompensed me,' as they have ' If I have requited those who have done evil to me.'

וָאֲחַלְּצָה yea-I-have-delivered, Pi. 1 s. fut. from חָלַץ vi. 5 with ו cop. and convers. iii. 6. Some persons have rendered this passage (the interpretation of which is somewhat doubtful) by ' And (if) I have *spoiled* him that without cause,' &c. The objection to this is that the verb never occurs in Pi. in the sense of *spoiling*, but always in that of *delivering*, although it is found in that sense in the corresponding conjugation of the Syriac.

רֵיקָם without-cause, adv. emptily, without cause. R. רִיק or רוּק ii. 1.

Verse 6. יִרַדֹּף Let-persecute, for יִרְדֹּף, Kal 3 m. s. fut. from רָדַף; it is a kind of hybrid form, half Kal and half Piel. Some MSS. have יִרְדֹּף and others יְרַדֵּף.

וְיַשֵּׂג and-take, Hiph. 3 m. s. fut. from נָשַׂג, not used in Kal.

חַיַּי my-life, subst. m. pl. (sing. חַי) with suff 1 s., the pl. form perhaps implying continuity or extension, חַיִּים being with a few exceptions used in the pl. to denote simply life. R. חָיָה to live; Pi. and Hiph. to make alive, to restore to life.

לֶעָפָר in-(the) dust, subst. m. with pr. לְ ii. 1. R. עָפַר, unused in Kal, to be whitish. The prefixes בְּ, כְּ, and לְ are always pointed with (ָ) when they displace the ה of the article and precede a guttural furnished with Kamets.

יַשְׁכֵּן lay, lit. cause to dwell, Hiph. 3 m. s. fut. from שָׁכַן to dwell.

Verse 7. בְּעַבְרוֹת because-of-(the) rage-of, pl. of עֶבְרָה subst. f., prop. overflowing of wrath, with pr. בְּ i. 1, which has here the force of against. The pl. denotes intensity. R. עָבַר to pass over, to pass by, metaphorically to transgress; Pi. and Hiph. to cause to pass over, to lead across; Hithp. to pour oneself forth in wrath, to be angry. Comp. Sans. *upari*, above, upon; Gr. ὑπέρ, περάω; Lat. *super;* Goth. *ufar, afar;* and Ger. über. The Syr. and Arab. seem to have read בְּעָרְךָ.

וְעוּרָה and-awake, Kal 2 m. s. imp. with ה parag. from עוּר.

אֵלִי for-me, the LXX., Vulg., Æth., and Arab. have יהוה אלי.

צִוִּיתָ Thou-hast-commanded, Pi. 2 m. s. pret. from צָוָה, not

PSALM VII. vv. 8–13.

used in Kal, to set up; Pi. to constitute, to appoint, to command.

Verse 8. תְּסוֹבְבֶךָ shall-compass-Thee-about, Poel 3 f. s. fut. from סָבַב iii. 7 with suff. 2 m. s.

וְעָלֶיהָ and-because-of-it, i. 3, with suff. 3 f. s.

לַמָּרוֹם on-high, verb. n. m. with pr. לְ ii. 1, from רוּם iii. 4.

Verse 9. יָדִין shall-judge, Kal 3 m. s. fut. from דִּין i. q. דּוּן.

וּכְתֻמִּי and-according-to-mine-integrity, subst. m. with וְ cop. i. 1, pr. כְּ i. 3, and suff. 1 s. R. תָּמַם to complete, to finish; Hithp. to act uprightly; in Hithp. only found in Ps. xviii. 26 and in the parallel passage in 2 Sam.

Verse 10. יִגְמָר־ Let-come-to-an-end, Kal 3 m. s. fut. from גָּמַר to complete, to finish, to leave off, intrans. to cut off, to fail. The word occurs only four times besides, viz. Ps. xii. 2, lvii. 3, lxxvii. 9, and cxxxviii. 8.

נָא I-pray-Thee, a primitive particle expressive of respectful entreaty or exhortation.

לִבּוֹת (the) hearts, pl. of לִבָּה subst. f., i. q. לֵב iv. 8.

וּכְלָיוֹת and-reins, subst. f. pl. with וְ cop. i. 1, from the unused sing. כִּלְיָה.

Verse 11. יִשְׁרֵי־ (the) upright-in, pl. constr. of יָשָׁר verb. adj. m. from יָשַׁר v. 9.

Verse 12. אֱלֹהִים שׁוֹפֵט צַדִּיק God-judgeth-(the) righteous, or *God is a righteous judge*, as in the Prayer-Book Version. The LXX. and Vulg. add the words 'both strong and patient.'

וְאֵל and-God, the LXX., Syr., Vulg., Æth., and Arab. read אֵל.

זֹעֵם is-angry (with the wicked), Kal pres. part. m. s. from זָעַם. The Chal. has 'And God is angry with the wicked.'

Verse 13. חַרְבּוֹ his-sword, verb. n. f. with suff. 3 m. s. from חָרַב to destroy, also to be dried up. Comp. Gr. κάρφω, to become dry; κράμβος, dry.

יִלְטוֹשׁ he-will-whet, Kal 3 m. s. fut. from לָטַשׁ to hammer, to forge, to sharpen.

קַשְׁתּוֹ his-bow, subst. com. gen. with suff. 3 m. s.; abs. form קֶשֶׁת, pl. קְשָׁתוֹת, constr. קַשְׁתוֹת. R. קוֹשׁ to bend as a bow, to wind, not used in Heb.

Verse 14. חִצָּיו His-arrows, pl. of חֵץ subst. m. with suff. 3 m. s. R. חָצַץ to divide.

לְדֹלְקִים against-(the) persecutors, Kal pres. part. m. pl. with pr. לְ ii. 1, from דָּלַק, prop. to burn, to flame, applied to the heat of persecution, to pursue hotly, (in the language of High Germany nachfeuern.) Comp. Gr. δέρκομαι, prop. to flame, to shine, applied to the power of seeing.

יִפְעָל He-maketh, Kal 3 m. s. fut. from פָּעַל v. 6. Or, 'He maketh His arrows burning.'

Verse 15. הִנֵּה Behold, demonstr. adj. or conj. i. q. הֵן with ה parag.

יְחַבֶּל־ he-travaileth (with), Pi. 3 m. s. fut. from חָבַל to twist, to bind; Pi. to writhe with pains or sorrows, to bring forth. (ֶ) not (ֵ), on account of the following Makkeph.

עָמָל mischief, verb. n. m. from עָמַל to labour (particularly to weariness).

שָׁקֶר falsehood, verb. n. m. from שָׁקַר Kal and Pi. to lie, to deceive. See ii. 8.

Verse 16. בּוֹר a-pit, verb. n. m. from בָּאַר to dig, not used in Kal. Comp. Lat. *forare* and Eng. *to bore*.

כָּרָה He-made, or digged, Kal 3 m. s. pret.

בְּשַׁחַת into-(the) pit (which), verb. n. f. (not used in the pl.), from שׁוּחַ to sink or bow down, with pr. בְּ i. 1.

The pron. אֲשֶׁר must be understood before יִפְעָל.

Verse 17. קָדְקֳדוֹ his-own-pate, subst. m. with suff. 3 m. s., the crown of the head, so called from the hair being there divided and separated. R. קָדַד to cleave.

חֲמָסוֹ his-violent-dealing, verb. n. m. with suff. 3 m. s. from חָמַס to tear off, to treat with violence.

יֵרֵד shall-come-down, Kal 3 m. s. fut. from יָרַד to go down, to descend; Hiph. to let down.

Verse 18. עֶלְיוֹן Most-High, verb. adj. m. (f. עֶלְיוֹנָה), from עָלָה i. 3.

The words 'I will praise the Lord according to *His* righteousness' are rendered in the Syr. Version 'I will give thanks unto the Lord according to *my* righteousness.'

PSALM VIII.

In this Psalm, which is one of those appointed for Ascension Day, God's name is glorified for the wondrous love which he has shewn to man. The Psalmist may possibly have composed it when, as a youth, he kept his father's flocks on the hills of Bethlehem, at which time of his life his nightly watches gave him frequent opportunities of observing the wonders of the heavens.

Verse 1. הַגִּתִּית Gittith, subst. f., the name of a musical instrument, perhaps invented at Gath, or so called from גַּת a wine-press, because used at the joyful season of vintage.

Verse 2. אַדִּיר excellent, verb. adj. m. from אָדַר, not found in Kal, the primary signification of which appears to have been, to be wide, broad, to be great, noble.

תְּנָה hast-set, this word is very perplexing; it may be Kal 2 m. s. imp. with ה parag. from נָתַן (which Glory of Thine do Thou set, &c.); according to some, תְּנָה is an irreg. form of the inf. constr. after the analogy of רְדָה Gen. xlvi. 3, (Thou, the setting of whose Glory is above the heavens); whilst others, with a change of vowel points, would read תֻּנָּה Hoph. 3 f. s. pret. from נָתַן; others again suppose תְּנָה to be a defective form for תָּנָה (Thou whose Glory is extended), תנה being supposed to be kindred with תנן and the Indo-Germanic root *tan*, whence Gr. τείνω, Lat. *tendere, tenuis,* and Ger. be̬hnen.

הוֹדְךָ Thy-glory, subst. m. with suff. 2 m. s. R. unused in Heb., to lift oneself up, to be beautiful. Luther has da man Dir baufet im Himmel; the LXX. ὅτι ἐπήρθη ἡ μεγαλοπρέπειά σου ὑπεράνω τῶν οὐρανῶν; Vulg. *quoniam elevata est magnificentia tua super coelos.*

Verse 3. עוֹלְלִים children, pl. of עוֹלֵל subst. m., the derivation of which is uncertain.

וְיֹנְקִים and-sucklings, Kal pres. part. m. pl. from יָנַק to suck.

יִסַּדְתָּ hast-Thou-ordained, or founded, Pi. 2 m. s. pret. from יָסַד ii. 2.

עֹז strength, verb. n. m. from עָזַז to be strong, to strengthen, to make strong.

לְהַשְׁבִּית that-Thou-mightest-still, lit. to cause to cease, Hiph. inf. constr. with pr. לְ ii. 1, from שָׁבַת to cease to do anything, to rest; Hiph. to cause to cease, to put an end to, to remove.

וּמִתְנַקֵּם and-(the)avenger, Hithp. pres. part. m. s. with ו cop. i. 1, from נָקַם to avenge.

Verse 4. The LXX., Æth., and Arab. read the word שמים without the suff.

מַעֲשֵׂה (the)work-of, verb. n. m. from עָשָׂה to make, to do.

אֶצְבְּעֹתֶיךָ Thy-fingers, pl. of אֶצְבַּע subst. f. (with suff. 2 m. s.), the finger, specially the fore-finger, which is used in dipping into anything. R. עָבַץ to dip in.

יָרֵחַ (the)moon, subst. m., prob. from the unused root יָרַח to be yellow.

וְכוֹכָבִים and-(the)stars, pl. of כּוֹכָב subst. m. R. כָּבַב, unused in Heb., to roll up as in a ball.

Verse 5. אֱנוֹשׁ man, subst. m.; in the sing. (except 2 Chron. xiv. 11) it is found only poetically, in Job, Isaiah, and the Psalms; (the prose expression is אָדָם); pl. אֲנָשִׁים, constr. אַנְשֵׁי (formed from the obs. sing. אֲנָשׁ), employed as the pl. of אִישׁ man, denoting men generally.

אָדָם man, subst. m.; this word has neither constr. state nor pl. form. R. אָדַם to be red.

תִּפְקְדֶנּוּ Thou-visitest-him, Kal 2 m. s. fut. with suff. 3 m. s. from פָּקַד to visit, to look after anything, to lay up, to deposit;

PSALM VIII. vv. 6–8.

Hiph. to set any one over anything, to commit to the care of any one.

Verse 6. וַתְּחַסְּרֵהוּ Thou-hast-made-him-lower, Pi. 2 m. s. fut. with ו convers. and suff. 3 m. s. from חָסֵר to be void of anything, to be lessened, in Pi. found elsewhere only in Eccles. iv. 8.

מֵאֱלֹהִים than-(the) angels, or than God. The LXX. and Chal. translate the word 'angels.' Luther's Version is Du wirst ihn lassen eine kleine Zeit von Gott verlassen sein.

וְהָדָר and-honour, verb. n. m. from הָדַר, prob. to be wide, broad, swollen, to adorn.

Verse 7. תַּמְשִׁילֵהוּ Thou-makest-him-to-have-dominion, Hiph. 2 m. s. fut. with suff. 3 m. s. from מָשַׁל to rule, also to make like, to assimilate, to put forth a parable, to use a proverb; Niph. to be compared, to be like; Pi. to use parables; Hiph. to compare, also to cause to rule.

יָדֶיךָ Thy-hands, dual of יָד, subst. f. with suff. 2 m. s.; abs. form יָדַיִם, constr. יְדֵי, pl. יָדוֹת. R. יָדָה vi. 6.

תַּחַת־ under, strictly a subst. m., the lower part, used as a prep. below, under, also sometimes in the place of, instead of.

רַגְלָיו his-feet, subst. f. dual with suff. 3 m. s.; abs. form sing. רֶגֶל, dual רַגְלַיִם, constr. רַגְלֵי, pl. רְגָלִים.

Verse 8. צֹנֶה Sheep, a collective noun com. gen., i. q. צֹאן denoting smaller cattle, the corresponding noun expressing an individual is שֶׂה. The word occurs also in Num. xxxii. 24 without the א.

וַאֲלָפִים and-oxen, pl. of אֶלֶף subst. epicene (with ו cop. ii. 6), an ox, animal of the ox kind, lit. tame cattle. This word only occurs in the pl. here and in Prov. xiv. 4. R. אָלַף to accustom oneself, to be familiar, to become tame, to join together, to associate; Hiph. (denom. from אֶלֶף) to bring forth or make thousands.

וְגַם and-moreover, prop. a subst., addition, accumulation, hence used as a conj. indicating accession, also.

בַּהֲמוֹת (the) cattle-of, = greater beasts, constr. of בְּהֵמוֹת, pl. of בְּהֵמָה subst. f., so called from being unable to speak. R. בָּהַם, unused in Heb., prop. to shut, specially the mouth, hence to be dumb.

שָׂדָי (the) field, subst. m., i.q. שָׂדֶה, but used only in poetry. R. שָׂדָה, unused in Heb., to level, to extend, to smooth or level with a harrow. Comp. Lat. *arvum* from *arare*.

Verse 9. צִפּוֹר (The) fowl-of, subst. com. gen., pl. צִפֳּרִים. R. צָפַר to chirp, to twitter.

וּדְגֵי and-(the) fishes-of, constr. of דָּגִים, pl. of דָּג verb. n. m. with ו cop. i. 1, from דָּגָה to be multiplied.

הַיָּם the-sea, subst. m. R. יָמַם, unused in Heb., to make a noise.

עֹבֵר (and whatsoever) passeth (through), Kal pres. part. m. s. from עָבַר vii. 7. The LXX., Vulg., Syr., Æth., and Arab. have the part. in the pl.; the Chal. reads, 'Leviathan traversing the paths of the sea.'

אָרְחוֹת (the) paths-of, constr. of אֳרָחוֹת, pl. of אֹרַח subst. com. gen., in Heb. used only in poetry. R. אָרַח to go.

Or perhaps, '(man) passeth the paths of the sea.' The Psalmist has here brought the subject to a climax. To have dominion over all cattle, the birds of heaven, and the fishes of the sea, was placing vast power in the hands of man, but to endue him with skill to navigate the sea was to set him still farther above the rest of living creatures. In the spirit of this remark Mendelssohn observes, in his comment on the verse: 'The word יָם hath brought the Psalmist to this thought, for passing the path of the sea requires the greatest effort of the mind of man. The great power of man is to keep alive in an element in which he was not born. Great must be his power and strength to stand before the raging of the sea and the tumult of its waves. Powerful must he be in the knowledge of the stars, their stations, and their orbits; passing the paths of the sea, this is his extreme boundary, and here he stops.'

PSALM IX.

A triumphant song of thanksgiving to God the righteous Judge of all men, who punishes the ungodly and defends the cause of the oppressed. This Psalm may possibly have been composed by David at the conclusion of the Syro-Ammonite war, or after one of his victories over the Philistines. This is the first of the eight Acrostic or Alphabetical Psalms (reckoning the ninth and tenth as forming one), the first verse beginning with the first letter of the Hebrew alphabet, and the other letters following in order at the beginning of each successive verse. In this case the alphabetical arrangement is not nearly so perfect as in the seven other Psalms of the same class, i.e. Psalms xxv, xxxiv, xxxvii, cxi, cxii, cxix, and cxlv.

Verse 1. מוּת לַבֵּן Muth-labben, lit. Death of the son. Some suppose this to be the name of a tune or of a musical instrument; others regard לְ as servile and בֵּן as the prop. name of a Levite, as in 1 Chron. xv. 18; whilst others suppose Absalom to be meant, and render it 'On the death of the son;' whilst others again take it as an anagram of *Nabal*, and render it 'On the death of the fool.' See 1 Sam. xxv. 25.

Verse 2. The LXX., Vulg., Æth., and Arab. read here אוֹדְךָ.

נִפְלְאוֹתֶיךָ Thy-marvellous-works, Niph. pres. part. f. pl. with suff. 2 m. s. from פָּלָא to separate, not used in Kal; Niph. to be great, extraordinary, to be difficult; Hiph. to make wonderful, to deal wonderfully; Hithp. to exert one's strength.

Verse 4. אָחוֹר backward, subst. m., hinder part, rear, end, used adverbially. R. אָחַר to be behind, after, also to stay, to tarry, only found once in Kal, Gen. xxxii. 5; Pi. to cause to retard, to hinder.

יִכָּשְׁלוּ they-shall-fall, Niph. 3 m. pl. fut. from כָּשַׁל, only found once in the fut. in Kal, Prov. iv. 16, elsewhere the fut. of Niph. is used; Pi. to cause to fall=to fell.

Verse 5. וְדִינִי and-my-cause, verb. n. m. from דִּין vii. 9, with suff. 1 s.

לְכִסֵּא on-(the)throne, subst. m. with pr. לְ ii. 1, pl. כִּסְאוֹת, a seat, lofty, and covered with a canopy or hanging, a throne. R. כָּסָא i. q. כָּסָה to cover.

Verse 6. רָשָׁע (the)wicked, sing. of i. 1 used collectively.

מָחִיתָ Thou-hast-put-out, Kal 2 m. s. pret. from מָחָה to rub or wipe away, to destroy.

Verse 7. The sing. הָאוֹיֵב is here to be regarded as a collect., and so taken with a pl. verb.

תַּמּוּ they-are-extinct, Kal 3 pl. pret. from תָּמַם vii. 9.

חֳרָבוֹת (they are made)desolations, or destructions, pl. of חָרְבָּה verb. n. f. from חָרַב vii. 13.

לָנֶצַח for-ever, strictly a subst. m., perpetuity, eternity, with pr. לְ ii. 4.

וְעָרִים and-cities, pl. of עָר subst. m., i.q. עִיר, prob. from a root, now extinct, signifying to surround; some derive the word from a root having the signification of frequenting and thronging; others from עוּר to be awake, to be vigilant. Some think that the word עָר signifies *an enemy*, from the unused root עִיר, prop. to be hot, ardent, applied to the heat of anger.

נָתַשְׁתָּ Thou-hast-destroyed, Luther's Version is, Die Schwerdter des Feindes haben ein Ende; die Städte hast Du umgekehret.

Verse 9. תֵּבֵל (the)world, subst. f., used in poetry for אֶרֶץ. R. יָבַל, unused in Kal, to flow, to run, poetically to go, to walk; Hiph. to bring, to carry, to bring forth, to produce, used only in poetry; Hoph. to be brought.

בְּמֵישָׁרִים in-righteousness, verb. n. m. pl. from יָשַׁר vii. 11, with pr. בְּ i. 1.

Verse 10. וִיהִי also-will-be, Kal 3 m. s. fut. apoc. from הָיָה with ו cop. prefixed. For יְהִי (.) is inserted under ו because two (֫) cannot come together at the beginning of a word, and the (֫) so inserted coalesces with the homogeneous י, so that it is written without (֫). The simple fut. of the verb is יִהְיֶה. The apoc. fut. (when one is found in the species) is used to express an imp. or subj. mood, and after ו convers.

מִשְׂגָּב a-refuge, or a high place, verb. n. m. from שָׂגַב, i. q. רוּם (but, except in Deut. ii. 36, used only in poetry), to rise, to be high; Niph. to be exalted; Pi. to raise up.

לַדָּךְ for-(the) oppressed, verb. adj. m. with pr. לְ ii. 1, from the unused root דָּכַךְ (i. q. דָּכָא and דָּכָה) to break in pieces, to crush.

בַּצָּרָה in-trouble, verb. n. f. from צָרַר iii. 2 with pr. בְּ i. 1.

Verse 11. The Syr. and Arab. have כל יודעי.

דֹּרְשֶׁיךָ them-that-seek-Thee, Kal pres. part. m. pl. with suff. 2 m. s. from דָּרַשׁ, prop. to rub, to tread with the feet, hence to go to a place, to frequent it, also to seek, to demand, to punish.

Verse 12. עֲלִילוֹתָיו His-doings, pl. of עֲלִילָה verb. n. f. with suff. 3 m. s. from עָלַל to do or perform anything.

Verse 13. אוֹתָם them, suff. 3 m. pl. joined with אֵת, marking the object, ii. 3, used as objective case of personal pronouns.

צַעֲקַת (the) cry-of, constr. of צְעָקָה verb. n. f. from צָעַק to cry, i. q. זָעַק.

עֲנָיִים (the) humble, or the afflicted, (to be read עֲנִיִּים), pl. of עָנִי verb. adj. m. from עָנָה to bestow labour or toil on anything, to till the ground, to bring the earth into cultivation, to suffer, to be oppressed; Pi. to oppress; Hithp. to humble oneself. The K'ri ענוים is pl. of עָנָו, which is also derived from the same root.

Verse 14. The Psalmist here passes from the language of triumph to that of supplication.

חָנְנֵנִי an unusual form for חָנֵּנִי iv. 2.

עָנְיִי my-trouble (which I suffer), verb. n. m. from עָנָה ix. 13 with suff. 1 s.

מִשַּׁעֲרֵי from-(the) gates-of, pl. constr. of שַׁעַר subst. com. gen. with pr. מִן ii. 3. R. שָׁעַר to cleave, to divide.

Verse 15. תְּהִלָּתֶיךָ Thy-praise, verb. n. f. from הָלַל v. 6 with suff. 2 m. s. We have here an instance of a sing. noun with suff. as if it were a pl.

בְּשַׁעֲרֵי in-(the)gates-of, the most public place of concourse in an Eastern city.

בַּת־ (the)daughter-of, subst. f., contracted from בְּנַת for בֶּנֶת, pl. בָּנוֹת. R. בָּנָה to build.

צִיּוֹן Zion, ii. 6. '*The daughter of Zion*' was a poetical personification, the ideal representative of its *inhabitants*.

Verse 16. טָבְעוּ are-sunk-down, Kal 3 pl. pret. from טָבַע to sink, to press into any soft material such as clay, hence to impress a seal, to seal. Comp. Gr. δύπτω, to dive; Goth. *diup;* Ger. *tief;* Eng. *deep;* also Ger. *taufen;* Ital. *tuffare,* to dip, to immerse; and with the letters transposed, Gr. βαθύς, deep; βυθός, depth.

בְּרֶשֶׁת־ in-(the)net, subst. f. with pr. בּ i. 1. R. יָרַשׁ to take possession, iv. 8.

זוּ which, pron. demonstr. com. gen. i.q. זֶה and זֹאת, used only in poetry.

Verse 17. The LXX., Vulg., Æth., and Arab. read the word עָשָׂה as if pointed עָשָׂה.

בְּפֹעַל in-(the)work-of, verb. n. m. from פָּעַל v. 6 with pr. בּ i. 1. This word is used exclusively in poetry.

נוֹקֵשׁ is-snared, or rather lays snares, sc. for himself; Kal pres. part. m. s. from נָקַשׁ to lay snares. Possibly נוֹקֵשׁ may be for נוֹקָשׁ, Niph. 3 m. s. pret. from a root יָקשׁ, according to the LXX. and Vulg.

הִגָּיוֹן Higgaion, subst. m., the sound of the harp when struck; sometimes meaning a meditation; הִגָּיוֹן סֶלָה probably means a grave, subdued symphony. R. הָגָה i. 2. The only other places where the word occurs are Ps. xix. 15, xcii. 4, and Lam. iii. 62.

Verse 19. אֶבְיוֹן (the)needy, verb. adj. m. from אָבָה, prop. to breathe after, hence to wish, to desire, to want, to need. Comp. Lat. *aveo.*

תִּקְוַת (the)expectation-of, constr. of תִּקְוָה subst. f. R. קָוָה to twist, to bind, in Kal found only in the part. קֹוֶה; Pi. to wait or look for; Niph. to be gathered together.

K'thiv עֲנִוִּים to be read עֲנָוִים; K'ri ענִיִּים.

תֹּאבַד shall-(not)perish, i. 6. The particle לֹא is to be repeated from the first member of the verse.

Verse 21. שִׁיתָה Put, Kal 2 m. s. imp. with ה parag. from שִׁית, see ii. 2.

מוֹרָה fear, i.q. מוֹרָא verb. n. m. from יָרֵא to fear. The LXX., Syr., Vulg., Arab., and Luther render the word as if מוֹרֶה a teacher or doctor, whilst some persons translate 'Lay on them *the razor*,' in which sense מורה occurs in Jud. xiii. 5 and elsewhere, which would imply the greatest dishonour in the East, where it is customary to let the beard grow. Luther has Gib ihnen, Herr, einen Meister.

PSALM X.

The Psalmist here calls on the Almighty to chasten the presumption of the wicked. The LXX. and Vulg. unite this Psalm with the preceding one.

Verse 1. בְּרָחוֹק afar-off, verb. adj. m. (remote, distant), with pr. ב i. 1, from רָחַק to be removed, used adverbially.

Verse 2. בְּגַאֲוַת in-(the) pride-of, constr. of גַּאֲוָה verb. n. f. with pr. ב i. 1, from גָּאָה, a poetical word, to be lifted up, to be exalted.

יִדְלַק doth-persecute, lit. burns.

יִתָּפְשׂוּ let-them-be-taken, Niph. 3 m. pl. fut. from תָּפַשׂ. We observe here a sudden change of number.

בִּמְזִמּוֹת in-(the) devices, pl. of מְזִמָּה subst. f. (with pr. ב ii. 11), counsel, device, specially evil counsel. R. זָמַם to purpose, to resolve, most frequently used in a bad sense, to meditate evil, to plot.

Verse 3. תַּאֲוַת desire, constr. of תַּאֲוָה subst. f., delight, object of desire. R. אָוָה to bend, to inflect, to desire, sometimes to mark, to designate, not used in Kal; Pi. to desire, to long for. Comp. Lat. *aveo*.

וּבֹצֵעַ and-(the)covetous, Kal pres. part. m. s. with ו cop. i. 1, from בָּצַע to heap up, to collect (particularly ill-gotten wealth), to tear in pieces, to spoil.

בֵּרֵךְ blesseth, Pi. 3 m. s. pret. from בָּרַךְ iii. 9.

נִאֵץ (whom)abhorreth, Pi. 3 m. s. pret. from נָאַץ to despise, to reject with contempt.

יְהֹוָה the-Lord, or it may perhaps be, 'and he blesseth the robber, he despiseth Jehovah;' or, 'the covetous blesseth (himself), he abhorreth the Lord.'

Verse 4. כְּגֹבַהּ according-to-(the)pride-of, verb. n. m. with pr. כ i. 3, from גָּבַהּ to be high, to be exalted, to be proud.

אַפּוֹ his-countenance, or his nostril.

בַּל־ not, i.q. בְּלִי, strictly a subst., failure, defeat, nothing, hence used as an adv. of negation, i.q. לֹא, but only in poetry. R. בָּלָה to fall or waste away, to fail, to perish, to grow old; Pi. to consume, to trouble.

אֵין אֱלֹהִים בָּל־מְזִמּוֹתָיו God-(is)not-(in)all-his-devices; or, 'all his devices (are, There is) no God.'

Verse 5. יָחִילוּ are-grievous, or perhaps are strong, i.e. prosper, Kal (Ges.), Hiph. (Fürst), 3 m. pl. fut. from חִיל or חוּל to be strong, also to turn, to twist, to be pained, to tremble, to delay; Pilel, to dance in a circle, also to bring forth; Pulal, to be born; Hithpolel, to writhe with pain, to wait for.

For the K'thiv דְּרָכָו (to be read דְּרָכּוֹ) the K'ri has דרכיו.

מָרוֹם high, vii. 8, used adverbially.

יָפִיחַ he-puffeth, i. e. in scorn or contempt, Hiph. 3 m. s. fut. from פּוּחַ to blow.

Verse 6. אֶמּוֹט I-shall-be-moved, Kal 1 s. fut. from מוֹט, in Kal and Niph. to move, quake, tremble; in Hiph. (to cause to fall) found only in Ps. lv. 4 and cxl. 11, K'thibh.

PSALM X. vv. 7, 8.

לְדֹר to-generation, subst. m., age, generation, habitation, with pr. לְ ii. 1; pl. יָמִ֫ and דֹּת. R. דּוּר to go around, to go in a circle, to dwell, in Heb. found only in Ps. lxxxiv. 11, though it occurs several times in Chal. in the Book of Daniel. Comp. Gr. δηρός, δηρόν, long, lasting; Lat. *durare*, to last, to remain; Ger. dauern, anciently turen, turen; Eng. *durable*, and to en*dure*.

בְרָע in-evil, v. 5, with pr. בְּ i. 1. The Chal. has 'from generation to generation I shall not be moved from doing evil;' the Syr. 'he meditates evil.' The LXX. omits the relat. altogether, and has merely ἄνευ κακοῦ.

Verse 7. אָלָה cursing, verb. n. f. from אָלָה to swear, to curse.

וּמִרְמוֹת and-deceits, pl. of v. 7. The LXX. has πικρία, probably confounding the word with מָרוֹת from מָרַר.

וָתֹךְ and-fraud, subst. m. with וְ cop. i. 2, from the obs. root תָּכַךְ to oppress, to rob. The word is written in full תּוֹךְ in Ps. lxxii. 14; pl. תְּכָכִים is found in Prov. xxix. 16.

וָאָוֶן and-vanity, or iniquity.

Verse 8. בְּמַאְרַב in-(the)lurking-place-of, constr. of מַאְרָב verb. n. m. with pr. בְּ i. 1, from אָרַב strictly to tie, fig. to lay snares, to lie in ambush.

חֲצֵרִים (the) villages, pl. of חָצֵר verb. n. com. gen. with pr. בְּ i. 1, from the unused root חָצַר to shut in, to surround. For חֲצֵרִים the LXX. reads עשירים 'the rich.'

בְּמִסְתָּרִים in-(the)secret-places, pl. of מִסְתָּר verb. n. m. with pr. בְּ i. 1, from סָתַר to hide, to conceal, in Kal found only in Prov. xxii. 3, K'thiv.

נָקִי (the) innocent, verb. adj. m. (pl. נְקִיִּים), from נָקָה to be pure; Pi. to acquit, to pardon.

לְחֵלְכָה against-(the)poor, adj. m. for חֵלְכָא with pr. לְ ii. 1 and ה parag. R. in Arabic to be dark, metaph. to be wretched. The word only occurs here and in vv. 10 and 14. In ver. 10 we find חל כאים substituted in the K'ri for חֵלְכָּאִים.

יִצְפֹּנוּ are-privily-set, lit. will hide (themselves), Kal 3 m. pl. fut. from צָפַן.

PSALM X. vv. 9, 10, 12, 14, 15, 17, 18.

Verse 9. בְּסֻכֹּה in-his-den, an unusual form for סֻכּוֹ subst. m. with pr. בְּ i. 1 and suff. 3 m. s. R. סָכַךְ v. 12.

בְּמָשְׁכוֹ when-he-draweth-him, Kal inf. constr. from מָשַׁךְ with pr. בְּ i. 1 and suff. 3 m. s.

Verse 10. וְדָכָה He-bends-down, or he will break himself, prob. for יִדְכֶּה the K'ri reading; Kal 3 m. s. fut. from דָּכָה i. q. דָּכָא to be crushed or bruised, in Kal found only in this passage. Or we may perhaps read וְדֻכָּה 'and crushed he (the humble) sinks down,' according to the K'thiv with a change of vowel points.

יָשֹׁחַ he-will-bow-down, Kal 3 m. s. fut. from שָׁחַח i. q. שׁוּחַ and שָׁחָה to sink down; Niph. and Hithp. to be cast down; Hiph. to bring down, to humble; in Hithpoel to be cast down, only found in Ps. xlii. 6, 12, and xliii. 5.

בַּעֲצוּמָיו by-his-strong-ones, meaning prob. his strong *claws* or *teeth*, recurring to the metaphor of the lion, ver. 9; pl. of עָצוּם verb. adj. m. from עָצַם vi. 3 with pr. בְּ i. 1 and suff. 3 m. s.

Verse 12. For the K'thiv עֲנִיִּים the K'ri has עֲנָוִים.

Verse 14. תַּבִּיט beholdest, Hiph. 2 m. s. fut. from נָבַט, not used in Kal.

לָתֵת to-put (it), for תֵּנֶת, Kal inf. constr. from נָתַן with pr. לְ ii. 4.

For בְּיָדְךָ sing. the LXX., Vulg., Syr., Æth., and Arab. have the plural.

יַעֲזֹב committeth (himself), lit. will leave himself.

יָתוֹם (the) fatherless, subst. m. R. יָתַם, unused in Heb., to be solitary, bereaved.

Verse 15. זְרוֹעַ (the)arm-of, subst. com. gen., rarely m.

Verse 17. אָזְנְךָ Thine-ear, subst. f. with suff. 2 m. s.; abs. form אֹזֶן, dual אָזְנַיִם. R. אָזַן v. 2.

Verse 18. יוֹסִיף he-shall-add, Hiph. 3 m. s. fut. from יָסַף, not used in the fut. in Kal.

עוֹד yet, prop. inf. abs. (but used only as an adv.) from עוּד to do or say over again, to repeat, to witness; Pi. to surround;

Hiph. to give evidence, to affirm solemnly; Pilel, to confirm, to restore; Hithpalel, to stand upright, found only in Ps. xx. 9.

לַעֲרֹץ to-oppress, or to terrify, Kal inf. constr. from עָרַץ to terrify, to oppress, with pr. לְ ii. 1 pointed with (ַ) because of the following (ֲ).

PSALM XI.

This Psalm, probably written by David either at the time of his persecution by Saul, or of the rebellion of his son Absalom, represents the Psalmist, having full trust in the providence and justice of God, rejecting the counsel of timorous advisers who urge him to take refuge in flight.

Verse 1. The LXX., Vulg., Chal., and two MSS. insert the word מִזְמוֹר before לְדָוִד.

אֵיךְ how, adv. abbreviated from אֵיכָה, compounded of אֵי, a mark of interrogation put before adverbs and pronouns giving them an interrog. sense, and כָּה i. q. כֹּה so, thus.

לְנַפְשִׁי has here the force of the pron. לִי as in iii. 3.

נוּדוּ flee, (to be read נֻדוּ), Kal 2 m. pl. imp. from נוּד to be agitated, to nod, to flee, followed by a dative, to pity, to comfort, to lament. Comp. Eng. *nod*. The K'ri נוּדִי f. s. imp. is followed by the ancient versions.

הַרְכֶם (to) your-mountain, some old versions have הַר כְּמוֹ.

צִפּוֹר (as) a-bird, viii. 9. The particle of similitude is omitted as in Ps. xxii. 14, xlviii. 8, and elsewhere.

Verse 2. יֶתֶר (the) string, subst. m., a cord, a rope, prop. something hanging over, redundant, the rest, the remainder, abundance, superfluity, sometimes used for excellence, dignity. R. יָתַר to be over and above, to be left, in Kal there only occurs part. יוֹתֵר that which is left, 1 Sam. xv. 15; Hiph. to let remain, to leave, also to make profit.

בְּמוֹ in, מוֹ an enclitic syllable, annexed to the prefixes בְּ (i. 1),

בְּ, and לְ to make them independent words, the signification not being affected thereby. · These lengthened forms are exclusively poetical.

אֹפֶל darkness, subst. m., a poetical word. R. אָפַל, unused in Heb., to set, spoken of the sun, to become dark, to fail, to be weak.

Verse 3. הַשָּׁתוֹת the-foundations, subst. f. pl. (sing. שָׁת unused). R. שִׁית, see ii. 2.

יֵהָרֵסוּן shall-be-destroyed, Niph. 3 m. pl. fut. from הָרַס to tear down, to destroy, with ן parag.

Verse 4. After עֵינָיו the LXX. has preserved a word dropped in the Heb. from its likeness to the preceding one: οἱ ὀφθαλμοὶ αὐτοῦ εἰς τὸν πένητα ἀποβλέπουσι, עֵינָיו עָנִי יֶחֱזוּ; this reading perfectly restores the parallelism with the following hemistich, and is supported by the Vulg., Æth., and Arab. The Chal. and Syr. have however followed the present Hebrew text.

יֶחֱזוּ behold, Kal 3 m. pl. fut. from חָזָה, used in poetry i. q. רָאָה to see.

עַפְעַפָּיו His-eyelids, subst. m. dual with suff. 3 m. s., the eyelids, so called from their volatile motion (die Flatternden). R. עוּף to cover, especially with feathers or wings, to fly.

Verse 6. יַמְטֵר May-He-rain, Hiph. 3 m. s. fut. from מָטַר to rain; not used in Kal; Hiph. to pour down rain, to water.

פַּחִים snares, pl. of פַּח verb. n. m. from פָּחַח, prob. to spread out; Hiph. to spread a net, to ensnare.

אֵשׁ fire, subst. com. gen. (rarely m.) Comp. Sans. *ush*, to burn; Lat. *aestus*, heat; Ger. heiß, hot.

וְגָפְרִית and-brimstone, subst. f., prop. pitch, the name of which was afterwards transferred to other inflammable materials, especially sulphur, brimstone. R. גָּפַר, unused in Heb., prob. i. q. כָּפַר to cover, to overspread.

וְזִלְעָפוֹת horrors, or heat, pl. of זִלְעָפָה subst. f., heat, glow. R. זָלְעַף i. q. יָעַף to be hot, to be angry.

מְנָת (the) portion-of, for מְנָאת verb. n. f. from מָנָה kindred to מָנַן ii. 3.

כּוֹסָם their-cup, subst. f. with suff. 3 m. pl.; pl. כּוֹסוֹת. The etymology of this word is somewhat uncertain.

Verse 7. פָּנֵימוֹ His-countenance, iii. 1 with suff. 3 m. s. The suff. יָמוֹ may be *sing.* as well as *pl.*, especially when used, as here, in reference to God. Some translate this passage, 'They that are upright shall behold His face,' יָשָׁר sing., but in a collective sense, and therefore followed by a plural predicate.

PSALM XII.

This Psalm is very similar to the two preceding. In the Syr. it is called, 'The battle of the evil one, and a prophecy concerning the Advent of Christ.'

Verse 2. For הוֹשִׁיעָה the LXX., Vulg., Æth., and Arab. have הוֹשִׁיעֵנִי.

פַּסּוּ fail, Kal 3 pl. pret. from פָּסַס (i. q. אָפֵס), only found in this passage.

אֱמוּנִים (the) faithful, Kal pass. part. m. pl. from אָמַן to stay, to support, intrans. to be firm, metaph. to be faithful; Hiph. to lean on, to confide in. Some consider the word as pl. of the subst. אֱמוּן faithfulness, and translate with the Vulg. 'Truth and faith have disappeared from among men.'

Verse 3. שָׁוְא vanity, subst. m., vanity, what is useless, to no purpose, what is false or deceitful, a lie. R. שׁוֹא i. q. שָׁאָה to make a noise, to crash, also to be laid waste, desolate.

אֶת־ with, prep., strictly a subst. denoting nearness, prob. for אֱנָת, not to be confounded with אֵת marking the definite object. R. אָנָה, not used in Kal, to approach, to draw near; Pi. to cause anything to happen; Pu. to be caused to meet, i. e. to light upon, to befal.

רֵעֵהוּ his-neighbour, verb. n. m. from רָעָה to feed (a flock), to pasture, also to take delight in, to associate with, with suff. 3 m. s.

שְׂפַת (with) a-lip-of, constr. of שָׂפָה subst. f., sometimes used for language, dual שְׂפָתַיִם, constr. שִׂפְתֵי; pl. only in the constr. state שִׂפְתוֹת, from the unused root שָׂפָה, which appears to have had the signification of devouring or licking up.

חֲלָקוֹת slipperinesses, or smooth things, pl. of חֲלָקָה verb. n. f. from חָלַק v. 10.

Verse 4. יַכְרֵת May-He-cut-off, Hiph. 3 m. s. fut. apoc. from כָּרַת Kal and Hiph. to cut, to destroy, joined with בְּרִית to make a covenant, because it was customary in making a covenant to slay and divide the victims; Niph. to be destroyed, to perish, i. q. אָבַד.

גְּדֹלוֹת great-things, f. pl. of גָּדוֹל verb. adj. from גָּדַל, prop. to twist or bind together, hence to be or become great; Pi. and Hiph. to make great, to magnify.

Verse 5. נַגְבִּיר will-we-prevail, Hiph. 1 pl. fut. from גָּבַר to be strong, powerful, construed with מִן to be stronger than, to prevail over; Hithp. to be proud.

Verse 6. מִשֹּׁד For-(the) oppression-of, verb. n. m. from שָׁדַד to be powerful, to be strong, to oppress, to destroy, with pr. מ ii. 3.

מֵאַנְקַת for-(the) sighing-of, constr. of אֲנָקָה subst. f. (with pr. מ iii. 5), only found in three other places, viz. Ps. lxxix. 11, cii. 21, and Mal. ii. 13. R. אָנַק, prop. to struggle, to be in anguish, to groan, to cry out, hence used of cries extorted by great anguish. See vi. 7.

בְּיֵשַׁע in-salvation, verb. n. m. with pr. ב i. 1, from יָשַׁע iii. 3.

יָפִיחַ לוֹ he-will-puff-at-him. Or it may be, 'I will place in safety him at whom they puff;' or perhaps, 'I will place in safety him who pants after it.'

Verse 7. אִמְרוֹת (The) words-of, pl. constr. of אִמְרָה verb. n. f. (used only in poetry) from אָמַר ii. 7.

טְהֹרוֹת pure, f. pl. of טָהוֹר verb. adj. from טָהֵר to shine, to be clean; Pi. to cleanse, to purify.

כֶּסֶף silver, subst. m., used also for money generally. R. כָּסַף to become pale, also to desire, to long for; in Kal found only in Job xiv. 15 and Ps. xvii. 12.

צָרוּף tried, or refined, Kal pass. part. m. s. from צָרַף to melt, to fuse, particularly to refine (gold, silver, &c. by the fire), metaph. to prove or examine any one, to purge.

בַּעֲלִיל in-a-furnace, subst. m. (only found in this passage), with pr. בְּ i. 1. R. עָלַל ix. 12.

מְזֻקָּק purified, Pu. pres. part. m. s. from זָקַק to pour out, to filter, to refine.

שִׁבְעָתָיִם seven-times, dual of שִׁבְעָה num. adj. m., constr. שִׁבְעַת; f. שֶׁבַע, constr. שְׁבַע. Comp. Sans. *sapta*, Zend *hapta*, Gr. ἑπτά, Lat. *septem*, in all which the letter *t* appears, which is not the case in the Phœnicio-Shemitic languages or in the Germanic; see Goth. *sibum*, Ger. ſieben, Eng. *seven*.

Verse 8. תשמרנו instead of תשמרם is the reading of the LXX., Vulg., Arab., Æth., and some MSS.

תִּצְּרֶנּוּ Thou-shalt-preserve-them, lit. him, i. e. every one of them; Luther has the 1st pers. pl. here and in the previous clause.

Verse 9. כְּרֻם at-raising, Kal inf. constr. from רוּם iii. 4 with pr. כְּ i. 3.

זֻלּוּת vileness, subst. f., vileness, or perhaps terror, trembling, or a shaking, an earthquake, a storm, a tempest; the word occurs only here. R. זָלַל to pour out, to shake, and as only those things are cast out which are counted worthless, intrans. to be vile, worthless; Niph. to be shaken, to tremble.

לִבְנֵי אָדָם of-(the) sons-of-men; or perhaps, like the rising of a tempest upon the sons of men. Bp. Horsley translates the verse, 'The impious shall be getting them out of the way' (will endeavour to escape and secrete themselves, but will not be able to effect it), 'when the scorn of the sons of men,' i. e. he whom the sons of men despised, 'is exalted.'

E

PSALM XIII.

In this Psalm we see a servant of God, sorely tried by the persecutions of his enemies, pouring out the deep sighing of his heart, and praying for preventing grace.

Verse 2. עַד־אָנָה How-long, lit. until when, עַד iv. 3; אָנָה adv. interrog. contraction of אַיִן whither, with ה local.

Verse 3. יָגוֹן sorrow, subst. m. R. יָגָה, unused in Kal, to be pained in mind, to be sad. After יומם the LXX. and some MSS. add וליֹלה.

Verse 4. הַמָּוֶת the-(sleep of) death. Before הַמָּוֶת the word שְׁנַת should be understood.

Verse 5. יְכָלְתִּיו I-have-prevailed-against-him, Kal 1 s. pret. with suff. 3 m. s. from יָכֹל to be able, construed with לְ of the person, to obtain the mastery over any one; in Kal found only in the pret.; in the fut. the conj. Hoph. is used.

Verse 6. אָשִׁירָה I-will-sing; this begins another verse in the Eng. Version. The LXX. adds the words 'and I will sing praise unto the name of the Lord most High,' and this is followed by the Prayer-Book Version, the Vulg., Arab., Æth., and Coptic.

PSALM XIV.

This Psalm and the next may be viewed as a pair; *the one* presenting us with the character of the ungodly, *the other* with that of the righteous. Both in Psalms xii and xiv, the singer complains of the oppression which the righteous suffer at the hands of the wicked. This Psalm (Jehovistic) appears again, with some variations, as Psalm liii (Elohistic), but it is uncertain which is the original poem.

PSALM XIV. vv. 1–5.

Verse 1. The LXX., Syr., Vulg., Æth., and some MSS. insert the word מִזְמוֹר before לְדָוִד.

נָבָל (The) fool, verb. adj. m. from נָבֵל i. 3.

הִשְׁחִיתוּ They-are-corrupt, Hiph. 3 pl. pret. from שָׁחַת, not used in Kal; Pi. and Hiph. to corrupt, to destroy, intrans. to behave wickedly, to sin.

הִתְעִיבוּ they-have-done-abominable, Hiph. 3 pl. pret. from תָּעַב v. 7.

For עֲלִילָה the Syr., Chal., and Vulg. have the suff. 3 pl. as if they read עֲלִילוֹתָם. The LXX., Vulg., Æth., Arab., Coptic, and our Prayer-Book Version add at the end of the verse the words 'no not one.'

Verse 2. הִשְׁקִיף looked-down, Hiph. 3 m. s. pret. from שָׁקַף, not used in Kal.

מַשְׂכִּיל that-did-understand, Hiph. pres. part. m. s. from שָׂכַל ii. 10.

Verse 3. סָר is-gone-aside, Kal 3 m. s. pret. from סוּר vi. 9.

נֶאֱלָחוּ they-are-become-filthy, Niph. 3 pl. pret. from אָלַח to become sour as milk, found only in Niph. to be corrupted. The word occurs elsewhere only in Ps. liii. 4 and Job xv. 16.

אֶחָד one, num. adj. m., constr. אַחַד; f. אֶחָת, constr. אַחַת, pl. אֲחָדִים. This cardinal number is used in commencing a series, or in naming the days of the month, as though it were an ordinal. Comp. Æth. *ahadu;* Sans. *eka*. Between this verse and the next one the Prayer-Book Version, following the Vulg. and a MS. of the LXX., inserts three verses which are not found in the Authorized Version: 'Their throat is an open sepulchre, with their tongues do they deceive,' &c.; but in the parallel passage in Ps. liii we find no such addition.

Verse 4. לֶחֶם bread, verb. n. com. gen. from לָחַם to eat, to consume, also to fight, only used in Kal in the signification of fighting in Ps. xxxv. 1 and lvi. 2, 3, though it frequently occurs in that signification in Niph.

Verse 5. שָׁם There, adv. of place and of time.

פָּחַד fear, verb. n. m. from פָּחַד. The LXX., Vulg., and Arab. add here, as in Ps. liii, 'where no fear was.'

Verse 6. מַחְסֵהוּ his-refuge, verb. n. m. from חָסָה ii. 12 with suff. 3 m. s.

Verse 7. יִשְׂרָאֵל Israel, prop. name m., a prince of God, or a wrestler with God, from שָׂרָה to contend, to struggle with a person, and אֵל v. 5.

שְׁבוּת (the) captivity-of, verb. n. f. from שָׁבָה to take or lead away captive.

יַעֲקֹב Jacob, prop. name m., taking hold of the heel, supplanter. R. עָקַב to be behind, to take hold of any one by the heel, to supplant.

PSALM XV.

This Psalm, in which David describes a citizen of Zion, (and which is one of the Proper Psalms for Ascension Day,) is supposed to have been written on the occasion of the removal of the Ark to Zion, and the Consecration of the Tabernacle. In its general subject it bears some resemblance to Ps. v, the doctrine of both being this: that righteousness is the qualification which alone may fit any one to be a guest in God's Tabernacle.

Verse 1. בְּאָהֳלֶךָ in-Thy-tabernacle, subst. m. with pr. ב i. 1 and suff. 2 m. s.; abs. form אֹהֶל, pl. אֹהָלִים, constr. אָהֳלֵי. The LXX., Syr., Vulg., Æth., Arab., and Chal. have וּמִי.

Verse 2. תָּמִים uprightly, verb. adj. m. from תָּמַם vii. 9, used substantively, (in) uprightness.

אֱמֶת truth, contraction of אֲמֶנֶת subst. f. R. אָמַן xii. 2.

Verse 3. רָגַל He-backbiteth, Kal 3 m. s. pret., denom. from רֶגֶל foot (see viii. 7), to run about, especially as a talebearer and as a spy; to calumniate, to spy out; in Kal found only in this passage.

וְחֶרְפָּה and-a-reproach, verb. n. m. from חָרַף Kal and Pi. to mock, to revile.

קְרֹבוֹ him-that-is-near-him, verb. adj. m. with suff. 3 m. s. from קָרַב to approach. The word קָרַב, when occurring in connection with עַל, indicates hostility (hence we have מִקְרָב war), i.e. parties meeting each other for hostile purposes.

Verse 4. נִבְזֶה is-contemned, Niph. pres. part. m. s. from בָּזָה i.q. בּוּז.

נִמְאָס a-vile-person, Niph. pres. part. m. s. from מָאַס to reject, to despise. The subject and the predicate are not clearly marked; some take נִבְזֶה as the subject, 'The despised person is rejected in his eyes;' others consider both נִבְזֶה and נִמְאָס as predicates, and render 'He (i.e. the subject of the Psalm) is despised and rejected in his own eyes.'

נִשְׁבַּע he-sweareth, Niph. 3 m. s. pret. from שָׁבַע to swear, in Kal found only in the part. pass.; Niph. to swear; Hiph. to make to swear, to bind by an oath.

לְהָרַע to-(his own)hurt, prob. for לְהָרֵעַ, Hiph. inf. constr. from רָעַע ii. 9. The LXX. has τῷ πλησίον, and so Syr., Vulg., Arab., Æth., Coptic, and our Prayer-Book Version, as if they read לְרֵעֵהוּ for לְהָרַע. Some suppose that it stands for לָרָע 'to the evil;' the Chal. has 'so as to afflict himself.'

יָמִר changeth, Hiph. 3 m. s. fut. from מוּר, not used in Kal, to change, to exchange, i.q. יָמֵר.

Verse 5. בְּנֶשֶׁךְ to-usury, verb. n. m. with pr. ב i. 1, from נָשַׁךְ to lend on usury.

וְשֹׁחַד and-a-reward, verb. n. m. from שָׁחַד to give a present.

אֵלֶּה these(things), demonstr. pron. com. gen., used as the pl. of זֶה and זֹאת.

PSALM XVI.

Psalms XVI and XVII form a pair, and express the Psalmist's joy in God, and adherence to Him in times of peril, with a firm belief in the doctrine of the Resurrection. Ps. xvi is interpreted with respect to Christ by St. Peter in Acts ii. 25–28, and also by St. Paul, Acts xiii. 35, in the synagogue of the Jews at Antioch in Pisidia. The Syr. and Arab. Versions entitle this Psalm, 'The election of the Church and the resurrection of Christ.'

Verse 1. מִכְתָּם Michtam, subst. m. (in the superscriptions of Psalms xvi, lvi–lx), most probably i. q. מִכְתָּב Is. xxxviii. 9 (by commutation of ם and ב), a writing, by way of eminence a song. Some render מִכְתָּם (as if from כֶּתֶם gold) a golden or most precious poem. Some suppose this title to be given to certain Psalms, either on account of their *peculiar excellence*, or because they were written in *golden* letters.

Verse 2. אָמַרְתְּ (O my soul) thou-hast-said, Kal 2 f. s. pret. from אָמַר ii. 7. This supposes an ellipsis of נַפְשִׁי; some take אָמַרְתְּ as a defective reading for אָמַרְתִּי, according to the LXX., Syr., Vulg., Arab., Æth., and some MSS. In Ps. cxl. 13 we find יָדַעְתָּ for יָדַעְתִּי.

אֲדֹנָי my-Lord = אֲדֹנִי ii. 4 with suff. 1 s.

טוֹבָתִי my-prosperity (extendeth), verb. n. f. from טוֹב iv. 7 with suff. 1 s.

בַּל־עָלֶיךָ not-upon-Thee, or I have no good beyond Thee, or without Thee, in addition to Thee, or my prosperity is not needful to Thee.

Verse 3. לִקְדוֹשִׁים To-(the) holy-ones, pl. of קָדוֹשׁ verb. adj. m. with pr. ל iv. 3, from קָדַשׁ ii. 6.

וְאַדִּירֵי the constr. form instead of the abs., as in Ps. xxiv. 7.

Verse 4. יִרְבּוּ shall-be-multiplied, Kal 3 m. pl. fut. from רָבָה to become many or numerous; Pi. and Hiph. to multiply, to increase, to make great.

עַצְּבוֹתָם their-sorrows, pl. of עַצֶּבֶת verb. n. f. with suff. 3 m. pl. from עָצַב to labour, to form, to fashion, to suffer pain; Niph. to be pained, to be grieved; Pi. and Hiph. to form, also to afflict; Hithp. to be grieved, to be angry. The LXX., Vulg., Arab., and Syr. render עַצְּבוֹתָם 'their sorrows,' whereas the Chal., Jerome, and Symmachus translate the word 'their idols.' In the former case it is the pl. of עֲצָבֹת, in the latter of עָצָב.

אַחֵר another (god), adj. m.; f. אַחֶרֶת, prop. following, another. R. אָחַר ix. 4.

מָהָרוּ (that) hasten (after), or give gifts to, Kal 3 pl. pret. from מָהַר to hasten after, also to buy (a wife), to marry.

נִסְכֵּיהֶם their-drink-offerings, pl. of נֶסֶךְ verb. n. m. from נָסַךְ ii. 6 with suff. 3 m. pl.

Verse 5. חֶלְקִי mine-inheritance, verb. n. m. with suff. 1 s. from חָלַק v. 10.

תּוֹמִיךְ maintainest; apparently this is Hiph. 2 m. s. fut. from a root יָמַךְ, which, however, does not exist either in Heb. or Arab. It may possibly be = תּוֹמֵךְ Kal pres. part. m. s. from תָּמַךְ.

גּוֹרָלִי my-lot, subst. m. with suff. 1 s. from an unused root גָּרַל, softened from גָּרָה, having the sense of roughness, especially used of a rough gravelly soil. Bp. Horsley translates these two words, 'Thy Thummim is my lot,' (substituting of course different vowel points.) 'That eternal perfect priesthood is allotted unto me, of which the Levitical is the general type; of the glory of which the brilliant gems on the High Priest's breastplate are the particular symbols.' See Deut. xxxiii. 8.

Verse 6. חֲבָלִים (The) lines, pl. of חֶבֶל subst. m. (once f. in Zeph. ii. 6), a cord, a rope, especially a measuring line, hence a measured field, a possession. Comp. Eng. and Fr. *cable*. R. חָבַל vii. 15.

בַּנְּעִימִים in-pleasant (places), pl. of נָעִים adj. m. with pr. בְּ i. 1. R. נָעֵם to be pleasant, lovely.

אַף־ yea, conj. signifying addition. R. perhaps אָפָה to cook, hence cooked, complete, whole.

נַחֲלָת an-inheritance, poet. form of נַחֲלָה ii. 8.

שָׁפְרָה has-been-goodly, or is beautiful, Kal 3 f. s. pret. from שָׁפַר to be fair, shining, bright; the notion of brightness being also applied to brilliancy of sound: according to some it also signifies to pierce through, to hollow, to be hollow.

Verse 8. שִׁוִּיתִי I-have-set, Pi. 1 s. pret. from שָׁוָה to be even; Pi. to make even, also to place, to put.

תָּמִיד always, subst. m., lit. meaning constant continuance, used as an adv. constantly, always, for ever. R. מוּד, unused in Heb., to be moved, agitated.

מִימִינִי at-my-right-hand, subst. com. gen. (mostly f.) with suff. 1 s. and pr. מ ii. 3, see ix. 10.

Verse 9. For כְּבוֹדִי my-glory, the LXX. has ἡ γλῶσσά μου, the Vulg. *lingua mea.*

בְּשָׂרִי my-flesh, subst. m. with suff. 1 s., once pl. בְּשָׂרִים Prov. xiv. 30. R. בָּשַׂר, unused in Kal, of which the primary sense appears to have been that of beauty; Pi. to make cheerful with glad tidings, to bear glad tidings.

Verse 10. נַפְשִׁי is here equivalent to the pers. pron. אוֹתִי me.

חֲסִידֶיךָ Thy-Beloved, or Thy godly One, prob. for חֲסִידְךָ in the sing. according to all the old versions, the K'ri, and a large number of MSS., though several modern critics are of opinion that it stands for חֲסִידֶיךָ 'Thy beloved Ones,' in the pl. St. Peter (Acts ii. 17) and St. Paul (Acts xiii. 35) quote the word in the sing.

שַׁחַת corruption; it is uncertain whether this is the same word as שַׁחַת vii. 16, or whether it is verb. n. m. from שָׁחַת xiv. 1.

Verse 11. שֹׂבַע fulness-of, verb. n. m. from שָׂבַע to be satisfied.

PSALM XVII.

This Psalm (which is somewhat similar to the preceding) was probably written at the time of David's persecution by Saul.

Verse 1. The LXX., Vulg., and Arab. have 'my righteousness,' as if they read צִדְקִי for צֶדֶק.

רִנָּתִי my-cry, verb. n. f. with suff. 1 s. from רָנַן v. 12.

Verse 2. יֵצֵא Let-go-forth, Kal 3 m. s. fut. from יָצָא to go out; Hiph. to cause to go out = to bring out.

For עֵינֶיךָ the LXX. reads עֵינַי.

PSALM XVII. vv. 3–5, 7, 8.

Verse 3. זַמֹּתִי I-am-purposed; some consider this word as Kal inf. constr. with suff. 1 s. from זָמַם x. 2, and render 'my thought varies not from (lit. passes not by יַעֲבָר) my mouth,' i.e. I do not think one thing and say another; others think that it stands for זַמּוֹתַי, pl. of זַמָּה verb. n. f. from זָמַם, and render 'my counsels,' i.e. my settled purpose, 'my mouth shall not overstep;' whilst others (as Gesenius) take it for Kal 1 s. pret. from זָמַם, and render '(that which) I purposed my mouth shall not transgress.' The LXX. has 'that my mouth may not *speak*,' instead of *transgress*, ידבר for יעבר.

Verse 4. לִפְעֻלּוֹת Concerning-(the) works-of, pl. of פְּעֻלָּה verb. n. f. from פָּעַל v. 6 with pr. ל iv. 3.

פָּרִיץ (the) destroyer, adj. m. R. פָּרַץ to tear, or break forth, to spread abroad, to disperse, to increase. Comp. Gr. ῥήσσω, Ger. reißen; and with a prefixed sibilant, Goth. *spreitan*, Ger. ſpreiẞen, to spread.

Verse 5. תָּמֹךְ To-maintain, Kal inf. abs. from תָּמַךְ. The inf. for the imp.

אֲשֻׁרַי my-goings, pl. of אָשׁוּר verb. n. f. with suff. 1 s. from אָשַׁר i. 1.

בְּמַעְגְּלוֹתֶיךָ in-Thy-paths, pl. of מַעְגָּלָה verb. n. f. with pr. בּ i. 1 and suff. 2 m. s. from עָגַל to roll, to revolve.

פְעָמָי my-footsteps, pl. of פַּעַם verb. n. f. (once m. in Jud. xvi. 28), with suff. 1 s. from פָּעַם to strike; Niph. to be agitated, disturbed; used sometimes with the art. as an adv. now; abs. form sing. פַּעַם, dual פַּעֲמַיִם, pl. פְּעָמִים and פְּעָמוֹת.

Verse 7. חוֹסִים them-who-seek-refuge (in Thee). The LXX., Syr., and Arab. have the suff. 2 m. s.

מִמִּתְקוֹמְמִים בִּימִינֶךָ from-those-that-rise-up-(against them) by-Thy-right-hand; or, 'that savest them which trust (in Thee) from those that rise up against Thy right hand.'

Verse 8. כְּאִישׁוֹן as-(the) apple, subst. m. (or perhaps in this instance com. gen.), dimin. from אִישׁ i. 1, homunculus, mannikin, little man; joined with עַיִן the little man in the eye, i.e. the apple of the eye, so called from the little image of himself which the beholder sees therein. Some derive the word from the unused root אָשַׁשׁ to be black, to be dark.

בְּצֵל under-(the) shadow-of, verb. n. m. (once f. in Is. xxxviii. 8), with pr. ב i. 1, from צָלַל to be shaded, to be dusky.

כְּנָפֶיךָ Thy-wings, subst. f. dual with suff. 2 m. s.; sing. כָּנָף, dual כְּנָפַיִם, pl. כְּנָפוֹת. R. כָּנַף, unused in Kal, to cover, to protect.

Verse 9. בְּנֶפֶשׁ against-(my) soul, or perhaps 'with the soul' = eagerly; Chal. 'with the desire of their souls;' Syr. 'enemies of my soul,' i. e. deadly enemies.

יַקִּיפוּ they-will-enclose, Hiph. 3 m. pl. fut. from נָקַף to make a circle, to go round, to revolve; Hiph. to surround, to encompass.

Verse 10. חֶלְבָּמוֹ their-own-fat, verb. n. m. with suff. 3 m. pl. from חָלָב, unused in Heb., to be fat.

בְגֵאוּת in-pride, verb. n. f. from גָּאָה x. 2 with pr. ב i. 1.

Verse 11. The K'thiv is סְבָבוּנִי (to be read סְבָבוּנִי); the K'ri is סבבונו.

Verse 12. דִּמְיֹנוֹ His-likeness, verb. n. m. (only found here), with suff. 3 m. s. from דָּמָה to be like, to resemble; sometimes meaning to cut off, to destroy, also to be dumb; Pi. to liken, to compare, to imagine, to think, to think of, to mention, to remember.

וְכִכְפִיר and-as-a-young-lion, subst. m. (with pr. כ ii. 9), a young lion already weaned, prop. hairy, covered with hair. R. כָּפַר to cover, specially with hair, to be hairy, shaggy; according to Fürst to be strong, to be powerful; Pi. to cover, i. e. to pardon (sin), to expiate (an offence).

Verse 13. קַדְּמָה prevent, Pi. 2 m. s. imp. with ה parag. from קָדַם, found only in Pi. to precede, to be beforehand, hence to do before, to do early in the morning, to fall upon, to meet.

הַכְרִיעֵהוּ cast-him-down, Hiph. 2 m. s. imp. with suff. 3 m. s. from כָּרַע to bend or let oneself down; Hiph. to cast down.

פַּלְּטָה deliver, Pi. 2 m. s. imp. with ה parag. from פָּלַט i. q.

מָלַט to be smooth, to slip away, to escape; Pi. to cause to escape = to deliver.

מֵרָשָׁע חַרְבֶּךָ from-(the) wicked-(which is) Thy-sword. Luther has mit Deinem Schwerdt, (the noun being in the acc. of the instrument.)

Verse 14. מְמְתִים־ From-men, subst. m. pl. from the unused sing. מֵת or מַת with pr. מ ii. 3.

מֵחֶלֶד of-(the)world, subst. m. with pr. מ iii. 5, length of life, life, world. This word occurs four times, besides this place, in the Old Testament, viz. Job xi. 17, Ps. xxxix. 6, xlix. 2, and lxxxix. 48. R. in Arab. to last, to endure.

וּצְפִינְךָ (to be read וְצָפוּנְךָ), and-Thy-hid(treasure); according to the K'thiv this is verb. n. m. from צָפַן to hide, to conceal; the K'ri וצפונך is Kal pass. part. m. s. from צָפַן with ו cop. i. 1 and suff. 2 m. s.

בִטְנָם whose-belly, subst. f. (abs. form בֶּטֶן), with suff. 3 m. pl. R. בָּטַן, unused in Heb., prop. to be empty, hollow.

יִשְׂבְּעוּ בָנִים they-are-full-of-children, or (their) children are full.

וְהִנִּיחוּ and-leave, Hiph. 3 pl. pret. with ו convers. from נוּחַ to rest, to sit down; Hiph. to set down, to deposit in any place.

Verse 15. תְּמוּנָתֶךָ Thy-likeness, subst. f. with suff. 2 m. s. R. מוּן or מִין, unused in Heb., prob. meaning to bear an appearance, to pretend, in Arab. signifying to lie, to speak falsehood. The LXX., Vulg., Arab., Æth., and Coptic have 'Thy Glory.'

PSALM XVIII.

In this magnificent Hymn, (which is also found with several variations in 2 Sam. xxii,) the sweet Psalmist of Israel praises God for the numerous blessings which he had received at His hands. There occur in it several words not found in any other part of the Old Testament. We find the expression 'the servant of the Lord' also in the Title of Ps. xxxvi. The Title in the Syriac Version is 'A Thanksgiving on the Ascension of Christ.' This is the first of the eight Psalms which, according to their

Inscriptions, are to be referred to David's persecution by Saul. The others are Psalms xxxiv, lii, liv, lvii, lix, lxiii, and cxlii.

Verse 1. לְעֶבֶד of-(the) servant-of, verb. n. m. with pr. לְ ii. 1, from עָבַד to labour, to serve.

הַשִּׁירָה the-song, verb. n. f. from שִׁיר vii. 1.

שָׁאוּל Saul, prop. name m. (asked for, R. שָׁאַל ii. 8, to ask, to demand), the first king of the Israelites, the son of Kish, of the tribe of Benjamin.

Verse 2. אֶרְחָמְךָ I-will-love-Thee-fervently, Kal 1 s. fut. with suff. 2 m. s. from רָחַם to be soft, to love, in Kal found only in this passage; Pi. to have compassion, to pity.

חִזְקִי my-strength, verb. n. m. (only found here), with suff. 1 s. from חָזַק to bind fast, to be strong; Pi. to strengthen; Hiph. to take hold of; Hithp. to strengthen oneself, i. e. to collect one's strength.

Verse 3. סַלְעִי my-rock, subst. m. (with suff. 1 s.), from the unused root סָלַע, having the signification of height, elevation.

וּמְצוּדָתִי and-my-fortress, subst. f. with וְ cop. i. 1 and suff. 1 s. R. צוּד to lie in wait, to hunt. The Syr. reads אלהי צורי, which seems to have been borrowed from the parallel passage 2 Sam. xxii.

צוּרִי my-strength, lit. my rock, subst. m. with suff. 1 s. R. צוּר to straighten, to press.

וְקֶרֶן and-(the) horn-of, (the horn being a symbol of strength,) subst. f. Comp. Gr. κέρας, Lat. *cornu*, Fr. *corne*, and Goth. *haurns*, whence Ger. *horn*.

Verse 4. מְהֻלָּל (who is worthy) to-be-praised, Pu. pres. part. m. s. from הָלַל v. 6. This word, by most of the older translators, is taken in an active sense, as if they read מְהַלֵּל. The LXX. has αἰνῶν ἐπικαλέσομαι, Vulg. *laudans*, Chal. 'In a hymn of praise do I utter my prayer.' The Syr. joins it to the previous word מְשַׂגְּבִי 'my glorious refuge.'

Verse 5. אֲפָפוּנִי compassed-me, Kal 3 pl. pret. from אָפַף, a poetic word, with suff. 1 s.

PSALM XVIII. vv. 6–11.

וְנַחֲלֵי and-(the) floods-of, constr. of נְחָלִים, pl. of נַחַל subst. m. (dual נְחָלַיִם); it properly denotes a river or stream, or a valley with a torrent. R. נָחַל, unused in Heb., i. q. נָהַל and נָהַר to flow.

בְלִיַּעַל ungodliness, subst. m. (compounded of בְּלִי (see x. 4) and יַעַל, prob. use, profit, from יָעַל i. q. עָלָה to ascend on high, to climb, also to be useful, not used in Kal; Hiph. to profit, to help); prop. unprofitableness, worthlessness, what is useless, hence wickedness, vileness, sometimes used for destruction.

יְבַעֲתוּנִי made-me-afraid, Pi. 3 m. pl. fut. with suff. 1 s. from בָּעַת, unused in Kal (Syr. to be afraid); Niph. to be afraid; Pi. to frighten; only used in poetry.

Verse 6. חֶבְלֵי (The) sorrows-of, or the cords of; in Sam. we find מִשְׁבְּרֵי billows or breakers, instead of bands or sorrows.

מוֹקְשֵׁי (the) snares-of, pl. constr. of מוֹקֵשׁ verb. n. m. from יָקֹשׁ to lay snares.

Verse 7. וישמע is the reading of the Syr., Vulg., and some MSS.

Verse 8. וַתִּגְעַשׁ Then-shook, Kal 3 f. s. fut. with ו convers. from גָּעַשׁ to push, to thrust, to be moved violently, to shake, to tremble; Hithp. to be moved, to roll, in Kal found only in this passage.

וּמוֹסְדֵי and-(the) foundations-of, constr. of מוֹסָדוֹת, from the unused sing. מוֹסָד verb. n. m. from יָסַד ii. 2 with ו cop. i. 1.

כִּי־ because, or when.

חָרָה there-was-wrath, the word אַף is understood.

Verse 9. עָשָׁן a-smoke, verb. n. m. from אָשֵׁן to smoke.

בְּאַפּוֹ in-His-anger, or in His nostril.

גֶּחָלִים coals, pl. of גַּחֶלֶת subst. f. R. unused in Heb., prob. to light a fire, to burn.

Verse 10. וַעֲרָפֶל and-thick-darkness, subst. m. with ו cop. ii. 6.

Verse 11. כְּרוּב a-cherub, subst. m., a poetical being in the writings of the Hebrews, whose form was compounded of that of a man, an ox, a lion, and an eagle, the well-known symbols of might and power. The etymology of the word is doubtful.

וַיָּ֫עׇף and-He-did-fly, Kal 3 m. s. fut. apoc. with ו convers. from דָּאָה. The ordinary fut. of the verb is יִדְאֶה. In the corresponding passage in Sam. we find וַיֵּרָא He was seen, He appeared, instead of וַיָּעׇף.

Verse 12. סִתְרוֹ His-secret-place, verb. n. m. from סָתַר x. 8 with suff. 3 m. s. The word is omitted in Sam.

חֶשְׁכַת־ darkness-of, constr. of חֲשֵׁכָה or חֲשֵׁכָה verb. n. f. from חָשַׁךְ to be dark. The only other passages where the word occurs are Gen. xv. 12, Ps. lxxxii. 5, cxxxix. 12, Is. viii. 22, and l. 10.

עָבֵי thick-clouds-of, constr. of עָבִים, pl. of עָב subst. com. gen. R. עוּב or עִיב to darken, to obscure, found only in the fut. Hiph. in Lam. ii. 1.

שְׁחָקִים (the)skies, pl. of שַׁחַק subst. m., i. q. שָׁמַיִם and רָקִיעַ the heavens, the sky, in the sing. found only in Ps. lxxxix. 7, 38.

Verse 13. מִנֹּגַהּ At-(the)brightness, verb. n. f. with pr. מ ii. 3, from נָגַהּ to shine, to be bright; Hiph. to enlighten.

בָּרָד hail(stones), verb. n. m. from בָּרַד to scatter, to sprinkle.

Verse 14. וַיַּרְעֵם also-thundered, Hiph. 3 m. s. fut. with ו convers. from רָעַם to be agitated, to tremble; Hiph. to thunder.

In Sam. we find '*from*' and not '*in* the heavens,' which is the reading here of the LXX., Chal., Vulg., Æth., and Arab.

The last three words of this verse, 'hailstones and coals of fire,' are wanting both in 2 Sam. and in the LXX.

Verse 15. וַיִּשְׁלַח And-He-sent-forth, Kal 3 m. s. fut. with ו convers. from שָׁלַח.

וַיְפִיצֵם and-scattered-them, Hiph. 3 m. s. fut. with ו convers. and suff. 3 m. pl. from פּוּץ i. q. נָפַץ to break or dash in pieces, to scatter, only found (in Kal) in fut., imp., and once in part. pass. in Zeph. iii. 10.

וּבְרָקִים and-lightnings, pl. of בָּרָק verb. n. m. with ו cop. i. 1, from בָּרַק to lighten, to send forth lightnings, used of God, only found in Ps. cxliv. 6.

רָב He-shot-out; some consider this as Kal 3 m. s. pret. from רָבַב to shoot arrows; others take it for an adv. '*in abundance*,' from רָבַב iii. 2.

וַיְהֻמֵּם and-discomfited-them, Kal 3 m. s. fut. with ו convers. and suff. 3 m. pl. from הָמַם to terrify, to confound.

Verse 16. אֲפִיקֵי (the) channels-of, pl. constr. of אָפִיק subst. m. (always used in the constr. state), channel, tube, so called from the idea of containing. R. אָפַק, unused in Kal, to hold, to hold fast, also to be strong; Hithp. to restrain oneself.

In 2 Sam. for מַיִם we find יָם, which is more suitable.

וַיִּגָּלוּ and-were-discovered, Niph. 3 m. pl. fut. with ו convers. from גָּלָה to uncover; Niph. to be uncovered, to be revealed; Hithp. to strip oneself.

מִגַּעֲרָתְךָ at-Thy-rebuke, constr. of גְּעָרָה verb. n. f. (with pr. מ ii. 3 and suff. 2 m. s.), from גָּעַר to chide, to rebuke.

מִנִּשְׁמַת at-(the)blast-of, constr. of נְשָׁמָה verb. n. f. with pr. מ ii. 3, from נָשַׁם to pant.

Verse 17. יַמְשֵׁנִי He-drew-me-out, Hiph. 3 m. s. fut. with suff. 1 s. from מָשָׁה. The only other places where the word occurs are the parallel passage 2 Sam. xxii. 17 and Ex. ii. 10.

Verse 18. מֵאֹיְבִי from-my-enemy, the word should be taken collectively.

עָז strong, verb. adj. m. from עָזַז viii. 3.

אָמְצוּ they-were-strong, Kal 3 pl. pret. from אָמֵץ to be strong, to be courageous; followed by מִן to prevail over; Pi. to strengthen, to establish; Hiph. intrans. to be strong, i.q. Kal; Hithp. to strengthen oneself, to collect one's strength.

Verse 19. אֵידִי my-calamity, subst. m. (with suff. 1 s.), prop. a burden, a load, hence a calamity. R. אוּד, unused in Heb., to load, to press down.

לְמִשְׁעָן for-a-stay, verb. n. m. with pr. ל ii. 1, from שָׁעַן, found only in Niph., to lean, to rest. The only other passages where the word occurs are 2 Sam. xxii. 19 and Is. iii. 1.

Verse 20. לְמֶרְחָב into-a-large-place, verb. n. m. with pr. לְ ii. 1, from רָחַב iv. 2.

Verse 21. כְּבֹר according-to-(the) cleanness-of, verb. n. m. with pr. כְּ i. 3, from בָּרַר to separate, to separate what is unclean, to purify; Hithp. to purify oneself, to shew oneself pure, found only in Ps. xviii. 27, the parallel passage in 2 Sam. and Dan. xii. 10. In the proper signification of purity it answers to the Lat. *purus*, Ger. *bar*, and Eng. *pure;* figuratively to the Lat. *verus* and Ger. *wahr*.

Verse 22. רָשַׁעְתִּי מֵאֱלֹהָי have-done-wickedly-(in departing) from-my-God. The verb רָשַׁע i. 1, construed with מִן, signifies to act wickedly against a person. The phrase is elliptical.

Verse 23. וְחֻקֹּתָיו and-His-statutes, pl. of חֻקָּה subst. f. with suff. 3 m. s. R. חָקַק ii. 7.

מֶנִּי from-me, poetic form for מִמֶּנִּי s. of ii. 3.

Verse 24. עִמּוֹ before-Him, lit. with Him, suff. 3 m. s. with עִם, lit. a subst. connexion, union, but used only as a prep. R. עָמַם iii. 7.

מֵעֲוֹנִי from-mine-iniquity, subst. m. with pr. מ iii. 5 and suff. 1 s., lit. perversity, depravity, sometimes used for the penalty of sin; calamity, misery; pl. יִם and וֹת. R. עָוָה, not used in Kal, to be crooked, to bend, to twist; Niph. to be bowed down, especially with pain, also to be perverse; Pi. to overturn, to destroy. In some MSS. the pl. מְעוֹנִים is found.

Verse 26. The LXX., Syr., Vulg., Arab., and some MSS. have וְעִם.

גְּבַר a-man, Chal. form for גֶּבֶר subst. m., i. q. אִישׁ, used almost exclusively in poetry. In the parallel passage in 2 Sam. we find גִּבּוֹר.

תִּתַּמָּם Thou-wilt-shew-Thyself-upright, for תִּתְתַּמָּם, Hithp. 2 m s. fut. from תָּמַם vii. 9.

Verse 27. נָבָר (the) pure, Niph. pres. part. m. s. from בָּרַר xviii. 21.

עִקֵּשׁ (the) froward, verb. adj. m. from עָקַשׁ to distort, pervert.

תִּתְפַּתָּל Thou-wilt-shew-Thyself-froward, Hithp. 2 m. s. fut. from פָּתַל to twist, to twine, not used in Kal; Niph. to be twisted, to wrestle, metaph. to be deceitful; Hithp. to act perversely.

Verse 28. רָמוֹת exalted, Kal pres. part. f. pl. from רוּם iii. 4.

תַּשְׁפִּיל wilt-make-low, Hiph. 2 m. s. fut. from שָׁפֵל to be made low, to sink; Hiph. to make low, to bring down.

Verse 29. נֵרִי my-candle, or lamp; a lamp lighted in a house is a common Heb. figure for *prosperity*, as its extinction is for *distress*; verb. n. m. with suff. 1 s. from the unused root נור to shine.

יַגִּיהַּ will-enlighten, Hiph. 3 m. s. fut. from נָגַהּ xviii. 13.

Verse 30. אָרֻץ I-have-run-through, Kal 1 s. fut. from רוּץ to run; Hiph. to cause to run = to bring quickly.

גְּדוּד a-troop, subst. m., pl. יִם and וֹת a troop, a band of soldiers (prop. a cutting in), so called as intended *to cut* or *break* in upon the enemy. R. גָּדַד to cut into, to cut.

אֲדַלֶּג־ have-I-leaped-over, Pi. 1 s. fut. from דָּלַג to leap, to spring; in Kal found only in Zeph. i. 9.

שׁוּר a-wall, subst. m.; pl. שׁוּרוֹת.

Verse 31. הָאֵל (As for) the-God, v. 5, with the art. i. 1, used emphatically.

Verse 32. מִבַּלְעֲדֵי save, compounded of בַּל not (x. 4) and עֲדֵי, poetic form for עַד unto (iv. 3), with pr. מ ii. 3; prop. not unto, nothing to, besides, without.

זוּלָתִי besides, strictly a subst. f., taking away, putting aside; used as a prep., besides, save, except, with Chirek compaginis. This final Yod or Chirek compaginis as it is called, or long connecting vowel, is the vowel originally employed to mark the relation of the gen. The old form of the stat. constr. had for its termination either Cholem, as in חַיְתוֹ אֶרֶץ, or Chirek, as in the compound names מַלְכִּי־צֶדֶק, אֱלִיעֶזֶר, and many others; in the part. אֹסְרִי לַגֶּפֶן Gen. xlix. 11, חַכְלִילִי עֵינַיִם 12, and in some prepositions מִנִּי, זוּלָתִי, בִּלְתִּי (poet.)

F

Verse 33. חָיִל strength, subst. m., strength, ability, power, hence wealth, riches. R. חוּל to be strong, x. 5.

Verse 34. כָּאַיָּלוֹת like-hinds'(feet), pl. of אַיָּלָה subst. f. with pr. כ i. 3, excluding the art., pointed with (ָ) because the next letter does not admit Dagesh.

בָּמוֹתַי my-high-places, i.e. secure places, pl. of בָּמָה subst. f. with suff. 1 s. from the unused root בּוּם, which appears to have had the meaning of height.

Verse 35. מְלַמֵּד He-teacheth, Pi. pres. part. m. s. from לָמַד to accustom oneself to anything, to learn; Pi. to teach.

לַמִּלְחָמָה to-war, verb. n. f. from לָחַם xiv. 4 with pr. ל ii. 1.

וְנִחֲתָה so-that-bend, Pi. 3 f. s. pret. from נָחַת to descend, to come down; Pi. to press down, to stretch. Some incorrectly consider it as Niph. 3 f. s. pret. from חָתַת to break. The verb is sing. with plur. noun. In the parallel passage in 2 Sam. we find the verb in the masc.

נְחוּשָׁה steel, prop. adj. f. brazen, denom. from נְחֹשֶׁת brass, subst. com. gen. from the unused root נָחַשׁ, prob. signifying to shine.

זְרוֹעֹתָי mine-arms, pl. of זְרוֹעַ x. 15 with suff. 1 s. The LXX., Vulg., and Jerome have 'Thou hast made my arms like a brazen bow.'

Verse 36. תִּסְעָדֵנִי hath-holden-me-up, Kal 3 f. s. fut. with suff. 1 s. from סָעַד to hold up, to support, to refresh. (Might it not possibly be 'with Thy right hand Thou wilt hold me up,' 2 m. s. instead of 3 f. s.?)

וְעַנְוָתְךָ and-Thy-gentleness, strictly f. of עָנָו ix. 13, used substantively, with suff. 2 m. s.

תַּרְבֵּנִי hath-made-me-great, Hiph. 3 f. s. fut. with suff. 1 s. from רָבָה xvi. 4; or perhaps it is 2 m. s. fut. '(with) Thy meekness Thou hast multiplied me.' Luther has 'when Thou humblest me Thou makest me great.'

Verse 37. צַעֲדִי my-step, verb. n. m. with suff. 1 s. from צָעַד to step, to go on slowly.

מָעֲדוּ did-slip, Kal 3 pl. pret. from מָעַד to totter, to slide; Hiph. to cause to shake.

PSALM XVIII. vv. 39, 41, 43–45.

קַרְסֻלָּי my-ancles, dual of קַרְסֹל subst. m., prop. dimin. from קֶרֶס a hook, with suff. 1 s., a joint, a little joint, specially the ancle, which is also in Ger. expressed by a dimin. Knöchel. R. קָרַס to bow oneself.*

Verse 39. אֶמְחָצֵם I-have-wounded-them, Kal 1 s. fut. with suff. 3 m. pl. from מָחַץ to agitate, to shake, to break or smite in pieces.

Verse 41. עֹרֶף (the)neck-of, subst. m.

אַצְמִיתֵם I-might-destroy-them, Hiph. 1 s. fut. with suff. 3 m. pl. from צָמַת, Kal and Pi. to root out, to cut off; Niph. to perish. The LXX. renders the verb in the 2nd person.

Verse 43. וְאֶשְׁחָקֵם And-I-did-grind-them, Kal 1 s. fut. with ו convers. and suff. 3 m. pl. from שָׁחַק to pound or bruise in pieces.

כְּטִיט as-(the) mire-of, subst. m. with pr. כ i. 3.

חוּצוֹת (the)streets, pl. of חוּץ subst. m., prop. a wall, hence especially the outside (of a house), what is without, the street; used sometimes for that which is without the city, i. e. the fields, as in Ps. cxliv. 13, Job v. 10, Prov. viii. 26; sometimes used as an adv. out-of-doors, abroad. R. חוּץ, unused in Heb., to enclose, to surround.

אֲדִקֵּם is the reading of the LXX., Syr., Chal., Vulg., Arab., several MSS., and 2 Sam. xxii.

Verse 44. מְרִיבֵי from-(the)strivings-of, constr. of רִיבִים, pl. of רִיב verb. n. m. from רִיב to contend or strive (with any one), with pr. מ iii. 7.

עַמִּי is the reading of 2 Sam. xxii.

Verse 45. לִשְׁמֹעַ At-(the)hearing-of, verb. n. m. with pr. ל ii. 1, from שָׁמַע to hear.

נֵכָר (the) stranger, or of foreignness, verb. n. m. from נָכַר, unused in Kal, to be foreign, strange; Hiph. to recognize, to acknowledge, also to contemplate; Hithp. to be recognized, also to dissimulate, to feign.

יְכַחֲשׁוּ shall-submit, Pi. 3 m. pl. fut. from כָּחַשׁ, prob. to lie, also to fail, in Kal found only in Ps. cix. 24; Pi. to deny, to lie, to deceive, also to feign, to flatter, used of the vanquished pretending subjection and love towards a victor.

Verse 46. וְיַחְרְגוּ and-be-afraid, Kal 3 m. pl. fut. from חָרַג, only found in this passage. In the corresponding passage in Sam. we find יַחְגְּרוּ from חָגַר to gird.

מִמִּסְגְּרוֹתֵיהֶם from-their-borders, subst. f. pl., close places, poet. used of fortified cities, borders, margins, from the unused sing. מִסְגֶּרֶת with pr. מ ii. 3 and suff. 3 m. pl. R. סָגַר to shut.

Verse 47. חַי־ liveth, lit. (is) living, (is) alive, verb. adj. m. from חָיָה vii. 6.

Verse 48. נְקָמוֹת avengements, pl. of נְקָמָה verb. n. f. from נָקַם to avenge.

Verse 51. וּלְזַרְעוֹ and-to-his-seed, verb. n. m. from זָרַע to scatter, to disperse, especially to scatter seed, to sow, with ו cop. i. 1, pr. ל ii. 1, and suff. 3 m. s.

PSALM XIX.

In this Psalm, which consists of two parts, David speaks first of the Glory of God as seen in the Heavens, and then of His Glory as manifested in His Law, concluding with an earnest prayer for grace. This Psalm is quoted by St. Paul, Rom. x. 18, and is one of the Proper Psalms appointed for Christmas Day.

Verse 2. הָרָקִיעַ the-firmament, verb. n. m. from רָקַע to spread out, with the art. i. 4.

Verse 3. יַבִּיעַ uttereth, Hiph. 3 m. s. fut. from נָבַע to spring, to flow; Hiph. to let flow out, to announce, to manifest.

אֹמֶר speech, subst. m., used only in poetry, i.q. אֵמֶר. R. אָמַר ii. 7.

יְחַוֶּה־ sheweth, Pi. 3 m. s. fut. from חָוָה, unused in Kal, prop. to breathe, to live, i.q. חָיָה; Pi. prop. to breathe out, hence to declare, to shew, found only in poetry.

דַּעַת knowledge, prop. inf. constr. from יָדַע i. 6, used as a subst. f.

קַוָּם Their-line, subst. m. (with suff. 3 m. pl.), a cord, a rope, the string of a harp, hence sound. R. קָוֶה ix. 19. Almost all the ancient versions read קוֹלָם, which has the authority of St. Paul, Rom. x. 18.

וּבִקְצֵה and-to-(the)end-of, constr. of קָצֶה i.q. קֵץ verb. n. m. with ו cop. i. 1 and pr. בּ ii. 11, from קָצַץ to cut off.

מִלֵּיהֶם their-words, pl. of מִלָּה subst. f. (with suff. 3 m. pl.), i.q. דָּבָר, but used only in poetry. R. מָלַל, in Aram. to speak, in Kal only in part. מוֹלֵל Prov. vi. 13.

לַשֶּׁמֶשׁ for-(the)sun, subst. com. gen. with pr. ל ii. 1.

Verse 6. כְּחָתָן as-a-bridegroom, subst. m. with pr. כּ i. 3. R. חָתַן to give one's daughter in marriage, to take in marriage.

מֵחֻפָּתוֹ of-his-chamber, subst. f. (with pr. מ iii. 5 and suff. 3 m. s.), prop. a covering, hence a bed with a canopy, a nuptial bed. R. חָפַף to cover, to protect.

כְּגִבּוֹר as-a-strong-man, verb. adj. m. from גָּבַר xii. 5 with pr. כּ i. 3.

Most of the ancient versions seem to have read אׇרְחוֹ for אֹרַח.

Verse 7. מוֹצָאוֹ His-going-forth, verb. n. m. from יָצָא xvii. 2 with suff. 3 m. s.

וּתְקוּפָתוֹ and-his-circuit, verb. n. f. (with ו cop. i. 1 and suff. 3 m. s.), from קוּף i.q. נָקַף xvii. 9. The LXX., Vulg., and some MSS. read עַד for עַל.

קְצוֹתָם (the)ends-of-it, lit. their ends, pl. of קָצָה verb. n. f. with suff. 3 m. pl. from קָצַץ to cut off.

מֵחַמָּתוֹ from-(the)heat-thereof, verb. n. f. from חָמַם to be warm, with pr. מ iii. 5 and suff. 3 m. s.

Verse 8. עֵדוּת (the)testimony-of, verb. n. f. from עוּד x. 18.

מַחְכִּימַת making-wise, Hiph. pres. part. f. s. from חָכַם to be or become wise; Pi. and Hiph. to make wise; Hithp. to think oneself wise, to act wisely.

פֶּתִי (the)simple, in pause for פְּתִי adj. m. simple, inexperienced, lit. open to every impression, easily seduced. R. פָּתָה to open; see v. 10.

Verse 9. פִּקּוּדֵי (The) statutes-of, constr. of פִּקּוּדִים, pl. of פִּקּוּד verb. n. m. from פָּקַד viii. 5.

מִצְוַת (the) commandment-of, constr. of מִצְוָה verb. n. f. from צָוָה vii. 7.

בָּרָה pure, f. of בַּר verb. adj. from בָּרַר xviii. 21.

Verse 11. הַנֶּחֱמָדִים Which-are-desirable, Niph. pres. part. m. pl. with ה prefixed as the relat., from חָמַד to desire, to take delight in, to covet.

מִזָּהָב more-than-gold, verb. n. m. with pr. מ ii. 3, from the unused root זָהַב to be bright, to shine.

וּמִפַּז and-than-pure-gold, subst. m. with ו cop. i. 1 and pr. מ ii. 3. R. פָּזַז, not used in Kal, to purify metals.

וּמְתוּקִים and-sweet, pl. of מָתוֹק verb. adj. m. with ו cop. i. 1, from מָתַק to suck, also to become sweet, sweet things being commonly sucked; Hiph. to render sweet or pleasant.

מִדְּבַשׁ more-than-honey, subst. m. with pr. מ ii. 3. R. דָּבַשׁ, unused in Heb., to work up a mass, to make it soft by kneading it.

וְנֹפֶת and-droppings-of, verb. n. f. from נוּף to swing, wave, move to and fro; Hiph. to scatter in small particles, to sprinkle.

צוּפִים honeycombs, pl. of צוּף verb. n. m. from צוּף to overflow. The only other passage in which the word occurs is Prov. xvi. 24.

Verse 12. נִזְהָר is-warned; Niph. pres. part. m. s. from זָהַר, not used in Kal, to shine; Niph. to be instructed; Hiph. to enlighten, to teach.

עֵקֶב reward, subst. m. R. עָקַב xiv. 7.

Verse 13. שְׁגִיאוֹת (As for) wanderings, or errors, pl. of שְׁגִיאָה subst. f. wandering, transgression. R. שָׁנָא i.q. שָׁגָה to wander about, to transgress; Hiph. metaph. to seduce, entice. The word occurs nowhere else.

Verse 14. מִזֵּדִים from-presumptuous (sins), pl. of זֵד verb. adj. m., used as a subst., with pr. מ ii. 3, from זוּד or זִיד Kal and Hiph. to act proudly, to deal wickedly.

חֲשֹׂךְ keep-back, Kal 2 m. s. imp. from חָשַׂךְ; or perhaps, 'preserve thy servant also from the proud,' i.e. from tyrannical or haughty governors, or from evil spirits. The LXX. has ἀπὸ ἀλλοτρίων, as if the reading were מִזָּרִים.

אֵיתָם shall-I-be-upright, for אֵתָם Kal 1 s. fut. from תָּמַם vii. 9.

Verse 15. וְגוֹאֲלִי and-my-redeemer, Kal pres. part. m. s. with suff. 1 s. from גָּאַל to demand back one's property, hence to redeem, to ransom.

PSALM XX.

Psalms XX and XXI form a pair, and express the prayers and thanksgivings of the people for the Lord's Anointed: *the first* being a litany before the king went forth to battle, *the second* a Te Deum on his return.

Verse 3. עֶזְרֶךָ thy-help, verb. n. m. from עָזַר to help, with suff. 2 m. s.

Verse 4. מִנְחֹתֶיךָ Thy-offerings, pl. of מִנְחָה verb. n. f. with suff. 2 m. s. from מָנַח, unused in Heb., to give. The LXX., Vulg., Æth., and some MSS. have the word in the sing.

וְעוֹלָתְךָ and-Thy-burnt-sacrifice, verb. n. f. with suff. 2 m. s. from עָלָה i. 3. The Arab., Syr., Chal., and some MSS. have the word in the plur.

יְדַשְּׁנֶה accept, or make fat, or turn to ashes, Pi. 3 m. s. fut. from דָּשֵׁן to wax fat; Pi. to make fat, to anoint, to pronounce (a burnt offering) fat = to accept it; according to some, to reduce to ashes.

Verse 6. נִדְגֹּל we-will-set-up-(our) banners, Kal 1 pl. fut. from דָּגַל to carry or raise up standards, denom. from דֶּגֶל subst. m. a standard, a banner. Some of the ancient MSS. have 'we will magnify,' as if they read נִגְדַּל. The LXX. has μεγαλυνθησόμεθα.

מִשְׁאֲלוֹתֶיךָ Thy-petitions, pl. of מִשְׁאָלָה verb. n. f. with suff. 2 m. s. from שָׁאַל to ask. The only other passage where the word occurs is Ps. xxxvii. 4.

Verse 7. בִּגְבוּרוֹת with-(the) strength-of, pl. of גְּבוּרָה verb. n. f. from גָּבַר xii. 5 with pr. בְּ ii. 11.

Verse 8. בְּרֶכֶב in-chariots, verb. n. m. from רָכַב to ride, with pr. בְּ i. 1, pointed with (ָ) because ר does not take Dagesh.

בַּסּוּסִים in-horses, pl. of סוּס subst. m. with pr. בְּ i. 1, perhaps from the unused root סוס to leap for joy.

Verse 10. יְהוָֹה הוֹשִׁיעָה הַמֶּלֶךְ יַעֲנֵנוּ בְיוֹם־קָרְאֵנוּ Save-Lord:-let-the-King-hear-us-in-the-day-of-our-calling. The LXX. and Vulg. render 'O Lord! save the king; hear us when we call.' The Syr. has 'Jehovah will preserve us, and our King will answer us.'

PSALM XXI.

This is one of the Proper Psalms appointed for Ascension Day.

Verse 2. K'thiv יָגִיל (to be read יָגִיל), K'ri יגל.

Verse 3. וַאֲרֶשֶׁת and-(the) request-of, subst. f. (only found in this passage), with וְ cop. ii. 6. R. אָרַשׁ, unused in Heb., to long for.

Verse 4. עֲטֶרֶת a-crown-of, constr. of עֲטָרָה verb. n. f. from עָטַר v. 13.

Verse 7. תְּחַדֵּהוּ Thou-wilt-make-him-rejoice, Pi. 2 m. s. fut. with suff. 3 m. s. from חָדָה to rejoice, in Pi. found only in this passage.

Verse 10. כְּתַנּוּר as-a-furnace-of, subst. m. with pr. כְּ i. 3, compounded of the unused word תָּן a furnace, R. תָּנַן, Syr. and Chal. to smoke (comp. Welsh *tân*, fire), and נוּר fire, from the unused root נור to give light.

Verse 13. שֶׁכֶם (the) shoulder, subst. m.

בְּמֵיתָרֶיךָ on-Thy-strings, subst. m. pl. with pr. בְּ i. 1 and suff. 2 m. s., i.q. יֶתֶר xi. 2.

PSALM XXII.

In this Psalm (which somewhat resembles the sixty-ninth, and which is one of the Proper Psalms for Good Friday) David prays to the Almighty for help in the midst of overwhelming distress and anguish. Independently of the circumstances of David's case, this Psalm is a foreshadowing of the Passion of Christ, and the first words of it were uttered by our Blessed Saviour when He hung upon the cross (see Matt. xxvii. 46), substituting for the Hebrew verb the corresponding word in the Aramæan dialect then in use among the Jews.

Verse 1. אַיֶּלֶת הַשַּׁחַר Aijeleth Shahar, (the Hind of the dawn,) compounded of אַיֶּלֶת subst. f., i.q. אַיָּלָה and שַׁחַר subst. m. R. שָׁחַר to break forth as light, or the dawn, in Kal only found in Prov. xi. 27; Pi. to seek, used only in poetry. The Title of this Psalm is difficult to explain; it may perhaps signify the name of some tune to which the Psalm was to be sung, or possibly the name of a musical instrument, so called on account of the tremulousness of its sound being like to the cry of a stag. Some critics suppose the words to be a description of the subject of the Psalm; *the hind*' being a figure of *persecuted innocence*, and *the morning* of *deliverance* after long distress.

Verse 2. שַׁאֲגָתִי my-roaring, verb. n. f. with suff. 1 s. from שָׁאַג to roar, to groan. Perhaps the passage may be rendered, ' Far from my salvation (are the) words of my roaring.'

Verse 3. דוּמִיָּה silence, verb. n. f. from the obs. root דּוּם i.q. דָּמַם iv. 5.

Verse 4. The LXX., Vulg., and Arab. read קֹדֶשׁ; the Æth. קָדְשֶׁךָ.

Verse 6. וְנִמְלָטוּ and-were-delivered, Niph. 3 pl. pret. from מָלַט, not used in Kal, to be smooth, slippery, hence to slip away, to escape; Niph. to be delivered; Pi. to let escape=to deliver.

Verse 7. תּוֹלַעַת a-worm, subst. m. R. תָּלַע, unused in Kal, to have a long neck, to be stretched out.

Verse 8. יַפְטִירוּ they-will-open, Hiph. 3 m. pl. fut. from פָּטַר to cleave, to burst open; in Hiph. found only in this passage.

Verse 9. גֹּל Cast (thyself), or roll (thyself). Some consider this as Kal 2 m. s. imp. from גָּלַל, others take it for the 3rd pret., and others again as Kal inf. abs. (At the beginning of this verse לֵאמֹר is understood as in Ps. ii. 3, Eccles. iv. 8, &c.)

Verse 10. גֹחִי taking-me-out, Kal pres. part. m. s. with suff. 1 s. from גּוּחַ or גִּיחַ to break out, trans. to cause to break forth, to bring forth.

שְׁדֵי (the) breasts-of, constr. of שָׁדַיִם, dual of שַׁד subst. m. R. perhaps שָׁדָה, unused in Heb., to cast forth, to pour out, to irrigate.

אִמִּי my-mother, subst. f. with suff. 1 s.; abs. form אֵם, pl. אִמּוֹת.

Verse 11. מֵרָחֶם from-(the)womb, subst. m. (once f. in Jer. xx. 17), with pr. מ iii. 7. R. רָחַם xviii. 2.

Verse 13. פָּרִים bulls, pl. of פַּר subst. m.

אַבִּירֵי strong-(bulls)of, pl. constr. of אַבִּיר adj. m. mighty, strong, noble, poetically used of bulls, sometimes metaph. of princes. R. אָבַר, which implies the notion of being above, being over, hence of passing over, surpassing, prop. to strive upward, to mount. Comp. Pers. *eber*; Gr. ὑπέρ.

בָּשָׁן Bashan, prop. name of a country beyond Jordan, between the rivers Jabbok and Arnon, celebrated for its pastures.

כִּתְּרוּנִי have-beset-me-round, Pi. 3 pl. pret. with suff. 1 s. from כָּתַר, not used in Kal; Pi. to surround.

Verse 14. Before אַרְיֵה the part. כ is understood, which is the reading of the LXX., Vulg., Chal., Syr., and Arab.

Verse 15. וְהִתְפָּרְדוּ and-have-separated-themselves, Hithp. 3 pl. pret. from פָּרַד to break off, to separate by breaking; Niph. to be divided.

כַּדּוֹנָג like-wax, subst. m. with pr. כ i. 3, from the unused root דָּנַג, which appears to have had the signification either of tenacity or else of melting.

נָמֵס it-is-melted, Niph. 3 m. s. pret. from מָסַס to dissolve, to melt; in Kal found only in inf. constr. in Is. x. 18.

בְּתוֹךְ in-(the)midst-of, constr. of תָּוֶךְ subst. m. with pr. בּ i. 1. R. תּוּךְ, unused in Heb., to cut up, to divide.

מֵעָי my-bowels, subst. m. (with suff. 1 s.), found only in the pl., from the unused root מָעָה, which appears to have had the signification of flowing down, or of softness.

Verse 16. כַּחֶרֶשׂ like-a-potsherd, subst. m. with pr. כְּ i. 3, so called from its roughness. R. חָרַשׁ i. q. חָרַם to scrape, to scratch, to be rough.

כֹּחִי my-strength, subst. m. with suff. 1 s.; abs. form כֹּחַ. R. כָּחַח, unused in Heb., prop. to pant, hence to exert one's strength.

מֻדְבָּק cleaveth-to, Hoph. pres. part. m. s. from דָּבַק to cleave to, to adhere.

מַלְקוֹחָי my-jaws, dual of מַלְקוֹחַ subst. m. (with suff. 1 s.), the jaws, by which food is taken. R. לָקַח to take hold of.

Verse 17. כְּלָבִים dogs, pl. of כֶּלֶב subst. m. a dog, so called from barking, from the unused root כָּלַב, apparently signifying to imitate the sound of beating or clapping, fig. applied to barking. Comp. Gr. κολάπτω, Ital. *colpo*, Fr. *coup*, Ger. flopfen, flappen, and Eng. *to clap*.

כָּאֲרִי they-pierced; the true interpretation of this word has been much discussed; most of the ancient versions translate it '*they pierced*,' '*bored through*,' considering that it stands for כָּאֲרוּ Kal 3 pl. pret. from כָּאַר, a lengthened form of כּוּר to pierce or bore through. Some take it for Kal pres. part. m. pl. from כָּאַר, formed in the Chal. manner for כָּאֲרִים (comp. Sans. *khur*, to cut up, to break in pieces, to scratch); whilst others, regarding the word as a subst., translate the passage '*as a lion (they gape upon, or threaten) my hands and my feet*,' i.e. they threaten to tear all my members; but this rendering would certainly involve a very strange ellipsis.

Verse 19. בְּגָדַי my-garments, subst. m. pl. with suff. 1 s., once f. in Lev. vi. 20; abs. form sing. בֶּגֶד, pl. בְּגָדִים; with the termination וֹת only in Ps. xlv. 9. R. בָּגַד, prop. to cover, hence to act covertly, perfidiously, to deal falsely.

לְבוּשִׁי my-vesture, verb. n. m. with suff. 1 s. from לָבַשׁ to put on (a garment).

Verse 20. אֱיָלוּתִי O-my-Strength, subst. f. with suff. 1 s., only found in this passage. R. אוּל iii. 3.

לְעֶזְרָתִי to-my-help, verb. n. f. from עָזַר to help, with pr. לְ ii. 1 and suff. 1 s.

Verse 21. יְחִידָתִי my-only-one, verb. n. f. (m. יָחִיד), from יָחַד to be united, with suff. 1 s.; the word occurs in the f. only here, in Ps. xxxv. 17, and Jud. xi. 34.

Verse 22. רֵמִים (the)buffalos, an abbreviated form of רְאֵמִים, pl. of רְאֵם subst. m. a wild animal, (prob. either the buffalo, the oryx, or the rhinoceros,) fierce and untamed, resembling an ox; some suppose that the word denotes a large and fierce species of antelope.

עֲנִיתָנִי Thou-hast-answered-me, or according to the LXX. and Syr. 'my humiliation.'

Verse 23. לְאֶחָי to-my-brethren, pl. of אָח subst. m. with pr. לְ ii. 1 and suff. 1 s.

קָהָל (the)congregation, verb. n. m. from קָהַל, not used in Kal, prob. to call, to call together (kindred to the root קוֹל iii. 5); Hiph. to assemble, to call together.

Verse 24. וְגוּרוּ and-fear, Kal 2 m. pl. imp. from גּוּר = יָגֹר.

Verse 25. בָזָה He-hath-despised, Kal 3 m. s. pret. i. q. בּוּז.

שִׁקַּץ abhorred, Pi. 3 m. s. pret. from שָׁקַץ to be abominable, not used in Kal; Pi. to loathe, to abhor.

עֱנוּת (the)affliction-of, subst. f. R. עָנָה ix. 13. The LXX. and Vulg. erroneously render the word 'cry.'

Verse 26. נְדָרַי my-vows, pl. of נֶדֶר or נֵדֶר verb. n. m. from נָדַר to vow, with suff. 1 s.

In the beginning of the verse God is spoken of in *the second*, but in the latter part in *the third* person.

Verse 27. Some of the ancient versions read לְבָבָם for לְבַבְכֶם.

Verse 28. For לְפָנֶיךָ the LXX., Vulg., Syr., Arab., and Jerome have לְפָנָיו.

מִשְׁפְּחוֹת (the)kindreds-of, constr. of מִשְׁפָּחוֹת, pl. of מִשְׁפָּחָה subst. f., kind, species, family. R. שָׁפַח, unused in Heb., to spread out.

Verse 30. דִּשְׁנֵי (the)fat-ones-of, pl. constr. of דָּשֵׁן verb. adj. m. from דָּשֵׁן xx. 4.

אֶרֶץ earth, a periphrasis for all men.

For וְנַפְשׁוֹ the LXX., Syr., Vulg., Æth., and Arab. have וְנַפְשִׁי.

לוֹ, instead of לֹא, is the reading of the LXX., Vulg., and Arab.

Verse 31. The LXX., Vulg., Æth., and Arab. read the word זֶרַע with the suff. 1 s.

Verse 32. נוֹלָד that-shall-be-born, Niph. pres. part. m. s. from יָלַד to beget; Niph. to be born. The pron. אֲשֶׁר must be understood before נוֹלָד.

PSALM XXIII.

In this Psalm David expresses his confidence in the grace of God, under the figure of a sheep lying down in rich pastures beneath the care of a tender and watchful shepherd.

Verse 2. בִּנְאוֹת in-pastures-of, subst. f. pl. (with pr. בּ ii. 11), used only in the constr. state and in poetry, a seat, a dwelling; when spoken of flocks—pastures. R. נָאָה, unused in Kal, to sit, to dwell; Pilel, followed by לְ, to be suitable for any one, to become any one, to sit well on any one.

דֶּשֶׁא tender-herb, verb. n. m. from דָּשָׁא to wax green, to flourish.

יַרְבִּיצֵנִי He-will-lay-me-down, Hiph. 3 m. s. fut. with suff. 1 s. from רָבַץ to lie down.

מְנֻחוֹת rest, pl. of מְנוּחָה verb. n. f. from נוּחַ xvii. 14.

יְנַהֲלֵנִי He-will-guide-me, Pi. 3 m. s. fut. with suff. 1 s. from נָהַל, not used in Kal, which had properly the signification of flowing and going, like the cognate נָהָר; Pi. to lead, specially to lead to water, hence with the notion of care and protection, to guard, to provide for, to sustain; Hithp. to go on.

Verse 4. בְּגֵיא through-(the)valley-of, constr. of גַּיְא subst. com. gen., generally m. (with pr. בּ i. 1), so called from the water flowing together there, from the unused root גָּיָא to flow together (as water).

צַלְמָוֶת (the) shadow-of-death, subst. f., lit. '*death shade*,' compounded of צֵל xvii. 8 and מָוֶת vi. 6, poetically used for very thick darkness. The LXX. has ἐν μέσῳ σκιᾶς θανάτου.

עִמָּדִי with-me, prep. עִמָּד i. q. עִם xviii. 24, but found only with suff. 1 s.

וּמִשְׁעַנְתֶּךָ and-Thy-staff, subst. f. (abs. form מִשְׁעֶנֶת), i. q. מִשְׁעָן xviii. 19.

יְנַחֲמֻנִי comfort-me, Pi. 3 m. pl. fut. with suff. 1 s. from נָחַם to pant, to groan, not used in Kal, but in Niph. signifying to grieve, to repent; Pi. to comfort; Hithp. to comfort oneself, to be comforted, to take vengeance.

Verse 5. שֻׁלְחָן a-table, subst. m., pl. שֻׁלְחָנוֹת, so called from its being extended, spread out. R. שָׁלַח to stretch out.

דִּשַּׁנְתָּ Thou-hast-anointed, or made fat.

בַשֶּׁמֶן with-oil, verb. n. m. with pr. בְּ i. 1, from שָׁמַן to be or become fat.

For 'my cup,' the LXX. and Arab. read 'Thy cup,' but the Chal., Syr., and Vulg. support our present Hebrew reading.

רְוָיָה (is) abundance, verb. n. f. (only found here and in Ps. lxvi. 12), from רָוָה to drink eagerly, to be satisfied with drink; Pi. and Hiph. to give to drink, to water, to moisten.

Verse 6. אַךְ Surely, adv., shortened from אָכֵן, prop. inf. abs. Hiph. from the root כּוּן i. 3, used only as an adv. of limitation.

וְשַׁבְתִּי and-I-will-dwell; some consider this as Kal inf. constr. from יָשַׁב with suff. 1 s., שַׁבְתִּי being for שִׁבְתִּי; others take it as a defective writing for יָשַׁבְתִּי Kal 1 s. pret. from יָשַׁב; and others again as Kal 1 s. pret. from שׁוּב.

PSALM XXIV.

This grand choral hymn (which was evidently intended to be sung in antiphonal measure) was probably composed and sung on the occasion of the removal of the Ark from the house of

Obed-Edom to the city of David on Mount Zion. It is one of the Proper Psalms appointed for Ascension Day.

Verse 1. וּמְלוֹאָהּ and-(the)fulness-thereof, verb. n. m. with ו cop. i. 1 and suff. 3 f. s. from מָלֵא to fill.

וְיֹשְׁבֵי the constr. form for the abs. as in Ps. xvi. 3.

Verse 2. נְהָרוֹת (the)floods, pl. of נָהָר subst. m. R. נָהַר to run, to flow, also to shine, to be bright, hence fig. to rejoice, to have a bright countenance.

Verse 3. בִּמְקוֹם in-(the)place-of, constr. of מָקוֹם verb. n. com. gen. (generally m.), from קוּם i. 5 with pr. ב ii. 11.

Verse 4. נַפְשׁוֹ his-soul, prob. for נַפְשׁוֹ, though some read נַפְשִׁי, according to the K'ri.

After לְמִרְמָה the LXX. and Vulg. add the words 'his neighbour.'

Verse 5. צְדָקָה is here, as in many other places, taken for mercy.

Verse 6. David here refers to himself in the third person. The K'ri reading is דורשיו for דֹּרְשָׁו.

פָּנֶיךָ יַעֲקֹב Thy-face-O-Jacob; some translate this clause, 'They that seek Thy face (are) Jacob' (used collectively), i.e. are the true Jacob, the true Israel of God; but the reading of the old versions, 'O God of Jacob,' is better. The LXX., Vulg., and Arab. have 'the face of the God of Jacob;' the Syr. has 'Thy face, O God of Jacob.'

Verse 7. שְׂאוּ Lift-up, for נְשׂאוּ pl. of iv. 7.

פִּתְחֵי O-doors-of, constr. of פְּתָחִים, pl. of פֶּתַח subst. m. R. פָּתַח v. 10.

עוֹלָם eternity; Luther has 'of the world.'

Verse 8. עִזּוּז strong, verb. adj. m. from עָזַז viii. 3. Besides this place the word occurs only in Is. xliii. 17.

Verse 9. For יִשָּׂאוּ some MSS. have the Niph. form הִנָּשְׂאוּ.

Verse 10. הוּא is, lit. he; but in use here, as elsewhere, for the substantive verb.

צְבָאוֹת Hosts, pl. of צָבָא verb. n. m. from צָבָא to go forth to war.

PSALM XXV.

In this Psalm (which is an acrostic or alphabetical one, the first verse beginning with the first letter of the Hebrew alphabet, and the other letters following *nearly*, though not *quite*, in order at the beginning of each successive verse), David expresses his confidence in prayer, and prays for forgiveness and help in trouble. The second verse begins with א instead of ב, the letter ו is altogether omitted, ר is repeated vv. 18, 19, whereas the former verse should have begun with ק, and a last verse, added to make up the number twenty-two, commences with פ. See introduction to Ps. ix. Luther put this Psalm into his Office for the Dying, to be used after the receiving of the Holy Communion.

Verse 5. אוֹתְךָ Thee, suff. 2 m. s. joined with אֶת, marking the object (ii. 3), used as objective case of personal pronouns. Some MSS., LXX., Vulg., Arab., and Syr. read וְאוֹתְךָ, making a fresh verse begin here, which would restore the alphabetical arrangement, as otherwise the letter ו is altogether omitted.

Verse 6. רַחֲמֶיךָ Thy-tender-mercies, subst. m. pl. with suff. 2 m. s. R. רָחַם xviii. 2.

Verse 7. חַטֹּאות (the) sins-of, pl. of חַטָּאת subst. f., sin, sinfulness, sometimes used for a sin-offering, the penalty of sin. R. חָטָא i. 1.

נְעוּרַי my-youth, subst. m. pl. with suff. 1 s. R. נַעַר a boy. Comp. Sans. *nara*, a man; *narî*, a woman: Zend *nara*: Gr. ἀνήρ.

טוּבְךָ Thy-goodness, verb. n. m. from טוֹב iv. 7 with suff. 2 m. s.

Verse 10. The ו of וֶאֱמֶת is pointed with (ֶ) instead of (ְ) because of the following (ֱ).

בְּרִיתוֹ His-covenant, subst. f. with suff. 3 m. s., so called from the idea of cutting, since it was the custom in making covenants to pass between the divided parts of victims. R. בָּרָה to cut.

PSALM XXV. vv. 11–14, 16–19, 21, 22.   81

וְעֵדֹתָיו and-His-testimonies, pl. of עֵדָה verb. n. f. from עוּד x. 18 with suff. 3 m. s.

Verse 11. וְסָלַחְתָּ pardon, Kal 2 m. s. pret. (with ו emphatic, used for the imperat.) from סָלַח, prop. to separate, to loosen, fig. to untie sin, i.e. to do away with it, to forgive it.

רַב־הוּא it-(is)great; the antecedent to הוּא is more naturally אָוֹן than שֵׁם, although by some critics הוּא is referred to the latter noun, 'for it is great,' i.e. Thy name, and because of it pardon my iniquity.

Verse 12. Luther has ben beſten Weg.

Before יִבְחָר the pron. אֲשֶׁר is understood.

Verse 13. תָּלִין shall-lodge, Kal 3 f. s. fut. from לוּן or לִין to lodge, to pass the night, to dwell; Niph. to be obstinate, also to murmur, to complain.

Verse 14. סוֹד (The)secret-of, for יְסוֹד, subst. m., prop. a couch, a cushion, hence a sitting together, an assembly, deliberation, secret. R. יָסַד ii. 2.

Verse 16. יָחִיד desolate, or alone, m. of xxii. 21.

Verse 17. מִמְּצוּקוֹתַי out-of-my-distresses, pl. of מְצוּקָה verb. n. f. with pr. מ ii. 3 and suff. 1 s. from צוּק to be narrow, compressed.

Verse 18. וְשָׂא for נְשָׂא; see iv. 7.

Verse 19. וְשִׂנְאַת and-(with)hatred-of, constr. of שִׂנְאָה subst. f., strictly Kal inf. constr. from שָׂנֵא v. 6.

Verse 21. וָיֹשֶׁר and-uprightness, verb. n. m. from יָשַׁר v. 9 with ו cop. i. 2.

After קִוִּיתִיךָ the LXX., Æth., and Arab. add יְהוָה, the Chal. קִוִּיתִי בִּדְבָרֶךָ.

Verse 22. The name of God is here אֱלֹהִים, whereas throughout the rest of the Psalm it is יְהוָה.

G

PSALM XXVI.

This Psalm, which somewhat resembles the last, differs from it in this respect, that the chief subject of Ps. xxv is the cry for mercy, whilst that of Ps. xxvi is the protestation of integrity. It was probably composed for the Temple service on some special occasion of a general visitation, possibly some plague or sickness.

Verse 1. אֲנִי I, emphatic.

Verse 2. וְנַסֵּנִי and-try-me, Pi. 2 m. s. imp. with suff. 1 s. from נָסָה, not used in Kal.

צְרוּפָה (to be read צָרְפָה) purify; according to the K'thiv this is Kal inf. abs. with ה parag. from צָרַף xii. 7; the K'ri צרפה is the imp.

Verse 4. נַעֲלָמִים hiders-of-themselves, Niph. pres. part. m. pl. from עָלַם v. 12. It is uncertain what class of men is here meant; the Vulg. translates, 'persons acting unjustly,' whose actions will not bear the light; the Syr. has rendered the word 'foolish,' as if denoting those persons from whom knowledge is hidden. It is perhaps better to take the word as signifying persons who conceal their sins; 'dissemblers,' as our English Version has it. Luther has mit den Falschen.

Verse 6. אֶרְחַץ I-will-wash, Kal 1 s. fut. from רָחַץ to wash used only in reference to the body; different from כָּבַס which applies to garments.

בְּנִקָּיוֹן in-innocency, verb. n. m. from נָקָה x. 8 with pr. בּ i. 1. Washing the hands was a common token of innocence among the Jews. Comp. St. Matt. xxvii. 24.

מִזְבַּחֲךָ Thine-altar, verb. n. m. with suff. 2 m. s. from זָבַח to slay to sacrifice.

Verse 7. לַשְׁמִעַ To-make-to-hear, for לְהַשְׁמִיעַ, Hiph. inf. constr. from שָׁמַע with pr. ל ii. 1.

תּוֹדָה thanksgiving, verb. n. f. from יָדָה vi. 6.

Verse 8. מְעוֹן (the) habitation-of, constr. of מָעוֹן verb. n. m. from the unused root עין to dwell. The LXX., Arab., and Vulg. have 'comeliness,' the Syr. 'ministry.'

מִשְׁכַּן (the) dwelling-of, constr. of מִשְׁכָּן subst. m., pl. יִם and וֹת. R. שָׁכַן to dwell.

Verse 10. זִמָּה mischief, verb. n. f. from זָמַם x. 2.

Verse 11. The LXX., Arab., Æth., and some MSS. read פְּדֵנִי יְהוָֹה.

Verse 12. בְּמִישׁוֹר in-an-even-place, verb. n. m. from יָשַׁר v. 9 with pr. ב i. 1.

בְּמַקְהֵלִים in-(the) congregations, subst. m. pl. with pr. ב i. 1. R. קָהַל xxii. 23. This word is nowhere else found in the masc. gender; it occurs in the fem. in Ps. lxviii. 27.

The LXX., Vulg., Æth., and Arab. read the word אברך with the suff. 2 m. s.

PSALM XXVII.

The first part of this Psalm (which may probably be referred to the time of Absalom's rebellion), is an expression of confidence in Jehovah, *the second* an earnest cry for help and comfort. The Title in the Syriac is 'A Psalm of David, on account of the sickness which fell on him.' The LXX., Vulg., and Arab. say that it was written before David was anointed.

Verse 1. מָעוֹז (the) strength-of, verb. n. m. from עָזַז viii. 3.

Verse 2. לִי is here pleonastic.

Verse 3. תַּחֲנֶה should-encamp, Kal 3 f. s. fut. from חָנָה to bow down, to incline, to set oneself down, to encamp.

מַחֲנֶה a-host, or a camp, subst. com. gen., f. only in Gen. xxxii. 9. R. חָנָה.

בְּזֹאת in-this, or in that case, even then.

Verse 4. אַחַת One (thing), f. constr. of אֶחָד xiv. 3. The noun שְׁאֵלָה is understood.

שִׁבְתִּי my-dwelling, Kal inf. constr. (used substantively) from יָשַׁב with suff. 1 s.

בְּנֹעַם־ upon-(the) beauty-of, verb. n. m. from נָעֵם to be pleasant to be lovely, with pr. בּ i. 1.

Verse 5. בסכו is the K'ri, supported by the LXX., Vulg Chal., and Syr.

Verse 6. תְּרוּעָה shouting, verb. n. f. from רוּעַ i. q. רָעַע t make a loud noise, not used in Kal; Hiph. to cry aloud, t rejoice, to triumph.

Verse 7. The LXX., Vulg., Syr., and Æth. omit the conj. before חָנֵּנִי.

Verse 8. The LXX. has 'My heart hath said to Thee, I hav sought Thy face,' as if reading בִּקַּשְׁתִּי for בַּקְּשׁוּ; the Syr. has 'M heart saith to Thee, and my face seeks Thy face,' and in the nex verse 'O Lord Thou wilt not hide Thy face from me.' Th Vulg. has 'Tibi dicit cor meum, Exquisivit te facies mea; faciem tuam, Domine requiram,' reading בְּקֶשׁ for בַּקְּשׁוּ.

Verse 12. עֵדֵי־ witnesses-of, constr. of עֵדִים, pl. of עֵד verb n. m. from עוּד ix. 18.

וִיפֵחַ and-he-who-breathes-out, constr. of יָפֵחַ verb. adj. m. only found besides in Hab. ii. 3, from יָפַח i. q. פּוּחַ to breathe, t puff, unused in Kal, with ו cop. ix. 10. The sing. is here used in a collective sense.

Verse 13. לוּלֵא (I had fainted) unless, a conditional negative conjunction (which has in most instances much the same sense as אִם), compounded of לוּ if, and לֵא i. q. לֹא not. The LXX. Vulg., Syr., Æth., and Arab. omit the word. See Ps. cxix. 92 where a similar sentence is found without ellipsis.

PSALM XXVIII.

Here the Psalmist, after first praying earnestly against his enemies, blesses God for hearing his supplications, and concludes with a prayer on behalf of the people. Some have supposed that this Psalm was written by Jeremiah, and others by Josiah, although in the Title it is attributed to David.

Verse 1. תֶּחֱרַשׁ be-silent, Kal 2 m. s. fut. from חָרַשׁ, Kal and Hiph. to be deaf, to be dumb, also to cut into, to inscribe letters (on a tablet), and to plough.

Verse 2. תַּחֲנוּנַי my-supplications, subst. m. (with suff. 1 s.), only found in the pl. R. חָנָה iv. 2.

בְּנָשְׂאִי when-I-lift-up, Kal inf. constr. from נָשָׂא with pr. בּ i. 1 and suff. 1 s. The lifting up of the hands is a posture of supplication in ordinary use among all nations, and the expression is of frequent occurrence in the Scriptures.

דְּבִיר (the)oracle-of, or perhaps the innermost part of, subst. m., only found here and in the Books of Kings and Chronicles. R. דָּבַר ii. 5.

Verse 3. תִּמְשְׁכֵנִי Draw-me-away, Kal 2 m. s. fut. from מָשַׁךְ with suff. 1 s. We find the words μὴ συναπολέσῃς added in the LXX.

Verse 4. וּכְרֹעַ and-according-to-(the)wickedness-of, verb. n. m. from רָעַע ii. 9 with ו cop. i. 1 and pr. כּ i. 3.

מַעַלְלֵיהֶם their-actions, subst. m. pl. with suff. 3 m. pl. R. עָלַל ix. 12.

כְּמַעֲשֵׂי is the reading of the LXX., Chal., Vulg., Syr., and Arab.

גְּמוּלָם their-desert, verb. n. m. from גָּמַל vii. 5 with suff. 3 m. pl.

Verse 5. כִּי has here the force of לְמַעַן.

Verse 6. Here commences the second portion of the Psalm.

Verse 7. וּמִשִּׁירִי and-out-of-my-song, subst. m. with ו cop. i. 1, pr. מ ii. 3, and suff. 1 s. R. שִׁיר vii. 1.

אֲהוֹדֶנּוּ will-I-praise-Him, poet. for אוֹדֶנּוּ. The LXX. has ἀνέθαλεν ἡ σάρξ μου, καὶ ἐκ θελήματός μου ἐξομολογήσομαι αὐτῷ, Vulg. *et refloruit caro mea et ex voluntate mea confitebor.*

Verse 8. עֹז־לָמוֹ strength-to-him, or to them. For לָמוֹ several MSS., the LXX., Vulg., Syr., and Arab. read לְעַמּוֹ, as in Ps. xxix. 11. The Prayer-Book Version has 'my strength.'

Verse 9. וּרְעֵם feed-them-also, or be their shepherd. The LXX. ποίμανον, Vulg. *rege*, whence our 'govern' in the Te Deum.

PSALM XXIX.

This Psalm is a magnificent description of a thunderstorm, and contains an exhortation to the mighty ones of the earth to give glory to God, Who manifests His power in the thunder and lightning which He sends upon the earth, and Who promises protection unto His people.

Verse 1. הָבוּ Give, Kal 2 m. pl. imp. from יָהַב a defective root used only in the imp. with the exception of Ps. lv. 23, where it occurs in the pret.

בְּנֵי אֵלִים O-ye-sons-of-(the)gods, or the mighty ones ; prob. poet. for angels, according to the Chal. rendering ; the Syr. takes the words as the acc. and renders 'young rams.'

Verse 2. בְּהַדְרַת־ in-(the)beauty-of, or in the majesty of, constr. of הֲדָרָה verb. n. f. with pr. בּ i. 1, from הָדַר viii. 6.

The LXX. has ἐν αὐλῇ ἁγίᾳ αὐτοῦ, Vulg. *in atrio sancto ejus*, which is also the rendering of the Syr. and Arab.

Verse 4. The two nouns בַּכֹּחַ and בֶּהָדָר are used in the place of adjectives.

Verse 5. אֲרָזִים (the)cedars, pl. of אֶרֶז subst. m., so called from the firmness of its roots. R. אָרַז, unused in Heb., to be firm.

הַלְּבָנוֹן the-Lebanon, prop. name of a great range of mountains between Syria and Palestine, so called because its summit is continually covered with snow. R. לָבַן to be white.

Verse 6. וַיַּרְקִידֵם And-He-maketh-them-to-skip, Hiph. 3 m. s. fut. with ו convers. and suff. 3 m. pl. from רָקַד to skip, to dance.

עֵגֶל a-calf, subst. m.

וְשִׂרְיוֹן and-Sirion, prop. name given to Mount Hermon by the Sidonians. The LXX. has ὁ ἠγαπημένος, 'the beloved,' for Sirion.

Verse 7. חֹצֵב divideth, or cutteth out, Kal pres. part. m. s. from חָצַב.

לַהֲבוֹת (the) flames-of, pl. constr. of לֶהָבָה subst. f. from the unused root לָהַב to burn, to flame.

Verse 8. יָחִיל shaketh, or putteth in pain, Hiph. 3 m. s. fut. from חִיל or חוּל x. 5.

מִדְבָּר (the) wilderness, subst. m., strictly an uninhabited plain country, fit for feeding flocks, not desert. R. דָּבַר ii. 5. Comp. Ger. Trift from treiben.

קָדֵשׁ Kadesh, prop. name of a town in the desert to the south of Palestine.

Verse 9. יְחוֹלֵל maketh-to-calve, or to be in pain, Pilel 3 m. s. fut. from חִיל or חוּל x. 5.

וַיֶּחֱשֹׂף and-discovereth, Kal 3 m. s. fut. from חָשַׂף to strip, or make bare.

יְעָרוֹת (the) forests, pl. f. of יַעַר subst. m. (which has both a masc. and fem. plur.), a forest, a thicket of trees, so called from the luxuriant growth of trees and shrubs. R. יָעַר, unused in Heb., prop. to boil, to boil over, the idea of which is applied to any sort of abundance as the luxuriant growth of plants.

כֻּלּוֹ all-of-it, or all that is therein.

Verse 10. לַמַּבּוּל upon-(the) flood, verb. n. m. with pr. לְ ii. 1, from יָבַל ix. 9. The word occurs nowhere else, except in the story of the Deluge, to which this verse is supposed to refer. Luther has der Herr sitzet, eine Sündfluth anzurichten.

PSALM XXX.

According to the Inscription, this Psalm was composed 'at the Dedication of the House,' by which expression some would understand the dedication of the spot on which the Temple afterwards stood; others conjecture that the purification and re-consecration of David's palace, which Absalom had defiled, is meant; whilst others suppose that it refers to the house which David built in his new city of Zion. However this may be, it must certainly have been composed after recovery from sickness.

This Psalm is the first which is called שִׁיר, and the only one in this Book.

Verse 1. חֲנֻכַּת (the) dedication-of, constr. of חֲנֻכָּה verb. n. f. from חָנַךְ to consecrate.

Verse 2. דִּלִּיתָנִי Thou-hast-lifted-me-up, Pi. 2 m. s. pret. with suff. 1 s. from דָּלָה to hang down, to let down (a bucket into a well), to draw (water); Pi. to draw up (out of a well), hence fig. to deliver, to set free.

Verse 4. מִיּוֹרְדִי from-among-them-that-go-down-to, prob. for מִיּוֹרְדֵי constr. of יוֹרְדִים, with pr. מ ii. 3; K'ri מִירְדִי 'that I might not descend,' Kal inf. constr. (יְרֹד for רֶדֶת), with pr. מ ii. 3 and suff. 1 s.

Verse 5. לְזֵכֶר at-(the) remembrance-of, or to the memorial of; comp. Ex. iii. 15.

Verse 6. בָּעֶרֶב in-(the) evening, subst. com. gen. with pr. ב, pointed with (ָ) because ע does not take Dagesh. R. עָרַב to set (as the sun), hence to grow dark, to become evening, to be black.

Verse 7. בְּשַׁלְוִי in-my-prosperity, subst. m. with pr. ב i. 1 and suff. 1 s. (abs. form שֶׁלִי). R. שָׁלָה to be quiet, to be safe. The noun occurs only in this place in the masc. form, but it is found in the fem. שַׁלְוָה in many passages.

Verse 8. For לְהַרְרִי Houbigant would read, with the LXX., Syr., Vulg., and Arab., לַהֲדָרִי 'in Thy favour Thou hast established strength for my beauty,' i.e. Thou hast given me that lasting comeliness of person which arises from a sound constitution.

Verse 10. In the beginning of this verse, in order to connect it with the preceding, the word לֵאמֹר should be understood.

בֶּצַע profit, verb. n. m. from בָּצַע x. 3.

בְּרִדְתִּי in-my-going-down, Kal inf. constr. from יָרַד vii. 17 with pr. בְּ i. 1 and suff. 1 s.

Verse 12. This verse, as well as the beginning of the Psalm, proves that the Psalmist wrote after his recovery.

מִסְפְּדִי my-mourning, verb. n. m. from סָפַד to mourn, to lament, with suff. 1 s.

לְמָחוֹל into-dancing, verb. n. m. with pr. לְ ii. 1, from חוּל x. 5. The pron. לְ is a pleonasm; see Gen. xxi. 16 and Ps. cxliv. 2.

פִּתַּחְתָּ Thou-hast-put-off, or loosed.

שַׂקִּי my-sackcloth, subst. m. with suff. 1 s., a thick cloth made of hair. R. שָׂקַק to strain, unused in Heb.

Verse 13. The LXX., Vulg., and Æth. read כְּבוֹדִי for כָּבוֹד. The Prayer-Book Version is 'every good man.'

PSALM XXXI.

In this Psalm David shews his confidence in God, to Whom he prays for help in his calamity, concluding by praising Him for His goodness to all who trust in Him. Some persons suppose that it was written by David when he fled from Saul to the wilderness of Maon (1 Sam. xxiii. 24); though others, notwithstanding the Title, attribute it to Jeremiah. The first part of ver. 6 was cited by our Blessed Lord when He hung upon the Cross, and St. Stephen used nearly the same words as he was expiring; see Acts vii. 59.

Verse 3. מְהֵרָה speedily, subst. f., haste, quickness; used as an adv., speedily.

Verse 4. The subst. verb הָיִיתָ is understood before סַלְעִי.

Verse 5. After מָעוּזִי the LXX., Æth., and Arab. add the word יְהֹוָה.

Verse 7. For שָׂנֵאתִי the LXX., Syr., Vulg., Æth., Arab., and some MSS. have the 2nd pers. 'Thou hatest,' but the Chal. retains the word in the 1st pers.

הַבְלֵי־ vanities-of, constr. of הֲבָלִים, pl. of הֶבֶל subst. m., strictly breath, breathing, used of anything transitory or frail, something vain and empty; used sometimes as an adv., vainly, emptily. R. הָבַל to breathe, to exhale, to act or speak vainly.

Verse 10. The ב of בְּעַם has the force of *propter*, because of.

Verse 11. וּשְׁנוֹתַי and-my-years, pl. of שָׁנָה subst. f. with ו cop. i. 1 and suff. 1 s. R. שָׁנָה to do the second time, to repeat; Pi. to change.

בַּעֲוֹנִי because-of-mine-iniquity, or my affliction. The LXX. has ἐν πτωχείᾳ, 'in poverty,' as if reading בְּעָנִי.

Verse 12. וְלִשְׁכֵנַי but-to-my-neighbours, pl. of שָׁכֵן a participial noun, from שָׁכַן to dwell, with pr. ל iv. 3 and suff. 1 s.

לִמְיֻדָּעַי to-mine-acquaintance, Pu. pres. part. m. pl. from יָדַע i. 6 with pr. ל iv. 3 and suff. 1 s.

נָדְדוּ fled, Kal 3 pl. pret. from נָדַד.

Verse 13. כְּמֵת as-a-dead-man, Kal pres. part. m. s. from מוּת vi. 6 with pr. כ i. 3.

Verse 14. דִּבַּת (the)slander-of, constr. of דִּבָּה subst. f. R. דָּבַב to creep about, used of a slanderer, hence simply to slander.

מָגוֹר fear, verb. n. m. from גּוּר to be afraid.

Verse 19. תֵּאָלַמְנָה Let-be-put-to-silence, Niph. 3 f. pl. fut. from אָלַם, not used in Kal, to bind, to be solitary, forsaken; Niph. to be dumb.

עָתָק a-hard-thing, adj. m., bold, independent; used adverbially, independently, wickedly. R. עָתַק vi. 8.

וָבוּז and-contempt, verb. n. m. from בּוּז to despise, with ו cop. i. 2.

Verse 20. After טוּבְךָ the LXX., Vulg., Æth., and Arab. add the word יְהוָה.

Before פָּעַלְתָּ the pron. אֲשֶׁר should be understood, or rather repeated from the former part of the verse.

Verse 21. מֵרֻכְסֵי from-(the)conspiracies-of, pl. constr. of רֹכֶס subst. m., league, plot, conspiracy, so called from the idea of being bound together, with pr. מ iii. 7. R. רָכַס to bind. The word is an ἅπαξ λεγόμενον.

For בְּסֻכָּה the Syr., Vulg., and Æth. have בְּסָכָּךְ.

Verse 22. מָצוֹר strength, verb. n. m. from צוּר xviii. 3.

Verse 23. בְחָפְזִי in-my-haste, Kal inf. constr. with pr. ב and suff. 1 s. from חָפַז to leap up, to be alarmed, perplexed, to make haste; Niph. to flee.

נִגְרַזְתִּי I-am-cut-off, Niph. 1 s. pret. from גָּרַז, found only in Niph., to be cut off, or taken away. Fourteen MSS. read נִגְזַרְתִּי.

אָכֵן nevertheless, prop. for הָכֵן Hiph. inf. abs. from כּוּן i. 4, used as an adv. of affirmation, surely, truly, certainly, but, yet.

Verse 25. הַמְיַחֲלִים ye-that-hope, Pi. pres. part. m. pl., with the art. and omission of Dagesh, from יָחַל to remain, not used in Kal; Pi. and Hiph. to expect, to hope, to wait for.

PSALM XXXII.

This is the first of the thirteen Psalms inscribed with the title of Maschil, and the second of the seven penitential Psalms (see Ps. vi). In it David describes the blessedness which consists in the remission of sins. The Syriac Version entitles this Psalm, 'Concerning the offence of Adam who presumptuously sinned, and a prophecy of the Messiah, through whom we are delivered from Gehenna.' The Arabic entitles it, 'The Psalmist speaks prophetically of redemption.' It is one of the Proper Psalms for Ash-Wednesday.

Verse 1. מַשְׂכִּיל Maschil, or giving instruction, subst. m. (strictly Hiph. pres. part. m. s. from שָׂכַל ii. 10), a Psalm of instruction or admonition, a didactic poem.

The form נְשׂוּי, instead of נָשׂוּא, is adopted on account of its similarity in form to כְּסוּי. The LXX., Vulg., Arab., Æth., and St. Paul, Rom. iv. 7, have the pl.

כְּסוּי covered (as to), Kal pass. part. m. s. from כָּסָה, in Kal only found here and in Prov. xii. 16.

חֲטָאָה sin, subst. f., sometimes used for a sacrifice for sin. R. חָטָא i. 1.

Verse 2. רְמִיָּה guile, verb. n. f. from רָמָה v. 7.

Verse 3. The ב of שַׁאֲגָתִי has the force of *because of*.

Verse 4. לְשַׁדִּי my-moisture, subst. m., juice, (from the idea of sucking,) moisture, vigour, with suff. 1 s. R. לָשַׁד, unused in Heb., to suck. The word occurs only here and in Num. xi. 8.

בְּחַרְבֹנֵי into-(the)drought-of, pl. constr. of חַרְבוֹן verb. n. m. from חָרַב vii. 13 with pr. ב i. 1.

קַיִץ summer, subst. m., harvest, prop. cutting off (of fruits), hence summer, as being the time when fruits are gathered. R. קוּץ to cut.

Verse 5. For פִּשְׁעֵי pl., the LXX., Syr., Vulg., and Arab. read the sing.

Verse 6. רַק surely, adv. of limitation and restriction only, except, surely; the word means primarily *thin*. R. רָקַק, prop. to beat, to pound, specially to spread out by beating, to make thin.

לְשֵׁטֶף in-(the)flood-of, verb. n. m. with pr. ל ii. 1, from שָׁטַף to flow out abundantly, to inundate.

יַגִּיעוּ they-shall-draw-near, Hiph. 3 m. pl. fut. from נָגַע to touch, to injure, to draw near.

Verse 7. רָנֵּי shouts-of, pl. constr. of רֹן, prop. inf. from רָנַן v. 12. The part. ב is understood before רָנֵּי, which occurs nowhere else as a noun substantive. The Syr. and Vulg. omit the word.

פַּלֵּט deliverance, verb. n. m., strictly Pi. inf. constr. from פָּלַט xvii. 13.

Verse 8. The LXX. has ἐπιστηριῶ ἐπὶ σὲ τοὺς ὀφθαλμούς μου, the Chal. 'I will set my eye on thee for good.'

Verse 9. כְּפֶרֶד as-(the) mule, subst. m. with pr. כ i. 3.

הָבִין understanding, Hiph. inf. constr. from בִּין.

בְּמֶתֶג with-a-bit, subst. m. with pr. ב i. 1, from the unused root מָתַג, which appears to have had the signification of spreading out.

וָרֶסֶן and-bridle, subst. m. with ו cop. i. 2. R. רָסַן, unused in Heb., to bind.

עֶדְיוֹ his-trapping, subst. m. with suff. 3 m. s.; abs. form עֲדִי ornament, harness; some attribute to the word the signification of mouth. R. עָדָה i. 3.

לִבְלוֹם to-hold-in, Kal inf. constr. from בָּלַם to bind together, to shut fast (with pr. ל ii. 1), only found in this passage.

בַּל קְרוֹב אֵלֶיךָ lest-they-come-near-unto-thee; some translate, (or else) they will not come nigh unto thee.

Verse 10. מַכְאוֹבִים sorrows, pl. of מַכְאוֹב verb. n. m. from כָּאַב to have pain, either in body or mind.

PSALM XXXIII.

This Psalm opens with the exhortation with which the latter closed, and is one of the few earlier Psalms without a Title.

Verse 1. נָאוָה comely, f. of נָאוֶה verb. adj. from נָאָה xxiii. 2. Some persons consider it as Niph. pres. part. f. s. from אָוָה x. 3.

Verse 2. בְּכִנּוֹר with-harp, or guitar, or lute, subst. m. with pr. ב i. 1, pl. יִם and וֹת. R. כָּנַר, unused in Heb., to give forth a tremulous sound. Comp. Gr. κίνυρα; Lat. *cithara*, a harp.

בְּנֵבֶל with-psaltery, subst. m. with pr. ב i. 1. R. נָבֵל i. 3. Comp. Gr. νάβλα, ναῦλα; Lat. *nablium*.

עָשׂוֹר (and an instrument of) ten (strings), subst. m., a ten, a decade.

Verse 3. For לוֹ the Chal. has לַיהוָה.

חָדָשׁ new, verb. adj. m. from חָדַשׁ to be new, not used in Kal; Pi. to make new, to renew.

הֵיטִיבוּ be-skilful, Hiph. 2 m. pl. imp. from יָטַב to be good, in Kal found only in the fut.; Hiph. to do well or rightly.

Verse 4. בֶּאֱמוּנָה in-truth, verb. n. f. from אָמַן xii. 2 with pr. בּ i. 1, pointed with (ֶ) instead of (ְ) because of the following (ֱ).

Verse 7. כֹּנֵס He-gathereth-together, Kal pres. part. m. s. from כָּנַס, in Pi. found only in Ps. cxlvii. 2, Ezek. xxii. 21 and xxxix. 28.

כַּנֵּד as-an-heap, subst. m. with pr. כּ i. 3. The only other places where the word occurs are Ex. xv. 8, Josh. iii. 13, 16, Ps. lxxviii. 13, and Is. xvii. 11. R. נוד to heap up, to accumulate. For נֵד some would read נֹאד a bottle. Luther has wie in einem Schlauch; the LXX. has ὡσεὶ ἀσκόν; the Vulg. sicut in utre.

בְּאוֹצָרוֹת in-storehouses, pl. of אוֹצָר verb. n. m. with pr. בּ i. 1, from אָצַר to heap up, to lay up.

תְּהוֹמוֹת (the)depths, pl. of תְּהוֹם subst. com. gen., a poetic word, prop. water making a noise. R. הוּם to put in motion, to disturb.

Verse 10. הֵפִיר hath-brought-to-nought, or made void, Hiph. 3 m. s. pret. from פּוּר i.q. פָּרַר to break, only found here and in Ezek. xvii. 19.

הֵנִיא He-hath-made-of-none-effect, Hiph. 3 m. s. pret. from נוּא or נִיא to remove, not used in Kal, except in Num. xxxii. 7; Hiph. to refuse, to hold back, to make of no effect, to bring to nothing.

מַחְשְׁבוֹת (the)devices-of, constr. of מַחֲשָׁבוֹת, pl. of מַחֲשָׁבָה or מַחֲשֶׁבֶת verb. n. f. from חָשַׁב to intend, to purpose.

After עַמִּים the LXX., Vulg., Arab., and Æth. add the words 'and frustrates' (Prayer-Book Version, 'casteth out') 'the counsels of princes.'

Verse 14. מִמְּכוֹן From-(the)place-of, verb. n. m. from כּוּן i. 4 with pr. מ ii. 3.

הִשְׁגִּיחַ He-hath-looked-down, Hiph. 3 m. s. pret. from שָׁגַח, only found here, in Is. xiv. 16, and Cant. ii. 9.

Verse 17. לִתְשׁוּעָה for-salvation, verb. n. f. from יָשַׁע iii. 3 with pr. לְ iv. 3.

Verse 18. The LXX., Vulg., Syr., Æth., and Arab. read עֵינֵי.

Verse 19. בְּרָעָב in-famine, verb. n. m. from רָעֵב to be hungry, with pr. בְּ xx. 8.

Verse 20. חִכְּתָה hath-waited, Pi. 3 f. s. pret. from חָכָה, in Kal found only in Is. xxx. 18.

Verse 22. כַּאֲשֶׁר according-as, i. 1 with pr. כְּ i. 3, pointed with (ֲ) because of the following (ֲ).

PSALM XXXIV.

In this Psalm (which is an acrostic or alphabetical one) is an exhortation to praise God. With the exception of there being no verse beginning with the letter ו, the alphabetical arrangement is preserved throughout. In order to make the number of verses correspond with that of the letters of the Hebrew alphabet, an additional verse, beginning with the letter פ, is added at the end. This Psalm and the next are the only two in which the expression 'Angel of the Lord' occurs. See Introduction to Psalms ix and xviii. The Title in the Syriac is ' A Psalm of David when he went to the House of the Lord, and gave first-fruits to the priest.' Verses 12-16 are quoted by St. Peter, 1 Ep. iii. 10-12.

Verse 1. טַעְמוֹ his-behaviour, or his judgment, or his reason, subst. m. (with suff. 3 m. s.), taste, especially pleasant taste, metaph. intellectual taste, wisdom, judgment. R. טָעַם to taste, metaph. to enjoy, to experience. The LXX. has τὸ πρόσωπον αὐτοῦ, Luther feine Geberbe.

אֲבִימֶלֶךְ Abimelech, Father of the King, or Father-King, a common title of the Philistine kings, as פַּרְעֹה of the Egyptian, compounded of אָב father, see iii. 1, and מֶלֶךְ sing. of ii. 2.

PS. XXXIV. vv. 3, 5, 6, 8, 9–11, 18, 19, 21; XXXV. v. 1.

Verse 3. תִּתְהַלֵּל shall-make-her-boast, lit. shall glory.

Verse 5. מְגוּרוֹתַי my-fears, pl. of מְגוּרָה verb. n. f. from גּוּר to be afraid, with suff. 1 s.

Verse 6. וְנָהָרוּ and-were-lightened, or flowed unto Him, as Luther renders it. The Welsh Version is *a hwy a oleuwyd*.

For וּפְנֵיהֶם the LXX., Vulg., Syr., Æth., Arab., and Kennicott read וּפְנֵיכֶם.

Verse 8. מַלְאַךְ־ (The) Angel-of, lit. messenger, verb. n. m. from obs. לָאַךְ to send, also to wait upon, to minister to.

Verse 9. הַגֶּבֶר the-man, subst. m., i.q. אִישׁ, but, with few exceptions, used only in poetry. R. גָּבַר xii. 5. There is an ellipsis of the pron. אֲשֶׁר before the word יֶחֱסֶה.

Verse 10. מַחְסוֹר want, verb. n. m. from חָסֵר viii. 6.

Verse 11. The LXX., Syr., Vulg., Arab., and Luther render כְּפִירִים by 'rich.'

רָשׁוּ have-lacked, Kal 3 pl. pret. from רוּשׁ to be poor, or in want.

Verse 18. The LXX., Vulg., Syr., Arab., Chal., and Bishop Lowth read צָעֲקוּ צַדִּיקִים וַיהוָֹה שָׁמֵעַ.

Verse 19. דַּכְּאֵי־ those-crushed-of, pl. constr. of דַּכָּא verb. adj. from דָּכָא i.q. דָּכַךְ ix. 10.

Verse 21. Before שֹׂמֵר the LXX., Vulg., Æth., and Arab. read the word יְהוָֹה.

נִשְׁבָּרָה is-broken. This is the prophecy to which St. John alludes, xix. 36.

PSALM XXXV.

In this Psalm, which was probably composed either during the persecution by Saul or the revolt of Absalom, David prays for his own safety and the overthrow of his enemies.

Verse 1. יְרִיבַי them-that-strive-with-me, pl. of יָרִיב verb. n. m. from רִיב with suff. 1 s.

PSALM XXXV. vv. 2–8, 10, 12, 13.

Verse 2. The words מָגֵן and צִנָּה both denote *shields*, but the latter was the larger, and covered the whole body of the warrior.

The בְ of בְּעֶזְרָתִי (in the character of help turned towards me) is the so-called *Beth essentiae*, used to introduce the predicate, as in Ex. xviii. 4, Prov. iii. 26, Is. xlviii. 10 (*tanquam argentum*), 'in my help,' i.e. as my helper, in that character, see Ex. vi. 2, בְּאֵל שַׁדַּי 'in the character of the Almighty God.'

Verse 3. חֲנִית (the) spear, subst. f. (pl. יִם and וֹת), so called from its flexibility. R. חָנָה xxvii. 3.

וּסְגֹר and-stop (the way), prob. Kal 2 m. s. imp. from סָגַר with ו cop. i. 1, though some consider it as a subst. = σάγαρις, battle-axe.

לִקְרַאת to-meet, Kal inf. constr. from קָרָא (i.q. קָרָה) to meet, to happen, with pr. ל iv. 3.

Verse 4. יִסֹּגוּ let-them-be-turned, Niph. 3 m. pl. fut. from סוּג or סוֹג (i.q. נָסַג) to depart; Niph. to decline, to fall away.

Verse 5. דֹּחֶה thrusting, Kal pres. part. m. s. from דָּחָה to thrust, to impel vehemently; in Kal found only in the Psalms.

Verse 6. וַחֲלַקְלַקֹּת and-slipperinesses, verb. n. f. pl. with ו cop. i. 1, from חָלַק v. 10. The word is found elsewhere only in Jer. xxiii. 12 and Dan. xi. 21, 34.

Verse 7. חִנָּם without-cause, adv., compounded of חֵן grace, favour, and the syllable ־ָם, with which adverbs are formed, gratis, gratuitously, without cause. R. חָנַן iv. 2.

Verse 8. שׁוֹאָה destruction, verb. n. f. from שׁוֹא xii. 3.

For בְּשׁוֹאָה the LXX. and Vulg. read בְּשַׁחַת; the Syriac Version is 'into the pit which he has digged, let him fall.'

Verse 10. מֵחָזָק from-him-who-is-strong, verb. adj. m. from חָזַק xviii. 2 with pr. מ iii. 5.

Verse 12. שְׁכוֹל (the) bereavement-of, verb. n. m. from שָׁכַל to bereave.

Verse 13. בַּחֲלוֹתָם in-their-sickness, Kal inf. constr. with pr.

בְ i. 1 and suff. 3 m. pl. from חָלָה, prop. to be rubbed, to b polished, to be worn down in strength, to be sick; Pi. to stroke, to smooth, to sooth, to caress, to flatter, also to mak sick.

בְּצוֹם with-fasting, verb. n. m. from צוּם to fast, with pr. בְ i. 1.

חֵיקִי my-bosom, subst. m. with suff. 1 s. R. prob. חָיִק or חוּק unused in Heb., to surround, to embrace.

Verse 14. כְּאָבֵל־ as-(one) mourning, constr. of אָבֵל verb adj. m. from אָבַל to mourn, to be languid, with pr. כ xxxiii. 22.

שַׁחוֹתִי I-bowed-down, Kal 1 s. pret. from שָׁחַח x. 10. The LXX., Syr., Vulg., and Arab. do not translate the word אֵם, but render the passage 'As one mourning and sore lamenting, so was I humbled;' but the Chal. adheres to the Heb.

Verse 15. וּבְצַלְעִי But-in-my-halting, verb. n. m. with ו co[i. 1, pr. בְ i. 1, and suff. 1 s. from צָלַע to halt, to limp.

נֵכִים (the) abjects, subst. m. pl., only found in this passage; word of doubtful signification; some take it in an active sense= 'smiters' (with the tongue), i. e. 'railers,' 'slanderers;' other give the word a passive sense, and render it 'the smitten,' i. poor, miserable, abject beings. The LXX. has μάστιγες; th Chal. 'the wicked who strike me with their words.'

Verse 16. בְּחַנְפֵי With-profane-of, pl. constr. of חָנֵף profan impious, verb. adj. m. from חָנֵף to be profaned, defiled, to trea contumeliously, to profane, to spit upon, with pr. בְ, which ha here the force of עַם.

לַעֲגֵי mockers-of, pl. constr. of לָעֵג adj. m., speaking in a ba barous or foreign tongue; a jester, buffoon, mocker. R. לָעַג ii. . The word occurs only here and in Is. xxviii. 11. לְעֻנִי is the read ing of the LXX., Vulg., Arab., and Æth.

מָעוֹג a-cake, subst. m., found only here and in 1 Kings xvii. 1: This passage is extremely difficult; some translate the word 'With profane jesting parasites' (mockers for a cake), who a the part of buffoons at the feasts of the wealthy for the sake ‹ dainty fare. Others, considering the word מָעוֹג as derived fro the root עוּג to go in a circle, to twist, to turn, would render 'With the profane in their foreign stammerings,' or 'Amongst profane, foreign, barbarous stammerers.'

חָרֹק to-gnash, Kal inf. abs. from חָרַק; inf. instead of pret.

Bishop Horsley translates, 'While I was (thus) contumeliously treated, they jeered me with their jeers, gnashing their,' &c.

Verse 17. מְשֹׁאֵיהֶם from-their-destructions, pl. of שׁוֹא verb. n. m. from שׁוֹא xii. 3 with pr. מ ii. 3 and suff. 3 m. pl.

Verse 19. לְ has here the force of בַּעֲבוּרִי.

Verse 20. The LXX., Vulg., and others read לְ instead of לֹא.

רִגְעֵי (the)quiet-ones-of, pl. constr. of רָגֵעַ verb. adj. m. from רָגַע vi. 11. The word is an ἅπαξ λεγόμενον.

Verse 26. שְׂמֵחֵי them-that-rejoice-at, pl. constr. of שָׂמֵחַ verb. adj. m. from שָׂמַח or שָׂמֵחַ.

בֹּשֶׁת shame, verb. n. f. from בּוֹשׁ to be ashamed.

PSALM XXXVI.

In this Psalm, David, after first describing the state of the unrighteous, extols the mercy of God, and concludes by beseeching Him for a continuance of His favour.

The expression 'the servant of the Lord' occurs also in the Title of Ps. xviii.

Verse 2. נְאֻם an-utterance-of, Kal part. pass. constr. from נָאַם to mutter, to speak in a low voice. The word is never used of common speech, but uniformly of oracular announcements. Some would translate the verse, 'That which Transgression saith to the wicked is within my heart,' i. e. forms the subject of my meditation, or, 'An utterance concerning the transgression of the wicked is within my heart;' others, supposing that לִבִּי is a mistake for לבּוֹ, (which latter reading is found in some MSS., the LXX., Syr., Vulg., Chal., Arab., and Æth.,) render, 'The wicked hath an oracle of transgression within his heart.'

Verse 8. יָקָר excellent, verb. adj. m. from יָקַר to be heavy, to be difficult, also to be dear, to be precious. The word is sometimes used (as in Ps. xxxvii. 20) as a subst., worth, costliness, splendour.

Verse 9. מִדֶּשֶׁן with-(the)fatness-of, verb. n. m. from דָּשֵׁן xx. 4 with pr. מ ii. 3.

עֲדָנֶיךָ Thy-pleasures, pl. of עֶדֶן verb. n. m. with suff. 2 m. s. from עָדַן, unused in Kal, which appears to have had the signification of softness; found only in Hithp. to enjoy oneself.

תַשְׁקֵם Thou-shalt-make-them-drink-of, Hiph. 2 m. s. fut. with suff. 3 m. pl. from שָׁקָה to drink, not used in Kal; Hiph. to give to drink, to water.

Verse 10. מְקוֹר (the)fountain-of, constr. of מָקוֹר verb. n. m. from קוּר to dig; see xxii. 17.

Verse 11. מְשֹׁךְ O-continue, lit. lengthen out, Kal 2 m. s. imp. from מָשַׁךְ to hold fast, to draw out, to prolong.

Verse 12. תְּנִדֵנִי let-remove-me, Hiph. 3 f. s. fut. with suff. 1 s. from נוד xi. 1.

PSALM XXXVII.

This is one of the Acrostic or Alphabetical Psalms, and contains an exhortation to patience and trust in God by a comparison of the different estate (even in this life) of the righteous and the wicked. See Introduction to Psalm ix. The whole of the first verse is to be found almost word for word in Prov. xxiv. 19.

Verse 1. תִּקַנֵּא be-thou-envious, Pi. 2 m. s. fut. from קָנָא, not used in Kal. The verb קָנָא, when construed with לְ, is used in a good sense, as to be emulous in promoting another's welfare; but when it is construed with בְּ it is employed in a bad sense.

עַוְלָה iniquity, verb. n. f. from עָוֶל vii. 4; in the pl. the word occurs only in Psalms lviii. 3 and lxiv. 7.

Verse 2. כֶּחָצִיר like-the-grass, verb. n. m. with pr. כְּ i. 3, from the obs. root חָצַר to be green; see vii. 6.

יִמָּלוּ they-shall-be-cut-down, perhaps Kal 3 m. pl. fut. from מוּל i.q. נָמַל, מָהַל, מָלַל, to cut off, or to be cut off; in Hiph. found only in Ps. cxviii. 10, 11, 12. Some persons consider it as Niph. 3 m. pl. fut. from נָמַל or מוּל.

וּכְיֶרֶק and-as-(the)greenness-of, subst. m. with וְ cop. i. 1 and pr. כְּ i. 3. R. יָרַק, unused in Heb., to be green, also to be gold-coloured, to be shining.

Verse 3. וּרְעֵה אֱמוּנָה and-feed-upon-faithfulness, or perhaps delight in, or seek after truth. The LXX., Vulg., Æth., and Arab. seem to have read הֲמוֹנָהּ 'and feed on its abundance;' the Chal. has 'be strong in faith;' Luther nähre Dich redlich.

Verse 4. וְהִתְעַנַּג Delight-thyself-also, Hithp. 2 m. s. imp. from עָנַג to live softly, not used in Kal; Hithp. to delight oneself, to be glad (in anything).

Verse 6. כַּצָּהֳרָיִם as-the-noon-day, prop. double, i.e. most splendid light, mid-day, noon; dual of צֹהַר subst. m. with pr. כְּ i. 3. R. צָהַר to shine.

Verse 7. Luther has Sei stille dem Herrn.

Verse 8. הֶרֶף Cease, for הַרְפֵּה Hiph. 2 m. s. imp. apoc. from רָפָה to be slack, to hang down, to be feeble; Hiph. to let down, to desist, to leave off.

Verse 16. מֵהֲמוֹן more-than-(the)plenty-of, constr. of הָמוֹן subst. m. (f. only in Job xxxi. 34), with pr. מִ iii. 5, sound, noise, multitude, abundance, riches. R. הָמָה to make a noise, to rage, to roar, to be disquieted, to sigh, to lament.

Verse 20. כִּיקַר כָּרִים as-(the) fat-of-lambs, or as the glory of the meadows, כִּיקָר xxxvi. 8; כָּרִים pl. of כַּר subst. m., a lamb, sometimes used figuratively for a meadow, a pasture. Luther has wie eine köstliche Aue. R. כָּרַר, not used in Kal, prop. to go or move in a circle, to dance, to leap.

For בְּעָשָׁן the LXX., Vulg., Syr., and Arab. read כְּעָשָׁן.

Verse 21. לֹוֶה borroweth, Kal pres. part. m. s. from לָוָה to adhere, or be joined closely to any one, to borrow; Hiph. to lend.

Verse 22. וּמְקֻלָּלָיו and-(they that are) cursed-of-Him, Pu. pres. part. m. pl. with וּ cop. i. 1 and suff. 3 m. s. from קָלַל to be light, to be diminished, to be despised; Pi. to curse; Hiph. to reckon lightly, to despise; Pilpel to move to and fro.

Verse 23. מִצְעֲדֵי (The) steps-of, pl. constr. of מִצְעָד verb. n. m. from צָעַד xviii. 37.

Verse 24. יוּטָל he-shall-be-utterly-cast-down, Hoph. 3 m. s. fut. from טוּל, not used in Kal.

Verse 27. The Chal. has 'inhabit eternal life.'

Verse 28. Up to this point the alphabetical arrangement has been strictly preserved. Here apparently the ע is omitted. Ewald supposes that the words עֹשֵׂי טוֹב have dropped out, whilst Delitzsch suggests that the ל in לְעוֹלָם goes for nothing, and that the ע is the acrostic letter.

Verse 30. חָכְמָה wisdom, verb. n. f. from חָכַם xix. 8.

Verse 35. עָרִיץ oppressing, verb. adj. m. from עָרַץ x. 18.

וּמִתְעָרֶה and-spreading-himself, Hithp. pres. part. m. s. with וּ cop. i. 1, from עָרָה, not used in Kal, to be naked; Pi. to make naked, hence to empty (a vessel), to pour it out. The LXX., Syr., Vulg., Æth., and Arab. seem to have read וּמִתְעַלֶּה.

כְּאֶזְרָח as-a-native-tree, subst. m. (with pr. כ i. 3), a tree still standing in its original soil and not transplanted, a native, one born in a place. R. זָרַח to rise, to sprout up. The LXX. has 'as the cedars of Lebanon,' the Vulg. 'a cedar,' Luther 'a laurel tree.'

רַעֲנָן green, verb. adj. m. from רָעַן, found only in Pilel רַעֲנַן to be green, to be covered with leaves.

Verse 36. The LXX., Vulg., Syr., and Houbigant read וָאֶעֱבֹר instead of וַיַּעֲבֹר; Luther has da man vorüber ging.

Verse 37. תָּם integrity, verb. adj. m. (used as a subst.), from תָּמַם vii. 9. The LXX., Vulg., Chal., and the ancients generally have 'Keep integrity and attend to uprightness;' English Version and most moderns, 'Mark the perfect (man), and behold the upright;' Luther has Bleibe fromm, und halte Dich recht.

אַחֲרִית (the) latter-end, verb. n. f. from אָחַר ix. 4.

Verse 38. נִשְׁמְדוּ shall-be-destroyed, Niph. 3 pl. pret. from שָׁמַד, not used in Kal.

Verse 39. תְּשׁוּעַת, instead of וּתְשׁוּעַת, is the reading of four Hebrew MSS., Syr., and Arab., and one MS. of the LXX., and is required, that the last stanza of the Psalm may commence with the last letter of the Hebrew alphabet.

The relat. pron. אֲשֶׁר must be understood before מָעֻזָּם.

PSALM XXXVIII.

In this Psalm, which somewhat resembles the twenty-second, David beseeches the Almighty to take compassion on his pitiful state. It is one of the penitential Psalms, and is appointed by the Church to be read on Ash-Wednesday. See Ps. vi.

Verse 1. לְהַזְכִּיר to-bring-to-remembrance, i.e. either as a memorial of suffering and deliverance, or 'to bring (me) into remembrance (with) God;' Hiph. inf. constr. from זָכַר with pr. לְ ii. 1 (also found in the Title of Ps. lxx). The LXX. adds the words περὶ Σαββάτου.

Verse 2. בְּקֶצְפְּךָ in-Thine-anger, verb. n. m. with pr. בְּ i. 1 and suff. 2 m. s. from קָצַף to break, to break forth into anger, to be angry, indignant.

In some MSS. and the Chal. the negative particle occurs a second time before תְיַסְּרֵנִי.

Verse 4. מְתֹם soundness, verb. n. m. from תָּמַם vii. 9.

זַעְמֶךָ Thine-indignation, verb. n. m. with suff. 2 m. s. from זָעַם to be angry.

Verse 5. כְמַשָּׂא as-a-burden, verb. n. m. from נָשָׂא to bear, with pr. כ i. 3.

כָבֵד heavy, verb. adj. m. from כָּבֵד or כָּבַד iii. 4.

Verse 6. הִבְאִישׁוּ stink, Hiph. 3 pl. pret. from בָּאַשׁ to stink; Hiph. to make fetid, and metaph. to make hateful.

נָמַקּוּ are-corrupt, or have dissolved, Niph. 3 pl. pret. from מָקַק, not used in Kal; Niph. to flow or run down, to consume, to waste away.

חַבּוּרֹתָי my-wounds, pl. of חַבּוּרָה subst. f. with suff. 1 s. R. חָבַר to bind, to join together, to fascinate (spoken of magic), to be marked with stripes, to be variegated.

אִוַּלְתִּי my-foolishness, verb. n. f. with suff. 1 s. from the obs. אָוַל to be foolish.

Verse 7. נַעֲוֵיתִי I-am-troubled, or I am bent down, Niph. 1 s. pret. from עָוָה xviii. 24.

Verse 8. כְסָלַי my-loins, pl. of כֶּסֶל subst. m. (with suff. 1 s.), the loin, the flank, the part near the kidneys to which the fat adheres; the word sometimes signifies confidence, hope, and sometimes folly. R. כָּסַל, hardly ever used as a verb, of which the primary meaning appears to be, to be fleshy, to be fat; it is also sometimes applied in a good sense to strength and boldness, and in a bad sense to languor, inertness, folly.

נִקְלֶה a-loathsome (disease), or dryness, or an inflammation, Niph. pres. part. m. s. from קָלָה to roast in the fire, to burn.

Verse 9. נְפוּגֹתִי I-am-become-feeble, Niph. 1 s. pret. from פּוּג to be cold, to be wearied; Niph. to be weak, feeble. The word occurs three times in Kal, Gen. xlv. 26, Ps. lxxvii. 3, and Hab. i. 4; in Niph. it occurs nowhere except in this place.

PSALM XXXVIII. vv. 11–15, 18–21.

מִנַּהֲמַת by-reason-of-(the) disquietness-of, constr. of נְהָמָה subst. f. with pr. מ ii. 3. R. נָהַם to roar as a lion, to rage or foam as the sea, to sigh, to groan. The noun נְהָמָה in the fem. gender is found but once besides this place, viz. Is. v. 30.

Verse 11. סְחַרְחַר panteth, Pilp. 3 m. s. pret. from סָחַר to go or move about (specially for the sake of trade), to traffic; Pilp. to flutter, to palpitate, only found here in Pilp.

The phrase 'the light of the eyes' occurs only in this place in the Heb., although found in another in our English Bible, Prov. xv. 30, where the word in the original is different, though from the same root.

Verse 12. נִגְעִי my-stroke, verb. n. m. with suff. 1 s. from נָגַע to touch, to smite.

Verse 13. The LXX. and Vulg. translate וַיְנַקְשׁוּ by 'they used violence,' the Syr. has 'they laid hold of me,' Arab. 'they oppressed me.'

Verse 14. כְחֵרֵשׁ as-a-deaf (man), verb. adj. m. from חָרַשׁ xxviii. 1 with pr. כ i. 3.

וּכְאִלֵּם and-as-a-dumb (man), verb. adj. m. from אָלַם xxxi. 19 with ו cop. i. 1 and pr. כ i. 3.

Verse 15. תּוֹכָחוֹת reproofs, pl. of תּוֹכַחַת verb. n. f. from יָכַח vi. 2.

Verse 18. וּמַכְאוֹבִי and-my-sorrow, or my sore, my wound.

Verse 19. אֶדְאַג I-will-be-sorry, Kal 1 s. fut. from דָּאַג to be afflicted or troubled about anything, to fear.

Verse 20. For חַיִּים some would read חִנָּם.

Verse 21. יִשְׂטְנוּנִי will-oppose-me, Kal 3 m. pl. fut. with suff. 1 s. from שָׂטַן to be hostile, to oppose, to persecute, to lie in wait for.

רָדוֹפִי (to be read רְדוֹפִי) my-pursuing, Kal inf. constr. from רָדַף with suff. 1 s. The K'ri is רדפי instead of רְדוֹפִי.

PSALM XXXIX.

This Psalm somewhat resembles the sixty-second, which has also the name of Jeduthun in the Title. It must have been written by David at a time either of bodily illness, or of some severe visitation of Providence. All the words in the concluding verse occur in different parts of the Book of Job. Comp. Job vii. 8, 19, 21, and x. 20, 21.

Verse 1. לִידִיתִין for-Jeduthun, (K'ri לִידוּתִין), praising, celebrating, from the obs. noun יְדוּת praise, praisings, with pr. לְ ii. 1; see ix. 10. R. יָדָה vi. 6; prop. name of a Levite set by David as chief over a choir. The name occurs also in the Titles of Psalms lxii and lxxvii.

Verse 2. מַחְסוֹם a-bridle, verb. n. m. from חָסַם to stop, to obstruct. The word occurs nowhere else.

Verse 3. For מִטּוֹב the Chal. has 'from the words of the Law;' Vulg. *silui a bonis.*

וּכְאֵבִי and-my-sorrow, verb. n. m. from כָּאַב xxxii 10 with וְ cop. i. 1 and suff. 1 s.

נֶעְכָּר was-stirred, Niph. 3 m. s. pret. from עָכַר to disturb, to trouble; in Niph. found only here and in Prov. xv. 6.

Verse 5. קִצִּי mine-end, i.q. קָצֶה xix. 5 with suff. 1 s.

וּמִדַּת and-(the)measure-of, constr. of מִדָּה verb. n. f. with וְ cop. i. 1, from מָדַד to stretch, to extend, to stretch out a measuring line, to measure. Comp. Sans. *mâ, mâd,* to measure; Gr. μέτρον; Lat. *metior;* Goth. *mitan;* A. Sax. *metan;* Ger. meſſen.

חָדֵל frail, verb. adj. m. from חָדַל to cease, to leave off.

Verse 6. טְפָחוֹת hand-breadths, pl. of טֶפַח verb. n. m. from טָפַח, unused in Kal, to be broad, spreading.

נִצָּב standing, Niph. pres. part. m. s. from נָצַב i.q. יָצַב to set, to place; Niph. to be placed, to stand.

Verse 7. בְּצֶלֶם in-a-shadow, subst. m. (with pr. בְּ i. 1), an image, a shadow, a likeness. R. צָלַם, unused in Heb., to be shady.

Verse 8. תּוֹחַלְתִּי my-hope, subst. f. with suff. 1 s.; abs. form תּוֹחֶלֶת. R. יָחַל xxxi. 25.

Verse 10. עָשִׂיתָ didst (it), i.e. the blow, נֶגַע, which we find in the following verse. The LXX., Arab., and Æth. have 'Thou art He that hath made me.'

Verse 11. מִתִּגְרַת by-(the)blow-of, constr. of תִּגְרָה subst. f. with pr. מ ii. 3, strife, contention. The word is an ἅπαξ λεγόμενον. R. גָּרָה v. 10.

Verse 12. כָּעָשׁ as-the-moth, subst. m. with pr. כְּ xviii. 34. Either 'as a moth (perishes),' or (as in Job xiii. 28) 'as a moth (consumes) a garment.'

Verse 13. גֵר a-stranger, subst. m. R. גּוּר v. 5. תּוֹשָׁב a-sojourner, verb. n. m. from יָשַׁב to dwell.

Verse 14. הָשַׁע Look-away, for הַשְׁעָה Hiph. 2 m. s. imp. apoc. from שָׁעָה.

מִמֶּנִּי from-me, i.e. keep not Thine eye fixed upon me in anger. The LXX. has ἄνες μοι. Comp. Job vii. 19, xiv. 6.

וְאַבְלִיגָה that-I-may-take-comfort, Hiph. 1 s. fut. from בָּלַג, in Kal not used in Heb., but in Arab. signifying to be bright, to shine forth as the dawn, to rejoice, to smile; Hiph. to cause to shine forth (in a figurative sense), intrans. to be joyful. The only other places where the word occurs are Job ix. 27, x. 20, and Amos v. 9.

בְּטֶרֶם before, strictly a subst., a cutting off, a part cut off, (with pr. בְּ i. 1,) always used as an adv. R. טָרַם, unused in Heb., to cut off.

PSALM XL.

In *the first* part of this Psalm David recounts the mercies of God in the time of past troubles, and in *the second* he prays for deliverance in the midst of present calamities. The verses 13–17 appear again in an independent form as Ps. lxx, though Ps. xl was probably the original poem. This is one of the Proper Psalms for Good Friday.

Verse 2. קַוֹּה Expecting, Pi. inf. abs. from קָוָה ix. 19, placed before the finite verb to increase the strength of it.

Verse 3. שָׁאוֹן noise, or destruction, verb. n. m. from שָׁאָה to make a noise; Hiph. to lay waste.

הַיָּוֵן the-mire, subst. m., only found here and in Ps. lxix. 3. R. יָוַן, unused in Heb., which appears to have had the signification of boiling or bubbling up, to be clammy, also to be weak, tender.

Verse 4. לֵאלֹהֵינוּ unto-our-God, iii. 3 with pr. לְ ii. 1 and suff. 1 pl. As two Sh'vas, simple or compound, cannot stand together at the beginning of a word, the לְ should take (ֵ) the vowel homogeneous to the compound (ֱ), and then (ֱֵ) are contracted into (ֵ).

Verse 5. The LXX., Vulg., Syr., Arab., and Æth. have '*the name* of the Lord,' the Chal. follows the Hebrew.

מִבְטָחוֹ his-confidence, verb. n. m. from בָּטַח to trust or confide in, with suff. 3 m. s.

רְהָבִים (the) proud, pl. of רָהָב subst. m., only found in this passage. R. רָהַב to rage, to be fierce, to attack; Hiph. to make strong or courageous.

וְשָׂטֵי and-those-who-turn-aside-to, Kal pres. part. m. pl. constr. from שׂוּט i. q. שָׂטָה to incline to anything, to turn aside; only found here.

Verse 6. עֲרֹךְ to-set-in-order, or to expound (them).

The LXX. has 'there is none to be compared to Thee.'

Verse 7. זֶבַח means *a bloody sacrifice*, and is used in opposition to מִנְחָה *an unbloody sacrifice*. Instead of 'mine ears hast Thou opened,' lit. digged, we find in the LXX. 'a body hast Thou prepared me,' which is the reading quoted by St. Paul, Heb. x. 5.

PSALM XL. vv. 8, 10, 11, 13, 16; XLI. v. 2.   109

Verse 8. בִּמְגִלַּת־ in-(the) roll-of, constr. of מְגִלָּה subst. f. (with pr. בּ ii. 11), a volume, a book rolled together as was the ancient custom. R. גָּלַל to roll.

סֵפֶר (the) book, verb. n. m. from סָפַר ii. 7.

Verse 10. The Syr., Vulg., and Arab. have צִדְקָתְךָ.

אֶכְלָא I-will-refrain, Kal 1 s. fut. from כָּלָא to shut up, to restrain; Niph. to be restrained, hence to cease. Comp. Gr. κλείω, κλαίς; Lat. *clavis, claudo*.

Verse 11. כִחַדְתִּי I-have-concealed, Pi. 1 s. pret. from כָּחַד (not used in Kal), perhaps to be invisible; Pi. and Hiph. to hide, also to deny.

Verse 13. מִסְפָּר number, verb. n. m. from סָפַר ii. 7.

מִשַּׂעֲרוֹת more-than-(the) hairs-of, pl. of שַׂעֲרָה verb. n. f. (with pr. מ ii. 3), from שָׂעַר to shudder, to quiver, used also of the hair standing on end, to rage, to roar, to sweep away; Niph. to be tempestuous.

Verse 16. יֵשֹׁמּוּ Let-them-be-desolate, Kal 3 m. pl. fut. from שָׁמַם to be desolate, to be laid waste, also to be astonished, to be struck dumb, to be struck with amazement, Lat. *stupere, obstupescere*.

PSALM XLI.

In this Psalm, which somewhat resembles the thirty-eighth, and which seems to have been written during recovery from sickness, David complains of the treachery of his enemies, and flees to God for succour. Part of ver. 9 (10) is quoted by our Lord in St. John xiii. 18 as applicable to the treacherous conduct of Judas.

Verse 2. מַשְׂכִּיל followed by the prep. אֶל occurs nowhere in the Hebrew Bible with the exception of this passage and Neh. viii. 13.

דַּל (the) poor, or the weak, or sick, verb. adj. m. from דָּלַל i.q. דָּלָה to be pendulous, to be languid, weak.

Verse 3. The K'thiv is יְאַשֵּׁר, and the K'ri וְאִשֵּׁר.

At the latter end of the verse we have a sudden change from the 3rd to the 2nd person with respect to Jehovah; though the LXX., Vulg., and Syr. have the 3rd person.

Verse 4. דְּוַי languishing, verb. n. m. from דָּוָה to be languid, to be sick.

בְּחָלְיוֹ in-his-sickness, verb. n. m. from חָלָה xxxv. 13 with pr. בּ i. 1 and suff. 3 m. s.

Verse 7. There is an ellipsis of אוֹתִי after לִרְאוֹת, which is supplied in the Syriac.

Verse 8. יִתְלַחֲשׁוּ whisper, Hithp. 3 m. pl. fut. from לָחַשׁ to whisper, not used in Kal; Pi. to whisper, to mutter, used of incantations, in Pi. found only in Ps. lviii. 6.

Verse 9. For דְּבַר־בְּלִיַּעַל the Syr. has 'word of iniquity,' Chal. 'perverse word.'

יָצוּק is-poured-out, Kal part. pass. m. s. from יָצַק to pour out (liquids), to cast (metal), hence יָצוּק hard, firm, like cast metal.

Verse 10. עָקֵב heel, subst. m., the heel, the rear, also a persecutor or a lier in wait; (in the pl. signifying *footprints*.) R. עָקַב xix. 12.

Verse 14. אָמֵן Amen, adv. truly, verily. R. אָמַן xii. 2.

This last verse is no part of the original Psalm, but is merely a later doxology appended here when the Psalms were collected, in order to mark the conclusion of the First Book. Similar doxologies occur at the end of the three following Books; see Psalms lxxii, lxxxix, cvi. We find the same form of words in 1 Chron. xvi. 36.

BOOK II, PSALMS XLII–LXXII.

PSALM XLII.

In Psalms XLII and XLIII, which evidently form a pair, and which in more than forty ancient MSS. are found joined together into one, the Psalmist speaks of his zeal in the service of God, encourages his soul to trust in Him, and prays to be restored to His Temple. If not written by David himself they were probably composed by some Korahite who accompanied him in his flight across Jordan. The Title in the Arabic is 'A Prayer for the Jews who had fallen.'

Verse 1. קֹרַח Korah, baldness, prop. name m. R. קָרַח to make smooth or bald. These words לִבְנֵי־קֹרַח are found in the Inscription of Psalms xlii–xlviii, lxxxiv, lxxxv, lxxxvii, and lxxxviii. Some suppose the Title to denote not the authors of the Psalms, but the Levitical singers and musicians for whom it was composed.

Verse 2. כְּאַיָּל As-a-hart, subst. com. gen., (always m. with the exception of this passage, where it is construed with the f.,) with pr. כְּ i. 3.

תַּעֲרֹג (which) panteth, Kal 3 f. s. fut. from עָרַג to ascend, followed by עַל or אֶל to long for anything; the word only occurs here and in Joel i. 20.

Verse 3. This particular form of expression אֶל חָי only occurs in three other places, viz. Josh. iii. 10, Ps. lxxxiv. 3, and Hos. i. 10.

For the Niph. אֵרָאֶה some persons, with Luther, would substitute the Kal, and translate 'that I may behold God's face.'

Verse 4. The Syr. and Arab. read בְּאָמְרָם for בֶּאֱמֹר.

אַיֵּה Where, adv. of interrog., i.q. אֵי with ה parag.

Verse 5. בַּסָּךְ with-the-throng, subst. m. (with pr. בּ i. 1), only found in this passage, prop. a thicket of trees, a thick wood, applied poetically to a dense crowd. The LXX. has ἐν τόπῳ σκηνῆς θαυμαστῆς, as if supposing the Tabernacle to be meant.

אֶדַּדֵּם I-marched-with-them, for אֶתְדַּדֵּם Hithp. 1 s. fut. with suff. 3 m. pl. from דָּדָה to move, to go slowly, spoken of the solemn slowness of a procession. The word occurs only here and in Is. xxxviii. 15.

חוֹגֵג keeping-a-feast, Kal pres. part. m. s. from חָגַג to dance, to keep a festival; in a bad sense, to reel, to be giddy.

Verse 6. תִּשְׁתּוֹחֲחִי art-thou-cast-down, or bowest thou thyself down, Hithpoel 2 f. s. fut. from שָׁחַח x. 10.

וּמַה־תֶּהֱמִי is the reading of four Hebrew MSS., LXX., Vulg., Arab., and Chal., of ver. 11 and of xliii. 5.

יְשׁוּעוֹת פָּנָיו (the) health-of-His-countenance, lit. the salvations of, or 'His presence (is) salvation.' Many of the best critics follow the ancient versions and some copies of the Heb., in joining the next word in the Heb. to this verse. Thus, without altering a single letter, they read 'the salvation of my countenance and my God,' so making all the three verses, 6, 12, and xliii. 5, alike. The LXX. (Alex.), Vulg., Syr., and one MS. of Kennicott read פָּנַי וֵאלֹהַי, and begin the next verse with עָלַי.

Verse 7. יַרְדֵּן Jordan, the largest river of Palestine, rising at the foot of Anti-libanus, and flowing into the Dead Sea, where it is lost.

וְחֶרְמוֹנִים and-(the) Hermonites, pl. of חֶרְמוֹן (prominent, rugged mountain; R. חָרַם, unused in Heb., perhaps to be high, to be prominent, sometimes to consecrate); prop. name of a spur of Anti-libanus, in the north-east of Palestine, now called Jebel-esh-Sheikh, and towards the south Jebel-el-Heish, consisting of several mountains, and therefore spoken of in the plural.

מִצְעָר Mizar (prop. smallness, R. צָעַר to be small), prop. name of a mountain on the eastern ridge of Lebanon.

Verse 8. צִנּוֹרֶיךָ Thy-cataracts, pl. of צִנּוֹר subst. m. with suff. 2 m. s.; the word occurs only here and 2 Sam. v. 8, where it is in the sing. R. צָנַר, unused in Heb., prop. to creak, to squeak, specially used of the stridulous sound of water flowing down violently.

מִשְׁבָּרֶיךָ Thy-waves, subst. m. pl., waves broken on the shore, billows, with suff. 2 m. s. R. שָׁבַר to break.

וְגַלֶּיךָ and-Thy-billows, pl. of גַּל subst. m. (with suff. 2 m. s.), a heap of stones, a fountain, a spring; (when used in the plur. it signifies waves.) R. גָּלַל to roll.

Verse 9. שִׁירֹה His-song, an unusual form for שִׁירוֹ, which is found in some MSS.

Verse 10. בְּלַחַץ because-of-(the)oppression-of, verb. n. m. with pr. בּ i. 1, from לָחַץ to press, to oppress.

Verse 11. בְּרֶצַח (As)with-a-sword, subst. m. (with pr. בּ i. 1), a wounding, slaughter, breaking in pieces. R. רָצַח to dash in pieces, to kill.

Verse 12. Instead of יְשׁוּעֹת the LXX., Vulg., Æth., and Arab. have the sing. יְשׁוּעַת.

PSALM XLIII.

Verse 2. זְנַחְתָּנִי hast-Thou-cast-me-off? Kal 2 m. s. pret. with suff. 1 s. from זָנַח to have an offensive smell, metaph. to be abominable, trans. to loathe, to reject.

Verse 3. יְבִיאוּנִי let-them-bring-me, Hiph. 3 m. pl. fut. from בּוֹא v. 8 with suff. 1 s. The K'ri is יבאוני (to be read יְבָאוּנִי) let come upon me.

Verse 4. גִּילִי my-joy, verb. n. m. with suff. 1 s. from גִּיל ii. 11. The LXX., Syr., Æth., Vulg., and Arab. have 'my youth.'

I

PSALM XLIV.

In this Psalm, which somewhat resembles Psalm lx, and which was perhaps composed on occasion of the invasion of the Edomites, the Psalmist calls to mind the great deeds which God had wrought for His people in the days of old; contrasts it with the present state of things, when they are given over into the hand of their enemies; declares that they have not forgotten God, and prays for His succour against their adversaries. Verse 10 occurs almost word for word in Psalm lx.

Verse 2. The relat. pron. אֲשֶׁר is to be understood after פֹּעַל.

קֶדֶם old, subst. m., prop. that which is before, the east; referring to time—former time, the past; poet.=עוֹלָם. R. קָדַם xvii. 13.

Verse 3. The LXX., Syr., Vulg., and Æth. omit the word אַתָּה.

וַתִּטָּעֵם and-didst-plant-them, Kal 2 m. s. fut. with suff. 3 m. pl. from נָטַע to set anything upright, to plant.

תָּרַע Thou-didst afflict, Hiph. 2 m. s. fut. from רָעַע ii. 9.

וַתְּשַׁלְּחֵם and-cast-them-out, or rather, 'Thou didst afflict (the) nations, but *them* (i. e. our fathers) Thou madest to spread abroad,' i. e. extended their borders.

Verse 5. The part. מְצַוֶּה is apparently the reading of the LXX. instead of צַוֵּה imp.

Verse 6. נְנַגֵּחַ we-will-push-down, Pi. 1 pl. fut. from נָגַח Kal and Pi. to push.

נָבוּס we-will-tread-under, Kal 1 pl. fut. from בּוּס. To tread with the feet is expressed in many languages by the syllable *pat* variously inflected; see Sans. *path*, to go; Zend *pathan*, a path, a way; Gr. πάτος, πατέω, πούς for ποδς; Lat. *pes;* Low Germ. patten, Pfad; Eng. *path*, *t* being changed by the Hebrews into a sibilant *pas, bas*.

Verse 10. The LXX., Syr., Vulg., and Æth. seem to have read וְעַתָּה for אַף.

PSALM XLIV. vv. 11–15, 17, 20, 21.

The Syr., Arab., and Chal. read וַנְּחִתָּנוּ.

After חְנָא the LXX. and Vulg. add the word אֱלֹהִים as in Ps. lx. 12.

Verse 11. מִנִּי from, poetic form for מִן ii. 3.

The Syr., Arab., and Chal. read לָנוּ for לָמוֹ.

Verse 12. מַאֲכָל food, verb. n. m. from אָכַל to eat.

זֵרִיתָנוּ hast-scattered-us, Pi. 2 m. s. pret. with suff. 1 pl. from זָרָה Kal and Pi. to scatter, to disperse. Comp. Sans. *sri*, to scatter; Lat. *sero*.

Verse 13. בְלֹא־הוֹן without-wealth, or for (that which is) not wealth = for nought, gratis; הוֹן subst. m. R. הוּן to be light, to be of little moment.

בִּמְחִירֵיהֶם by-their-price, pl. of מְחִיר subst. m. with pr. בְּ ii. 11 and suff. 3 m. pl. R. מָחַר, unused in Heb., to interchange, to buy, to sell. The word occurs nowhere else in the plural.

Verse 14. לַעַג a-scorn, verb. n. m. from לָעַג ii. 4.

וָקֶלֶס and-a-derision, verb. n. m. with ו cop. i. 2, from קָלַס, not used in Kal; Pi. to mock, to scorn.

Verse 15. מָשָׁל a-by-word, subst. m., a proverb, a byword, a parable, a figurative discourse generally, hence a song, a poem. R. מָשַׁל viii. 7.

מְנוֹד־ a-shaking-of, constr. of מָנוֹד verb. n. m. from נוּד xi. 1. The word is an ἅπαξ λεγόμενον.

Verse 17. וּמְגַדֵּף and-blasphemeth, Pi. pres. part. m. s. with ו cop. i. 1, from גָּדַף, found only in Piel.

Verse 20. תַּנִּים jackals, prop. howlers, pl. of תַּן subst. m. R. תָּנַן, not used in Heb., (Ges.) to stretch out, to extend; (Fürst) to call, to cry. Comp. Sans. *tan*, to extend; Lat. *tendo, tenuis;* Goth. *thanjan;* Ger. dehnen.

Verse 21. וַנִּפְרֹשׂ and-stretched-out, Kal 1 pl. fut. with ו convers. from פָּרַשׂ to break in pieces, to spread or stretch out; Pi. to scatter.

זָר strange, Kal pres. part. m. s. from זוּר, a kindred root to סוּר

to turn aside, to depart, to turn from the way, to lodge at any one's house, hence to be a stranger, to be strange or foreign.

Verse 22. תַּעֲלֻמוֹת (the) secrets-of, subst. f. pl. R. עָלַם v. 12. The only other places where the word occurs are Job xi. 6 and xxviii. 11.

Verse 23. טִבְחָה (the) slaughter, verb. n. f. from טָבַח to slaughter. See Rom. viii. 36.

PSALM XLV.

Under the type of the nuptials of a Jewish king (probably Solomon) with a foreign princess—by some supposed to be the daughter of Pharaoh, king of Egypt, and by others of Hiram, king of Tyre—is prefigured the marriage of Christ and His Church. Some persons refer the Psalm to the marriage of Ahab with Jezebel, daughter of Ethbaal, king of the Zidonians; whilst others think that Joram, the son of Jehoshaphat, is the king intended, and Athaliah (who was of Tyrian origin and of the royal family of Israel) the queen. Verses 7 and 8 are quoted by St. Paul, Hebr. i. 8, 9. This is one of the Proper Psalms appointed for Christmas Day.

Verse 1. שֹׁשַׁנִּים (the) lilies, pl. of שׁוֹשָׁן subst. m., a lily, prop. what is white, the name of a musical instrument, perhaps so called from its resemblance to a lily, though some persons suppose that it was the name of the melody to which the Psalm was to be sung. The same Inscription occurs in the Titles of Psalms lxix and lxxx, and a similar one in Ps. lx. Luther has von den Rosen. R. שׁוּשׁ, unused in Heb., which appears to have had the signification of whiteness.

יְדִידֹת loves, or beloved ones, f. pl. of יָדִיד one beloved, a friend, also loveliness, used as an adj. meaning lovely, pleasant. R. יָדַד, unused in Heb., i. q. דּוּד to love.

Verse 2. רָחַשׁ boileth, or bubbleth up, Kal 3 m. s. pret., to swell or boil up (as a fountain and boiling water). The verb occurs nowhere else.

עֵט (the)pen-of, subst. m. R. עוּט, unused in Heb., prob. meaning to cut into, to engrave.

מָהִיר quick, verb. adj. m. from מָהַר xvi. 4.

Verse 3. יָפְיָפִיתָ Thou-art-fair, Pu. 2 m. s. pret. from יָפָה to be fair, to be beautiful; Pi. to make beautiful, to adorn; Pu. to be very beautiful.

Verse 4. יָרֵךְ thigh, subst. m., perhaps so called from softness. R. יָרַךְ, unused in Heb., to be soft, tender.

Luther's Version is Gürte Dein Schwerdt an Deine Seite, und schmücke Dich schön.

Verse 5. The two first words of this verse are omitted in the Syriac.

For וַהֲדָרְךָ the LXX. seems to read הַדְרֵךְ tread or bend, i. e. the bow קֶשֶׁת, as in Ps. vii. 13.

וְצֶדֶק is the reading of two Hebrew MSS., Chal., LXX., Vulg., Æth., and Arab.

Verse 6. שְׁנוּנִים whetted, Kal pass. part. m. pl. from שָׁנַן to sharpen; Hithpoel to be wounded.

Verse 7. מַלְכוּתֶךָ Thy-kingdom, subst. f. with suff. 2 m. s. R. מָלַךְ to reign.

Verse 8. שָׂשׂוֹן gladness, verb. n. m. from שָׂשָׂה i. q. שׂוּשׂ to rejoice, to be glad.

מֵחֲבֵרֶיךָ above-Thy-fellows, pl. of חָבֵר verb. n. m. from חָבַר xxxviii. 6 with pr. מ iii. 5 and suff. 2 m. s.

Verse 9. מֹר Myrrh, subst. m., so called from flowing down, distilling. R. מָרַר to flow, to drop.

וַאֲהָלוֹת and-aloes, subst. m. pl. with ו cop. ii. 6, a very valuable odoriferous Indian tree, in Gr. ἀγάλλοχον, in later writers ξυλαλόη.

קְצִיעוֹת cassia, pl. of קְצִיעָה subst. f., only found here, cassia, so called from its being peeled. R. קָצַע, unused in Kal, to cut off, to scrape, to peel, also to rimple, to fold. Some translate the passage '*the folds* of all thy garments.'

מִנִּי (the) stringed-instruments. This is a very difficult word; some suppose that it is an apocopated pl. of מִנִּים viols, stringed instruments, subst. m. pl., prop. slender threads, so called from their being divided. R. מָנָה ii. 3. Others think that it is a repetition of the מִן preceding (in its poetical form), and render 'out of ivory palaces whence they gladden Thee,' whilst others suppose that מִנִּי may mean a province of Armenia (as in Jer. li. 27) according to the Chal. rendering.

The LXX. has ἐξ ὧν ηὔφρανάν σε.

Verse 10. בְּיִקְּרוֹתֶיךָ among-Thy-honourable-women, or thy beloved ones, f. pl. of יָקָר xxxvi. 8 with pr. בְּ i. 1; see ix. 10. Luther has Jn Deinem Schmuck gehen der Könige Töchter.

שֵׁגַל (the) Queen-Consort, subst. f. R. שָׁגַל to lie with a woman.

בְּכֶתֶם in-fine-gold-of, subst. m. (with pr. בְּ i. 1), i. q. זָהָב, but used only in poetry; prop. that which is hidden away in treasuries, that which is precious. R. כָּתַם, unused in Kal, perhaps to hide away, to lay up; according to some, to separate (dross from metal), to purify, to cleanse.

אוֹפִיר Ophir, a celebrated region abounding in gold, by some supposed to have been in India, and by others in Arabia.

Verse 12. יָפְיֵךְ thy-beauty, subst. m. with suff. 2 f. s.; abs. form יֳפִי. R. יָפָה xlv. 3.

Verse 13. צֹר Tyre, a rock, rock-city, i.q. צוּר (comp. Rupella, la Rochelle); a city of the Phœnicians celebrated for its traffic, and very rich.

יְחַלּוּ shall-entreat, lit. smooth, or stroke, Pi. 3 m. pl. fut. from חָלָה xxxv. 13.

עֲשִׁירֵי (the) rich-of, pl. constr. of עָשִׁיר verb. adj. m. from עָשַׁר to prosper, to be happy, to be rich; Hiph. to make rich, to enrich, intrans. to become rich.

Verse 14. כְּבוּדָּה glorious, lit. all glory, nothing but glory, incorrect orthography for כְּבֻדָּה, either (as in Ezek. xxiii. 41) verb. n. f., or else (as in Jud. xviii. 21) f. of כָּבֹד verb. adj. from כָּבַד iii. 4.

פְּנִימָה within, iii. 1 with ה local; prop. to the wall of the house, or room, or court which is opposite to the door, where the throne stood in royal palaces; 'all splendid (sits) the daughter of the King (the Queen) פְּנִימָה by the wall,' i.e. is seated on the throne. Some persons derive the word from a root פָּנַם, unused in Heb., to conceal, considering that it means a thing concealed, hidden, hence as an adv. within, inwardly, signifying that the Bride, the Church, must be pure within.

מִמִּשְׁבְּצוֹת of-embroiderings-of, subst. f. pl. with pr. מ ii. 3, cloth embroidered or interwoven with gold thread. R. שָׁבַץ, not used in Kal, to mingle; Pi. to weave together.

Verse 15. לִרְקָמוֹת In-raiment-of-needlework, pl. of רִקְמָה subst. f. with pr. ל iv. 3, a variegation of colour, a parti-coloured cloth or garment. R. רָקַם to variegate, to work cloth with various colours; Pu. found only in Ps. cxxxix. 15. Comp. Span. *recamar*; Ital. *ricamare*; Fr. *récamer*, to embroider.

בְּתוּלוֹת (the) virgins, pl. of בְּתוּלָה subst. f., prop. separated from intercourse with a man. R. בָּתַל, unused in Heb., to divide, to separate.

מוּבָאוֹת are-brought, Hoph. pres. part. f. pl. from בּוֹא v. 8.

Verse 17. לְשָׂרִים for-princes, pl. of שַׂר verb. n. m. from שָׂרַר to have dominion, to rule, with pr. ל ii. 1.

Verse 18. For אַזְכִּירָה the LXX., Vulg., Chal., and Syr. have the plur.

PSALM XLVI.

This Psalm and the two following are hymns of triumph, composed on the occasion of some great deliverance. They probably commemorate the destruction of the army of Sennacherib, recorded in 2 Kings xix and Is. xxxvii, though they are by some persons referred to the victory of Jehoshaphat over the combined Moabites, Ammonites, and Edomites. This Psalm was a special favourite of the Reformer Luther in times of peculiar danger; he founded on it the well-known hymn Ein' feste Burg ist unser Gott, and it is admirably adapted for the solace of the Church in all her afflictions.

Verse 1. עֲלָמוֹת Alamoth, pl. of עַלְמָה subst. f., a girl, a virgin. R. עָלַם, unused in Heb., to be young, to be vigorous. The words עַל־עֲלָמוֹת probably mean that the Psalm was to be sung *in the manner of virgins*, i.e. with the virgin voice, soprano, opposed to שְׁמִינִית basso; see vi. 1.

Verse 2. Luther, after the LXX. and Vulg., renders the last words of the verse, 'in the great distresses which have come upon us.'

Verse 3. בְּהָמִיר in-changing, Hiph. inf. constr. from מוּר xv. 4 with pr. ב i. 1.

Verse 4. יֶחְמְרוּ are-turbid, Kal 3 m. pl. fut. from חָמַר to be agitated, to boil up, to ferment, also to be red.

Verse 5. For מִשְׁכְּנֵי the LXX., Vulg., and Syr. read מִשְׁכָּנוֹ, and render 'the Most High hath sanctified His Tabernacle.'

Verse 6. לִפְנוֹת at-(the)appearing-of, lit. at the turning of.

Verse 7. מַמְלָכוֹת (the)kingdoms, pl. of מַמְלָכָה verb. n. f. from מָלַךְ to reign.

תָּמוּג will-dissolve, Kal 3 f. s. fut. from מוּג to flow, to melt; Niph. to despond (from fear); Pilel to soften, to melt; Hithpalpel to melt, to despond.

Verse 8. The epithet 'the Lord of Hosts' first occurs in the mouth of Hannah, 1 Sam. i. 11.

Verse 9. מִפְעָלוֹת (the)works-of, pl. constr. of מִפְעָלָה verb. n. f. from פָּעַל v. 6.

שַׁמּוֹת desolations, pl. of שַׁמָּה subst. f., elsewhere found only in the sing.

Verse 10. עֲגָלוֹת (the) chariots, pl. of עֲגָלָה subst. f., a wagon, a chariot, so called from rolling, wheeling. R. עָגַל i.q. גָּלַל to roll, to revolve. The Chal. and LXX. have 'shields.'

Verse 11. We find a change of person in this verse, Jehovah Himself being introduced as the speaker.

PSALM XLVII.

This is one of the Proper Psalms for Ascension Day. The words in verse 4, 'He shall subdue the people under us,' are the same as in Ps. xviii. 48.

Verse 2. תִּקְעוּ clap-ye, Kal 2 m. pl. imp. from תָּקַע to strike, to clap, to blow with a trumpet.

Verse 5. The LXX. and Vulg. have 'his inheritance.'

גְּאוֹן (the) excellency-of, constr. of גָּאוֹן subst. m., greatness, majesty, pride. R. גָּאָה x. 2.

Verse 6. שׁוֹפָר a-trumpet, subst. m., pl. וֹת. R. שָׁפַר xvi. 7.

Verse 7. The LXX., Vulg., Æth., and Arab. have לֵאלֹהֵינוּ.

Verse 8. מַשְׂכִּיל with-understanding, lit. causing to understand, or every one that hath understanding.

Verse 10. נְדִיבֵי (The) princes-of, pl. constr. of נָדִיב subst. m., one noble in rank, a prince; as an adj. voluntary, giving voluntarily, liberal, noble-minded. R. נָדַב to drive on, to excite; Hiph. to excite oneself, to shew oneself willing, to give willingly.

We find in the LXX., followed by the Vulg. and Luther, that the word עַם is taken as the prep. עִם, as the verse is rendered, 'The princes of the people were joined *to* the people of the God of Abraham.' The Welsh Version is *sef pobl Duw Abraham.*

אַבְרָהָם Abraham, (father of a multitude, compounded of אָב, see iii. 1, and רָהָם multitude; R. רָהַם, unused in Heb., which appears to have had the signification of raging); the founder and father of the Jewish nation, the son of Terah, born in Mesopotamia, whose name was changed from אַבְרָם to אַבְרָהָם.

מָגִנֵּי (the) shields-of, i.e. 'chiefs;' the word is rendered 'rulers' in Hos. iv. 18; the LXX. has κραταιοί.

PSALM XLVIII.

The mention of 'ships of Tarshish,' in verse 7 of this Psalm, harmonises well with the supposition of its referring to the victory of Jehoshaphat. (See Introduction to Psalm xlvi.) This is one of the Proper Psalms for Whit-Sunday.

Verse 3. יְפֵה Beautiful-in, constr. of יָפֶה verb. adj. m. from יָפָה xlv. 3.

נוֹף elevation, subst. m., height, elevation. R. נוּף xix. 11. The word is an ἅπαξ λεγόμενον.

מְשׂוֹשׂ (the) joy-of, constr. of מָשׂוֹשׂ verb. n. m. from שִׂישׂ or שׂוּשׂ to rejoice.

Luther, with Jerome, (departing from the LXX. and Vulg.,) renders the verse, 'Mount Zion is like a beautiful branch,' after the Mishna-Talmudic נוֹף a branch.

יַרְכְּתֵי (on the) sides-of, constr. of יַרְכָתַיִם, dual of יַרְכָּה or יְרֵכָה subst. f. R. יָרַךְ xlv. 4.

צָפוֹן (the) north, subst. com. gen., prop. hidden, obscure, inasmuch as the ancients regarded the north as obscure and dark. R. צָפַן to hide, to conceal.

קִרְיַת (the) city-of, constr. of קִרְיָה subst. f., i.q. עִיר, but used almost exclusively in poetry. R. קָרָה to meet, to happen; Pi. to lay beams or joists, prop. to make the beams to meet one another; Hiph. to cause to meet, hence to bring to a person.

Verse 4. בְּאַרְמְנוֹתֶיהָ in-her-palaces, pl. of אַרְמוֹן subst. m. with pr. בְּ i. 1 and suff. 3 f. s. R. prob. רָם to be high.

Verse 5. נוֹעֲדוּ were-assembled, or were met, Niph. 3 pl. pret. from יָעַד i. 5.

Verse 6. נֶחְפְּזוּ hasted-away, or were seized with panic, Niph. 3 pl. pret. from חָפַז xxxi. 23.

Verse 7. חִיל pain, subst. m., pain (especially of childbirth). R. חִיל or חוּל x. 5.

כַּיּוֹלֵדָה as-of-a-woman-in-travail, Kal pres. part. f. s. from יָלַד with pr. כ i. 3.

Verse 8. קָדִים east, verb. adj. m. from קָדַם xvii. 13.

תְּשַׁבֵּר Thou-breakest; this may be either Pi. 2 m. s. fut. or 3 f. s. fut. from שָׁבַר, so that the passage may be rendered either 'Thou breakest (them as Thou breakest) the ships,' &c., or '(They were broken as) with the East wind which breaketh,' &c.

אֳנִיּוֹת (the) ships-of, pl. of אֳנִיָּה subst. f.

תַּרְשִׁישׁ Tarshish, Tartessus, the prop. name of a city and country in Spain, situated between the two mouths of the river Bætis (Guadalquiver), a very flourishing colony of the Phœnicians. Some suppose that it was a city of Cilicia, and others of India.

Verse 11. קַצְוֵי (the) ends-of, subst. m. pl. from the unused sing. קָצֶו, found only in the construct state. R. קָצָה to cut off.

Verse 12. יְהוּדָה Judah, (praise, R. יָדָה vi. 6); prop. name of the fourth son of Jacob, used collectively to signify the whole land of Judæa.

At the end of this verse the LXX., Syr., Vulg., Arab., and Æth. add the word יְהוָה.

Verse 13. מִגְדָּלֶיהָ her-towers, pl. of מִגְדָּל subst. m. with suff. 3 f. s.; pl. יִם and וֹת. R. גָּדַל xii. 4.

Verse 14. שִׁיתוּ לִבְּכֶם Set-ye-your-heart, i. e. pay attention to.

לְחֵילָה to-(the) bulwark, perhaps subst. f., i.q. חֵיל, with pr. ל ii. 1, though it is better to consider it as a mistaken reading for לְחֵילָהּ subst. m. with pr. ל ii. 1 and suff. 3 f. s., according to the LXX., Vulg., Syr., Chal., Jerome, and eighteen MSS.

פַּסְּגוּ consider, Pi. 2 m. pl. imp. from פָּסַג, not used in Kal; Pi. perhaps to divide, to fix the limits of, to review all over. The word only occurs here. Luther has erhöhet.

אַחֲרוֹן following, verb. adj. m. from אָחַר ix. 4.

Verse 15. יְנַהֲגֵנוּ will-lead-us, Pi. 3 m. s. fut. with suff. 1 pl. from נָהַג, prop. to pant, specially used of those who are exhausted by running; causat. to urge on in a course, to drive, to lead.

עַל־מוּת perhaps for עַל־מָוֶת unto-death, or beyond death, though some MSS. read עַלְמוּת one word, 'youth;' Chal. 'as in the days of youth;' Luth. Er führet uns wie die Jugend. Bishop Horsley thinks that the words עַל־מוּת undoubtedly belong to the Title of the following Psalm.

PSALM XLIX.

The Psalmist here declares that neither wealth, nor glory, nor wit can save the soul; he comforts the righteous in their oppression and affliction by the glorious hope of resurrection and of everlasting life with God. The Title of this Psalm in the Syriac is, 'The doctrine of the Divine judgment.'

Verse 3. The expressions בְּנֵי אָדָם and בְּנֵי־אִישׁ are frequently used to signify, the former *men of low degree*, the latter *the great ones of the earth*. Comp. the distinction between ἄνθρωπος and ἀνήρ, and between *homo* and *vir*.

Verse 4. וְהָגוּת and-(the) meditation-of, verb. n. f. from הָגָה to meditate, i. 2.

תְּבוּנוֹת understandings, pl. of תְּבוּנָה verb. n. f. from בִּין to understand.

Verse 5. חִידָתִי my-dark-saying, subst. f. with suff. 1 s., lit. something intricate or complicated, a riddle or a parable. R. חוּד to tie knots, to propose an enigma or a parable.

Verse 7. עָשְׁרָם their-riches, verb. n. m. from עָשַׁר xlv. 13 with suff. 3 m. pl.

Verse 8. פָּדֹה redeeming, Kal inf. abs. from פָּדָה, placed before the finite verb to increase the strength of it.

כָּפְרוֹ his-ransom, verb. n. m. with suff. 3 m. s. from כָּפַר xvii. 12.

Verse 9. פִּדְיוֹן (the) redemption-of, verb. n. m. from פָּדָה to redeem. The only other place where the word occurs is in Ex. xxi. 30.

וְחָדַל לְעוֹלָם and-it-ceaseth-for-ever, i.e. there is an end of it, it must be given up.

Verse 11. חֲכָמִים wise-men, pl. of חָכָם verb. adj. m. from חָכַם xix. 8.

כְּסִיל (the) fool, subst. m., only found in the Psalms, Proverbs, and Ecclesiastes. R. כָּסַל xxxviii. 8.

וָבַעַר and-(the) brutish-person, subst. m. with ו cop. i. 2. R. בָּעַר ii. 12.

Verse 12. For קִרְבָּם 'their inward thought,' the Chal., LXX., Vulg., Arab., Æth., and Syr. read קִבְרָם 'their grave (graves) are their house for ever.'

בָּתֵּימוֹ their-houses, i.e. their families.

אֲדָמוֹת (their) lands, pl. of אֲדָמָה subst. f., perhaps so called from being red or tawnyish, only found in the plur. in this passage. R. אָדַם to be red. The LXX., Vulg., and Arab. read אַדְמוֹתָם.

Verse 13. בִּיקָר in-honour, subst. m. with pr. בּ i. 1, see ix. 10. R. יָקַר xxxvii. 20.

For יָלִין the LXX., Vulg., Arab., and Syr. read יָבִין as in ver. 21.

נִדְמוּ they-are-like; according to some 'they are destroyed,' according to others 'they are dumb;' Niph. 3 pl. pret. from דָּמָה xvii. 12.

Verse 14. The LXX. has σκάνδαλον, as if reading כֶּשֶׁל, which rendering is followed by the Syr., Vulg., and Arab.

Verse 15. שַׁתּוּ they-(indef.) lay (them), or place (them) = they are laid, perhaps for שָׁתוּ iii. 7, or possibly Kal 3 pl. pret. from שָׁתַת i.q. שִׁית.

יִרְעֵם shall-feed-them, or shepherd them; the LXX. ποιμανεῖ αὐτούς.

וְצִירָם (to be read וְצִירָם) and-their-strength, subst. m., form, shape, with suff. 3 m. pl. R. צוּר to cut, to form, to fashion, also to press, to beset. The K'ri is וצורם.

מִזְּבֻל from-(the)dwelling, verb. n. m. (with pr. מ ii. 3), from זָבַל to dwell, found only in Gen. xxx. 20.

לוֹ to-it, i.e. to each one taken distributively.

Verse 19. וְיוֹדֻךָ and-(men) will-praise-thee; we have here one of those sudden changes of person so frequent in the Psalms.

For לָךְ the LXX., Syr., Vulg., and Arab. read לוֹ.

Verse 20. תָּבוֹא It-shall-come, i.e. the soul, though some consider it as 2 m. s. fut., and render 'Thou must go each to the generation of his fathers;' the older versions read יָבוֹא instead of תָּבוֹא. The Syr. seems to have read תָּבִיא 'Thou shalt bring (him).'

דּוֹר אֲבוֹתָיו (the) generation-of-his-fathers, or habitation of, the house of their fathers, i.e. the grave.

PSALM L.

In this sublime Psalm, the only one in this Book ascribed to Asaph, the divine Lawgiver, appearing on Zion in glory similar to that of Sinai, summons the whole creation to witness His judgment of His people. With regard to *the first* table of the Decalogue, He charges them with formalism, losing sight of the purpose of their outward rites, and the spirituality of His worship. With respect to *the second*, He severely rebukes the hypocrites who professed to serve Him whilst they violated all

His moral commands; and He then concludes with a warning and a promise.

Verse 1. לְאָסָף of-Asaph, or for Asaph, (collector, R. אָסַף to collect); prop. name of a Levite, one of David's chief musicians (with pr. לְ ii. 1), to whom the twelve Psalms, l, lxxiii–lxxxiii, are ascribed in their Titles.

מִמִּזְרַח־ from-(the)rising-of, verb. n. m. with pr. מ ii. 3, from זָרַח xxxvii. 35.

מְבֹאוֹ (the) going-down-thereof, verb. n. m. from בּוֹא v. 8 with suff. 3 m. s.

Verse 2. מִכְלַל־ (the)perfection-of, subst. m., an ἅπαξ λεγόμενον. R. כָּלַל i. 3.

הוֹפִיעַ hath-shined, Hiph. 3 m. s. pret. from יָפַע, found only in Hiph.; to shine, to give light, used particularly of Jehovah.

Verse 9. מִמִּכְלְאֹתֶיךָ out-of-thy-folds, pl. of מִכְלָה or מִכְלָא verb. n. f. with pr. מ ii. 3 and suff. 2 m. s. from כָּלָא xl. 10.

עַתּוּדִים he-goats, pl. of עַתּוּד subst. m., perhaps meaning ready and prompt for fighting. R. עָתַד, not used in Kal, Arab. to be ready; Pi. to make ready.

Verse 10. חַיְתוֹ־ beast-of, the older form of the stat. constr. for חַיַת, used only in poetry, constr. of חַיָה verb. n. f. from חָיָה vii. 6. The word is sometimes used to signify *a beast, an animal,* and sometimes *a people, a band of men, a troop,* sometimes also *life,* i.q. חַיִּים.

בְּהַרְרֵי־אָלֶף on-the-mountains-of-a-thousand, i.e. where a thousand are, or where they are by thousands; אֶלֶף num. adj. com. gen., dual אַלְפַּיִם, pl. אֲלָפִים (see ii. 8); perhaps prop. a joining together. R. אָלַף viii. 8. The LXX., Vulg., Æth., Arab., and Syr. translate the word as if it meant *oxen*.

Verse 11. עוֹף (the)fowl-of, subst. m., prop. a wing, hence collect. birds, fowls. R. עוּף xi. 4.

For הָרִים the ancient versions seem to have read שָׁמַיִם.

וְזִיז and-(the) wild-beast-of, subst. m., prop. any moving thing, only found in two other passages, viz. Ps. lxxx. 14 and Is. lxvi. 11. R. זיז, unused in Heb., to move oneself. We find in the LXX. ὡραιότης, as if the word were זִיו lustre, or beauty, which rendering is followed by the Chal. and Vulg.; the Syr. has 'beast.'

Verse 13. הַאוֹכַל Shall-I-eat; הַ interrog. is changed into הַ before Sh'va and the gutturals א, ה, ח, and ע, if furnished with any vowels except Kamets; it is changed into הֶ before the gutturals provided with Kamets.

Verse 17. מוּסָר instruction, subst. m., warning, correction, instruction, chastisement. R. יָסַר ii. 10.

Verse 18. גַנָּב a-thief, verb. n. m. from גָּנַב to steal, also to deceive.

וַתִּרֶץ then-Thou-wast-pleased, Kal 2 m. s. fut. with ו convers. from רָצָה v. 13. Luther has, after the LXX. and Chal., derived the form falsely from רוּץ to run.

מְנָאֲפִים adulterers, Pi. pres. part. m. pl. from נָאַף, prop. to go astray, to be faithless, to commit adultery.

Verse 19. תַּצְמִיד frameth, Hiph. 3 f. s. fut. from צָמַד to bind, to fasten; Niph. found only in the phrase נִצְמַד לְבַעַל־פְּעֹר to join or consecrate oneself to Baal-peor; Hiph. joined with מִרְמָה to frame deceit. Possibly it may be Hiph. 2 m. s. fut. '(with) thy tongue thou hast set forth deceit,' as in the Prayer-Book Version.

Verse 20. דֹּפִי slander, or a thrust, or destruction, subst. m., only found here. R. דָּפָה, unused in Heb., to thrust, to push.

Verse 21. הֱיוֹת being, Kal inf. constr. (instead of inf. abs.), from הָיָה, placed before the finite verb to increase the intensity of it. The Prayer-Book Version, with the LXX., reads הַוּוֹת wickedness.

Verse 22. '*He*' instead of '*I* tear (you) in pieces' is found in most of the versions; but Jerome and the Targum have '*I*.'

Verse 23. Luther, following the LXX., Vulg., and Syr., reads שָׂם instead of שָׁם. The Welsh Version follows the present Hebrew text.

PSALM LI.

In this Psalm, which is appointed by the Church to be read on Ash-Wednesday, and which is the fourth of the penitential Psalms (see Psalm vi), David, after making confession of his sins, prays for forgiveness and sanctification, declares that God delighteth not in sacrifice but in sincerity, and concludes by a prayer for the Church. The third verse, which contains only seven Hebrew words, is rendered in English by twenty-two words according to the Bible Version, and by twenty-one in the Prayer-Book Version.

Verse 2. נָתָן Nathan, (a bestower, giver; R. נָתַן to give,) prop. name masc.

הַנָּבִיא the-prophet, subst. m. R. נָבָא, not used in Kal, (prob. i.q. נָבַע) to bubble up, hence to pour forth (words) abundantly; Niph. to speak (as a prophet), to prophesy.

בַּת־שֶׁבַע Bathsheba, in pause for בַּת שֶׁבַע daughter of an oath, שֶׁבַע for שְׁבוּעָה, comp. Gen. xxvi. 33, 34; or daughter of seven (sc. years), the wife of Uriah, defiled by David, who married her after her husband was killed, and by whom she was the mother of Solomon.

Verse 4. הֶרְבֵה (to be read הַרְבֵּה) Increase-Thou, probably Hiph. 2 m. s. imp. from רָבָה xvi. 4; the K'ri הרב is the apoc. form. It *may*, however, be the inf. abs. used adverbially.

כַּבְּסֵנִי wash-me, Pi. 2 m. s. imp. with suff. 1 s. from כָּבַס, prop. to tread, to trample with the feet, hence to wash garments by treading on them when under water; in Kal it only occurs in the part. כּוֹבֵס a washer of garments, a fuller.

Verse 5. For פְּשָׁעַי pl. the LXX., Vulg., Æth., and Arab. read the sing. פִּשְׁעִי, which agrees better with the parallel line.

K

Verse 6. בְּדָבְרֶךָ in-Thy-speaking, apparently Kal inf. constr. from דָּבַר ii. 5 with pr. בְּ i. 1 and suff. 2 m. s., though the verb is usually found in Kal only in the part.

תִּזְכֶּה be-clear, Kal 2 m. s. fut. from זָכָה to shine, to be clear, to be innocent; Pi. to justify.

בְּשָׁפְטֶךָ in-Thy-judging, Kal inf. constr. from שָׁפַט with pr. בְּ i. 1 and suff. 2 m. s. This is active, *not* passive, as in the LXX., Vulg., and Luther, and as it is quoted in Rom. iii. 4.

Verse 7. חוֹלָלְתִּי I-was-brought-forth, Pu. 1 s. pret. from חוּל x. 5.

וּבְחֵטְא and-in-sin, verb. n. m. from חָטָא i. 1 with ו cop. i. 1 and pr. בְּ i. 1.

Verse 8. בַטֻּחוֹת in-(the)inward-parts, subst. f. pl. (with pr. בְּ i. 1), only found here and in Job xxxviii. 36; the reins, so called from being covered with fat. R. טוּחַ to smear, to cover over. Comp. Gr. τέγγω; Lat. *tingo;* Ger. taudjen.

Verse 9. בְאֵזוֹב with-hyssop, subst. m. (with pr. בְּ i. 1), prob. the caper plant, capparis spinosa, used by the Hebrews in sacred purifications.

וּמִשֶּׁלֶג and-more-than-snow, subst. m. with ו cop. i. 1 and pr. מ ii. 3, so called from its whiteness. R. שָׁלַג, unused in Kal, to be white; Hiph. to whiten, to bleach.

אַלְבִּין shall-I-be-white, Hiph. 1 s. fut. from לָבַן to be white, not used in Kal.

Verse 10. Before the verb דִּבִּיתָ the relat. pron. אֲשֶׁר is to be understood.

Verse 20. חוֹמוֹת (the)walls-of, pl. of חוֹמָה subst. f. R. חָמָה, unused in Heb., to guard, to surround with a wall.

יְרוּשָׁלָם (written defectively for יְרוּשָׁלַיִם) Jerusalem, (dwelling of peace,) prop. name of the chief city of Palestine, situated on the borders of the tribes of Judah and Benjamin.

Verse 21. וְכָלִיל and-whole-burnt-offering, verb. adj. m. (used substantively) from כָּלַל i. 3.

PSALM LII.

The Psalmist, after condemning the spitefulness of Doeg, prophesies his destruction, at which, he says, the righteous shall rejoice. He concludes by an expression of confidence in the mercy of God, to Whom he gives thanks for His mercy towards him. Doeg here stands as a general type of the enemies of the Christian Church. See Introduction to Ps. xviii.

Verse 2. דּוֹאֵג Doeg, (fearful, R. דָּאַג xxxviii. 19); prop. name of an Edomite, chief of the herdsmen in the court of Saul.

הָאֲדֹמִי the-Edomite, prop. name (with the art. i. 1) of the descendants of Edom or Esau, the inhabitants of Idumea or Edom, the mountainous tract between the Dead Sea and the Ælanitic gulf of the Red Sea, afterwards called Gebalene. R. אָדַם to be red; see Gen. xxv. 30.

אֲחִימֶלֶךְ Ahimelech, (brother of the king); a priest living at Nob, the father of Abiathar, the intimate friend of David, and therefore slain by Saul. The LXX., Æth., and Arab. read *Abimelech* instead of *Ahimelech*.

Verse 3. הַגִּבּוֹר O-mighty-man, xix. 6, with the art. as the sign of the vocative. The word evidently occurs here in a bad sense; the Prayer-Book Version has 'O tyrant.'

In the LXX. there is nothing about *the goodness of God;* the rendering is Τί ἐγκαυχᾷ ἐν κακίᾳ ὁ δυνατὸς ἀνομίαν, ὅλην τὴν ἡμέραν ἀδικίαν ἐλογίσατο ἡ γλῶσσά σου, reading, perhaps, חָמָם for חֶסֶד.

Verse 4. כְּתַעַר like-a-razor, subst. m. with pr. כ i. 3. R. (according to Gesenius) עָרָה xxxvii. 35, (according to Fürst) תָּעַר, unused in Heb., to cut off.

Verse 6. בָלַע devouring, in pause for בֶּלַע verb. n. m. from בָּלַע to swallow down, to devour. The Syr. seems to have read דִּבְרֵי בְלִיַּעַל *loquentes iniquitatem*. All the other ancient versions take דברי as a subst.

לְשׁוֹן מִרְמָה. (O thou)tongue-of-deceit, or, and the deceitful tongue.

Verse 7. וְשֵׁרֶשְׁךָ and-root-thee, Pi. 3 m. s. pret. with ו convers. and suff. 2 m. s. from שָׁרַשׁ, not used in Kal, to be knotted or twisted; Pi. (privative) to root out, to extirpate. The LXX., Syr., Æth., and Arab. take the word as a subst.

Verse 8. Observe the paronomasia וְיִירְאוּ וְיִירָאוּ.

Verse 9. The word לֵאמֹר should be supplied before הִנֵּה.

Verse 10. כְּזַיִת like-an-olive-tree, subst. m. with pr. כ i. 3; pl. זֵיתִים. R., according to Gesenius, זָיָה, unused in Heb., to shine, to be fair; according to Fürst, זוז to have a sweet pleasant smell, to be juicy.

Verse 11. Luther has und will harren auf Deinen Namen, denn Deine Heiligen haben Freude daran.

PSALM LIII.

This is only a variation of Ps. xiv, which was probably the original poem. It differs from it in two respects: *first*, in the use of the word אֱלֹהִים instead of יְהוָֹה, a peculiarity which is characteristic of all the Psalms in the Second Book; and *secondly*, in the deviation of verse 6 from the language of the parallel passage, verses 5 and 6 of Ps. xiv.

Verse 1. מָחֲלַת Mahalath; the meaning of this word is uncertain; it occurs again in the Title of Ps. lxxxviii, with the addition of לְעַנּוֹת (from עָנָה) to sing; possibly it may mean that the Psalm was to be sung in a sad mournful tone=andante messo. R. חָלָה xxxv. 13.

Verse 6. פִּזַּר hath-scattered, Pi. 3 m. s. pret. from פָּזַר, in Kal found only in part. pass., Jer. l. 17.

חֹנָךְ him-that-encampeth-against-thee, for הֹנֶה Kal pres. part.

m. s. from חָנָה xxvii. 3 with suff. 2 m. s., which is here equivalent to עָלָיו.

Verse 7. The LXX., Syr., and Chal. have יְהוָֹה instead of אֱלֹהִים.

PSALM LIV.

This Psalm, according to the Title, refers to the time of Saul's persecution of David; it contains a prayer to God for deliverance from his enemies, and a promise of thanksgiving for the mercy which he confidently expects in answer to his prayer. See Introduction to Ps. xviii. It is one of the Proper Psalms for Good Friday.

Verse 2. הַזִּיפִים the-Ziphites, the inhabitants of זִיף, (melting-place, R. זוּף to melt or flow down, not used in Heb.,) a city in the tribe of Judah, in the vicinity of which was a desert of like name.

Verse 5. Instead of זָרִים many MSS. have זֵדִים (the proud), which was the reading also of the Chal., is followed by Luther in his version, and occurs in the parallel passage in Ps. lxxxvi. 14.

Verse 6. The בְ of בְּסֹמְכֵי (see xxxv. 2) is not meant to imply that God is one out of many who uphold the Psalmist's threatened life; but rather that He comes within the category of such, and fills it up in Himself alone.

Verse 7. The K'thiv has יָשׁוּב (to be read יָשׁוּב) Kal 3 m. s. fut. from שׁוּב, but the K'ri ישיב is Hiph. instead of Kal.

Verse 8. בִּנְדָבָה with-free-will, verb. n. f. from נָדַב xlvii. 10 with pr. בְ ii. 11.

PSALM LV.

In this Psalm, written probably during Absalom's rebellion, (the treacherous friend being Ahithophel,) David earnestly entreats the Almighty for deliverance from his enemies, expresses a longing desire to escape from the hostility to which he is exposed, prays that the wickedness and treachery of his enemies may be brought to nought, and concludes by comforting himself in God's preservation of his life and confusion of his enemies.

Verse 3. אָרִיד I-roam-about, prob. Hiph. 1 s. fut. from רוּד to wander about, to ramble, specially used of beasts which have broken the yoke; the word occurs only in three other passages, viz. Gen. xxvii. 40, Jer. ii. 31, and Hos. xii. 1; according to some it is the Kal, from a verb רִיד, and not Hiph. from רוּד. The LXX. and Chal. have 'I mourn.'

בְּשִׂיחִי in-my-complaint, verb. n. m. with pr. בְּ i. 1 and suff. 1 s. from שִׂיחַ.

Verse 4. עָקַת (the) oppression-of, constr. of עָקָה subst. f., occurring only in this passage. R. עוּק, found only in Hiph., to press.

יַשְׂטִמוּנִי they-hate-me, Kal 3 m. pl. fut. with suff. 1 s. from שָׂטַם cognate with שָׂטַן to lie in wait for, to hate.

Verse 5. וְאֵימוֹת and-(the) terrors-of, pl. of אֵימָה verb. n. f. from אָיַם, unused in Heb., to be violently moved, to be terrified, to frighten.

Verse 6. פַּלָּצוּת horror, subst. f., only found in three other passages, viz. Job xxi. 6, Is. xxi. 4, and Ezek. vii. 18. R. פָּלַץ, unused in Kal, to be broken in pieces, to be amazed, terrified.

Verse 7. אֵבֶר a-wing, subst. m. R. אָבַר xxii. 13.

כַּיּוֹנָה as-a-dove, subst. f. with pr. בְּ i. 3; pl. יוֹנִים. R. perhaps יָנַף xl. 3.

וְאֶשְׁכְּנָה and-will-be-at-rest, lit. will dwell, i.e. have some fixed and settled place of abode.

Verse 9. מִפְלָט a-deliverance, verb. n. m. from פָּלַט xvii. 13.

סֹעָה storming, Kal pres. part. f. s. from סָעָה to rush or tear along, only found here.

מִסַּעַר from-(the) tempest, subst. m. with pr. מִ ii. 3. R. סָעַר to storm, to rage. The LXX. has προσεδεχόμην τὸν σώζοντά με ἀπὸ ὀλιγοψυχίας καὶ καταιγίδος, which reading is followed by the Vulg.;

the Syr. has 'a tempestuous wind.' וּמִסָּעַר is the reading of two Hebrew MSS., LXX., Vulg., and Arab.

Verse 10. בַּלַּע Destroy, or swallow up.

Verse 12. יָמִישׁ depart, Hiph. 3 m. s. fut. from מוּשׁ to yield, to remove.

מֵרְחֹבָהּ from-her-street, verb. n. f. with pr. מ iii. 7 and suff. 3 f. s. from רָחַב iv. 2.

Verse 13. Before יֶחָרְפֵנִי the relat. pron. אֲשֶׁר should be supplied.

Verse 14. כְּעֶרְכִּי mine-equal, lit. according to my rank, verb. n. m. from עָרַךְ v. 4 with pr. כ i. 3 and suff. 1 s.

אַלּוּפִי my-guide, subst. m., a familiar or intimate friend, with suff. 1 s. R. אָלַף to accustom oneself.

Verse 15. For נַמְתִּיק 1 pers. pl. the LXX. has 2 pers. s.

בְּרֶגֶשׁ in-company, subst. m. (only found here), with pr. ב i. 1. R. רָגַשׁ ii. 1; see ii. 8.

Verse 16. יַשִּׁימָוֶת (to be read יְשִׁימוֹת) Let-death-seize; it is uncertain whether we should consider this word according to the K'thiv as pl. of יְשִׁימָה subst. f., desolation, R. יָשַׁם i.q. שָׁמַם to be waste, desolate; or, according to the K'ri, מוֹת (ישיא) ישי 'Let Death deceive (and rush) on them,' i. e. let Death surprise them, come upon them unawares, which is the reading of the LXX., Syr., Vulg., and Arab.; Hiph. 3 m. s. fut. from נָשָׁא, not used in Kal, perhaps to err, to go astray; Hiph. to lead into error, to deceive, and מָוֶת vi. 6. Ten MSS. read יַשִּׁי מָוֶת 'Let Death exact from them,' perhaps Hiph. 3 m. s. fut. from נָשָׁה to borrow, also to lend; Hiph. to lend, also to exact, to demand payment back. ('This night thy soul shall be required of thee.')

Verse 18. וְאֶהֱמֶה and-cry-aloud, or be disquieted.

Verse 19. מִקְּרָב־ from-(the) battle, subst. m. (as in ver. 22) with pr. מ ii. 3. R. קָרַב xv. 3. Some render the word 'so that they come not,' considering it as Kal inf. constr.

The ב of בְרַבִּים, which is the *Beth essentiae* (see xxxiv. 5), serves, as it does frequently, to denote the qualification of the subject.

עִמָּדִי with-me, xxiii. 4, not *with* me=on my side, but *opposed* to me, *against* me; comp. Eng. to fight with=to fight *against*, to be angry with=to be angry *against*.

Verse 20. וַיְעַנֵם and-afflict-them, or answer them; it is uncertain whether this is Kal 3 m. s. fut. from עָנָה *to hear*, or Hiph. 3 m. s. fut. from עָנָה *to afflict*, with suff. 3 m. pl. The LXX., Vulg., and Luther take the word in the latter sense.

חֲלִיפוֹת changes, pl. of חֲלִיפָה verb. n. f. from חָלַף to pass by, also to come up, hence to revive or flourish as a plant; Pi. and Hiph. to change, to alter.

Verse 22. מַחֲמָאֹת (the)butterinesses-of, subst. f. pl., only found here. R. perhaps חָמָא, not used in Heb., to become thick, to curdle (as milk). The Chal., Syr., Symmachus, and Jerome seem to read מֵחֲמָאוֹת in the comparative sense, '(smoother) *than* butter,' in order to suit the parallelism מִשֶּׁמֶן.

פִּיו his-mouth, v. 10,=his words drop from his lips like cream or butter. For פִּיו read דִּבְרֵי פִּיו; the ellipsis is supplied in the Chal.

פְּתִחוֹת drawn-swords, pl. of פְּתִיחָה subst. f. R. פָּתַח v. 10.

Verse 23. יְהָבְךָ thy-burden, or gift, subst. m., only found in this passage, what is given, allotted, hence fate, lot, with suff. 2 m. s. R. יָהַב to give. Comp. 1 Pet. v. 7. Hupfeld thinks it is the perfect of the verb, with omission of the relat. '(that which) He (i. e. God) hath given thee.'

יְכַלְכְּלֶךָ shall-sustain-thee, Pilpel 3 m. s. fut. with suff. 2 m. s. from כּוּל to measure, only found once in Kal in Is. xl. 12; Pilpel to take in, to contain, also to hold, to sustain.

Verse 24. יְהֹוָה instead of אֱלֹהִים is the reading of the LXX., Vulg., and Arab.

לִבְאֵר into-(the)pit-of, subst. f., a well, a pit, with pr. לְ iv. 3. R. בָּאַר vii. 16.

יֶחֱצוּ shall-halve, Kal 3 m. pl. fut. from חָצָה to separate, to split to divide.

PSALM LVI.

David here prays to God for help against his enemies, expresses his confidence in His word, and promises to praise Him.

Verse 1. יוֹנַת אֵלֶם רְחֹקִים Jonath-elem-rechokim, lit. the dove of silence (in places) far off, the silent dove in far-off lands, probably the name of a tune to which this Psalm was to be sung; יוֹנַת constr. of lv. 7; אֵלֶם subst. m. dumbness; R. אָלַם xxxi. 19; רְחֹקִים pl. of x. 1. For אֵלֶם some would punctuate אֵלִם, as if by incorrect orthography for אֵלִים 'the dove of the distant terebinths,' whilst Fürst would read יוֹנַת אֵל מֶרְחָק־יָם 'dove of God from the far sea,' or 'from the remoteness of the sea.' Some suppose that the Inscription of this Psalm is intended to describe David's situation as a wanderer in a strange country; he being like *the dove* in his innocence, *silent* in his patience and defencelessness, and among *the distant* ones or strangers, i. e. the Philistines.

פְּלִשְׁתִּים (the) Philistines, the inhabitants of פְּלֶשֶׁת, (prop. the land of wanderers, strangers; R. פָּלַשׁ, unused in Heb., to wander, to emigrate,) Philistia, a country in the south-western part of Palestine.

בְּגַת in-Gath, (wine-press,) prop. name of the chief of the five princely cities of the Philistines, with pr. ב i. 1. R. יָגַן, unused in Heb., to press.

Verse 2. שְׁאָפַנִי would-swallow-me-up, or panteth for me, Kal 3 m. s. pret. with suff. 1 s., to draw breath, to breathe vehemently, hence to breathe for the purpose of devouring or swallowing. The LXX. and Vulg. have 'has trodden me down.'

Verse 3. מָרוֹם O-Thou-most-High, so the Chal., Aquila, Jerome, and others; or possibly '*proudly*,' '*loftily*,' LXX. ἀπὸ ὕψους, vii. 8, used adverbially. As the word is not elsewhere found in Scripture as an epithet of the Deity, it is perhaps better to render it adverbially instead of considering it as a noun in the vocative. Luther has ſtolziglich; the Welsh Version is *O Dduw Goruchaf.*

Verse 4. For יוֹם read with the Syr., Symmachus, Houbigant and Bishop Lowth בְּיוֹם.

There is an ellipsis of the pron. אֲשֶׁר before the verb אִירָא.

Verse 5. In this verse the Deity is spoken of in the 3rd person.

בָּשָׂר flesh = man in general, used rather as a term of contempt.

Verse 6. יְעַצֵּבוּ they-wrest, (they twist and pervert them give them a wrong meaning, falsely misrepresent me); Pi. 3 m pl. fut. from עָצַב xvi. 4. The LXX. has ἐβδελύσσοντο, as if the reading were יְתָעֲבוּ instead of יְעַצֵּבוּ.

Verse 7. The K'thiv יִצְפִּינוּ (to be read יַצְפִּינוּ) is Hiph. 3 m pl. fut. from צָפַן, but the K'ri יצפונו is Kal.

Verse 8. פַּלֶּט־ cause-to-escape, i. e. deliver; this may be either Pi. 2 m. s. imp. from פָּלַט xvii. 13, or else it may be a subst., see xxxii. 7. For פַּלֶּט some persons would read פַּלֵּס 'weigh out to them,' 'requite them on account of (their) iniquity, Pi. 2 m. s. imp. from פָּלַס, not used in Kal, to tear asunder, to break through, fig. to weigh.

Verse 9. נֹדִי my-wandering, verb. n. m. from נוּד xi. 1 with suff. 1 s.

בְּנֹאדֶךָ into-Thy-bottle, subst. m. (with pr. ב i. 1 and suff. 2 m. s.), so called from its hollow shape. R. נָאד, unused in Heb. to be hollow. The LXX., Vulg., Syr., Symmachus, and Jerome render it as if it were בְּנֶגְדֶּךָ.

בְּסִפְרָתֶךָ in-Thy-book, verb. n. f. from סָפַר ii. 7 with pr. ב i. and suff. 2 m. s. The word occurs only here; the older interpreters, for the most part, render it not *book* = סֵפֶר, but *numbers reckoning.*

Verse 10. The reading of the LXX. seems to have been לִי אַתָּה and אֶקְרָאֶךָ.

Verse 14. The LXX. and Syr. leave out the negation. מִדֶּחִי from-falling, subst. m., only found here and in Ps. cxvi. 8 (with pr. מ ii. 3). R. דָּחָה xxxvi. 13.

PSALM LVII.

In this Psalm, which is in many respects like the last, and, like it, was probably written by David, the Psalmist prays to God to be liberated from the dangers to which he was exposed; and, his petition being granted, he proceeds to praise and give thanks to the Author of this deliverance for His great mercy and righteousness. (See Introduction to Ps. xviii.) This is one of the Proper Psalms for Easter Day, and it suggests to us to transfer our ideas from David's escape to the Resurrection of Christ from the grave. The latter part of this Psalm, from verse 8 to the end, is repeated at the commencement of Ps. cviii.

Verse 1. אַל־תַּשְׁחֵת Al-taschith, destroy not, אַל iv. 5; תִּשְׁחֵת Hiph. 2 m. s. fut. from שָׁחַת, not used in Kal. The meaning of these words is difficult to understand; אַל־תַּשְׁחֵת may perhaps be the opening words of some poem to the tune of which this Psalm was to be sung; the same expression occurs in the Titles of Psalms lviii, lix, and lxxv.

בַּמְּעָרָה in-the-cave, i.e. the cave of Adullam, verb. n. f. with pr. ב i. 1, from עוּר, unused in Heb., to dig, to bore.

Verse 2. חָסָיָה hath-found-refuge, an unusual form for חָסְתָה, the י being substituted for ת.

הַוּוֹת calamities, or destructions, subst. f. pl. with a verb. sing. masc. to be taken distributively, until every one of the calamities is gone by.

Verse 3. The LXX., Vulg., Æth., and Arab. seem to have read גֹּמֵל for גֹּמֵר.

Verse 4. שֹׁאֲפִי he-who-pants-for-me, or that would swallow me up, Kal pres. part. m. s. from שָׁאַף lvi. 2 with suff. 1 s. The older translators make God the subject of the verb חֵרֵף 'He hath brought reproach upon (put to shame) him that would devour me;' some render the words, 'God shall ... save me, even He whom my persecutor (the man that would swallow me up) hath reproached.' The LXX. has καταπατοῦντάς με, Vulg. concultantis me.

Verse 5. לְבָאִם lions, subst. m. pl. from the unused sing. לָבִי. R. לָבָא to roar.

לֹהֲטִים them-that-are-set-on-fire, or those who are ready to devour, Kal pres. part. m. pl. from לָהַט to lick, to devour; of fire, to burn, to consume; Pi. to set on fire, to burn up.

חַדָּה sharp, verb. adj. f. from חָדַד to be sharp. Before לֹהֲטִים the word בְּתוֹךְ must be repeated, and also before בְּנֵי אָדָם. Again, before שְׁנֵיהֶם and לְשׁוֹנָם there is an ellipsis of the pron. אֲשֶׁר.

Verse 7. כָּפַף he-hath-bowed-down. The LXX. has κατέκαμψαν τὴν ψυχήν μου.

שִׁיחָה a-pit, verb. n. f. from שׁוּחַ vii. 16.

Verse 9. אָעִירָה שָּׁחַר I-will-awake-early, or (at) dawn. It should rather be 'I will wake the morning dawn;' for first, the verb is transitive Hiph.; and secondly, the noun '*dawn*' is never used adverbially to express a part of time. The point in the initial letter of שַּׁחַר is Dagesh euphonic, (see Gesenius' Grammar, Sect. 20,) uniting the syllable, in pronunciation, with the last syllable of the preceding word.

PSALM LVIII.

David here reproves the unrighteous judges, describes the swift judgment which is soon to overtake them, and the joy of the righteous at beholding their overthrow. In the person of Saul, and his evil counsellors, may be represented the enemies of Christ and the Church.

Verse 2. הַאֻמְנָם Indeed, adv., verily, truly, certainly, (with

PSALM LVIII. vv. 5–9.

ה interrog. 1. 13,) from אֵמֶן subst. m. (with the adverbial termination ־ָם), faithfulness, truth. R. אָמֵן xii. 2.

אֵלֶם (in) silence, perhaps subst. m., dumbness, silence. R. אָלַם xxxi. 19. See the Title of Ps. lvi, the only other place in which the word occurs. Some would change the punctuation and read אֵלֶם defective for אֵלִים (as in Ex. xv. 11) 'O ye gods;' others would give to אֵלֶם the meaning of 'band,' 'congregation,' from אָלַם to bind, to tie up. The Prayer-Book Version has 'O ye congregation.' The LXX., Vulg., Æth., and Arab. seem to have read אוּלָם or אֵלֶם.

Verse 5. כִּדְמוּת according-to-(the)likeness-of, verb. n. f. from דָּמָה xvii. 12 with pr. כ ii. 9.

The LXX. and Vulg. omit the second חֲמַת.

נָחָשׁ a-serpent, verb. n. m. from נָחַשׁ, not used in Kal, to hiss, to whisper; Pi. to practise enchantment, to augur, to forebode.

פֶּתֶן an-adder, subst. m., so called from stretching or extending itself. R. פָּתַן, unused in Heb., to bend, to twist, to stretch.

The relat. pron. אֲשֶׁר is to be understood before יַאְטֵם.

Verse 6. חֲבָרִים charms, pl. of חָבֶר verb. n. m. from חָבַר xxxviii. 6.

Verse 7. מַלְתְּעוֹת (the) great-teeth-of, subst. f. pl., only found here, prop. something biting or grinding. R. לָתַע, unused in Heb., to bite.

Verse 8. יִמָּאֲסוּ Let-them-melt-away, for יִמַּסּוּ Niph. 3 m. pl. fut. from מָאַס, found only in Niph.

For the K'thiv חִצּוּ (to be read חִצָּו) the K'ri has the pl. חִצָּיו.

יִתְמֹלָלוּ let-them-be-cut-in-pieces, either Hithpalel 3 m. pl. fut. from מוּל to cut off, or else Hithpo. 3 m. pl. fut. from מָלַל xxxvii. 2.

Verse 9. שַׁבְּלוּל a-snail, subst. m., so called from leaving moisture behind it, like the Gr. λείμαξ from λείβω. The word is an ἅπαξ λεγόμενον. R. שָׁבַל, not used in Heb., to bubble up, to flow, to be slimy, metaph. to go, to walk. The LXX., Syr., Vulg., Arab., and Æth. translate the word *wax*.

תֶּמֶס (in) melting, subst. m., not found elsewhere, a melting away, a flowing off, slime. R. מָסַס xxii. 15.

נֵפֶל an-abortion-of, subst. m., a premature birth, an abortion. R. נָפַל to fall, see v. 11.

אֵשֶׁת a-woman, constr. of אִשָּׁה subst. f.; pl. usually נָשִׁים for אֲנָשִׁים, from the sing. אִנְשָׁה, constr. נְשֵׁי. Here the constr. state is put for the abs. The LXX., Vulg., and Syr. read נָפַל אֵשׁ 'fire hath fallen.'

Verse 10. סִירֹתֵיכֶם your-pots, pl. of סִיר subst. (usually) m. with suff. 2 m. pl., fem. only in 2 Kings iv. 38 and Ezek. xxiv. 6, prop. a thing hollowed out, a kettle, a pot. R. סור to cut out, to deepen. The word סִיר signifies both a pot and a thorn; but in the former case it has a fem. pl. and in the latter a masc.

אָטָד a-thorn, verb. n. m. from אָטַד, not used in Heb., to pierce. The word occurs, besides this place, only in Gen. l. 10, 11, and Jud. ix. 14, 15.

Verse 11. נָקָם (the) vengeance, verb. n. m. from נָקַם to avenge.

Verse 12. The word אָדָם is here used collectively.

PSALM LIX.

The Psalmist here prays for deliverance from his enemies, expresses his confidence in the Almighty, and concludes by a curse upon the wicked, and joyful acknowledgment of God's goodness to himself. Verse 8 is nearly the same as ver. 4 in Ps. ii. See Introduction to Ps. xviii.

Verse 2. The LXX., Syr., and Arab. read אֱלֹהִים instead of אֱלֹהַי.

Verse 4. לֹא stands here for בְּלֹא.

Verse 5. וְיִכּוֹנָנוּ and-set-themselves, Hithp. 3 m. pl. fut. from כּוּן i. 4 with compensation of the ת charact. by Dagesh.

Verse 8. יַבִּיעוּן they-belch-out, or they utter.

מִי שֹׁמֵעַ who-doth-hear?=no one hears, an affirmative interrogation has a negative sense, as in Ps. xix. 13.

Verse 10. For עֻזּוֹ the LXX. has τὸ κράτος μου=עֻזִּי, which is found in some MSS., and is also the reading of the Vulg., Chal., and Arab.

Verse 11. חַסְדּוֹ my-mercy, perhaps for חַסְדִּי, which is found in the K'ri; some would read אֱלֹהֵי חַסְדִּי '(as for) my God, His mercy,' &c. The LXX. has Ὁ Θεός μου, τὸ ἔλεος αὐτοῦ προφθάσει με; Vulg. *Deus meus, misericordia ejus preveniet me;* the Syr. ' O God, Thy goodness;' Luther has Gott erzeiget mir reichlich seine Güte.

Verse 12. The LXX., Syr., and some MSS. have *my shield* for *our shield*.

Verse 13. וּמִכַּחַשׁ and-because-of-lying, verb. n. m. from כָּחַשׁ xviii. 45 with ו cop. i. 1 and pr. מ ii. 3.

Verse 14. After the verb כַּלֵּה there is evidently an ellipsis of the accusative אוֹתָם.

Verse 16. יְנוּעוּן (to be read יָנוּעוּן) shall-wander, Kal 3 m. pl. fut. from נוּעַ xxii. 8. The K'ri יְנִיעוּן is Hiph.

וַיָּלִינוּ then-they-murmur; so the LXX., Vulg., and Luther. Some translate ' they will pass the night.'

Verse 17. וּמָנוֹס and-refuge, verb. n. m. from נוּס to flee, with ו cop. i. 1.

PSALM LX.

The Psalmist here laments over past disasters, appeals to God's word and promise as the sufficient pledge that his prayers will be answered, and expresses a triumphant hope and anticipation of victory.

Verse 1. שׁוּשַׁן עֵדוּת Shushan-eduth, (the lily of testimony); שׁוּשָׁן subst. m., a white lily. R. שׁוּשׁ xlv. 1; עֵדוּת xix. 8; an instrument of music, properly so called from its resemblance to a lily. 'Upon Shushan-eduth' is rendered in the LXX. 'On account of those who will be changed;' the same rendering as is given to Shoshannim in Ps. xlv.

Verse 2. אֲרַם Syria-of, (height, high region; R. אָרַם xlviii. 4); prop. name of the land lying between Phœnicia and the Euphrates, of which the chief city is Damascus.

נַהֲרַיִם (the) two-rivers, i.e. the Euphrates and Tigris; the Greek word μεσοποταμία is nearly of the same import, lit. denoting '*between the rivers,*' from μέσος, middle, midst, and ποταμός, a river.

צוֹבָה Zobah, (prop. plantation, settlement; R. צוּב, unused in Heb., to plant, to found); the Syr. interpreters take Zobah to be Nisibis in Mesopotamia.

יוֹאָב Joab, (whose father is Jehovah,) prop. name m., compounded of יְהוֹ subst. m., God, same as יָהּ, abridged from יְהֹוָה = יְהוָה, but only placed at the commencement of human names, and אָב, see iii. 1.

אֱדוֹם Edom, the mountainous territory called by Greek writers Ἰδουμαῖα, extending from the southern extremity of the Dead Sea to the Ælanitic gulf of the Red Sea, inhabited by the descendants of Edom or Esau; see Gen. xxv. 30.

מֶלַח salt, subst. m. R. perhaps מָלַח, not used in Heb., intrans. to spring, to flow of the sea, then to be like the sea, to be salt.

שְׁנֵם עָשָׂר twelve, שְׁנֵם constr. of שְׁנַיִם num. adj. m. pl.; fem. שְׁתַּיִם, constr. שְׁתֵּי or שְׁתֵּים; R. שָׁנָה xxxi. 11; עָשָׂר num. adj. m. (fem. עֶשְׂרֵה) used only in composition with the units to express the numbers from 11 to 19. R. עָשַׁר, unused in Heb., to put together, to bind.

Verse 3. פְּרַצְתָּנוּ Thou-hast-scattered-us, or broken us.

Verse 4. פְּצַמְתָּהּ Thou-hast-cleaved-it, Pi. 2 m. s. pret. with suff. 3 f. s. from פָּצַם, only found in this passage.

רְפָה heal, for רְפָא, Kal 2 m. s. imp. from רָפָא.

שְׁבָרֶיהָ (the) breaches-thereof, pl. of שֶׁבֶר or שֵׁבֶר verb. n. m. from שָׁבַר to break in pieces, with suff. 3 f. s.

Verse 5. קָשָׁה a-hard-thing, verb. adj. f. from קָשָׁה to be hard. The fem. is here used neutrally.

יַיִן (as) wine, subst. m.

תַּרְעֵלָה astonishment, or trembling, giddiness, verb. n. f. (only found here and in Is. li. 17, 22), from רָעַל to tremble, to shake, found only in Hoph. Comp. Eng. *to reel*. The LXX. has 'the wine of stupefaction,' the Chal. 'of malediction,' the Vulg. 'of compunction.' Perhaps the passage may be rendered, 'Thou hast given us to drink infatuation, or bewilderment, (as men drink) wine.' Luther's Version is Du haſt uns einen Trunk Wein gegeben, daß wir taumelten.

Verse 6. נֵס a-banner, verb. n. m. from נָסַס, not used in Kal, prob. to lift up, to exalt.

לְהִתְנוֹסֵס that-they-may-betake-themselves-to-flight, or that they may muster round it; this may be either Hithpalel inf. constr. (with pr. לְ ii. 1), from נוּס to flee, Hithp. to flee, to betake oneself to flight; or Hithpo. inf. constr. from נָסַס.

קֹשֶׁט (the) truth, subst. m., prop. firmness, hence fidelity, truth. R. קָשַׁט, not used in Heb., perhaps to make firm, to establish. The only other passage where the word occurs is Prov. xxii. 21. The LXX., Vulg., Æth., Arab., and Syr. read קֶשֶׁת for קֹשֶׁט.

Verse 7. The LXX. and Vulg. follow the K'ri וַעֲנֵנִי, whilst Luther adopts the K'thiv וַעֲנֵנוּ (to be read וַעֲנֵנוּ).

Verse 8. שְׁכֶם Shechem, prop. name of a city belonging to the tribe of Ephraim, situated between Mount Ebal and Mount Gerizim.

וְעֵמֶק and-(the) valley-of, verb. n. m. from עָמַק to be deep.

סֻכּוֹת Succoth, (booths,) prop. name of a city in the tribe of Gad.

Verse 9. גִלְעָד Gilead, i. q. גַּלְעֵד the hill of witness, compounded of גַּל sing. of גַּלִּים xlii. 8 and עֵד subst. m.; R. עוּד x. 18; the name of a mountain and province beyond Jordan; see Gen. xxxi. 47.

L

מְנַשֶּׁה Manasseh, (one who forgets; R. נָשָׁה to forget); prop. name of a son of Joseph, adopted by Jacob his grandfather. The word is here used to signify the territory of the tribe of Manasseh, part of which was on each side of Jordan.

וְאֶפְרַיִם Ephraim-also, (perhaps fruitful, double land, twin land; R. פָּרָה i. 3); prop. name of the younger son of Joseph and of the tribe descended from him.

Verse 10. מוֹאָב Moab, (water, i.e. seed, progeny of a father); prop. name of a son of Lot by his own daughter, and of the country occupied by his descendants, extending to the east of the Dead Sea, as far as Arnon.

רַחְצִי my-washing, verb. n. m. from רָחַץ xxvi. 6 with suff. 1 s.

נַעֲלִי my-shoe, verb. n. f. from נָעַל to bolt a door, to put on a shoe, with suff. 1 s.

הִתְרוֹעָעִי raise-a-shout-of-joy, Hithpalel 2 f. s. imp. from רוּעַ xxvii. 6, i.e. 'Hail me with loud acclamations as thy sovereign.' The Syr. reads here as in Ps. cviii, 'Over Philistia will I triumph;' the LXX. has ἀλλόφυλοι ὑπετάγησαν.

Verse 11. By עִיר מָצוֹר is probably meant Petra.

Verse 12. The Chal. has יְהוָה instead of אֱלֹהִים.

Verse 13. מִצָּר from-trouble, or against the enemy.

תְּשׁוּעַת (the)help-of, or the salvation of.

PSALM LXI.

This Psalm consists partly of humble prayer, and partly of thanksgiving to God for His mercies. The King mentioned in the seventh verse is Christ Himself.

Verse 1. The constructive state of נְגִינָה is here put by enallage for the absolute.

Verse 3. בַּעֲטֹף in-fainting, Kal inf. constr. with pr. בְ i. 1, from עָטַף to cover, to clothe, to faint, to languish.

Before יָרוּם there is an ellipsis of אֲשֶׁר. The LXX., Syr., Vulg., Æth., and Arab. have תְּרוֹמְמֵנִי.

Verse 6. יְרֻשַּׁת (the) heritage-of, constr. of יְרֻשָּׁה verb. n. f. from יָרַשׁ iv. 8.

Verse 8. מַן O-prepare, prob. Pi. 2 m. s. imp. apoc. from מָנָה i.q. מָנַן ii. 3. The Chal. renders it 'from the Lord of the world,' and therefore perhaps reads מִן יְהוָה; the LXX., Syr., and Arab. take the word as an interrog. pron., which it is in Arabic but not in Hebrew.

PSALM LXII.

This Psalm commences with a declaration of the writer's trust in God, and ends by placing in forcible contrast with this the folly of reliance on man. It is remarkable that there is no *prayer* in this Psalm.

Verse 3. רַבָּה much, verb. adj. f. from רָבַב iii. 2, used adverbially. The Chal. adds בְּיוֹם עָקָה 'I shall not be moved in the day of great trouble.'

Verse 4. תְּהוֹתְתוּ will-ye-rush, Poel 2 m. pl. fut. from הוּת or הָתַת, found only here, perhaps meaning to rush against a person in a tumultuous manner.

תְּרָצְחוּ will-ye-break-down, prob. irregular form for תְּרַצְּחוּ Pi. 2 m. pl. fut. from רָצַח to break or dash in pieces.

כָּקִיר as-a-wall, subst. m. with pr. בְ i. 3; pl. קִירוֹת. R. קוּר to dig; see xxii. 17.

גָּדֵר a-fence, subst. com. gen. R. גָּדַר to build a wall, to wall up.

הַדְּחוּיָה tottering, Kal pass. part. f. s. from דָּחָה xxxv. 5.

Verse 5. There is here a sudden change of person from the 2nd to the 3rd.

מִשְׂאֵתוֹ from-his-excellency, subst. f., exaltation, excellence, majesty; strictly Kal inf. constr. from נָשָׂא to lift up, with pr. מ ii. 3 and suff. 3 m. s.

לְהַדִּיחַ to-cast-(him)down, viz. אוֹתוֹ *him*, the man placed in dignity.

בְּפִיהֶם is the reading of the ancient versions.

Verse 8. The LXX., Syr., Vulg., Æth., and Arab. have וִימַחְסִי.

Verse 9. The Chal. has 'O people of the house of Israel.'

Verse 10. בְּמֹאזְנַיִם in-(the)balances, subst. f. dual with pr. ב i. 1. R. אָזַן to weigh, found only in Piel in Eccles. xii. 9.

The ל in לַעֲלוֹת has the force of לְמַעַן.

Verse 11. בְּעֹשֶׁק in-oppression, verb. n. m. with pr. ב i. 1, from עָשַׁק to oppress.

וּבְגָזֵל and-in-robbery, verb. n. m. from גָּזַל to tear away violently, to rob, with ו cop. i. 1 and pr. ב i. 1.

יָזוּב, instead of יָנוּב, is apparently the reading of the LXX.

Verse 12. The phrase *once and twice* is a Hebraism for *many times*.

שָׁמַעְנוּ is the reading of some MSS., the Talmud, and the Arabic Version.

Verse 13. כְּמַעֲשֵׂהוּ according-to-his-work. Comp. Rom. ii. 6.

PSALM LXIII.

The Psalmist here expresses the longing of his heart, and then anticipates the destruction of his enemies, and his own triumph in consequence. The whole Psalm is applicable to the circumstances of Christ in the flesh and to those of His people in the world. See Introduction to Ps. xviii.

Verse 1. The Chal., Aquila, and Symmachus have 'the wilderness of Judah,' but the LXX., Arab., Æth., Jerome, and the Vulg. 'the wilderness of Idumæa.'

PSALM LXIII. vv. 2, 4, 6, 7, 9–12.

Verse 2. כָּמַהּ pineth, Kal 3 m. s. pret. The word only occurs in this passage; the LXX. and Vulg. have rendered it as if it were written כַּמָּה; the Chal. has 'desires,' the Syr. 'expecting.'

צִיָּה dryness, subst. f. R. צָיָה, unused in Heb., to glow, to burn, hence to be dry, arid.

וְעָיֵף and-weary, verb. adj. m. from עָיֵף to faint, to be weary.

בְּלִי־ without, i. q. בַּל x. 4.

Verse 4. יְשַׁבְּחוּנְךָ shall-praise-Thee, Pi. 3 m. pl. fut. with suff. 2 m. s. and נ epenth. from שָׁבַח, not used in Kal, prop. to soothe, to stroke; Pi. and Hiph. to still, to quiet, also to praise; Hithpael, followed by ב, to boast in anything.

Verse 6. רְנָנוֹת shoutings-for-joy, pl. of רְנָנָה verb. n. f. from רָנַן v. 12.

Verse 7. יְצוּעַי my-bed, Kal pass. part. m. pl. with suff. 1 s. from יָצַע to spread for a bed, to lay under, used as a substantive.

בְּאַשְׁמֻרוֹת in-(the) night-watches, pl. of אַשְׁמֻרָה verb. n. f. from שָׁמַר to keep, with pr. ב i. 1.

Verse 9. דָּבְקָה hath-followed-hard, lit. has cleaved.

Verse 10. The LXX. and Vulg. translate לְשׁוֹאָה (for destruction) as if it were לְשָׁוְא.

בְּתַחְתִּיּוֹת into-(the) lowest-parts-of, adj. f. pl. from the unused sing. תַּחְתִּי with pr. ב i. 1.

Verse 11. יַגִּירֻהוּ They-shall-make-him-run-out (like water), Hiph. 3 m. pl. fut. from נָגַר, not used in Kal, prob. to flow; Hiph. to pour out, with suff. 3 m. s. to be taken distributively, referring to each one of those who sought David's life.

שֻׁעָלִים jackals, pl. of שׁוּעָל subst. m., a jackal, (perhaps so called from its yellowish red colour,) from the root שָׁעַל to be brown, to be yellowish red; according to Gesenius from the unused root שָׁעַל to burrow, to make a hole.

Verse 12. David here speaks of himself in the 3rd person.

יִסָּכֵר shall-be-stopped, Niph. 3 m. s. fut. from סָכַר to shut up, not used in Kal, i. q. סָגַר. Comp. the Maltese *sakkara*, a belt.

PSALM LXIV.

The first part of this Psalm contains a description of the wicked and their devices, and *the second* the destruction which shall assuredly come upon them, and which shall fill the righteous with joy. This Psalm was probably composed either during the rebellion of Absalom or the persecution by Saul.

Verse 2. בְּשִׂיחִי in-my-prayer, or meditation.

תִּצֹּר preserve, or Thou wilt preserve; the fut. has the force of supplicating.

Verse 3. מֵרִגְשַׁת from-(the) insurrection-of, or the assembling or conspiracy of, fem. constr. of רֶגֶשׁ lv. 15 with pr. מ iii. 7.

Verse 4. Here occurs a paronomasia in שָׁנְנוּ and לְשׁוֹנָם.

מַר bitter, verb. adj. m. (in pause), from מָרַר to be bitter; Pi. to irritate, to provoke. Comp. Lat. *amarus*, bitter; *moereo*, to be sad: and Eng. *to mourn*.

Verse 5. פִּתְאֹם suddenly, adv. for פִּתְעָם, from פֶּתַע with the adverbial termination ם‎. R. פָּתַע (i. q. פָּתַח), not used in Heb., to open.

Observe the paronomasia יֹרֻהוּ and יִירָאוּ. For יִירָאוּ many MSS. give יֵרָאוּ, the fut. Niph. from רָאָה, which is apparently the reading of the Syriac.

Verse 7. יַחְפְּשׂוּ They-will-search-out, Kal 3 m. pl. fut. from חָפַשׂ, in Kal found only in a figurative sense.

תַּמְנוּ they-have-ended; some consider that this stands for תַּמּוּ ix. 7, others for טָמְנוּ they have hidden (i. e. in their heart), and this latter rendering is followed by Luther.

חֵפֶשׂ a-search, verb. n. m. from חָפַשׂ lxiv. 7.

עָמֹק deep, verb. adj. m. from עָמַק to be deep.

Verse 8. מַכּוֹתָם their-wounds, pl. of מַכָּה verb. n. f. from נָכָה iii. 8 with suff. 3 m. pl.

Verse 9. יִתְנוֹדָדוּ shall-flee-away, Hithpoel 3 m. pl. fut. from נָדַד xxxi. 12. The Syr. has 'they shall fear;' the LXX., Chal., Vulg., Æth., and Arab. 'were troubled.'

Verse 10. Luther, in his Version, Und alle Menschen die es sehen werden sagen, apparently reads וַיִּרְאוּ instead of וַיִּירְאוּ, and this is also the reading of our Prayer-Book Version.

PSALM LXV.

In this Psalm, (which was no doubt composed on the occasion of an abundant harvest, and intended to be sung as a hymn of thanksgiving,) is a celebration of the mighty acts of the Lord. It concludes by a special thanksgiving for the refreshing rain which God has sent, and for an abundant harvest. The Psalm may have been written at the end of the three years' famine mentioned in 2 Sam. xxi.

Verse 2. דֻמִיָּה silence (is for), xxii. 3. The LXX. has Σοὶ πρέπει, Vulg. *decet*, Syr. 'is fit.'

After the word נֶדֶר the Vulg., Æth., Arab., and our Prayer-Book Version add the words 'in Jerusalem.'

Verse 4. דְּבַר is here redundant, as in many other places; see Psalms xxxv. 20, xlv. 5, and cv. 27.

At the word פְּשָׁעֵינוּ we find a change of number. The Psalmist passes from the consideration of his own sins to that of the sins of the people in general.

Verse 5. After אַשְׁרֵי we must supply אֲשֶׁר.

נִשְׂבְּעָה let-us-be-satisfied; or it may be the part. Niph., in which case it is sing. The LXX. has πλησθησόμεθα, the Vulg. *replebimur;* Luther has the sing., and the Welsh Version the plur.

Verse 7. The poet had up to this verse been addressing the Deity; he now speaks of Him in the 3rd person, and so continues to ver. 9, where he returns to the 2nd.

For בְּכֹחוֹ the LXX. and Vulg. have the suff. of the 2 pers. m. s.

נָאְזָר (being) girded-about, for נֶאְזָר Niph. pres. part. m. s. from אָזַר.

Verse 9. קְצָוֹת (the) uttermost-parts, pl. of קָצֶה contracted from the unused sing. קִצְוָה or קַצְוָה. R. קָצָה to cut off.

מֵאוֹתֹתֶיךָ at-Thy-signs, pl. of אוֹת subst. com. gen., sign, standard, pledge, token, sometimes used for sacred rites, religious institutions, with pr. מ iii. 5, (which has here the meaning *because of*,) and suff. 2 m. s. R. prob. אָוָה to mark, to describe, to designate, x. 3.

Verse 10. וַתְּשֹׁקְקֶהָ and-waterest-it, Pilpel 2 m. s. fut. with ו convers. and suff. 3 f. s. from שׁוּק, not used in Kal, to run, to run after, to desire; Hiph. to run over, to overflow; Pilpel to cause to overflow, i. e. to water abundantly.

Verse 11. תְּלָמֶיהָ Its-furrows, pl. of תֶּלֶם subst. m. with suff. 3 f. s. R. תָּלַם, not used in Heb., prob. to break or cut into.

רַוֵּה water-Thou, Pi. 2 m. s. imp. from רָוָה xxiii. 5. Some consider that רַוֵּה stands for רָווֹ, the inf. abs. put for the full form רַוֵּה תְרַוֶּה 'Thou wilt surely water.'

נַחֵת break-down, Pi. 2 m. s. imp. from נָחַת xviii. 35.

גְּדוּדֶיהָ its-ridges, pl. of גְּדוּד verb. n. m. with suff. 3 f. s. from גָּדַד to cut into, to cut.

בִּרְבִיבִים with-showers, subst. m. pl. (with pr. ב ii. 11), showers of rain, so called from the multitude of drops. R. רָבַב iii. 2.

תְּמֹגְגֶנָּה Thou-wilt-dissolve-it, Pilel 2 m. s. fut. with suff. 3 f. s. from מוּג xlvi. 7.

צִמְחָהּ its-budding, verb. n. m. with suff. 3 f. s. from צָמַח to sprout or germinate.

Verse 12. עִטַּרְתָּ שְׁנַת טוֹבָתֶךָ Thou-hast-crowned-(the)year-with-Thy-goodness, lit. the year of Thy goodness.

Verse 13. גְּבָעוֹת (the) hills, pl. of גִּבְעָה subst. f. from the root גָּבַע, not used as a verb, having the sense of elevation like a mountain or hill; specially, round like a cup or the head. Comp. Gr. κεφαλή; Lat. *caput*.

Verse 14. The Chal. interprets the word בָרִים in the sense of 'rams.'

בָר corn, subst. m., prop. cleaned from chaff. R. בָּרַר xviii. 21.

PSALM LXVI.

The Psalmist here celebrates God's great deeds in behalf of His people, and calls upon all nations to join in thanksgiving to Him, concluding by promising to bring large offerings in grateful acknowledgment of His goodness. In the LXX. it is styled, 'A Psalm of the Resurrection.' This Psalm occurs in our Forms of Prayer to be used at Sea, as a thanksgiving after a storm.

Verse 3. The word מַעֲשֶׂיךָ must be taken distributively.

Verse 6. לְיַבָּשָׁה into-dry (land), verb. n. f. with pr. לְ ii. 1, from יָבֵשׁ to be dried up.

Verse 7. הַסּוֹרְרִים the-rebellious, Kal pres. part. m. pl. from סָרַר to be refractory, to be stubborn, with ה prefixed.

The K'thiv יָרִימוּ (to be read יָרִימוּ) is Hiph., but the K'ri ירומו is Kal.

Verse 9. לַמּוֹט for-the-moving, verb. n. m. from מוֹט x. 6 with pr. לְ ii. 1.

Verse 10. כִּצְרָף like-(the) refining-of, Kal inf. constr. with pr. כ ii. 9, from צָרַף xii. 7.

Verse 11. מוּעָקָה a-heavy-weight, verb. n. f. from עוּק lv. 4. The word is an ἅπαξ λεγόμενον.

בְמָתְנֵינוּ upon-our-loins, subst. m. dual with pr. ב i. 1 and suff. 1 pl. from the unused root מָתַן to be strong.

Verse 12. לְרֹאשֵׁינוּ is the reading of the LXX., Vulg., Arab., and several MSS.

לִרְוָיָה to-abundance, or moisture; the LXX. has εἰς ἀναψυχήν, reading probably לִרְוָחָה.

Verse 14. פָּצוּ have-uttered, lit. have opened.

Verse 15. מֵחִים fatlings, or marrow, pl. of מֵחַ subst. m. R. מָחַח, unused in Heb., to be soft, tender.

קְטֹרֶת (the) incense-of, verb. n. f. from קָטַר, not used in Kal; Arab. to emit fragrance; Pi. to burn incense in honour of a god.

אֵילִים rams, pl. of אַיִל subst. m. R. אוּל v. 5.

בָּקָר bullocks, a collective noun denoting neat cattle without distinction of age or sex; for the sing. either בֶּן־בָּקָר or else the word שׁוֹר is used.

Verse 17. וְרוֹמָם and-(His) praise (was), subst. m., exaltation, praise. R. רוּם iii. 4.

תַּחַת has here the force of 'by means of.'

PSALM LXVII.

This Psalm (beginning with words borrowed from the High Priest's benediction in Num. vi. 24–26) is, like the last, an anonymous one, and probably much later than the age of David. It contains a song of thanksgiving to God for His great mercies to man, and is a part of our Evening Service, to be read occasionally after the Second Lesson, and is also introduced into the Marriage Service.

Verse 2. The Vulg., followed by our Prayer-Book Version, repeats at the end of the verse the words 'and be merciful unto us.'

Verse 5. מִישֹׁר (in) righteousness, xxvi. 12, used adverbially. The LXX., Vulg., Chal., Æth., and Arab. have בְּמִישֹׁר.

Verse 7. יְבוּלָהּ her-increase, verb. n. m. from יָבַל ix. 9 with suff. 3 f. s.

PSALM LXVIII.

This Psalm, which is prophetic of the final restoration of Israel, was probably composed on the occasion of the removal of the Ark to Mount Zion, as related in 2 Sam. vi and 2 Chron. xv. Conformably with this notion it has been appointed as one of the

Proper Psalms for Whit-Sunday. It contains first of all a prayer at the removing of the Ark, and next an exhortation to praise God for His mercies, for His care of the Church, and for His great works. There are no less than thirteen words in this Psalm which do not occur in any other part of Holy Scripture. We find the second verse in Num. x. 35, with this difference, that the 2nd person is used there, whilst the Psalmist here employs the 3rd.

Verse 3. כְּהִנְדֹּף As-(the)driving-away-of, a peculiar form for הִנָּדֵף Niph. inf. constr. from נָדַף with pr. כ i. 3.

כְּהִמֵּס as-(the)melting-of, for הִמָּסֵם Niph. inf. constr. from מָסַס lviii. 9 with pr. כ i. 3.

Before יֹאבְדוּ the LXX., Vulg., Æth., and Arab. add כִּי.

Verse 5. סֹלּוּ exalt, Kal 2 m. pl. imp. from סָלַל to raise, to cast up, to heap or pile up, to prepare (a way, a street). The LXX. has 'make a highway,' the Chal. 'praise ye.'

בָּעֲרָבוֹת upon-(the) heavens, or upon the plains, pl. of עֲרָבָה subst. f. (with pr. ב xxx. 6); by some supposed to signify *a plain, a desert*, (alluding to God's guiding His people through the plains of the wilderness); whilst others think that the word signifies *the clouds, the highest heavens*, which are free from stars, and therefore may be called a desert. The LXX. has ἐπὶ δυσμῶν, 'the West,' which is followed by the Vulg.; the Syr. has 'the East;' Luther has der da sanft herfahret, deriving it from עָרַב to be sweet, pleasant.

בְּיָהּ by-Jah, an abbreviation of יְהֹוָה i. 2 with *Beth essentiae* (see xxxv. 2), which here, as in Is. xxvi. 4, stands beside the subject: 'His name is (exists) in יָהּ,' i.e. His essential name is יָהּ. This contraction is first used in the Song of Moses, Ex. xv. 2.

Verse 6. וְדַיַּן and-a-Judge-of, verb. n. m. from דִּין or דּוּן to judge, vii. 9.

אַלְמָנוֹת (the) widows, pl. of אַלְמָנָה verb. n. f. from אָלַם xxxi. 19.

Verse 7. אֲסִירִים prisoners, pl. of אָסִיר verb. n. m. from אָסַר to bind.

בְּבוֹשָׁרוֹת into-prosperities, subst. f. pl., prosperity, abundance, with pr. בְּ i. 1. The word is an ἅπαξ λεγόμενον. R. כָּשַׁר to be straight, to grow, to prosper, to succeed.

צְחִיחָה a-dry-land, subst. f., only found here, a dry land, shined upon and parched by the sun. R. צָחַח to be white and shiny, to be dry.

Verse 8. בְּצֵאתְךָ in-Thy-going-out, contracted from צֵאת Kal inf. constr. from יָצָא xvii. 2 with pr. בְּ i. 1 and suff. 2 m. s.

בִּישִׁימוֹן through-(the) wilderness, verb. n. m. with pr. בְּ ii. 1 (see ix. 10), from יָשֵׁם i. q. שָׁמַם to be laid waste, to be desolate, found only in the fut.

Verse 9. סִינַי Sinai, prop. name of a mountain in the peninsula of Arabia, between the two gulfs of the Red Sea, celebrated as the scene of the giving of the Mosaic Law.

Verse 10. גֶּשֶׁם A-shower-of, verb. n. m. from גָּשַׁם, not used in Kal; Hiph. to cause to rain.

וְנִלְאָה and-when-it-was-wearied, Niph. part. f. s. from לָאָה to labour, to be wearied.

Verse 11. חַיָּתְךָ Thy-congregation, l. 10 with suff. 2 m. s. The LXX. has ζῶα σου.

Verse 12. הַמְבַשְּׂרוֹת the-women-who-publish-the-tidings, Pi. pres. part. f. pl. from בָּשַׂר xvi. 9 with ה prefixed as the relat. This refers to the custom of the Israelitish women going out with timbrels and dances to meet the victorious army on its return from battle.

Verse 13. וּנְוַת בַּיִת and-she-who-dwelt-in-(the) house, וּנְוַת constr. of נָוֶה verb. adj. f. from נָוָה to sit down, to rest, with וְ cop. i. 1. Luther, following the LXX., Vulg., and Syr., has 'the ornament of the house,' die Hausehre, i. e. the mistress of the household, so called as keeping house, whilst her husband goes forth to battle.

שָׁלָל (the) spoil, verb. n. m. from שָׁלַל to draw, to draw out, to plunder, to spoil.

Verse 14. בֵּין among, prop. constr. state of the noun בַּיִן interval, space between, used as a prep. R. בִּין v. 2.

PSALM LXVIII. vv. 15–18.

שְׁפַתַּיִם (the) cattle-pens, subst. m. dual, i. q. מִשְׁפְּתַיִם. When ye shall lie down among the folds, i. e. when (the toils of war being over) ye shall enjoy rural and domestic repose, ye shall be as the wings of, &c. R. שָׁפַת to set, to place, possibly sometimes to heap up. The word occurs only here and in Ezek. xl. 43.

נֶחְפָּה covered, Niph. pres. part. f. s. from חָפָה.

בִּירַקְרַק with-brightness-of, subst. m. with pr. בּ i. 1 (see ix. 10). The word occurs elsewhere only in Lev. xiii. 49 and xiv. 37. R. יָרַק xxxvii. 2.

חָרוּץ fine-gold, subst. m., a poetical word for gold. R. חָרַץ, unused in Heb., perhaps to glitter, to shine.

Verse 15. שַׁדַּי the-Almighty, an epithet of Jehovah, subst. m. pl. from the sing. שַׁד. R. שָׁדַד xii. 6.

תַּשְׁלֵג בְּצַלְמוֹן it-will-be-white-like-snow-in-Salmon; so the LXX. and Vulg.; Luther has ſo wird es helle, wo es dunkel ist; בְּצַלְמוֹן (shady, R. צָלַם xxxix. 7), prop. name of a mountain in Samaria not far from Sichem, with pr. בּ i. 1. The Chal. seems to read צַלְמָוֶת.

Verse 16. The LXX. has πίον, as if the reading were דָּשֵׁן for בָּשָׁן, and this is followed by the Vulg.

גַּבְנֻנִּים heights, subst. m. pl. (found only here and in the next verse), from the unused sing. גַּבְנֹן protuberances, knots; הַר גַּבְנֻנִּים a mountain having many summits. R. גָּבַן, unused in Heb., to be bent, to be drawn together (into a mass), spoken of a hill.

Verse 17. תְּרַצְּדוּן look-ye-enviously, Pi. 2 m. pl. fut. with ן parag. from רָצַד, only found in this passage, probably meaning to observe invidiously, to look askance.

Verse 18. רִבֹּתַיִם twenty-thousand, lit. two ten thousands, dual of רִבּוֹת subst. f., ten thousand, a myriad, i. q. רְבָבָה. R. רָבַב iii. 2. This numeral in the dual form is found nowhere else in Holy Scripture.

אַלְפֵי שִׁנְאָן thousands-of-repetition, i. e. many thousands, pl. constr. of אֶלֶף l. 10 and verb. n. m. from שָׁנָה xxxi. 11. The word does not occur elsewhere. The LXX. has εὐθηνούντων, 'of those abounding,' 'flourishing.' The Targum has 'thousands of angels,' and this rendering is followed by the Prayer-Book Version.

Before סִינַי the particle כ of similitude is understood.

Verse 19. שֶׁבִי captivity, verb. n. m. from שָׁבָה to lead or make captive. For Dagesh euphonic, see Gesenius' Grammar, Sect. 20.

מַתָּנוֹת gifts, pl. of מַתָּנָה verb. n. f. from נָתַן to give.

בָּאָדָם for-men, or in men; some translate it among men = upon earth, in opposition to heaven. St. Paul, in Eph. iv. 8, corrects the LXX. interpretation, and renders it ἔδωκε δόματα τοῖς ἀνθρώποις.

Verse 20. יַעֲמָס־ loadeth, Kal 3 m. s. fut. from עָמַס, signifying both to put a burden upon another, and to bear a burden. (,) on account of the following Makkeph.

לָנוּ us-(with benefits). Some render the verse, 'Blessed be the Lord day by day, He will bear (all, i. e. our burden) for us: God is our Salvation:' others, 'Praised be the Lord every day, they lay burdens on us,' &c.

Verse 21. לְמוֹשָׁעוֹת of-salvations, verb. n. f. pl. from יָשַׁע iii. 3 with pr. לְ ii. 1. The word is an ἅπαξ λεγόμενον.

תּוֹצָאוֹת (the) outgoings-of, verb. n. f. pl. from יָצָא xvii. 2, lit. means of escape *for* death, or with reference to, i.e. *against*, or *from* death.

Verse 22. שֵׂעָר hair-of, verb. n. m. from שָׂעַר xl. 13.

בַּאֲשָׁמָיו in-his-trespasses, pl. of אָשָׁם verb. n. m. from אָשַׁם v. 11 with prefix ב i. 1 and suff. 3 m. s.

Verse 23. מִמְּצֻלוֹת from-(the) depths-of, pl. of מְצוּלָה subst. f. (with pr. מ ii. 3), i. q. צוּלָה. R. צוּל, unused in Heb., prob. i. q. צָלַל to be sunk.

Verse 24. תִּמְחַץ Thou-shalt-dash, Kal 2 m. s. fut. from מָחַץ lxviii. 23. תִּמְחַץ is perhaps a mistaken reading for תִּרְחַץ, according to Ps. lviii. 11. The LXX., Syr., Vulg., and Luther have 'that may be tinged or coloured.'

מִנֶּהוּ from-it, poetic form for מִמֶּנּוּ. The Syr. and Arab. omit the word and read מֵאֹיְבָיו.

Verse 25. הֲלִיכוֹתֶיךָ Thy-goings, verb. n. f. pl. from הָלַךְ i. 1 with suff. 2 m. s.

Verse 26. For שָׁרִים *singers*, the LXX. and Vulg. read שָׂרִים *princes*.

תּוֹפֵפוֹת playing-on-timbrels, Kal pres. part. f. pl. from תָּפַף to strike, specially a timbrel. Comp. Sans. *tup*, to smite, to kill; Gr. τύπτω.

Verse 27. At the beginning of this verse some such word as לֵאמֹר is understood.

There is an ellipsis of אֲשֶׁר before מִמְּקוֹר.

Verse 28. בִּנְיָמִן צָעִיר little-Benjamin, so called either because their ancestor was the youngest son of Jacob, or because it was in reality the smallest tribe; צָעִיר verb. adj. m. from צָעַר to be small.

רִגְמָתָם their-company, subst. f., (only found here,) with suff. 3 m. pl., perhaps meaning a pile of stones, or a throng, an assembly. R. רָגַם to heap together. The LXX. has ἡγεμόνες αὐτῶν, 'their leaders;' Luther has mit ihren Haufen.

זְבֻלוּן Zebulun, (dwelling, R. זָבַל to dwell, xlix. 15,) prop. name of the tenth son of Jacob (by Leah).

נַפְתָּלִי Naphthali, the son of Jacob by Bilhah. R. פָּתַל xviii. 27.

Verse 29. The older versions read צִוָּה אֱלֹהִים.

עוּזָּה strengthen, for עֻזָּה Kal 2 m. s. imp. from עָזַז with ה parag.

Verse 30. שַׁי presents, subst. m., found only in the phrase הוֹבִיל שַׁי in Ps. lxxvi. 12 and Is. xviii. 7. R. prob. שָׁיָא, unused in Heb., to bring.

Verse 31. חַיַּת קָנֶה (the) company-of-spear-men, or perhaps the wild beast of the reeds, i. e. the crocodile or the hippopotamus, as a symbol of Egypt, the most powerful heathen kingdom then existing; קָנֶה subst. m. a cane, a reed, a spear (which is long like a reed). Comp. Gr. κάννα; Lat. *canna*; Eng. *cane*. R. קָנָה, prop. to erect, to set upright, also to get, to obtain, to buy. *The* *leaders* or *princes* of the people are compared to *bulls*, and the common soldiers to *calves*.

מִתְרַפֵּס (till every one) submit-himself, Hithp. pres. part. m. s. from רָפַס to tread with the feet; Hithp. to let oneself be trodden on, hence to submit.

בְּרַצֵּי־ with-pieces-of, pl. constr. of רַץ verb. n. m. with pr. בְּ i. 1, from רָצַץ Kal and Pi. to smite or dash in pieces, to bruise; Hithpolel to struggle. The word occurs nowhere else.

The LXX., Vulg., Syr., Arab., and Æth. have בַּדֵּי for בְּ.

Verse 32. יֶאֱתָיוּ shall-come, Kal 3 m. pl. fut. from אָתָה, in Heb. used only in poetry.

חַשְׁמַנִּים Chashmannim, subst. m. pl., found only in this passage, prob. princes, nobles, though others render the word as a Gentile noun Chasmoneans, inhabitants of the Egyptian province Aschmunim. In the LXX. we find the word πρέσβεις; in the Vulg. *legati*; Luther has *princes*. R. perhaps חָשַׁם to be fat, to be rich.

מִצְרַיִם Egypt, prop. name dual.

כּוּשׁ Cush, subst. f., Æthiopia; it is uncertain whether this was the southern part of Arabia or a country in Africa. The verb is in the fem., Cush or Æthiopia being, as is usual with names of countries, regarded as fem.; but, by a confusion not unusual in Hebrew, we have the suff. of the masc. pron. '*his* hands,' instead of '*her* hands.'

Verse 36. מִמִּקְדָּשֶׁיךָ out-of-Thy-holy-places, pl. of מִקְדָּשׁ verb. n. m. from קָדַשׁ ii. 6 with pr. מִ ii. 3 and suff. 2 m. s. The LXX., Vulg., Æth., and Arab. have the suff. of the 3rd pers. m. s.

וְתַעֲצֻמוֹת and-powers, subst. f. pl. R. עָצַם to be strong. The word is an ἅπαξ λεγόμενον.

PSALM LXIX.

The Psalmist here complains of his affliction, prays for deliverance, devotes his enemies to destruction, and concludes by praising and thanking God. This is one of the Proper Psalms for Good

Friday, and next to the twenty-second is the one most frequently quoted in the New Testament; see St. John ii. 17, xv. 25, Acts i. 20, Rom. xi. 9, xv. 3. If the Psalm was written by David, the last two verses must be considered as a later liturgical addition.

Verse 3. מָעֳמָד standing-place, verb. n. m. from עָמַד i. 1.

בְּמַעֲמַקֵּי into-deep-places-of, constr. of מַעֲמַקִּים subst. m. pl. with pr. בְּ i. 1. R. עָמַק to be deep.

וְשִׁבֹּלֶת and-(the)flood, subst. f.; pl. שִׁבֳּלִים. R. שָׁבַל lviii. 9.

Verse 4. נִחַר is-parched, or has been burned, Niph. 3 m. s. pret. from חָרַר to be hot, burnt, dried.

Verse 5. Comp. St. John xv. 25. For מַצְמִיתַי the Syr. has מֵעַצְמוֹתַי 'more numerous than my bones.'

Verse 7. יְהוָה written with the vowel points of אֱלֹהִים.

Verse 9. מוּזָר a-stranger, Hoph. pres. part. m. s. from זוּר xliv. 21.

וְנָכְרִי and-an-alien, verb. adj. m. from נָכַר xviii. 45.

Verse 10. קִנְאַת (the) zeal-of, constr. of קִנְאָה verb. n. f. from קָנָא xxxvii. 1.

Verse 11. The Chal. has rendered the first three words of this verse by, 'and I wept in the fasting of my soul;' the LXX. paraphrases it by, 'and I bowed my soul in fasting.'

Verse 13. שֵׁכָר strong-drink, verb. n. m. from שָׁכַר i. q. רָוָה to drink to the full, to be intoxicated.

Verse 16. תֶּאְטַר let-shut, Kal 3 f. s. fut. from אָטַר, only found in this passage.

Verse 18. מַהֵר speedily, adv. R. מָהַר xvi. 4.

Verse 21. וָאָנוּשָׁה and-I-am-sick, Kal 1 s. fut. with וְ cop. and convers. iii. 6, and ה parag., from נוּשׁ i. q. the more common אָנַשׁ to be sick, used metaphorically of the soul. The word is only found here.

Verse 22. בְּבָרוּתִי as-my-food, verb. n. f. from בָּרָה to eat,

M

i. q. בָּרָא, with pr. בּ i. 1 (the so-called *Beth essentiae*, see xxxv. 2) and suff. 1 s. The word is an ἅπαξ λεγόμενον.

רֹאשׁ gall, subst. m., a poisonous plant, which grows in the fields, bears fruit in clusters, and is bitter. In Hos. x. 4 the same word is translated 'hemlock.'

וְלִצְמָאִי and-for-my-thirst, verb. n. m. from צָמֵא to thirst, with pr. לְ iv. 3 and suff. 1 s.

חֹמֶץ vinegar, verb. n. m. from חָמֵץ to be sour, to be bitter, fig. to act violently, like the kindred חָמַס; Hithp. to be pained or grieved, in Hithp. found only in Ps. lxxiii. 21.

Verse 26. טִירָתָם their-encampment, subst. f. with suff. 3 m. pl. R. טוּר, unused in Heb., to surround.

Verse 27. חֲלָלֶיךָ Thy-wounded, pl. of חָלָל verb. adj. m. from חָלַל v. 1 with suff. 2 m. s.

The LXX. rendering of יְסַפֵּרוּ is 'they added to,' as if the word were יֹסִיפוּ, and this is followed by the Vulg., Syr., Arab., and Æth.

Verse 28. תְּנָה־עָוֹן עַל־עֲוֹנָם Add-iniquity-unto-their-iniquity, i.e. let them advance from one degree of wickedness to another; or it may mean *punishment* of iniquity.

Verse 32. וְתִיטַב And-it-shall-be-good, viz. תּוֹדָה the song of thanksgiving which is contained in the preceding verse.

מִשּׁוֹר more-than-ox, subst. epic. denoting an animal of the ox kind, without regard to age or sex, with pr. מ ii. 3; pl. שְׁוָרִים. R. שׁוּר, unused in Heb., to be strong.

מַקְרִן horned, Hiph. pres. part. m. s. from קָרַן, see xviii. 3.

מַפְרִיס hoofed, Hiph. pres. part. m. s. from פָּרַס to break, to divide, in Kal found only in the phrase פָּרַס לֶחֶם to break one's bread to any one, i.e. to distribute out; Hiph. to have a split hoof, to part the hoof. וּמַפְרִים is the reading of the LXX., Vulg., Syr., Arab., and several MSS.

Verse 33. The LXX., Vulg., and Arab. read יִרְאוּ.

The LXX., Vulg., Æth., and Arab. read דִּרְשׁוּ the imperat., and are followed by our Prayer-Book Version; the Welsh Version follows the Hebrew.

PSALM LXX.

This Psalm is a repetition, with some variations, of the last five verses of Ps. xl, and contains a prayer of David to God for speedy deliverance from some imminent danger. Some persons consider that this Psalm should be joined to Ps. lxxi, as the latter has no Title.

PSALM LXXI.

In this Psalm, which was perhaps composed by David during the rebellion either of Absalom or else of Adonijah, the Psalmist prays for himself and against the enemies of his soul; it is called in the LXX. 'A Psalm of the sons of Jonadab, and those who were first taken captive,' and is used in our Service for the Visitation of the Sick after the Absolution.

Verse 3. Some MSS., LXX., Chal., Vulg., and Arab. read מָעוֹן for מָעוֹז.

The Syr. translates צַוִּיתָ as if it were an imperative.

Verse 6. גוֹזִי bestowing-upon-me, Kal pres. part. m. s. with suff. 1 s. from גָּזָה, prob. to recompense, to bestow benefits.

Verse 7. כְּמוֹפֵת as-a-wonder, subst. m. with pr. כ i. 3. R., according to Gesenius, יָפָה xlv. 3, (as if the word meant a beautiful or splendid deed); according to Fürst, יָפַת, unused in Heb., to select, to mark out.

Verse 8. תִּפְאַרְתֶּךָ Thine-honour, subst. f. with suff. 2 m. s.; abs. form תִּפְאֶרֶת. R. פָּאַר, not used in Kal, prop. to shine, to glitter, to be beautiful; Pi. to adorn, to beautify; Hithpael to be glorified, to boast oneself.

Verse 9. זִקְנָה old-age, verb. n. f. from זָקֵן to be old.

Verse 11. לֵאמֹר Saying, for לֶאֱמֹר Kal inf. constr. from אָמַר ii. 7 with pr. לְ; see iii. 3.

Verse 12. In place of חִישָׁה (to be read חִישָׁה) the K'ri substitutes חוּשָׁה, which is the form exclusively found elsewhere.

Verse 13. For יִכְלוּ the Syr. reads יִכָּלְמוּ.

יַעְטוּ let-be-covered (with), Kal 3 m. pl. fut. from עָטָה, in Hiph. found only in Ps. lxxxix. 46.

Verse 15. סְפֹרוֹת (the) numbers (thereof), subst. f. pl., only found here. R. סָפַר ii. 7.

Verse 18. וְשֵׂיבָה and-grey-hairs, verb. n. f. from שִׂיב to have grey hairs.

We must supply אֲשֶׁר before יָבוֹא.

Verse 20. The verbs הִרְאָה, חִיָּה, and הֶעֱלָה have the suff. 1 *sing.* according to the K'ri; *plur.* according to the K'thiv.

Verse 21. גֻּדְלָּתִי my-greatness, verb. n. f. from גָּדַל xii. 4 with suff. 1 s.

וְתִסֹּב and-Thou-wilt-turn, Kal (Gesenius), Niph. (Fürst) 2 m. s. fut. from סָבַב.

Verse 22. The expression 'Holy One of Israel' occurs in the Psalms only in two other places, viz. Ps. lxxviii. 41 and lxxxix. 19. Isaiah uses it thirty times, Habakkuk once, Jeremiah twice.

PSALM LXXII.

This Psalm, (probably composed by David a little before he commanded Nathan and Zadok to set Solomon on the throne,) contains, *first*, a prayer that the reign of the King may be a reign of righteousness, peace, and prosperity, and that it may endure for ever; *secondly*, that His dominion may know no bounds, save those of the world itself; *thirdly*, follows the reason why such a dominion should be granted Him,—He is worthy to receive riches, and honour, and glory, and might, for He is the righteous Saviour

PSALM LXXII. vv. 1, 4, 6–9.

of the poor and the afflicted; *lastly*, the prayer is repeated both for prosperity and a universal dominion. The Psalm, of course, is prophetic of the Messiah, as there are several passages in it which cannot possibly refer to the reign of Solomon or of any earthly monarch. Verse 12 occurs almost word for word in Job xxix. 12.

Verse 1. לִשְׁלֹמֹה (A Psalm) for-Solomon, or of Solomon, (peaceable,) prop. name (with pr. ל iv. 3) of the son of David (by Bathsheba), who succeeded him as king, compounded of שָׁלוֹם iii. 1 and the termination ה or י. Compare the Saxon name *Friedrich*, Frederick, i. e. peaceable. The Syr. has 'A Psalm of David when he appointed Solomon king;' Arab. 'To Solomon, the son of David;' the LXX. Εἰς Σαλωμών.

Verse 4. וִידַכֵּא and-may-He-break-in-pieces, Pi. 3 m. s. fut. from דָּכָא i.q. דָּכַךְ ix. 10.

Verse 6. כְּמָטָר like-rain, verb. n. m. from מָטָר xi. 6 with pr. כ i. 3.

גֵּז (the) mown-grass, verb. n. m. from גָּזַז to shear (sheep), to mow (corn or grass). We find in the LXX. the word πόκον, 'fleece;' Luther has 'the skin.'

זַרְזִיף a-pouring-rain-of, subst. m., a violent shower, found only in this passage. R. זָרַף, unused in Heb., to flow.

Verse 7. יִפְרַח־ Let-flourish, Kal 3 m. s. fut. from פָּרַח to burst forth (as of a young brood), to blossom, to flourish.

The LXX., Vulg., Syr., Æth., and Arab. read צֶדֶק for צַדִּיק.

Verse 8. וְיֵרְדְּ And-let-Him-have-dominion, Kal 3 m. s. fut. apoc. from רָדָה. Jebb says, 'He shall come down,' reading the word with different vowel points, as he considers it the same as in ver. 6.

וּמִנָּהָר and-from-(the) river, probably referring to the river Euphrates.

Verse 9. צִיִּים They-that-dwell-in-the-wilderness, subst. m., found only in the pl., inhabitants of the desert, used of men as well as of animals; denom. from צִיָּה dryness, aridity; see lxiii. 2. Some, as the LXX., have assumed that the Ethiopians are here meant; the Syr. has 'the islands,' reading אִיִּים for צִיִּים, as in ver. 10.

יְלַחֵכוּ let-lick, Pi. 3 m. pl. fut. (in pause) from לָחַךְ, in Kal found only in Num. xxii. 4. Comp. Sans. *lih=lingere;* Gr. λείχειν; Ger. lecken; Eng. *to lick.*

Verse 10. וְאִיִּים and-of-(the) isles, pl. of אִי subst. m., more frequently found in the pl., habitable dry land in opposition to water; sea-coast, island, often perhaps in a more general sense remote coasts, distant lands, lands beyond sea.

שְׁבָא Sheba, a country in Arabia Felix, celebrated for affording incense, spicery, gold, and precious stones, and for carrying on commerce.

וּסְבָא and-Seba, prop. name (with ו cop. i. 1) of a people derived from Cush and their territory; according to Josephus probably Meroë, a province of Ethiopia surrounded by the branches of the Nile.

אֶשְׁכָּר gifts, subst. m. (with prosth. א), a gift, a present, only found here and in Ezek. xxvii. 15. The noun is sing., but used in a collective sense. R. שָׁכַר i.q. שָׂכַר to hire, to reward.

Verse 13. יָחֹם He-shall-spare, Kal 3 m. s. fut. from חוּם to have compassion, to pity, construed with עַל of the person; also to be grieved or troubled, with עַל of the thing.

Verse 16. פִּסַּת־ an-handful-of, constr. of פִּסָּה subst. f. R. prob. פָּסַס to spread out. This word occurs nowhere else; according to some it means *handful;* according to the Syr. Version and others, *abundance, plenty.* The masc. פַּס is found in Gen. xxxvii. 3, 23, 32, and 2 Sam. xiii. 18, 19.

וְיָצִיצוּ and-let-flourish, or spring forth, Hiph. 3 m. pl. fut. from צוּץ to shine, also to put forth flowers, to blossom.

מֵעִיר of-(the) city, i.q. עָר, see ix. 7, with pr. מ iii. 5. עִיר may stand for the city Jerusalem, or it may be taken collectively for cities in general.

כְּעֵשֶׂב like-grass-of, subst. m. with pr. כ i. 3, pl. constr. עִשְׂבוֹת. R. עָשַׂב, unused in Heb., to shine, to glitter, hence to grow, to be green.

Verse 17. יִנּוֹן (to be read יָנִין) shall-flourish, according to the K'thiv this is Hiph. 3 m. s. fut., and according to the K'ri יִנּוֹן Niph. 3 m. s. fut. from נוּן to sprout, to put forth, to increase, fig. to endure.

After בוֹ the LXX., Vulg., Syr., Æth., and Arab. add the words כָּל־שִׁבְטֵי אָרֶץ.

Verse 18. The word אֱלֹהִים is wanting in the LXX., Vulg., Syr., and Arab.

Verse 20. כָּלּוּ are-ended, for כֻּלּוּ Pu. 3 pl. pret. from כָּלָה ii. 9.

יִשַׁי Jesse, (perhaps wealthy, from the root יָשָׁה vii. 4); prop. name of a shepherd of Bethlehem, the father of king David.

Verses 18 and 19 are a later doxology, appended here to mark the close of the Second Book of the Psalter. See the end of Ps. xli.

BOOK III, Psalms LXXIII–LXXXIX.

PSALM LXXIII.

This begins the Third Book, which contains eleven Psalms (lxxiii–lxxxiii) by Asaph; five by the Korahites (lxxxiv, lxxxv, lxxxvii–lxxxix); and only one (lxxxvi) ascribed to David.

In this Psalm, (which, if composed on any particular occasion, was probably either on that of Sennacherib's invasion, or on the great distress of the country in the days of Ahaz,) the Psalmist, *first*, tells the story of the doubts which had assailed him, the temptation to which he had nearly succumbed; and *secondly*, he confesses the sinfulness of these doubts, and explains how he had been enabled to overcome them. The Title of this Psalm in the Syriac is, 'On the Death of Absalom.'

Verse 2. נָטוּי (to be read נָטוּי) turned-aside, Kal part. pass. m. s.; according to the K'ri נטיו 3 pl. pret. from נָטָה vi. 7.

שֻׁפְּכָה (to be read שֻׁפְּכָה) were-poured-out, Pu. 3 f. s. pret. from שָׁפַךְ. (Note—the verb in the sing. is frequently found with a pl. noun.) According to the K'ri שפכו it would be 3 pl. pret.

Verse 4. חַרְצֻבּוֹת bands, subst. f. pl., tight cords or bands, pains, torments; the word occurs only here and in Is. lviii. 6. R. חָרְצַב, unused in Heb., to bind a cord fast.

וּבָרִיא but-firm, lit. (is) fat, adj. m. with ו cop. i. 1. R. בָּרָא to eat, to grow fat. Comp. Gr. βόρω; Lat. *vorare*.

אוּלָם their-strength, subst. m. with suff. 3 m. pl. R. אוּל v. 5. Luther has Denn sie sind in keiner Gefahr des Todes, sondern stehen fest wie ein Pallast.

Verse 5. אָדָם here means the whole human race.

Verse 6. עֲנָקַתְמוֹ compasseth-them-about-as-a-chain, Kal 3 f. s. pret. from עָנַק, with (poetic) suff. 3 m. pl. The Kal occurs only in this passage.

שִׁית a-garment, verb. n. m. from שִׁית, see ii. 2.

Verse 7. For עֵינֵמוֹ their-eye, the LXX., Syr., and Vulg. read עֲוֺנֵמוֹ their iniquity. We have here a dual noun with a verb in the sing.

מַשְׂכִּיּוֹת (the) imaginations-of, pl. of מַשְׂכִּית subst. f., an image, a picture, an idea, a thought. R. שָׂכָה, unused in Heb., to look at, to contemplate.

Perhaps, 'the thoughts of their heart overflow,' namely, in the wicked and proud speeches mentioned in the next verse.

Verse 8. יָמִיקוּ They-scoff, Hiph. 3 m. pl. fut. from מוּק, found only in this passage, to mock, to revile. Comp. Gr. μωκάω; Fr. *se moquer;* Eng. *to mock.*

The LXX. has εἰς τὸ ὕψος ἐλάλησαν; Vulg. *in excelso locuti sunt;* Luther, und reden und lästern hoch her; Welsh Version, *yndywedyd yn uchel.*

Verse 9. תִּהֲלַךְ walketh, poet. form for תֵּלֵךְ.

Verse 10. The K'thiv is the Hiph. יָשִׁיב and the K'ri the Kal ישוב.

The LXX., Syr., Vulg., Æth., and Arab. read עַמִּי for עַמּוֹ.

הֲלֹם hither, adv. of place.

מָלֵא a-full (cup), verb. adj. m., used as a subst., from מָלָא to be full.

יִמָּצוּ are-wrung-out, Niph. 3 m. pl. fut. from מָצָה to swallow down, to drink with eagerness; Niph. to be wrung out. The LXX., Vulg., Syr., Æth., and Arab. have 'shall be found in them,' reading יִמָּצְאוּ for יִמָּצוּ.

Verse 11. אֵיכָה How, adv. compounded of אֵי, a mark of interrogation put before adverbs and pronouns giving them an interrogative sense, and כָּה i. q. כֹּה thus.

דֵּעָה knowledge, verb. n. f. from יָדַע i. 6.

Verse 12. וְשַׁלְוֵי and-(the)prosperous-of, pl. constr. of שָׁלֵו verb. adj. m. from שָׁלָה or שָׁלָו xxx. 7.

For עוֹלָם we find in the LXX. εἰς τὸν αἰῶνα.

הִשְׂגּוּ have-increased, Hiph. 3 pl. pret. from שָׂנָה i. q. שָׂנָא to become great, to grow; Hiph. to increase.

Verse 14. וְתוֹכַחְתִּי and-my-rebuking, or chastisement.

Verse 16. עָמָל grievousness, or labour.

הִיא it (was); it is unimportant whether we adopt the K'thiv הִיא or the K'ri הוּא, but either must be taken equally in a neuter sense.

Verse 18. לְמַשּׁוּאוֹת into-ruins, subst. f. pl. with pr. לְ ii. 1, treacherous, deceitful places; the word occurs only here and in Ps. lxxiv. 3. R. perhaps שׁוֹא xii. 3, or possibly נָשָׁא lv. 16.

Verse 19. סָפוּ they-have-come-to-an-end, Kal 3 pl. pret. from סוּף i. q. אָסַף, prop. to snatch away, to carry away, to make an end, to leave off; Hiph. to destroy, to make an end of.

בַּלָּהוֹת terrors, subst. f., only found in the sing. in Is. xvii. 14. R. בָּלַהּ, found only in Piel, to terrify.

Verse 20. כַּחֲלוֹם As-a-dream, verb. n. m. (pl. חֲלוֹמוֹת), from חָלַם to dream, with pr. כ xxxiii. 22.

מֵהָקִיץ when-(one)awaketh, Hiph. inf. constr. from קוּץ iii. 6 with pr. מ iii. 5.

בָּעִיר when-(Thou)awakest, or stirrest up Thyself; this may possibly be a contracted form of the Hiph. inf. for בְּהָעִיר, used intransitively, or it may mean 'in the city,' lv. 10. Luther has ' in the city,' the Welsh Version is ' when Thou awakest.'

תִּבְזֶה Thou-shalt-despise, Kal 2 m. s. fut. from בָּזָה i. q. בּוּז.

Verse 21. אֶשְׁתּוֹנָן I-was-pricked, Hithpo. 1 s. fut. from שָׁנַן.

Verse 24. כָּבוֹד (to) glory, or (in) glory; the LXX. Version is μετὰ δόξης. Houbigant, upon the authority of the Syr., reads בִּכְבוֹדְךָ.

Verse 25. After בַשָׁמַיִם the Chal. adds אלא את *nisi tu*.

וְעִמְּךָ and-beside-Thee, lit. with Thee, either in comparison of Thee, or (so long as I am) with Thee.

Verse 26. שְׁאֵרִי My-flesh, subst. m. (with suff. 1 s.) i. q. בָּשָׂר, but used almost exclusively in poetry. R. prob. שָׁאַר to swell, to be thick.

Verse 27. רְחֵקֶיךָ they-that-are-far-from-Thee, pl. of רָחֵק verb. adj. m. from רָחַק to be removed, with suff. 2 m. s.

Verse 28. קִרְבַת (the) drawing-near-to, constr. of קִרְבָה verb. n. f. from קָרַב xv. 3.

מַלְאֲכוֹתֶיךָ Thy-works, pl. of מִלְאָכָה (a Syriacism for מַלְאָכָה) verb. n. f. with suff. 2 m. s. from לָאַךְ xxxiv. 8.

At the end of this verse the LXX., Vulg., Coptic, Æth., and Arab. add, 'in the gates of the daughter of Zion,' whence it has passed into our Prayer-Book Version; but it does not occur in the Heb., Syr., and English Bible Translation.

PSALM LXXIV.

The Psalmist here, complaining of the desolation of the sanctuary, prays that God would remember His people and His covenant. Some persons consider that this Psalm was composed about the time either of the destruction of the first Temple and the Babylonian Captivity, or of that of Antiochus Epiphanes, when the Temple and city of Jerusalem were burnt (see 1 Macc. i. 31 and iv. 38); whilst others think that it refers to the destruction of the Temple by Titus.

Verse 1. The ב of בְּצֹאן has the force of *against*.

מַרְעִיתֶךָ Thy-pasture, verb. n. f. with suff. 2 m. s. from רָעָה to feed.

Verse 2. שֵׁבֶט (the) rod-of, or the tribe of. Luther has und Dir zum Erbtheil erlöset hast. זֶה here stands for אֲשֶׁר.

Verse 3. פְּעָמֶיךָ Thy-steps, or feet; the LXX. rendering is *Thy hands.*

Verse 4. מוֹעֲדֶךָ Thy-congregation, verb. n. m. with suff. 2 m. s. from יָעַד i. 5. The Chal. and a large number of MSS. have the pl. מוֹעֲדֶיךָ as in ver. 8.

Verse 5. The Chal. omits the word יִוָּדַע.

לְמָעְלָה upward, verb. n. f. from עָלָה i. 3 with pr. לְ ii. 1.

בִּסְבָךְ on-(the) thicket-of, verb. n. m. from סָבַךְ to interweave, with pr. בְּ ii. 11.

קַרְדֻּמּוֹת axes, pl. of קַרְדֹּם subst. m. R. perhaps קָדַם (with ר inserted), unused in Heb., to cut, to hew.

Verse 6. וְעַתּ for וְעַתָּה (ii. 10), which is found in the K'ri.

פִּתּוּחֶיהָ (the) carved-work-thereof, pl. of פִּתּוּחַ verb. n. m. from פָּתַח v. 10 with suff. 3 f. s.

בְּכַשִּׁיל with-axe, subst. m. (only found here) with pr. בְּ i. 1. R. כָּשַׁל ix. 4.

וְכֵילַפּוֹת and-hammers, subst. f. pl., only found in this passage. R. כָּלַף, unused as a verb, onomatopoët. imitating the sound of beating or striking. Comp. Gr. κολάπτω; Lat. *colaphus;* Ital. *colpo;* Fr. *coup;* Ger. Klopfen and Klappen.

Verse 7. Several MSS. read מִקְדָּשֶׁיךָ in the plural.

Verse 8. נִינָם Let-us-destroy-them, or break them, Kal 1 pl. fut. with suff. 3 m. pl. from יָנָה to break or to destroy. The LXX. has ἡ συγγένεια αὐτῶν, 'their kindred,' and this rendering is followed by the Vulg., Arab., and Æth. The Chal. has 'their children.'

Verse 9. אֹתוֹתֵינוּ our-signs, i. e. the signs of God's presence. The last two words of this verse עַד־מָה are omitted by the Syr. and Vulg.

Verse 11. For חֻקְּךָ (to be read חוֹקְךָ) we find in the K'ri חֵיקְךָ.

PSALM LXXIV. vv. 13–17, 19. 173

For כֵּלָה one MS. reads סֶלָה; the Syr. does not translate the word, as it hardly ever does סֶלָה; the LXX. has εἰς τέλος.

Verse 13. פוֹרַרְתָּ didst-divide, or break, Poel 2 m. s. pret. from פּוּר i.q. פָּרַר.

תַנִּינִים. (the) dragons, or whales, pl. of תַּנִּין subst. m. R. תָּנַן xliv. 20.

Verse 14. לִוְיָתָן Leviathan, subst. m., never found in the pl., lit. the twisted animal, hence any great sea monster, a great serpent, a crocodile, and so an emblem of Pharaoh, king of Egypt. R. לָוָה, in Arab. signifying to weave, to twist.

For לְצִיִּים the LXX. has λαοῖς τοῖς Αἰθίοψι.

Verse 15. מַעְיָן (the) fountain, subst. m. denom. from עַיִן v. 6 with מ formative.

אֵיתָן might, or continuance, (i. e. continually flowing,) verb. n. m. from obs. יָתַן to be perennial. The Chal. calls these rivers Arnon, Jabbok, and Jordan.

Verse 16. מָאוֹר (the) light, verb. n. m. from אוֹר iv. 7.

Verse 17. גְּבוּלוֹת (the) borders-of, or the bounds of, pl. of גְּבוּלָה verb. n. f. from גָּבַל to bound, to set up a boundary, to limit; also to make dense or thick, to cause to become a thick arched mass, applied to a mountain or hill, as a thing heaped together and bound into a solid mass.

וָחֹרֶף and-winter, rather autumn, subst. m. with ו cop. i. 2. R. חָרַף to gather.

Verse 19. לְחַיַּת unto-(the) multitude-of (the wicked), or, perhaps, to the beast of, sc. the field or the earth, which words are respectively supplied by Aben Ezra and the Chal. The LXX. has τοῖς θηρίοις.

תּוֹרֶךָ Thy-turtle-dove, subst. m. with suff. 2 m. s. The pious and faithful worshippers of God are compared here to a turtle-dove, which is put forward as an emblem of innocence, fidelity, and amiableness. The LXX., Syr., Arab., Æth., and Jerome seem to read 'the soul (which) confesseth (or giveth thanks) to

Thee;' the Chal. apparently reads תּוֹרָתְךָ 'the souls (of them that teach) Thy Law.'

Verse 20. מַחֲשַׁכֵּי־ (the) dark-places-of, pl. constr. of מַחְשָׁךְ verb. n. m. from חָשַׁךְ to be dark.

PSALM LXXV.

The Psalmist here praises God for all His wondrous works, promises to judge uprightly, rebukes the proud for their folly and pride, and concludes by expressing a determination to publish the praise of Jehovah for ever. There is a close resemblance between many of the expressions in this Psalm and parts of the Song of Hannah, 1 Sam. ii.

Verse 2. The LXX. has ἐξομολογησόμεθά σοι ὁ Θεὸς, ἐξομολογησόμεθα καὶ ἐπικαλεσόμεθα τὸ ὄνομά σου, διηγήσομαι πάντα τὰ θαυμάσιά σου, reading וְקָרָאנוּ בְשִׁמְךָ אֲסַפֵּר instead of וְקָרוֹב שְׁמֶךָ סִפְּרוּ. With this version the Syr. coincides, reading only סִפַּרְנוּ instead of אֲסַפֵּר; but it is unsupported by any existing MSS.

Verse 3. כִּי אֶקַּח מוֹעֵד When-I-shall-receive-(the) congregation. The noun מוֹעֵד would here be better rendered *time*, or *set time*, 'when I shall take a set time,' &c.; the LXX. καιρόν, Vulg. *tempus*.

Verse 4. תִּכַּנְתִּי I-bear-up, or measure out, Pi. 1 s. pret. from תָּכַן to make even, to level, to weigh, metaph. to prove, to examine accurately; Pi. to weigh out, to measure, to establish.

עַמּוּדֶיהָ (the) pillars-of-it, pl. of עַמּוּד verb. n. m. from עָמַד i. 1 with suff. 3 f. s.

Verse 6. Before תְּדַבְּרוּ the particle אַל must be repeated. בְּצַוָּאר with-a-neck, subst. m. with pr. בְּ i. 1.

Verse 7. וּמִמַּעֲרָב nor-from-(the)West, verb. n. m. with וְ cop. i. 1 and pr. מִ ii. 3, from עָרַב xxx. 6.

מִמְּדְבָּר is found in some MSS. for מִמִּדְבַּר.

הָרִים promotion, lit. lifting up; this is probably Hiph. inf. constr. from רוּם iii. 4, employed as a noun, as if it were רָמָה. Ewald has translated it as if it were מִן הָהָרִים. The LXX. has οὔτε ἀπὸ ἐρήμων ὀρέων, which is also the rendering of the Vulg., Chal., Syr., and Luther.

Verse 8. זֶה יַשְׁפִּיל וְזֶה יָרִים lit. this He will make low, and this He will lift up.

Verse 9. חָמַר is-red, or is thickened, rendered turbid by stirring up the lees, and mixing intoxicating dregs, Kal 3 m. s. pret.; see xlvi. 4.

מֶסֶךְ mixture, verb. n. m. from מָסַךְ to mix. Comp. Gr. μίσγω; Lat. *misceo*.

שְׁמָרֶיהָ (the) dregs-thereof, subst. m. pl. (with suff. 3 f. s.), the lees or dregs of wine, so called from their *preserving* the strength and colour of the wine, which was left to stand upon them. R. שָׁמַר to keep, to preserve.

Verse 10. The LXX., Æth., and Arab. have אֲגִיל for אַגִּיד.

Verse 11. אֲגַדֵּעַ will-I-cut-off, Pi. 1 s. fut. from גָּדַע to break in pieces.

PSALM LXXVI.

This Psalm is entitled in the LXX. 'A Song respecting the Assyrian,' and its whole tenor agrees well with the supposition that it refers to the miraculous destruction of Sennacherib's army (2 Kings xix. 35). It triumphantly celebrates the deliverance of Jerusalem by a signal Divine interposition, which destroyed the army during the slumbers of the night; and it then urges this intervention as a reason why all men, and especially all princes, should fear God's judgments.

Verse 3. בְּשָׁלֵם In-Salem, prop. name, i. q. יְרוּשָׁלָם li. 20 with pr. בְּ i. 1. In the LXX., which is followed by the Vulg., we find the word translated as if it were שָׁלוֹם *peace*, but the Syr. and Chal. have rendered it *Jerusalem*.

Verse 4. רִשְׁפֵי־ (the) arrows-of, or the lightnings of, pl. constr. of רֶשֶׁף subst. m., a flame, strong heat, the lightning, a burning pestilence. R. רָשַׁף, unused in Heb., to burn, to kindle. The פ of רִשְׁפֵי is without Dagesh. See another instance of this unusual punctuation in יַלְדוּת Ps. cx. 3.

Verse 5. טֶרֶף prey, in pause for טֶרֶף verb. n. m. from טָרַף to tear in pieces. The LXX. has ἀπὸ ὀρέων αἰωνίων, Vulg. *a montibus aeternis*.

Verse 6. אֶשְׁתּוֹלְלוּ Have-been-spoiled, Aramaic form for הִשְׁתּוֹלְלוּ Hithpoel 3 pl. pret. from שָׁלַל lxviii. 13.

נָמוּ they-have-slumbered, Kal 3 pl. pret. from נוּם i. q. יָשֵׁן.

שְׁנָתָם their-sleep, verb. n. f. from יָשֵׁן to sleep, with suff. 3 m. pl.

לֹא־מָצְאוּ ... יְדֵיהֶם have-not-found-their-hands, i. e. they have not been able to use them for resistance. We find in the LXX. ταῖς χερσὶν αὐτῶν, 'they found nothing *with their hands*,'=they were able to do nothing with them.

For חַיִל the LXX. has τοῦ πλούτου.

Verse 7. נִרְדָּם are-cast-into-a-dead-sleep, Niph. pres. part. m. s. from רָדַם, found only in Niph., to sleep heavily.

Verse 10. We have here a change of person: God, who had before been addressed in the 2nd person, is here spoken of in the 3rd.

Verse 11. שְׁאֵרִית (the) remainder-of, verb. n. f. from שָׁאַר to remain, to survive; Niph. to be left.

תַּחְגֹּר shalt-Thou-restrain, or perhaps Thou girdest Thyself with, Kal 2 m. s. fut. from חָגַר to enclose, to gird about. The LXX. and Vulg. have, 'shall celebrate to Thee a feast,' reading תְּחָגֶּךָ for תַּחְגֹּר.

Verse 12. לְמוֹרָא unto-Him-that-ought-to-be-feared, lit. to the fear, verb. n. m. from יָרֵא to fear, with pr. ל ii. 1.

Verse 13. יִבְצֹר He-cutteth-off, Kal 3 m. s. fut. from בָּצַר to cut off, to separate, to fortify (of walls, cities, &c.); Niph. to be restrained, hindered, difficult.

נְגִידִים princes, pl. of נָגִיד subst. m., a prince, a leader, so called from preceding. R. נָגַד v. 6.

PSALM LXXVII.

In this Psalm, probably composed either at the time of Sennacherib's invasion, or of the Babylonish Captivity, the Psalmist first of all expresses his deep sorrow and disquietude, and secondly, tells how he rose above them. In ver. 17 we find an allusion to the miraculous dividing of the waters of the Red Sea and of Jordan.

Verse 1. The K'thiv is יְדִיתוּן, and the K'ri ידותון.

Verse 2. וְהַאֲזִין and-He-gave-ear, or and do Thou give ear, prob. Hiph. 2 m. s. imp. from אָזַן v. 2; though some take it as the pret. with change of vowels for הֶאֱזִין.

Verse 3. נִגְּרָה hath-been-stretched-out, i. e. in prayer, Niph. 3 f. s. pret. from נָגַר lxiii. 11.

מֵאֲנָה hath-refused, Pi. 3 f. s. pret. from מָאֵן, not used in Kal.

Verse 5. שְׁמֻרוֹת (the) watches-of, pl. of שְׁמֻרָה verb. n. f. from שָׁמַר to keep, to watch. Some persons understand שְׁמֻרוֹת as denoting *eyelids*, which may be called *the preservers* of the eyes in shutting them; others consider it to be identical with אַשְׁמֻרוֹת *watches of the night*. The word is an ἅπαξ λεγόμενον.

Verse 7. For וַיְחַפֵּשׂ *the third* person, the LXX., Vulg., and Jerome have *the first* person.

Verse 10. חַנּוֹת to-be-gracious, verb. n. f. pl. from חָנַן iv. 2.

Verse 11. חַלּוֹתִי my-infirmity, or (that which) has made me sick, prob. Pi. inf. constr. with suff. 1 s. from חָלָה xxxv. 13.

N

Some persons translate the word *my wounding*, as if it were derived from חָלַל instead of חָלָה.

שְׁנוֹת (the) years-of; some consider this as a noun, i. e. constr of שָׁנָה xxxi. 11; others as Kal inf. constr. from שָׁנָה. The LXX. Syr., and Chal. render it 'changes.'

יְמִין עֶלְיוֹן (the) right-hand-of-the-Most-High; or, perhaps, that the right hand of the Highest hath changed. Luther renders the verse Ich muß das leiden; die rechte Hand des Höchsten kann Alles ändern.

Verse 12. The K'thiv is the Hiph. אַזְכִּיר (to be read אַזְכִּיר) the K'ri the Kal אֶזְכּוֹר.

פִּלְאֶךָ Thy-wonder, used collectively, verb. n. m. from פָּלָא ix. with suff. 2 m. s. The word is sing. (though the ancient versions and many MSS. have the plur.) here, and also in ver. 14.

Verse 13. For 'Thy work,' sing., the LXX., Syr., Vulg. Chal., and Arab. have the plur.

Verse 14. The Chal. has 'as the God of Israel,' the LXX. Vulg., Syr., and Arab. have the suff. 1 pl.

Verse 16. וְיוֹסֵף and-Joseph, (i. e. adding, or that shall add or addition; R. יָסַף to add); prop. name of the youngest son (except Benjamin) of Jacob, who became prime minister to Pharaoh, king of Egypt.

Verse 18. זֹרְמוּ Overflowed, or were poured forth with, Poel 3 pl. pret. from זָרַם i. q. יָרַד to flow, to inundate. The word occurs only here and in Ps. xc. 5.

חֲצָצֶיךָ Thine-arrows, pl. of חֵץ subst. m. (i. q. חֵי) with suff 2 m. s., a small stone, an arrow, poetically used of lightning.

Verse 19. רַעַמְךָ Thy-thunder, verb. n. m. from רָעַם xviii. 1. with suff. 2 m. s.

בַּגַּלְגַּל in-the-whirlwind, verb. n. m. with pr. בּ i. 1, from גָּלַל to roll.

Verse 20. וּשְׁבִילֶיךָ and-Thy-paths, pl. of שָׁבִיל subst. m., only found besides in Jer. xviii. 15, with ו cop. i. 1 and suff. 2 m. s

R. שָׁבַל lviii. 9. The Masorites, Chal., and Luther read the sing. of the word וּשְׁבִילְךָ, but the LXX., Vulg., and Syr. have the pl. וּשְׁבִילֶיךָ.

וְעִקְּבוֹתֶיךָ and-Thy-footsteps, pl. of עָקֵב xli. 10 with a fem. termination and suff. 2 m. s.

Verse 21. מֹשֶׁה Moses, the great leader, legislator, and prophet of the Israelites, the son of Amram, of the tribe of Levi. R. מָשָׁה to draw out.

וְאַהֲרֹן and-Aaron, prop. name of the first High Priest, the progenitor of the priestly family, and the elder brother of Moses.

PSALM LXXVIII.

In this, the longest of the historical Psalms, the opening of which is similar to that of Ps. xlix, the history of Israel is briefly recapitulated, from the time of the Exodus to the final union of the tribes under David, and the establishment of the kingdom in his family. In ver. 13 is a quotation from the Song of Miriam, Ex. xv. 8. In ver. 15 is an allusion to the miracle at Horeb.

Verse 4. וְעֱזוּזוֹ and-His-strength, verb. n. m. from עָזַז to be strong, with ו cop. xxv. 10 and suff. 3 m. s.

Verse 9. רוֹמֵי throwing-forth, or shooting, Kal pres. part. m. pl. (constr.) from רָמָה v. 7. Ephraim is put as a valiant tribe before all the others, and is here compared to the bow that fails at the moment of need.

Verse 12. The Prayer-Book Version has *our* instead of *their* fathers.

שְׂדֵה־ (the) field-of, constr. of שָׂדֶה verb. n. m. (pl. שָׂדוֹת) from שָׂדָה viii. 8.

צֹעַן Zoan, prop. name of an ancient city of Lower Egypt, in Gr. called Tanis, situated on the east of the Tanitic branch of the

Nile. The LXX. renders this by ἐν πεδίῳ Τάνεως, and the Chal by טאנס.

Verse 14. בְּעָנָן with-the-cloud, subst. m. with pr. בּ i. 1 (see vii. 6). R. עָנַן, not used in Kal, to cover.

Verse 15. We must understand אוֹתָם after וַיַּשְׁקְ.

Verse 16. נוֹזְלִים streams, Kal pres. part. m. pl., used substantively, from נָזַל to flow down. The word denotes *streams* pure *running* water, as opposed to *stagnant* and *putrid* waters.

Verse 17. לַמְרוֹת to-rebel-against, for לְהַמְרוֹת Hiph. inf. constr from מָרָה v. 11 with pr. לְ ii. 1.

Verse 18. אֹכֶל food, verb. n. m. from אָכַל to eat, to consume.

Verse 21. נִשְּׂקָה was-kindled, Niph. 3 f. s. pret. from נָשַׂק, not used in Kal.

Verse 23. וְדַלְתֵי and-(the)doors-of, constr. of דְּלָתַיִם, dual o דֶּלֶת subst. f. R. דָּלָה to hang down, xxx. 2. פֶּתַח denotes th *aperture* or *doorway*, and דֶּלֶת *the leaf* of the door.

Verse 24. מָן manna, subst. m., a sort of resin or gum, swee like honey, that exudes in drops from certain trees.

Verse 25. The Chal. has 'food that came down from th angels' dwelling place;' the LXX., Vulg., and Luther have 'th bread of the angels.'

צֵידָה provision, subst. f. R. צוּד to lie in wait, to hunt.

Verse 26. יַסַּע He-caused-to-blow, or to go, Hiph. 3 m. s fut. from נָסַע, prop. to pull up, especially the stakes of a ten when a camp moves, to strike one's tents=to set out; Hiph. t cause to go, to lead.

תֵּימָן (the)south-wind, subst. m. (fem. only in Is. xliii. 6), prop the light, clear quarter of the world, i. e. the south, metaph. th south wind. The verse may perhaps be rendered, 'He brough in the south wind in its strength.'

Verse 27. וּכְחוֹל and-like-as-(the) sand-of, subst. m. (with cop. i. 1 and pr. בּ i. 3), probably so called either from the idea o rolling and sliding, or as being rolled about by the wind. R. חוּל x. 5.

Verse 28. After וַיַּפֵּל we must understand אוֹתָו.

Verse 31. בְּמִשְׁמַנֵּיהֶם among-their-fat-ones, pl. of מִשְׁמָן verb. n. m. from שָׁמַן to be fat, with pr. בּ i. 1 and suff. 3 m. pl.

וּבַחוּרֵי and-(the) chosen-of, or the young men of, pl. constr. of בָּחוּר verb. n. m. from בָּחַר to choose, to select, or perhaps to mature, to ripen.

Verse 33. בַּבֶּהָלָה in-terror, verb. n. f. from בָּהַל ii. 5 with pr. בּ i. 1.

Verse 36. וַיְפַתּוּהוּ And-they-did-flatter-Him, Pi. 3 m. pl. fut. with ו convers. and suff. 3 m. s. from פָּתָה to part asunder, to open; Pi. to make wide (the heart or mind), to make accessible, hence to persuade, to entice, to deceive; see v. 10.

Verse 38. רַחוּם merciful, verb. adj. m. (used only of God), from רָחַם xviii. 2.

Verse 40. יַמְרוּהוּ did-they-provoke-Him, or rebel against Him, Hiph. 3 m. pl. fut. with suff. 3 m. s. from מָרָה v. 11.

Verse 41. הִתְווּ they-limited, or perhaps afflicted, or grieved, Hiph. 3 pl. pret. from תָּוָה, not used in Kal, to mark, to determine, also to be astonished, metaph. to be vexed; Hiph. to afflict, to grieve.

Verse 42. The Chal. has 'the miracles of His hand.'

Verse 44. יְאֹרֵיהֶם their-rivers, (the first plague,) pl. of יְאֹר subst. m. (with suff. 3 m. pl.), an Egyptian word used almost exclusively of the Nile.

Verse 45. עָרֹב flies, (the fourth plague,) subst. m., prob. a kind of stinging fly or beetle, so called from sucking (blood). R. עָרַב to suck.

וּצְפַרְדֵּעַ and-frogs, (the second plague,) subst. m. (collect. fem.) with ו cop. i. 1.

Verse 46. לֶחָסִיל unto-(the) caterpillar, (the eighth plague,) subst. m. with pr. לְ ii. 1 (see vii. 6), prob. the name of a kind of locust which devours the fruits of the field. R. prob. חָסַל to eat off, to tear off.

וִיגִיעָם and-their-labour, verb. n. m. with ו cop. ix. 10 and suff. 3 m. pl. from יָגַע to labour.

לָאַרְבֶּה unto-the-locust, subst. m. with pr. לְ (and the art.) ii. 1, a locust, especially that kind which appears in swarms. R., according to some, רָבָה xvi. 4; according to others אָרַב, unused in Heb., to browse.

Verse 47. גַּפְנָם their-vine, subst. com. gen. (masc. only in 2 Kings iv. 39 and Hos. x. 1) with suff. 3 m. pl. R. גָּפַן, unused in Heb., to be bent, to be crooked. The noun is sing. but to be understood collectively.

וְשִׁקְמוֹתָם and-their-sycomore-trees, subst. f. pl. from the unused sing. שִׁקְמָה, with suff. 3 m. pl.; a tree frequently found in the lower districts of Palestine, resembling the mulberry-tree in its leaves and appearance, with fruit like that of the fig. In the five other passages where the word occurs it is written שִׁקְמִים. R. perhaps שָׁקַם, unused in Heb., prob. to be firm, to be durable.

בַּחֲנָמַל with-frost, or great hailstones, (the seventh plague,) subst. m. with pr. בְּ i. 1. The word is an ἅπαξ λεγόμενον. R. חָנַם, not used in Heb., to be hard, firm.

Verse 48. בְּעִירָם their-cattle, subst. m. collect. with suff. 3 m. pl. R. בָּעַר to eat up, to consume.

וּמִקְנֵיהֶם and-their-flocks, pl. of מִקְנֶה subst. m. with ו cop. i. 1 and suff. 3 m. pl., something bought, a possession. R. קָנָה lxviii. 31.

Verse 49. מִשְׁלַחַת a-sending-of, verb. n. f. from שָׁלַח, with pr. מ ii. 3.

Verse 50. נָתִיב a-path, subst. m. R. נָתַב, unused in Heb., to tread down.

וְחַיָּתָם לַדֶּבֶר but-their-life-to-(the) pestilence, or their beasts to the murrain, (the fifth plague); דֶּבֶר subst. m. with pr. לְ ii. 1, prop. a snatching away, hence destruction, pestilence. R. דָּבַר ii. 5.

Verse 51. בְּכוֹר (the) first-born, (the tenth plague,) verb. n. m. from בָּכַר, in Heb. not used in Kal, but in Arab. signifying to come first, to precede.

רֵאשִׁית (the) first-fruits-of, or the beginning of, subst. f. denom. from רֹאשׁ head, with fem. termination ית.. R. רֹאשׁ iii. 4.

אוֹנִים (their) strength, lit. strengths, pl. of אוֹן subst. m. R. אָוֶן iii. 3.

חָם Ham, prop. name of the youngest son of Noah, whose descendants occupied the southern regions of the earth. R. חָמַם to be hot. The word is used poetically as a designation of the land of Egypt.

Verse 52. כָּעֵדֶר like-the-flock, verb. n. m. with pr. כ xviii. 34, from עָדַר to set in order, to arrange.

Verse 54. גְּבוּל (the) border-of, verb. n. m. from גָּבַל lxxiv. 17. Before קָנְתָה the word אֲשֶׁר must be understood.

Verse 55. וַיַּפִּילֵם and-allotted-them, lit. made them to fall, (in allusion to the throwing of the lot.)

Verse 58. וּבִפְסִילֵיהֶם and-with-their-graven-images, subst. m. pl. from the unused sing. פָּסִיל, with ו cop. i. 1, pr. ב ii. 11, and suff. 3 m. pl. R. פָּסַל to hew, to carve. This verse refers to Deut. xxxii. 16, 17.

Verse 60. שִׁלוֹ Shiloh, prop. name of a town of the Ephraimites, (variously written שִׁילוֹ, שִׁלוֹ, and שִׁלֹה,) situated on a mountain to the north of Bethel, where the holy Tabernacle was set for some time. For 'the tent which He placed (lit. caused to dwell) among men,' the LXX., Vulg., and Luther have 'where He dwelt among men.'

Verse 61. Luther, after the example of the LXX. and Vulg., has *their* strength and *their* glory.

Verse 63. הוּלָּלוּ were-given-in-marriage, lit. praised or celebrated (in nuptial songs), for הֻלָּלוּ; Pu. 3 pl. pret. from הָלַל v. 6 (in pause). Luther has 'and their maidens must remain unmarried.'

Verse 64. כֹּהֲנָיו Their-priests, or His priests, probably referring to Hophni and Phineas, pl. of כֹּהֵן verb. n. m. (with suff. 3 m. s.), from כָּהַן, not used in Heb., to perform, to execute (e. g. the offices of worship).

Verse 65. וַיִּקַץ Then-awaked, Kal 3 m. s. fut. with ו convers. from יָקַץ, used only in the fut.

כְּיָשֵׁן as-(one) sleeping, verb. adj. m. with pr. כ i. 3, from יָשֵׁן.

מִתְרוֹנֵן that-shouteth, prob. Hithp. pres. part. m. s. from רָנַן v. 12, not from רוּן to conquer, to overcome, (as a mighty man overcome by wine); Vulg. *crapulatus a vino.* Gesenius and Fürst derive the word from רוּן.

Verse 69. The Chal. and LXX. read רָמִים for רָמִים.

Verse 71. עָלוֹת (the ewes) giving-suck, Kal pres. part. f. pl. from עוּל or עִיל, only used in the part. f. pl., to be wet, to suck; trans. to suckle.

Verse 72. The LXX., Vulg., Chal., Syr., and Arab. read בְּתֹם for כַּתֹם.

PSALM LXXIX.

This Psalm, probably composed on the destruction of Jerusalem by Nebuchadnezzar, consists first of a complaint, and then of a prayer that God would visit His people again in mercy, and pour out His vengeance upon their enemies; and concludes by promising the gratitude with which God's mercy will be acknowledged. Verses 2 and 3 are quoted in 1 Macc. vii. 16, 17; verse 4 is a repetition of Ps. xliv. 14; verses 6 and 7 are almost entirely the same as Jer. x. 25; and the first half of the tenth verse is word for word from Joel ii. 17.

Verse 1. טָמְאוּ they-have-defiled, Pi. 3 pl. pret. from טָמֵא to be unclean; Pi. to pollute, to defile.

לְעִיִּים in-heaps, pl. of עִי subst. m. with pr. ל ii. 1. R. עָוָה xviii. 24.

Verse 2. נִבְלַת (The) dead-bodies-of, constr. of נְבֵלָה subst. f., prop. the sunk, the fallen, hence a corpse. R. נָבֵל i. 3. The sing. is here put collectively for the plur.

Verse 6. For אֶל fourteen MSS. have עַל.

מַמְלָכוֹת (the) kingdoms (as the kingdoms of Nineveh and Babylon).

Verse 7. אָכַל they-have-devoured, or he has devoured, one has devoured, indefinitely (Fr. '*on*'); אָכַל is the received reading, but the LXX., both our versions, and sixteen MSS. read אָכְלוּ; in Jer. x. 25 the verb is in the plur.

נָוֵהוּ his-dwelling-place, or pasture, verb. n. m. with suff. 3 m. s. from נָוָה to sit down, to rest, to dwell.

Verse 8. עֲוֹנֹת רִאשֹׁנִים (the) iniquities-of-former-times, or perhaps the iniquities of them that were before us, pl. of רִאשׁוֹן, ord. adj. m. denom. from רֹאשׁ iii. 4.

Verse 10. יִוָּדַע בַּגּוֹיִם let-Him-be-known-among-the-heathen, or rather, let there be made known ... the revenging of, &c., as the subject to the verb יִוָּדַע is not אֱלֹהִים but נִקְמַת, though the verb and the noun do not agree in gender, which is frequently found to be the case. The K'ri is בגוים.

Verse 11. כְּגֹדֶל according-to-(the)greatness-of, verb. n. m. from גָּדַל xii. 4 with pr. כ i. 3.

בְּנֵי תְמוּתָה (the) sons-of-death, i. e. those who are doomed,— whom Death already claims as his own; תְמוּתָה subst. f., used only in the phrase בֶּן־תְמוּתָה. R. מוּת vi. 6.

PSALM LXXX.

In this Psalm, (probably composed in the days of Hezekiah, and entitled in the LXX. ὑπὲρ τοῦ Ἀσσυρίου,) the writer, under the figure of a vine, pourtrays the going out of Israel from Egypt by Divine direction, and concludes with a prayer to God for help. Portions of verse 13 are repeated in Ps. lxxxix. 4.

Verse 1. For אֶל fourteen MSS. have עַל.

Verse 2. Joseph is here put for all Israel.

הוֹפִיעָה shine-forth, (as in the days of old, 'when the Lord ... shined forth from Paran,' Deut. xxxiii. 12); Hiph. 2 m. s. imp. from יָפַע l. 2 with ה parag.

Verse 4. The Syr., Æth., and some MSS. insert the word צְבָאוֹת after אֱלֹהִים, as in the following verse.

הֲשִׁיבֵנוּ turn-us-again, or bring us back; Luther has 'comfort us.'

Verse 5. אֱלֹהִים being in the abs. state, shows that there is an ellipsis of אֱלֹהֵי before צְבָאוֹת, which is also the case in ver. 15 of this Psalm, as well as in Ps. lix. 6.

Verse 6. שָׁלִישׁ (in) great-measure, subst. m. (denom. from שָׁלֹשׁ three), the name of a measure, used in the accusative as a determinative, by measure, i. e. abundantly. The only other place where the word occurs is Is. xl. 12.

Verse 7. מָדוֹן a-strife, verb. n. m. from דִּין vii. 9.

The LXX., Syr., Æth., Arab., Vulg., and Jerome read לָנוּ for לָמוֹ.

Verse 10. וַתַּשְׁרֵשׁ and-when-she-had-rooted, Hiph. 3 f. s. fut. with ו convers. from שָׁרַשׁ lii. 7.

שָׁרָשֶׁיהָ her-roots, pl. of שֹׁרֶשׁ verb. n. m. from שָׁרַשׁ lii. 7 with suff. 3 f. s.

וַתְּמַלֵּא־ then-it-filled, Pi. 3 f. s. fut. with ו convers. from מָלָא. Or it may be, 'and Thou hast rooted her roots, and hast filled with her the land,' as the verbs may be either 3 *pers. f. s.* or 2 *pers. m. s.* fut. The LXX., Vulg., Luther, and the Welsh Version have 'Thou hast made her strike her roots, and she filled,' &c.

Verse 11. For כָּסּוּ the LXX., Vulg., Bishop Hare, and others read כָּסָה.

וַעֲנָפֶיהָ and-(the) boughs-thereof, pl. of עָנָף subst. m. with suff. 3 f. s. R. עָנַף, unused in Heb., perhaps meaning either to cover or else to sprout, to grow.

Verse 12. קְצִירֶיהָ her-boughs, pl. of קָצִיר subst. m. (with suff. 3 f. s.), prop. mowing, reaping, hence harvest, also a branch, a bough. R. קָצַר to cut off, specially grain, hence to reap, also to shorten.

יוֹנְקוֹתֶיהָ her-young-shoots, pl. of יוֹנֶקֶת subst. f. (with suff. 3 f. s.), prop. sucking, fig. a sucker of a tree, as if it sucked nourishment from a mother. R. יָנַק to suck. (She extended her conquests to the Mediterranean Sea and the river Euphrates.)

Verse 14. יְכַרְסְמֶנָּה doth-waste-her, Pi. 3 m. s. fut. with suff. 3 f. s. from כָּסַם to cut off, with ר inserted. The quadriliteral occurs only in this place.

חֲזִיר (the) boar, (i. e. the Assyrian king,) subst. m. from the unused root חָזַר, prob. to be strong.

מִיַּעַר is written with suspended ע, according to Kiddushin, because this ע is the middle letter of the Psalter, as ו of נחון, Lev. xi. 42, is the middle letter of the Torah.

Verse 16. וְכַנָּה And-(the)plant; it is very uncertain whether this word, which occurs nowhere else, is to be considered as a verb or as a noun. According to the Targum, Chal., Syr., Kimchi, and the Authorized Version it is a subst. fem., a shoot, a plant, prob. from the root כָּנַן, unused in Heb., to stand fast, to set, to plant. The LXX., Vulg., and others consider it as a verb, either as if it were=וּכֹנְנָה from כּוּן, or else Kal 2 m. s. imp. with ה parag. from כָּנַן to cover, to protect. Luther has Und halte ihn im Bau. There is apparently no satisfactory reason why the Masorites thought fit to write the כ larger than the other letters.

The LXX., Vulg., Arab., Syr., and Æth. have 'the son of man.' The pron. אֲשֶׁר should be understood before אִמַּצְתָּה.

Verse 18. אִישׁ יְמִינֶךָ (the) man-of-Thy-right-hand, (Hezekiah, whom Thou hast advanced to the throne.)

Verse 20. וְהָאֵר is the reading of the LXX. and Vulg.

PSALM LXXXI.

This Psalm, (apparently intended to be sung at one or more of the great national festivals,) contains an exhortation to a solemn praising of God, and then to obedience.

Verse 3. זִמְרָה a-song, verb. n. f. from זָמַר iii. 1.

תֹף (the) timbrel, subst. m.   R. תָּפַף lxviii. 26.

Verse 4. בַחֹדֶשׁ in-the-new-moon, subst. m., new moon, or month, with pr. בּ i. 1.   R. חָדַשׁ xxxiii. 3.

בַּכֶּסֶה at-the-full-moon, or in the time appointed, subst. m. (with pr. בּ i. 1), i. q. כֶּסֶא (the way in which the word is written in Prov. vii. 20, the only other passage where it occurs), a festival, a feast day, principally used of the feast held at the new moon of Tisri. The Syr., Chal., and some MSS. have the plur.   R. prob. כָּסָא, unused in Heb., to appoint, to determine.

חַגֵּנוּ our-solemn-Feast, i. e. the Feast of Tabernacles, which was also called pre-eminently '*the Feast;*' subst. m. with suff. 1 pl. R. חָגַג xii. 5.   Luther has in unferm Feſt der Laubrüſte.

Verse 6. בִּיהוֹסֵף in-Joseph, poet. form for יוֹסֵף lxxvii. 16 with pr. בּ i. 1 (see ix. 10).

בְּצֵאתוֹ in-His-going-out, referring to God, not to Joseph or Israel.

עַל־ before, or over, or against.

יָדַעְתִּי I-understood, i. e. Israel.

אֶשְׁמָע I-heard; the LXX. and Vulg. have the 3rd pers. 'he heard,' and Luther the 3rd pers. pl.

Verse 7. מִסֵּבֶל from-(the) burden, verb. n. m. with pr. מ ii. 3, from סָבַל to lift (a burden), to carry; fig. to endure.

מִדּוּד from-(the) basket, (i. e. the bricklayers' basket,) subst. m. (with pr. מ ii. 3), a basket, a kettle, prop. a thing woven.   R. perhaps דּוּד, not used in Heb., to weave, to bind together.

תַּעֲבֹרְנָה ceased, lit. passed away. The LXX. Version apparently reads תַּעֲבֹרְנָה for תַּעֲבֹרְנָה.

Verse 8. מְרִיבָה Meribah, (strife, R. רִיב to contend); prop. name of a rock-fountain in the desert not far from Sinai.

Verse 9. בָּךְ unto-thee, or against thee.

The particle אִם has here the force of 'Oh that!'

Verse 13. בִּשְׁרִירוּת unto-(the) stubbornness-of, or hardness, subst. f. with pr. בּ ii. 11. R. שָׁרַר v. 9. The word occurs only once in the Pentateuch (Deut. xxix. 18), but several times in Jeremiah.

Verse 14. לוּ Oh-that, a primitive particle applied as an interjection of wishing.

Verse 15. אַכְנִיעַ I-would-put-down, Hiph. 1 s. fut. from כָּנַע, unused in Kal, to bend down; Niph. to humble oneself; Hiph. to subdue.

Verse 17. וַיַּאֲכִילֵהוּ And-He-made-them-eat, (the 3rd person instead of the 1st, which recurs again in the next clause.)

חִטָּה wheat, subst. f.; pl. חִטִּים. R. prob. חָנַט, by some supposed to mean to be of a yellowish red colour; and by others, to spice or season.

אַשְׂבִּיעֶךָ should-I-satisfy-thee-with; the LXX., Vulg., Æth., Arab., and one of Kennicott's MSS. read *He* and *them*, which certainly agrees better with the first part of the verse.

PSALM LXXXII.

In this Psalm, (which in its general strain somewhat resembles Ps. lviii, and which was probably composed in the days of Hezekiah,) the Psalmist solemnly rebukes the judges and magistrates for their corrupt practices, admonishing them to act uprightly. Verse 6 is quoted in St. John x. 34.

Verse 1. בַּעֲדַת־אֵל in-the-congregation-of-(the) mighty, lit.

of God, i. e. the courts of the magistrates. The LXX. has Θεῶν; the Syr. 'of angels;' our Prayer-Book Version 'of princes.'

בְּקֶרֶב אֱלֹהִים among-(the) gods; this name '*gods*' is applied to the Judges of Israel in the Pentateuch.

יִשְׁפֹּט doth-He-judge, Kal 3 m. s. fut. from שָׁפַט. Coleman, pointing the word differently, considers it as Niph. fut.; regarding the Psalm as prophetic of the Messiah, he translates the verse, 'God standeth in the divinely constituted Council, God in the midst thereof is condemned.' Dr. Kay has 'in the midst shall God judge,' as, in his opinion, the rendering 'among the gods' would require הָאֱלֹהִים.

Verse 2. The word לֵאמֹר is understood at the beginning of this verse.

עָוֶל (in) iniquity, vii. 4, used adverbially.

Verse 3. הַצְדִּיקוּ do-justice-to, lit. justify, i. e. give them their due.

PSALM LXXXIII.

This Psalm, which was probably composed when the Moabites and Ammonites joined together against Judah, in the reign of Jehoshaphat (see 2 Chron. xx. 14), contains first a complaint to God of the enemies' conspiracies, and then a prayer against those who oppress the Church.

Verse 2. דֳּמִי silence, verb. n. m. from דָּמָה xvii. 12.

Verse 4. יַעֲרִימוּ they-have-craftily-devised, Hiph. 3 m. pl. fut. from עָרַם to bind, to mix together, metaph. to spin, to devise, only found once in Kal, 1 Sam. xxiii. 22; Hiph. to act craftily.

וְיִתְיָעֲצוּ and-consulted, Hithp. 3 m. pl. fut. from יָעַץ i. 1. The Hithp. is found only in this passage.

Verse 5. מִגּוֹי from-(being) a-nation, i. e. so that they shall be no longer a nation. The מִן is here used in a privative sense.

Verse 7. The tents or tabernacles are here put for their inhabitants.

וְיִשְׁמְעֵאלִים and-(the) Ishmaelites, prop. name of the descendants of Ishmael, the son of Abraham by Hagar, compounded of יִשְׁמַע and אֵל 'God heareth,' or 'will hear.' The Chal. has אַרְבָאֵי Arabians.

וְהַגְרִים and-(the) Hagarenes, (fugitives, R. הָגַר, unused in Heb., to flee; comp. Arab. *Hejrah*, the Flight of Mahomet); prop. name of an Arabian people who dwelt on the other side of Jordan in the east of Gilead.

Verse 8. גְבָל Gebal, (mountain land, R. גְּבָל lxxiv. 17); prop. name of a mountain district inhabited by the Edomites, at the south of the Dead Sea in Arabia Petræa.

וְעַמּוֹן and-Ammon, (from the subst. עָם iii. 7 with the addition of the syllable וֹן); prop. name of the son of Lot by his own daughter, and of the tribe descended from him, who dwelt north-east of Moab, between the rivers Arnon and Jabbok.

וַעֲמָלֵק and-Amalek, prop. name (with וְ cop. ii. 6) of a people dwelling between Palestine and Arabia on the south-west of Edom; (perhaps signifying 'inhabitants of the valley,' from עָמַק to be deep.)

Verse 9. אַשּׁוּר Asshur, prop. name of the second son of Shem, the ancestor of the Assyrians, and therefore of the Semitic people the Assyrians themselves, who dwelt on the east side of the Tigris north-west of Elam.

לִבְנֵי־לוֹט (the) children-of-Lot, i.e. the Moabites and Ammonites; לוֹט a covering, a veil; R. לוּט to cover over, to hide; prop. name of the nephew of Abraham, who migrated into Canaan, and was the ancestor of the Moabites and Ammonites.

Verse 10. כְּמִדְיָן as-(unto) Midian, (strife, R. דִּין or דּוּן to judge); prop. name of a son of Abraham by Keturah, and of the Arabian tribe descended from him, with pr. כ i. 3.

כְּסִיסְרָא as-(unto) Sisera, prop. name of a general of Jabin, king of Canaan, with pr. כ i. 3.

כְּיָבִין as-(unto)Jabin, (intelligent, R. בִּן v. 2); prop. name (with pr. כ i. 3) of the Phœnician kings of Northern Palestine, who resided commonly at Hazor.

קִישׁוֹן Kishon, (the winding, meandering one, R. קוּשׁ vii. 13); prop. name of a brook or river rising in Mount Tabor, and flowing into the Mediterranean at the foot of Carmel.

Verse 11. בְּעֵין־דּאֹר at-En-dor, (fountain of habitation); prop. name of a city and district in Manasseh, (with pr. כ i. 1,) four miles south of Mount Tabor, whose ruins still exist.

דֹּמֶן dung, verb. n. m. from דָּמַן, not used in Heb., to heap together, to heap up (dung).

Verse 12. כְּעֹרֵב like-Oreb, (a raven, R. עָרַב to be dark); prop. name (with pr. כ i. 3) of a Midianite prince who was slain in battle.

וְכִזְאֵב and-like-Zeeb, (a wolf, so called from its tawny and yellow colour; R. זָאַב, unused in Heb.,=זָהַב to be shining like gold, to be of a yellow colour); prop. name (with pr. כ ii. 12) of a Midianite prince.

וּכְזֶבַח and-like-Zebah, (a slaying, R. זָבַח to slay); prop. name (with ו cop. i. 1 and pr. כ i. 3) of a Midianite king.

וּכְצַלְמֻנָּע and-like-Zalmunna, (from צֵל=צָל xvii. 8 and מָנַע=מְנָע one denied protection, i.e. abandoned); prop. name (with ו cop. i. 1 and pr. כ i. 3) of a Midianite king.

נְסִיכֵמוֹ their-princes, pl. of נָסִיךְ subst. m., a molten image, what is poured out, a libation, also one dedicated or anointed, hence a sovereign, a prince, with (poetic) suff. 3 m. pl.

Verse 14. כַּגַּלְגַּל like-the-wheel, or whirlwind.

כְּקַשׁ as-stubble, subst. m. with pr. כ i. 3. R. קָשַׁשׁ to be dried up.

Verse 15. The pron. אֲשֶׁר is understood before תְּבְעַר and תְּלַהֵט.

Verse 16. וּבְסוּפָתְךָ and-with-Thy-hurricane, subst. f., prop. a thing sweeping away, carrying all before it, a whirlwind, a hurricane, with ו cop. i. 1, pr. כ i. 1, and suff. 2 m. s.

Verse 17. קָלוֹן shame, verb. n. m. from קָלָה i.q. קָלַל, not used in Kal; Niph. to make light of.

PSALM LXXXIV.

In this Psalm, which resembles the forty-second, and which was probably composed on the same or a similar occasion, the writer, who seems to be an exile in a foreign land, dwells on the blessedness of God's service in His house, and the supreme happiness of those who are permitted to take their part in it, and prays to be restored unto it.

Verse 4. וּדְרוֹר and-(the) swallow, subst. com. gen. with ו cop. i. 1, prop. running round about, roving, hence a bird that flies round about swiftly, a swallow, a swift bird. R. דָּרַר, unused in Heb., to fly in a circle, to rove about. The LXX., Syr., and Targum have rendered the word 'turtle-doves.'

קֵן a-nest, subst. m., a nest, a cell. R. קָנַן to form, to prepare.

אֶפְרֹחֶיהָ her-young, pl. of אֶפְרֹחַ subst. m., young brood (of birds), chicken, with suff. 3 f. s. The only other passages in which the word occurs are Deut. xxii. 6 and Job xxxix. 30. R. פָּרַח lxxii. 7.

Verse 5. עוֹד still, i. e. always, continually.

Verse 6. The pron. אֲשֶׁר is to be understood before עוֹז and מְסִלּוֹת.

מְסִלּוֹת (the) ways, pl. of מְסִלָּה subst. f., a way cast up, a highway. R. סָלַל lxviii. 5. The LXX. and Vulg. seem to have read מַעֲלוֹת. The Syr. has מְסִלּוֹתָיו.

Verse 7. הַבָּכָא Bacha, or of mulberry-trees, or perhaps of weeping, or lamentation, as Luther renders it; subst. m., prop. resin-dropping, hence the name of a tree like the balsam, now growing about Mecca; Bacha, so called from the dropping of a resin when its leaves are cut; the word also signifies weeping, lamentation. According to Josephus it is the name of a valley in the neighbourhood of the Rephaim valley near Jerusalem, through which the pilgrims travelled to the Holy City. R. בָּכָא, unused in Heb., to flow out, to trickle forth (as in drops).

בְּרָכוֹת blessings, pl. of בְּרָכָה iii. 9, though some, with the change of a single vowel, read בְּרֵכוֹת pools, as in the English Version.

יַעְטֶה filleth, or covereth.

מוֹרֶה (the) rain, subst. m., prop. Hiph. pres. part. m. s. from יָרָה i. 2. Some, as Hengstenberg, translate 'the teacher is even covered with blessing;' Luther has und die Lehrer werden mit viel Segen geſchmückt. The LXX. has καὶ γὰρ εὐλογίας δώσει ὁ νομοθετῶν.

Verse 8. מֵחַיִל אֶל־חָיִל from-strength-to-strength, or from company to company. Our Prayer-Book Version has 'and unto the God of gods appeareth every one of them in Sion;' the ancient versions have 'the God of gods shall be seen in Zion,' as if they read אֶל for אֶל־; Luther has daß man ſehen muß, der rechte Gott ſei zu Zion.

Verse 11. הִסְתּוֹפֵף to-stand-at-the-threshold, Hithpo. inf. constr. from סָפַף, not found elsewhere; or, 'I would choose rather to sit at the threshold.'

מִדּוּר more-than-to-dwell, Kal inf. constr. from דּוּר x. 6 with pr. מ ii. 3. Instead of the mere *dwelling*, Luther has falsely substituted *long dwelling*.

PSALM LXXXV.

This Psalm, supposed to have been written after the return from the Babylonish Captivity, and in the days of Ezra and Nehemiah, contains first of all a thanksgiving for God's mercy to His people in having brought them out of captivity, and then a prayer for a continuance of the Divine favour, and for deliverance from present distress. In the twelfth verse of this Psalm we have the words אמת מארץ תצמח 'Truth shall spring from the earth,' in which we observe the same reading whether we take them from right to left horizontally; or perpendicularly, beginning at the right hand:

ת	מ	א
צ	אר	מ
מח	צ	ת

This is one of the Proper Psalms for Christmas Day.

Verse 2. שְׁבוּת (the) captivity-of, i. q. שְׁבִית xii. 7. The K'ri is שבית.

Verse 4. אָסַפְתָּ Thou-hast-gathered-in, or withdrawn.

מֵחֲרוֹן אַפֶּךָ from-(the) fierceness-of-Thine-anger, or 'Thou hast turned Thine anger from waxing hot.'

Verse 5. שׁוּבֵנוּ Turn-us; the Vulg. has *converte nos;* the Chal. תּוּב לְוָתָנָא 'turn unto us.'

וְהָפֵר and-cause-to-cease, or make void, Hiph. 2 m. s. imp. from פָּרַר.

עִם does not always express companionship, but sometimes the reverse.

Verse 9. לְכִסְלָה to-folly, verb. n. f. from כָּסַל xxxviii. 8 with pr. לְ ii. 1. The LXX. has 'and to them who turn (their) heart to Him.'

Verse 11. נִפְגָּשׁוּ have-met-together, Niph. 3 pl. pret. from פָּגַשׁ, (kindred to the root פָּגַע,) to strike against, to fall upon, metaph. to light upon, to meet, (in pause.)

PSALM LXXXVI.

This Psalm, (the only one in the Third Book which is ascribed to David,) was composed in some period of great distress, and contains a mixture of earnest prayer, of full confidence in God's goodness and power, and of resolution to persevere in His worship and service. The eleventh verse is borrowed word for word from Ps. xxvii. 11, and the fourteenth verse from Ps. liv. 3.

Verse 5. וְסַלָּח and-ready-to-forgive, verb. adj. m. from סָלַח xxv. 11. The word occurs nowhere else.

Verse 6. תַּחֲנוּנוֹתַי my-supplications, xxviii. 2. This peculiar form of the word is not found elsewhere.

Verse 8. For בָּאֱלֹהִים the Targum has 'high angels.'

Verse 11. For יַחֵד imp. from יָחַד the LXX., Syr., and Vulg. seem to have read יִחַד from חָדָה.

לְיִרְאָה to-fear, ii. 11 with pr. לְ ii. 1, though some consider it as a verb in the infinitive.

Verse 15. וְחַנּוּן and-gracious, verb. adj. m. from חָנַן iv. 2.

אֶרֶךְ אַפַּיִם slow-of-anger, אֶרֶךְ constr. of אָרֵךְ verb. adj. m. from אָרַךְ to be or to grow long; אַפַּיִם dual of אַף ii. 5.

Verse 16. אֲמָתֶךָ Thy-handmaid, subst. f. with suff. 2 m. s.

PSALM LXXXVII.

This Psalm first of all celebrates the glory of Zion as the city of God, and then declares that other nations shall be gathered to her as children of one mother.

Verse 1. יְסוּדָתוֹ His-foundation, verb. n. f. with suff. 3 m. s. from יָסַד ii. 2. The fem. form is found only in this place. Luther has Sie ist fest gegründet.

Verse 3. נִכְבָּדוֹת Glorious-things, Niph. pres. part. f. pl. from כָּבֵד iii. 4, used adverbially.

Verse 4. רַהַב Rahab, (fierceness, pride; R. רָהַב xl. 5); poetic name of Egypt.

וּבָבֶל and-Babylon, prop. name (with וְ cop. i. 1) of the celebrated metropolis of Babylonia, situated on the river Euphrates, and so called from the confusion of tongues; see Gen. xi. 9. R. בָּלַל to pour over, to pour together, to confound, intrans. to be poured over, anointed.

לְיֹדְעָי to-them-that-know-Me, or rather, among them that know Me, lit. as belonging to (the number of) them that know Me.

Verse 5. וּלֲצִיּוֹן יֵאָמַר And-to-Zion-it-shall-be-said; we find in the LXX. not 'it shall be said to (or of) Zion,' but 'Mother Zion shall say,' Μήτηρ Σιὼν ἐρεῖ.

Verse 6. Before זֶה the word לֵאמֹר should be understood.

Verse 7. The LXX. and Vulg. read שָׂרִים for שָׁרִים, connect it with the preceding verse, and then render the last clause 'Ὡς εὐφραινομένων πάντων ἡ κατοικία ἐν σοί; Vulg. Sicut laetantium omnium habitatio est in te; Luther has Und die Sänger, wie am Reigen, werden alle in Dir singen, eins um's andere.

PSALM LXXXVIII.

This Psalm, (although ascribed to Heman the Ezrahite,) was probably composed during the time of the Babylonish Captivity. It is prophetic of the sufferings of Christ, and has therefore been appointed by the Church as one of the Psalms for Good Friday. The first clause of verse 5 is from Ps. xxviii. 1, with the change of נֶחְשַׁבְתִּי into נִמְשַׁלְתִּי.

Verse 1. מָחֲלַת לְעַנּוֹת Mahalath-Leannoth; this has been variously rendered 'upon Mahalath (a harp or stringed instrument, see liii. 1) to answer,' or to sing, or to afflict; Pi. inf. constr. from עָנָה to sing, to answer, also to suffer; see ix. 13.

לְהֵימָן of-Heman, prop. name (with pr. לְ ii. 1) of a Levite of the family of the Kohathites, a leader of David's choir.

הָאֶזְרָחִי the-Ezrahite, a descendant of אֶזְרָח or of זֶרַח with the art. i. 1.

Verse 5. אֱיָל strength, subst. m., only found here. R. אוּל v. 5.

Verse 6. חָפְשִׁי Free, or perhaps infirm, weak, verb. adj. m. from חָפַשׁ, not used in Kal, to flow, or run along freely, hence to be loose, free to spread out, also to be prostrate, to be weak. Some consider it as a subst. m. (with suff. 1 s.), a spreading out, a couch, 'Among the dead is my couch.'

Verse 7. בִּמְצֹלוֹת in-(the) deeps, i. q. מְצֹלוֹת lxviii. 23 with pr. בּ ii. 11.

Verse 8. סָמְכָה lieth-hard, or has held, Kal 3 f. s. pret. from סָמַךְ.

The accusative נִי is wanted to the verb עִנִּיתָ.

Verse 9. תּוֹעֵבוֹת abominations, pl. of תּוֹעֵבָה verb. n. f. from תָּעַב v. 7.

כָּלֻא shut-up, for כָּלוּא Kal pass. part. m. s. from כָּלָא xl. 10.

Verse 10. דָאֲבָה melteth-away, Kal 3 f. s. pret. from דָאַב to melt away, to languish, to mourn, only found here and in Jer. xxxi. 12 and 25.

שִׁטַּחְתִּי I-have-stretched-forth, Pi. 1 s. pret. from שָׁטַח; in Pi. found only here.

Verse 11. רְפָאִים (the) dead, subst. m. pl., flaccid, feeble, weak, i. e. manes, shades living in Hades. R. prob. רָפָה xxxvii. 8. The LXX., deriving the word from רָפָא to heal, has translated it by ἰατροί, and the Vulg. by *medici*. The Syr. has 'strong men,' or 'giants.'

Verse 12. בָּאֲבַדּוֹן in-destruction, subst. m. with pr. בּ pointed with (ָ) because of the following א. R. אָבַד i. 6.

Verse 13. The Chal. has 'in the darkness of hell.'

נְשִׁיָּה forgetfulness, verb. n. f. from נָשָׁה to forget; Luther has ba man nichts gedenket.

Verse 16. מִנֹּעַר from-(my) youth-up, subst. m. denom. from נַעַר, see xxv. 7. The only other passages in which the word occurs are Job xxxiii. 25, xxxvi. 14, and Prov. xxix. 21.

אֵמֶיךָ Thy-terrors, subst. m. pl. with suff. 2 m. s. R. אָיֹם lv. 5.

אָפוּנָה I-am-distracted, Kal 1 s. fut. with ה parag. from פּוּן, only found here, perhaps to be cold, or to writhe with pain, to be distracted.

Verse 17. בְּעִוּתֶיךָ Thy-horrors, subst. m. pl., only found here and in Job vi. 4, with suff. 2 m. s. R. בָּעַת xviii. 5.

צִמְּתֻתֻנִי have-cut-me-off, Pilpel 3 pl. pret. from צָמַת xviii. 41 with suff. 1 s. This form occurs nowhere else.

PSALM LXXXIX.

In *the first* part of this Psalm, (which was perhaps composed at the time of the death of Josiah,) the author praises God for His great goodness to His people; whilst in *the second* he laments over the distresses which have befallen his king and people, and pleads earnestly with God that He would not suffer his enemies to triumph. It is one of the Proper Psalms for Christmas Day.

Verse 1. לְאֵיתָן of-Ethan, prop. name m. with pr. ל ii. 1.

Verse 2. חַסְדֶּיךָ, instead of חַסְדֵי, is apparently the reading of the LXX.

There is an ellipsis of ל before עוֹלָם.

Verse 3. For אָמַרְתִּי the LXX., Vulg., Syr., and Jerome have the 2nd person.

Verse 4. A change of persons here takes place.

לִבְחִירִי with-My-chosen, verb. adj. m. from בָּחַר with pr. ל iv. 3 and suff. 1 s.

Verse 7. יַעֲרֹךְ shall-(one)set-in-order, or compare.

Verse 9. חֲסִין mighty, verb. adj. m. from חָסַן, not used in Kal, to be firm, to be strong, also to be wealthy, to heap up; Niph. to be laid up. The word is found only in this passage.

Verse 10. בְּשׂוֹא when-arise, for נְשׂוֹא xxviii. 2.

Verse 13. תָּבוֹר Tabor, (mountain-height, mountain-top; R. probably תָּבַר, unused in Heb., to be high); prop. name of a mountain situated on the border of Zebulun and Naphtali between the plain of Jezreel and Scythopolis.

Verse 15. מָכוֹן (the) habitation-of, or the establishment of.

Verse 18. The K'thiv is the Hiph. תָּרִים (to be read תָּרִים), but the K'ri תרום is the Kal form.

Verse 20. בְחָזוֹן in-a-vision, subst. m. with pr. בּ i. 1. R. חָזָה xi. 4.

לַחֲסִידֶךָ to-Thy-beloved-one, i. e. Nathan, the godly one of Jehovah; comp. 1 Chron. xvii. 15, 2 Sam. vii. 17, though some think that it refers to Samuel, and others to David himself; חָסִיד xvi. 10 with pr. לְ x. 18. Some MSS., the LXX., Vulg., Chal., Syr., Aquila, Jerome, and others, have the plur., as though referring to the nation at large.

Verse 23. יַשִּׁיא shall-exact, Hiph. 3 m. s. fut. from נָשָׁא i. q. נָשָׁה to lend; Hiph. to exact (what has been lent).

Verse 24. אֶגּוֹף plague, or smite.

Verse 26. בַיָּם on-the-sea, i. e. the Mediterranean. וּבַנְּהָרוֹת and-on-the-rivers, i. e. the Euphrates.

Verse 29. K'thiv אֶשְׁמוּר (to be read אֶשְׁמוֹר), K'ri אשמר.

Verse 34. אָפִיר I-will-make-void, or break off, Hiph. 1 s. fut. from פָּרַר.

Verse 35. מוֹצָא שְׂפָתַי what-is-gone-out-of-my-lips, an elegant paraphrase for דְּבָרַי.

Verse 38. Some persons consider that 'the faithful witness in heaven' signifies *the moon*, whilst Luther and others suppose *the rainbow* to be meant.

Verse 40. נֵאַרְתָּה Thou-hast-made-void, Pi. 2 m. s. pret. with ה parag. from נָאַר, not used in Kal, to push down, to abhor; Pi. to abhor, to reject. The only other passage where the word occurs is Lam. ii. 7.

נִזְרוֹ his-crown, subst. m. with suff. 3 m. s., a diadem (perhaps prop. the token by which any one is separated from the people at large), specially that of a king. R. נָזַר, not used in Kal, to consecrate, to vow, (also, according to Fürst, to surround, to encircle); Niph. to separate oneself from anything, to consecrate oneself to anything.

Verse 41. גְּדֵרֹתָיו his-hedges, pl. of גְּדֵרָה verb. n. f. from גָּדַר lxii. 4 with suff. 3 m. s.

מִבְצָרָיו his-strong-holds, pl. of מִבְצָר verb. n. m. (fem. only in Hab. i. 10), with suff. 3 m. s. from בָּצַר lxxvi. 13.

מְחִתָּה a-ruin, subst. f., destruction, terror. R. חָתַת to break, to be broken, to be terrified; Pi. and Hiph. to frighten.

Verse 42. שַׁסֻּהוּ have-spoiled-him, Kal 3 pl. pret. from שָׁסַם i.q. שָׁסָה with suff. 3 m. s.

Verse 45. מִטְּהָרוֹ from-his-glory, subst. m., splendour, brightness, majesty, with pr. מ ii. 3 and suff. 3 m. s. R. טָהֵר xii. 7.

מִגַּרְתָּה Thou-hast-cast-down, Pi. 2 m. s. pret. from מָגַר, in Kal found only in Ezek. xxi. 17.

Verse 46. עֲלוּמָיו his-youth, subst. m. pl. with suff. 3 m. s. R. עָלַם lxviii. 26.

בּוּשָׁה shame, verb. n. f. from בּוּשׁ vi. 11.

Verse 48. חָלֶד (the)age, xvii. 14. Bishop Horsley has 'what a reptile (lit. weasel) I am,' apparently reading חֹלֶד.

Verse 50. Before נִשְׁבַּעְתָּ the pron. אֲשֶׁר is to be understood.

Verse 51. עַבְדְּךָ is the reading of the Syr. and of several MSS.

Verse 52. אֲשֶׁר Wherewith, or because.

מְשִׁיחֶךָ Thine-Anointed; the Chal. has 'They have scoffed at the tardiness of Thy Messiah's footsteps.'

Verse 53. This ends the Third Book of the Psalter. See note at the end of Ps. xli.

BOOK IV, Psalms XC–CVI.

PSALM XC.

Here begins the Fourth Book, containing all the Psalms from xc to cvi inclusive. *The first* part of this Psalm, (which forms a part of the Burial Service,) contains a meditation on the eternity of God, as contrasted with the weakness of man and the shortness of human life; and *the second* a prayer for the knowledge and sensible experience of God's good providence. This Psalm is entitled 'A Prayer of Moses, the man of God.'

Verse 2. וַתְּחוֹלֵל or-ever-Thou-gavest-birth-to; according to the punctuation this may be Pilel 2 m. s., as in the English Version, or 3 f. s. fut. with ו convers. from חִיל or חוּל x. 5, as the Syr. takes it, 'or ever it (i. e. the earth) brought forth' (i.e. plants, animals). But a very slight change of punctuation would give us the passive תְּחוֹלַל, which is the rendering of the Chal., LXX., Vulg., Jerome, and Luther, 'or ever the earth was formed,' lit. born.

Instead of אַתָּה אֵל the LXX. Version transfers the אֵל to the next verse, and reads אֵל־תָּשֵׁב.

Verse 3. דַּכָּא dust, subst. m., bruising, crushing, poet. dust. R. דָּכָא i. q. דָּכַךְ ix. 10.

Verse 4. אֶתְמוֹל yesterday, adv. of time, of which the derivation is uncertain.

יַעֲבֹר it-passeth, or when he hath passed (them).

Verse 5. יַחֲלֹף groweth-up, or is changed.

Verse 6. יְמוֹלֵל it-is-cut-down, either Poel 3 m. s. fut. from מָלַל, or else Pilel from מוּל xxxvii. 2.

Verse 8. For שַׁתָּ the K'ri has שתה.

עֲלֻמֵנוּ our-secret(sins), for עֲלוּמֵינוּ Kal part. pass. m. pl. from עָלַם v. 12 with suff. 1 pl. The LXX., Vulg., Arab., and Æth. have 'our life.'

Verse 9. הֶגֶה a-thought, or a meditation, verb. n. m. from הָגָה i. 2. The word occurs elsewhere only in Job xxxvii. 2 and Ezek. ii. 10, in the last of which passages it is rendered 'mourning.' The Chal. has 'as the vapour (or breath) of the mouth in winter;' comp. St. James iv. 14. The LXX., Vulg., and Syr. have 'as a spider.'

Verse 10. שִׁבְעִים seventy, num. adj. com. gen., pl. of שֶׁבַע; see xii. 7.

שְׁמוֹנִים eighty, num. adj. com. gen., pl. of שְׁמֹנֶה eight.

וְרָהְבָּם yet-their-pride, subst. m. (only found here) with suff. 3 m. pl. R. רָהַב xl. 5.

גָּז it-is-cut-off, Kal 3 m. s. pret. from גּוּז to flee, to escape, to pass away.

חִישׁ quickly, adv. of time. R. חִישׁ i. q. חוּשׁ to make haste.

Verse 12. וְנָבִיא that-we-may-gain, lit. cause to come.

Verse 15. The form יְמוֹת, instead of יְמֵי, occurs only here and in Deut. xxxii. 7.

PSALM XCI.

This Psalm, which in the Hebrew has no Inscription, is entitled in the LXX. 'Praise of an ode,' or 'A song of praise of David.' If composed by David it was probably on the occasion of the plague sent for his numbering the people (see 2 Sam. xxiv. 15), though some persons suppose it to have been written by Moses in the wilderness, shortly after the plague of the fiery serpents (see Num. xxi. 6). The lesson to be learnt from this Psalm is that confidence in God amidst trouble and peril is the privilege of those who are wholly devoted to Him. Verses 11 and 12 were quoted by Satan when he tempted our Blessed Lord to cast Himself down from a pinnacle of the Temple.

Verse 2. For אָמַר, the 1st person, the LXX., Vulg., Syr., and Luther have the 3rd person, reading either אֹמֵר or יֹאמַר.

Verse 3. יָקוּשׁ (the) fowler, subst. m. R. יָקַשׁ to lay snares.

מִדֶּבֶר הַוּוֹת from-the-pestilence-of-wickednesses. We find in the LXX. ἀπὸ λόγου ταραχώδους.

Verse 4. וְסֹחֵרָה and-buckler, subst. f., so called from surrounding, i. e. defending; the word is an ἅπαξ λεγόμενον. R. סָחַר to surround, to enclose.

Verse 6. מִקֶּטֶב for-(the) destruction, subst. m. with pr. מ ii. 3; the word occurs elsewhere only in Deut. xxxii. 24 and Is. xxviii. 2. R. קָטַב, unused in Heb., to cut off, to destroy.

יָשׁוּד (that) wasteth, Kal 3 m. s. fut. from שׁוּד i. q. שָׁדַד to be strong, to act with violence, also to rule. The pron. אֲשֶׁר is to be understood before the verb.

Verse 7. מִצִּדְּךָ at-thy-side, subst. m. (abs. form צַד) with pr. מ ii. 3 and suff. 2 m. s. R. צָדַד, unused in Heb., to turn away from any one, to be hostile.

Verse 8. וְשִׁלֻּמַת and-(the) reward-of, constr. of שִׁלֻּמָה verb. n. f. from שָׁלַם, see iii. 1.

Verse 10. תְאֻנֶּה There-shall-befall, Pu. 3 f. s. fut. from אָנָה xii. 3.

Verse 12. בָּאֶבֶן against-the-stone, subst. com. gen. (usually fem.) with pr. ב lxxxviii. 12. R. אָבַן, unused in Heb., prob. meaning to be hard, to be firm.

Verse 13. שַׁחַל (the) lion, subst. m., used only in poetry, prop. the roarer, from the unused root שָׁחַל to roar.

Verse 14. God is here the speaker.

חָשַׁק he-hath-set-his-love, Kal 3 m. s. pret., prop. to join together, hence to cleave to any one, i. e. to be attached with very great love.

PSALM XCII.

This Psalm, which contains an exhortation to give thanks to God for His wonderful works, for His judgments on the wicked, and for His goodness to the godly, may perhaps have been composed by David when God had given him rest from all his enemies round about, although by a tradition of the Rabbis it has been attributed to Adam.

Verse 1. הַשַּׁבָּת the-Sabbath, subst. com. gen., usually fem. R. שָׁבַת viii. 3.

Verse 11. There is an ellipsis of קֶרֶן before רְאֵמִים.

בַּלֹּתִי I-am-anointed, prob. Kal 1 s. pret. from בָּלַל lxxxvii. 4, though the LXX. by the rendering τὸ γῆράς μου, 'my being grown old,' seems to have taken the word as Pi. inf. from בָּלָה x. 4.

Verse 12. בְּשׁוּרָי upon-them-that-lie-in-wait-for-me, pl. of שׁוּר subst. m. with pr. בּ i. 1 and suff. 1 s. R. שׁוּר to look around or about.

Verse 13. כַּתָּמָר as-the-palm-tree, subst. m. with pr. כּ i. 3. R. תָּמַר, unused in Heb., to be lofty.

Verse 16. עַלָתָה unrighteousness, to be read עֲלָתָה, instead of the more common עוֹלָה (עוֹלָתָה), which the K'ri prefers.

PSALM XCIII.

This Psalm, which is entitled in the LXX. 'A Psalm of praise of David, on the day before the Sabbath, when the earth was founded,' and which still forms a part of the Jewish Service for Friday, extols the majesty, power, and holiness of Christ's kingdom. Psalms xciii–xcix celebrate the coming of Jehovah as King. The beginning and end of the first verse occur word for word again in Ps. xcvi. 10.

Verse 1. For תִּכּוֹן the LXX., Syr., Vulg., Arab., and Luther read תָּכֵן.

Verse 3. דָּכְיָם their-roaring, subst. m. (abs. form דֳּכִי), with suff. 3 m. pl. R. דָּכָה x. 10. The word occurs only in this passage.

PSALM XCIV.

By the LXX. this is called 'A lyric Psalm of David for the Fourth Day of the week,' (τετράδι σαββάτου,) and it still forms part of the Jewish Service for Wednesday. By some it is supposed to have been written in the time of the Maccabees, whilst others refer it to that of Saul and Ishbosheth, and others again to the rebellion of Absalom. In it the Psalmist, in the person of the Church, complains of the corrupt and troublous times, and teaches that God is the defender of the afflicted.

Verse 2. גֵּאִים (the)proud, pl. of גֵּאֶה verb. adj. m. from גָּאָה x. 2.

Verse 6. We find in the LXX. that the words 'fatherless' and 'stranger' are transposed, and the latter rendered 'proselyte.'

Verse 10. The LXX. has 'He that instructs the nations,' and the Chal. 'He that gives the Law to His people.'

Verse 17. We must supply הָיָה before יְהֹוָה.

דּוּמָה silence, subst. f., poetically used of Hades. R. דּוּם i. q. דָּמַם iv. 5.

Verse 19. שַׂרְעַפַּי my-thoughts, subst. m. pl. (with suff. 1 s.), found only here and in Ps. cxxxix. 23. R. prob. שָׂעַף, not used in Heb., to meditate, to think.

תַּנְחוּמֶיךָ Thy-comforts, subst. m. pl. with suff. 2 m. s. R. נָחַם xxiii. 4.

יְשַׁעַשְׁעוּ delight, Pilpel 3 m. pl. fut. from שָׁעַע, prop. to stroke, to overspread; in Kal once intrans. to be smeared over (used of the eye), to be blinded, Is. xxix. 9; Pilpel to delight, intrans. to delight oneself.

Verse 20. יְחָבְרְךָ Shall-have-fellowship-with-thee, or shall be joined to thee. Gesenius considers this as = יְחֻבָּרְךָ Pu. 3 m. s. fut. from חָבַר xxxviii. 6 with ה interrog. l. 13 and suff. 2 m. s., though Dr. Perowne and also Hengstenberg take it as Kal with interposed vowel for יַחְבָּרְךָ.

Verse 21. יָגוֹדּוּ They-gather-themselves-in-troops, or, They break in upon, Kal 3 m. pl. fut. from גָּדַד to cut into, also to collect together.

PSALM XCV.

This Psalm, which in the Hebrew has no Inscription, and which is called in the LXX. 'A Song of praise of David,' forms part of our Morning Service, to be read before the Psalms of the day. It celebrates the greatness of God, and His power as displayed in the works of creation; it also contains an exhortation to obedience. It is thought by some to have been written by David, probably on the occasion of bringing the Ark to Mount Zion.

Verse 2. בִּזְמִרוֹת with-psalms, pl. of זְמִיר (Gesenius) verb. n. m. from זָמַר iii. 1 with pr. ב ii. 11; Fürst considers it as pl. of the fem. זְמִירָה.

Verse 4. מֶחְקְרֵי (the) deep-places-of, pl. constr. of מֶחְקָר i. q. חֵקֶר, that which is known by searching, inmost depth. R. חָקַר to search, to investigate.

וְתוֹעֲפוֹת and-(the) heights-of, subst. f. pl.; according to Gesenius, weariness, labour, hence wealth derived from labour, from the root יָעַף to be fatigued; according to Fürst the word signifies splendour, things glittering afar, i. e. heights. R. יָעַף to shine, to glitter, fig. to be high. The LXX., Syr., Vulg., Luther, and the Welsh Version have 'the heights of.'

Verse 5. וְיַבֶּשֶׁת and-(the) dry (land), verb. n. f. from יָבֵשׁ to be dried up.

Verse 8. מַסָּה Massah, (temptation, trial; R. נָסָה xxvi. 2); the name of a place in the desert.

Verse 10. אַרְבָּעִים Forty, num. adj. com. gen., pl. of אַרְבַּע four.

אָקוּט was-I-grieved, Kal 1 s. fut. from קוט to loathe; Hithp. to be disgusted with.

Verse 11. מְנוּחָתִי My-rest, i. e. the land of Canaan, sing. of מְנוּחוֹת xxiii. 2 with suff. 1 s. This is quoted by St. Paul, Heb. iv. 5.

PSALM XCVI.

We find this Psalm, with little variation, as a part of the poem in 1 Chron. xvi. 8–36, which David composed to celebrate the carrying up of the Ark from the house of Obed-Edom to Mount Zion. From the Title in the LXX. it seems also to have been used on the occasion of dedicating the Second Temple, after the return from the Babylonish Captivity. It contains an exhortation to praise God for His greatness, for His kingdom, and for His general judgment.

Verse 5. אֱלִילִים idols, (or non-entities, nullities,) pl. of אֱלִיל subst. m. R. אָלַל iv. 5.

Verse 8. מִנְחָה an-offering, (the collect. sing. for the plur.)

Verse 9. בְּהַדְרַת־קֹדֶשׁ in-(the) beauty-of-holiness, or in the glorious sanctuary.

חִילוּ tremble; here, as in xcviii. 4, the verb is plur.

Verse 10. For תָּבוֹן the LXX., Syr., Vulg., Arab., and Luther read תִּכֹּן, as they do in xciii. 1.

Verse 13. The second כִּי בָא is omitted in several MSS. and in the Syr.

PSALM XCVII.

This Psalm, which in the LXX. is entitled 'A Psalm of David when his land was restored,' describes the majesty of God's kingdom, the joy of the Church at His judgments upon idolaters, and an exhortation to gladness. The first part of the sixth verse is from Ps. l. 6, and part of the seventh verse is quoted in Heb. i. 6 as applicable to Christ.

Verse 5. This name of God, 'the Lord of the whole earth,' occurs first in Josh. iii. 11, 13, where the Ark (at the passage of the Jordan) is called 'the Ark of Jehovah, the Lord of the whole earth;' the only other places where the same phrase is found are Mic. iv. 13, Zech. iv. 14 and vi. 5 (comp. Is. liv. 5).

Verse 7. פֶּסֶל a-graven-image, subst. m. R. פָּסַל to hew, to carve.

The LXX., Vulg., and Syr. have 'all ye angels of His.'

Verse 11. The LXX. ἀνέτειλε, 'hath sprung up,' 'arisen,' and so the other ancient versions, as if they read זָרַח for זָרֻעַ, as in Ps. cxii. 4.

PSALM XCVIII.

This Psalm, which closely resembles Ps. xcvi, is the only one entitled מִזְמוֹר, 'a Psalm,' without any addition. By the LXX. and Vulg. it is ascribed to David; in the Syriac the Inscription runs, 'Of the redemption of the people from Egypt.' It forms part of the Church of England Evening Service, to be read after the Second Lesson, and contains an exhortation to all creatures to praise God. The first two lines of this Psalm are taken from Ps. xcvi. 1; verses 2, 3 from Is. lii. 10, lxiii. 5; 'His right hand helped him' is from Is. lix. 16. The first clause of ver. 7 is from Ps. xcvi. 11.

Verse 4. פִּצְחוּ Make-a-loud-noise, Kal 2 m. pl. imp. from פָּצַח to break asunder, fig. to break out (into joy).

Verse 6. בַּחֲצֹצְרוֹת With-trumpets, pl. of חֲצֹצְרָה subst. f. with pr. בְּ i. 1.

Verse 8. יִמְחֲאוּ Let-clap, Kal 3 m. pl. fut. from מָחָא to smite, to strike, used poetically for הִכָּה.

PSALM XCIX.

In this, the last of the Psalms which celebrate the coming of Jehovah as King, the Psalmist exhorts all men to worship God at His holy hill, and cites Moses, Aaron, and Samuel as examples of obedience to God.

Verse 1. תָּנוּט let-be-moved, or stagger, Kal 3 f. s. fut. from נוּט, only found here, i. q. מוֹט.

Verse 3. קָדוֹשׁ הוּא it-(is) holy, or He (is) holy.

Verse 5. לַהֲדֹם רַגְלָיו at-His-footstool, lit. at the stool of His feet; הֲדֹם subst. m. with pr. לְ x. 18, prop. the lower part or step of the throne, put for the throne itself; always used metaphorically. R. הָדַם, unused in Heb., perhaps to tread down.

Before קָדוֹשׁ the LXX., Vulg., and Arab. read כִּי.

Verse 6. וּשְׁמוּאֵל and-Samuel, (heard of God,) prop. name (with ו cop. i. 1) of a famous judge and prophet of the Hebrews, of the tribe of Levi.

Verse 7. וְחֹק נָתַן־לָמוֹ and-(the) statute-(that) He-gave-them; Hengstenberg has, 'they kept His testimonies, and He gave them the Law.'

PSALM C.

In this Psalm, which forms a part of our Morning Service, to be read after the Second Lesson, is an exhortation to praise God cheerfully for His greatness and for His power. The Chal. calls it 'A Psalm of thankoffering,' i. e. to be used at the time of presenting the thankoffering sacrifice (Lev. vii. 12).

Verse 3. The K'ri וְלוֹ is often preferred to the K'thiv וְלֹא; it is supported by the Chal. and Jerome, whereas the LXX.,

Vulg., and Syr. have adopted the word in the text. There are several passages in the Old Testament in which, according to the Masora, לֹא is written, and לוֹ ought to be read, viz. Ex. xxi. 8, Lev. xi. 21, xxv. 30, 1 Sam. ii. 3, 2 Sam. xvi. 18, xix. 7, 2 Kings viii. 10, 1 Chron. xi. 20, Ezra iv. 2, Job vi. 21, xiii. 15, xli. 4, Ps. c. 3, cxxxix. 16, Prov. xix. 7, xxvi. 2, Is. ix. 2, xlix. 5, lxiii. 9, though several of these are considered doubtful.

PSALM CI.

The Psalmist here declares the principles upon which as king he has resolved to govern himself and his kingdom. It is one of the Proper Psalms for the Accession.

Verse 3. עֲשֹׂה־ the-work-of, lit. the doing of, for עֲשׂוֹת; the Chal. and Vulg. seem to have read עָשָׂה, the Syr. עָשִׂי.

סֵטִים them-that-turn-aside, subst. m., deviations, faults, those that turn aside. Besides this place it occurs only in Hos. v. 2, where it is written שֵׂטִים, which in our Version is translated 'revolters.' R. סוּט i. q. שׂוּט or שָׂטָה.

Verse 5. מְלָשְׁנִי (to be read מְלָושְׁנִי) Whoso-slandereth, Poel pres. part. m. s. from לָשַׁן v. 10 with Chirek-compaginis (xviii. 32). The K'ri מלשני for מְלָשְׁנִי is Piel, like תִּרְצְחוּ lxii. 4.

גְּבַהּ־ (the)proud-of, adj. m., used only in the constr. state, i. q. גָּבֵהַּ. R. גָּבַהּ x. 4.

וּרְחַב and-(the)wide-of, constr. of רָחָב verb. adj. m. from רָחַב iv. 2 with ו cop. i. 1.

Verse 6. יְשָׁרְתֵנִי he-shall-serve-me, Pi. 3 m. s. fut. from שָׁרַת, not used in Kal, with suff. 1 s.

PSALM CII.

This is one of the penitential Psalms (see Ps. vi), and was probably composed during the Captivity. It is also one of the Proper Psalms for Ash-Wednesday. In it the prophet makes a grievous complaint, comforts himself in the eternity and mercy of God, and sustains his weakness by a recollection of the unchangeableness of the Almighty. Verses 26–28 are quoted in the Epistle to the Hebrews (i. 10–12) as addressed to Christ.

Verse 4. בְעָשָׁן in-smoke; the true reading is probably כְּעָשָׁן 'as smoke,' which is supported by some MSS., the LXX., Vulg., Chal., and Arab.

כְּמוֹקֵד as-a-firebrand, subst. m., burning, conflagration, dry wood, faggot, with pr. בּ i. 3. The word signifies either the wood which is set on fire, or the pot which is heated by it, or the hearth on which the fire burns. R. יָקַד to burn.

Verse 5. הוּכָּה is-smitten, for הֻכָּה, as in Hos. ix. 16, Hoph. 3 m. s. pret. from נָכָה iii. 8.

The מ in מֵאֲכֹל has the force of a negative.

Verse 7. לִקְאַת to-a-pelican-of, constr. of קָאַת subst. f. with pr. לְ iv. 3, probably so called from vomiting, as the pelican is accustomed to vomit sea-shells and other things which it has swallowed. R. קָאָה, unused in Heb., to spue, to vomit, perhaps also to cry out.

כְּכוֹס like-an-owl-of, subst. f. with pr. בּ i. 3, an unclean bird dwelling amongst ruins, perhaps the pelican or cormorant.

Verse 8. בּוֹדֵד lonely, Kal pres. part. m. s. from בָּדַד to divide, to separate.

גָּג (the) house-top, subst. m., pl. גַּגּוֹת. R., unused in Heb., perhaps to spread out.

Verse 9. בִּי נִשְׁבָּעוּ are-sworn-against-me; or swear by me, i. e. use my name as a curse; 'May he be like this man;' see Is. lxv. 15, Jer. xxix. 22.

Verse 10. אֵפֶר ashes, subst. m. R. אָפַר, unused in Heb., perhaps to be ground to powder.

וְשִׁקֻּוַי and-my-drink, subst. m. pl. with suff. 1 s. R. שָׁקָה xxxvi. 9.

Verse 15. Luther has Denn Deine Knechte wollten gerne, daß sie gebauet würde, und sähen gerne, daß ihre Steine und Kalk zugerichtet würden.

Verse 18. הָעַרְעָר the-destitute, adj. m. with the art. (see i. 1), found only here and in Jer. xvii. 6. R. עָרַר to make oneself naked, to be naked; in Kal found once imp. with ה parag. in Is. xxxii. 11; Hithpalpel to be made naked, i. e. utterly overthrown.

Verse 24. The K'thiv בֹּחוֹ (to be read כֹּחוֹ) 'his strength' is adopted by the LXX. and Vulg., but the K'ri כֹּחִי 'my strength' is more suitable.

Verse 25. בַּחֲצִי in-(the)midst-of, subst. m. with pr. בּ i. 1. R. חָצָה lv. 24.

Verse 26. לְפָנִים Of-old, xvii. 2; the word is here employed adverbially.

PSALM CIII.

The Psalmist here, (perhaps after recovery from a dangerous sickness,) begins with an exhortation to bless God for His great goodness in forgiving iniquities, in redeeming the soul from death, and for His general care of mankind. After speaking of the changeableness and uncertainty of human life, he triumphantly concludes by expressing his joy in the remembrance of God's goodness to himself and his people. In some MSS. this Psalm is connected with the following one.

Verse 3. עֲוֺנֵכִי thine-iniquity, xviii. 24 with Aramaic form of suff. 2 f. s. The LXX., Vulg., Chal., and Arab. have the word in the plur.

תַּחֲלוּאָיְכִי thy-diseases, subst. m. pl. with Aramaic suff. 2 f. s. R. חָלָא i. q. חָלָה to be sick.

Verse 5. The Syr. translates עֶדְיֵךְ 'thy body,' the LXX. 'desire' (ἐπιθυμίαν), the Chal. 'old age;' Luther's Version and the Welsh have 'thy mouth.'

תִּתְחַדֵּשׁ renews-itself, Hithp. 3 f. s. fut. from חָדַשׁ xxxiii. 3. The verb does not agree in either gender or number with נְעוּרָיְכִי, which is the subject of it.

כַּנֶּשֶׁר like-the-eagle, subst. m. with pr. כ i. 3. R. נָשַׁר, unused in Heb., to rend or tear in pieces.

Verse 7. For עֲלִילוֹתָיו 'His acts,' we find in the LXX. θελήματα αὐτοῦ, 'His inclinations.'

Verse 9. יִטּוֹר He-keepeth (His anger), Kal 3 m. s. fut. from נָטַר i. q. שָׁמַר, but used chiefly in poetry.

Verse 11. כִּגְבֹהַּ as-(the) height-of, Kal inf. constr. with pr. כ ii. 9, from גָּבַהּ x. 4.

Verse 12. מִזְרָח (the) East, or sunrise.

מִמַּעֲרָב from-(the) West, or sunset.

Verse 14. יִצְרֵנוּ our-frame, or our fashioning, verb. n. m. with suff. 1 pl. from יָצַר to form, to fashion.

Verse 15. כְּצִיץ as-a-flower-of, verb. n. m. with pr. כ i. 3, from צִיץ lxxii. 16.

Verse 20. Before מַלְאָכָיו the LXX., Vulg., Æth., and Arab. add the word כָּל, which would correspond with the two following verses.

Verse 22. מֶמְשַׁלְתּוֹ His-dominion, subst. f. with suff. 3 m. s. R. מָשַׁל to rule.

PSALM CIV.

This Psalm, which in the LXX. is entitled 'A Psalm of David on the formation of the world,' is a hymn of praise to Jehovah as the Supreme and Almighty Creator of all things. In language of the richest poetical beauty it recounts the six days' work viewed as perpetually prolonged in the preservation of all. The order of creation as given in Genesis is exactly followed: comp. ver. 2, the light; 2–4, the heavens; 5–18, the dry land; 19–23, the heavenly bodies; 24–26, fish and fowls; 27–30, man and beast. It closes appropriately by celebrating God's lasting glory and delight in His works, and His power to destroy what He has made, by expressing grateful confidence in Him, and by praying that His creation may no more be defiled by the presence of sin. This Psalm is one of the Proper Psalms for Whit-Sunday.

Verse 2. כַּשַּׂלְמָה as-the-garment, subst. f. (with pr. כ i. 3) with the letters transposed for שִׂמְלָה. R. שָׂמַל, unused in Heb., to gird, to surround.

כַּיְרִיעָה like-the-curtain, subst. f. with pr. כ i. 3, a veil, a curtain, so called from its tremulousness. R. יָרַע to tremble, to flutter.

Verse 3. בַמַּיִם in-the-waters, i. e. the waters above that make the clouds.

עֲלִיּוֹתָיו His-chambers, lit. upper chambers, ὑπερῷα, pl. of עֲלִיָּה subst. f. with suff. 3 m. s. R. עָלָה i. 3.

רְכוּבוֹ His-chariot, verb. n. m. from רָכַב to ride, with suff. 3 m. s.

Verse 4. עֹשֶׂה מַלְאָכָיו רוּחוֹת (Who)maketh-His-angels-spirits; or perhaps, He maketh (the) winds His messengers.

Verse 6. כִּסִּיתוֹ Thou-coveredst-it-with,. abbreviated for כִּסִּיתָהוּ.

Verse 8. יַעֲלוּ הָרִים They-go-up-(by the)mountains, or the mountains go up, i. e. they *seemed* to rise as the waters subsided.

בְּקָעוֹת (the)valleys, pl. of בִּקְעָה subst. f., a valley, (as if a cleaving and separation of mountains.) R. בָּקַע to cleave, to divide. Or perhaps, They (the waters) climbed up mountains, they ran down vallies.

Verse 11. יִשְׁבְּרוּ quench, or break, (a phrase which occurs only here.)

פְּרָאִים (the) wild-asses, pl. of פֶּרֶא subst. com. gen., prop. *a swift runner*, hence a wild ass, onager. R. פָּרָא to run. The wild ass is specially mentioned because living in the desert.

Verse 12. עֳפָאיִם (the) branches, pl. of עֳפִי subst. m.; the word occurs nowhere else except in the Chal. part of Daniel, chap. iv. 9, 11, and 18. R. עָפָה, unused in Heb., to flourish, to grow luxuriantly. The LXX., Vulg., and Syr. have 'the rocks,' as if they read כֵּפִים.

קוֹלָם is the reading of the Arab.

Verse 13. Houbigant and Bishop Horsley read מַעֲשָׂיו for מַעֲשָׂיךָ.

Verse 14. לַעֲבֹדַת for-(the) service-of, constr. of עֲבֹדָה subst. f. with pr. ל x. 18. R. עָבַד to labour, to serve.

Verse 15. We must understand אֲשֶׁר before יְשַׂמַּח.

Verse 17. חֲסִידָה (the) stork, subst. f., prop. the pious (bird), so called from its love towards its parents and young. R. חָסַד iv. 4.

בְּרוֹשִׁים (the) cypresses, pl. of בְּרוֹשׁ subst. m. R. בָּרַשׁ, unused in Heb., by some supposed to mean, to cut, to cut into; and by others, to be firm, to be durable. The LXX. and Vulg. read בְּרֹאשָׁם among the head of them.

Verse 18. הַגְּבֹהִים The-high, pl. of גָּבֹהַּ verb. adj. m. from גָּבַהּ x. 4.

לַיְּעֵלִים for-the-wild-goats, pl. of יָעֵל subst. m., the ibex or chamois, with pr. ל ii. 1, prop. a climber. R. יָעַל xviii. 5.

לַשְׁפַנִּים for-the-conies, pl. of שָׁפָן (Hyrax Syriacus) subst. m. with pr. ל ii. 1.

Verse 24. קִנְיָנֶיךָ Thy-riches, or Thy creatures, pl. of קִנְיָן verb. n. m. from קָנָה lxviii. 31 with suff. 2 m. s. The LXX., Vulg., and Jerome read the word in the sing.

Verse 25. וּרְחַב יָדַיִם and-broad, lit. wide of two hands; the Chal. has 'spacious of bounds.'

רֶמֶשׂ moving-things, verb. n. m. from רָמַשׂ to creep, to crawl.

מִסְפָּר a-number, verb. n. m. from סָפַר ii. 7.

קְטַנּוֹת small, fem. pl. of קָטָן verb. adj. from קטֹן to be small.

Verse 26. For *Leviathan* Luther has *whale*.

בּוֹ therein; or perhaps, with him; comp. Job xli. 5. The LXX. has ἐμπαίζειν αὐτῷ, Vulg. *ad illudendum ei*.

Verse 27. יְשַׂבֵּרוּן wait, Pi. 3 m. pl. fut. (in pause with ן parag.) from שָׂבַר to look at, to view; Pi. to expect, to wait for.

Verse 34. For עָלָיו Bishop Horsley reads, with the LXX., Vulg., and Jerome, אֵלָיו 'Let my meditation be pleasing unto Him.'

PSALM CV.

This Psalm, (the first fifteen verses of which are found, with some slight variations, in 1 Chron. xvi. 8–22,) is the first of a number of Psalms beginning with the word הוֹדוּ 'Give thanks,' (cv, cvii, cxviii, cxxvi.) It is entitled in the LXX. *Hallelujah*, as are also the two following. Like the seventy-eighth and the one hundred-and-sixth, it has for its theme the early history of Israel, and God's wonders wrought on behalf of His nation. Psalms cv and cvi form a pair, probably composed during or after the exile to Babylon, and derived in part from the old sanctuary service, in which the beginning of Ps. cv and the end of Ps. cvi are to be found. Verse 1 is taken word for word from Is. xii. 4; ver. 13 alludes probably to the patriarchs moving about from one to another of the nations of Canaan; and ver. 14 to Pharaoh, Gen. xii. 17, and Abimelech, Gen. xx. 3, 17, 18.

Verse 6. יִשְׂרָאֵל, instead of אַבְרָהָם, is the reading of twenty-one MSS. and of 1 Chron. xvi. 13.

For עַבְדּוֹ the LXX. reads עֲבָדָיו ye His servants.

The Syr. has בְּחִירוֹ instead of בְּחִירָיו.

Verse 8. In 1 Chron. xvi we find 'remember ye.'
The relat. אֲשֶׁר is to be understood after דָּבָר.

Verse 9. וּשְׁבוּעָתוֹ and-His-oath, verb. n. f. from שָׁבַע xv. 4 with ו cop. i. 1 and suff. 3 m. s.

לְיִשְׂחָק unto-Isaac, for יִצְחָק laughter, prop. name m. with pr. ל ii. 1. R. שָׂחַק to laugh; Pi. to jest, to make sport of any one, to mock. The name is written thus only in three other passages, i.e. Jer. xxxiii. 26, Amos vii. 9 and 16; elsewhere it is always יִצְחָק.

Verse 11. כְּנַעַן Canaan, (perhaps the depressed, low region, from the root כָּנַע lxxxi. 15 with the addition of ן., opposed to the loftier country אֲרָם); prop. name of the country and people of Canaan, including what was afterwards called Palestine and Phœnicia.

חֶבֶל (the) lot-of, or the cord of.

Verse 12. In 1 Chron. xvi. 19 we find בִּהְיוֹתְכֶם, which is also the reading here of the Chal., Syr., and several MSS.

מְתֵי מִסְפָּר a-few-men-in-number, lit. mortals of a number, i.e. men easily numbered.

Verse 15. At the beginning of this verse we must understand לֵאמֹר.

Verse 16. מַטֵּה־ staff-of, subst. m. (once fem. in Mic. vi. 9); pl. מַטּוֹת.

Verse 18. בַּכֶּבֶל with-the-fetter, subst. m. (with pr. ב i. 1), only found here and in Ps. cxlix. 8. R. כָּבַל, unused in Heb., to tie or bind fast.

The K'thiv has רַגְלָיו (to be read רַגְלָיו) pl., and the K'ri the sing. רגלו.

Verse 20. וַיַּתִּירֵהוּ and-loosed-him, Hiph. 3 m. s. fut. with ו convers. and suff. 3 m. s. from נָתַר to tremble, to quake; Hiph. to cause to tremble, to shake off, to loose.

וַיְפַתְּחֵהוּ and-let-him-go-free, lit. and opened unto him.

Verse 21. קִנְיָנוֹ his-substance, or possession.

Verse 22. For לֶאְסֹר the LXX. and Vulg. seem to have read לְיַסֵּר to tutor.

וּזְקֵנָיו and-his-elders, pl. of זָקֵן verb. adj. m. from זָקֵן to be old, with ו cop. i. 1 and suff. 3 m. s.

Verse 25. לְהִתְנַכֵּל to-deal-subtilly, Hithp. inf. constr. with pr. לְ ii. 1, from נָכַל to act fraudulently; in Hithp. only found elsewhere in Gen. xxxvii. 18.

Verse 28. מָרוּ they-rebelled-against, i. e. Moses and Aaron, who, and not the Egyptians (as some think), must be the subject of the verb. We find the negative particle omitted in the LXX., (which is also the case in the Syr., Arab., and Æth.,) whence in the Prayer-Book Version, 'and they were not obedient unto His word.'

The K'thiv has דְּבָרָיו (to be read דְּבָרָיו), the K'ri דברו is sing.

Verse 29. וְנָתָם their-fish, (the first plague,) the sing. to be taken in a collective sense.

Verse 30. The second plague.

בְּחַדְרֵי in-(the)chambers-of, constr. of חֲדָרִים, pl. of חֶדֶר verb. n. m. with pr. בְ i. 1, from חָדַר to surround, to enclose.

Verse 31. כִּנִּים lice, (the third plague,) pl. of כֵּן subst. m., only found once in the sing., Is. li. 6; prob. a gnat, a kind of stinging insect.

Verse 33. וּתְאֵנָתָם and-their-fig-trees, subst. f., (used collectively); pl. תְּאֵנִים, with ו cop. i. 1 and suff. 3 m. pl.

Verse 34. וְיֶלֶק and-(the)grasshopper, subst. m., a species of locust with wings. R. יָלַק, unused in Heb., to lick, to lick up, to browse upon.

Verse 37. כּוֹשֵׁל one-stumbling, i. e. so as not to be able to travel.

Verse 39. לְמָסָךְ for-a-covering, verb. n. m. from סָכַךְ v. 12 with pr. לְ ii. 1.

Verse 40. The LXX., Vulg., and Luther read שָׁאֲלוּ for שָׁאַל.

שְׂלָו quails, subst. com. gen., a quail, (used collectively,) so called from its fatness. R. שָׁלָה, unused in Heb., to be fleshy, to be fat. For שְׂלָו the K'ri has שליו.

Verse 41. The LXX., Vulg., and Chal. read the pl. נְהָרוֹת.

Verse 45. בַּעֲבוּר That, prop. a subst., passing over, transition. R. עָבַר vii. 7. With the pr. בְּ (i. 1) it becomes a prep., signifying because of, for the sake of; or a conj. that.

PSALM CVI.

This, which is the first of a series of Hallelujah Psalms, opens with an exhortation to praise God, recounts the story of the people's rebellion and God's mercy, and concludes with a prayer for deliverance from present calamity. The first verse is the same as 1 Chron. xvi. 34; ver. 14 is supposed to allude to Num. xi. 4; and verses 47, 48 are from 1 Chron. xvi. 35, 36, the latter being merely a Doxology added at a time subsequent to the composition of the Psalm, to mark the close of the Fourth Book, which is predominantly the Book of the 'Captivity,' as the Fifth is of the 'Restoration.' See the end of Ps. xli.

Verse 2. The pron. מִי must be repeated before יַשְׁמִיעַ.

Verse 3. The LXX., Vulg., Chal., Syr., and Arab. read עֹשִׂי for עֹשֵׂה.

Verse 4. The LXX., Syr., Arab., and Æth. read the verbs זְכָר and פָּקַד with the suff. 1 pers. pl., but the Chal. retains the sing.

Verse 7. We find in the LXX. ἀναβαίνοντες, as if reading עֹלִים for עַל־יָם, and this is followed by the Vulg.

סוּף Suph, subst. m., rush, reed, sea-weed; יַם־סוּף 'the weedy sea,' i. e. the Arabian Gulf, which abounds in sea-weed. The etymology of the word is unknown.

Verse 15. שְׁאֶלָתָם their-request, verb. n. f. from שָׁאַל with suff. 3 m. pl.

רָזוֹן leanness, (Syr. and Vulg. *satiety*, LXX. *fulness*,) verb. n. m. from רָזָה to spread out, to make thin and lean, hence to consume, to destroy; Niph. to waste away.

Verse 16. Aaron is here called '*the holy one of the Lord*' on account of his priestly office.

Verse 17. In Num. xvi. 30, 32, and xxvi. 10 the fuller expression occurs, 'the earth opened her mouth.'

דָּתָן Dathan, (perhaps of or belonging to a fountain,) from דֹּת=דָּת a Chal. word, a well, a fountain,) prop. name of one of the fellow conspirators of Korah.

אֲבִירָם Abiram, (father of loftiness,) prop. name masc.

Verse 19. בְּחֹרֵב in-Horeb, (dry desert, R. חָרַב vii. 13,) prop. name (with pr. בְּ i. 1) of one of the summits of Mount Sinai.

לְמַסֵּכָה to-(the)molten-image, verb. n. f. with pr. לְ ii. 1, from נָסַךְ ii. 6.

Verse 20. בְּתַבְנִית for-(the)likeness-of, subst. f., structure, manner of building, model, likeness, figure, with pr. בְּ i. 1. R. בָּנָה to build.

Verse 23. בַּפֶּרֶץ in-the-breach, verb. n. m. from פָּרַץ to break through, with pr. בְּ i. 1.

Verse 24. חֶמְדָּה desire, or beauty, verb. n. f. from חָמַד xix. 11.

Verse 26. After the word 'His hand,' the Chal. has added 'with an oath.' Lifting up the hand is a sign of swearing.

Verse 28. לְבַעַל פְּעוֹר to-Baal-peor, the name of a Moabite deity, with pr. לְ ii. 1.

Verse 29. We must understand אֹתוֹ after the verb וַיַּכְעִיסוּ.

מַגֵּפָה (the)plague, verb. n. f. from נָגַף to smite.

Verse 30. פִּינְחָס Phinehas, ('mouth of brass,' compounded of פִּי v. 10 and נְחָס i. q. נְחֹשֶׁת,) the son of Eleazar.

וַיְפַלֵּל and-executed-judgment, not (as in the Prayer-Book Version, following the Chal. and Syr.) '*prayed*' (i.e. interceded), a meaning which the verb never has in Piel, but only in Hithpael; Pi. 3 m. s. fut. with ו convers. from פָּלַל iv. 2.

וַיֵּעָצַר and-(so) was-stayed, Niph. 3 f. s. fut. with ו convers. from עָצַר to shut, to hold back, to restrain; see Num. xxv. 7, 8.

Verse 32. וַיֵּרַע and-it-went-ill, Kal 3 m. s. fut. with ו convers. from רָעַע ii. 9.

Verse 33. הִמְרוּ they-provoked, or made to rebel, Hiph. 3 pl. pret. from מָרָה v. 11.

רוּחוֹ his-spirit; there is a doubt here whether the affix to the noun has for its antecedent אֵל or מֹשֶׁה; the Chal. refers it to the former, for it has 'because they rebelled against His Holy Spirit.'

וַיְבַטֵּא and-he-spake-unadvisedly, Pi. 3 m. s. fut. with ו convers. from בָּטָא to babble, to talk idly. Comp. Gr. βαττολογεῖν; Lat. blaterare.

Verse 35. וַיִּתְעָרְבוּ But-they-mixed-themselves, Hithp. 3 m. pl. fut. with ו convers. from עָרַב, prop. to mix, to exchange articles of traffic, to barter, to become surety (for any one), to give a pledge; hence Gr. ἀρραβών, earnest money, Lat. *arrhabo*, a word peculiar to traders, which the Greeks and Romans seem to have borrowed from the Phœnicians, the originators of traffic; Hithp. to mingle oneself, to intermingle.

Verse 36. עֲצַבֵּיהֶם their-idols, pl. of עָצָב, (only found in the pl.,) verb. n. m. from עָצַב xvi. 4 with suff. 3 m. pl.

Verse 37. לַשֵּׁדִים to-the-idols, or devils, subst. m. pl. (found only here and in Deut. xxxii. 17), with pr. לְ ii. 1. R. שׁוּד xci. 6.

Verse 43. וַיָּמֹכּוּ and-they-were-bowed-down, or impoverished, or weakened, Kal 3 m. pl. fut. with ו convers. from מָכַךְ to melt away, to pine, to perish, only found here in Kal.

Verse 44. The LXX. and Arab. insert the word יְהוָה after וַיַּרְא.

Verse 45. Both our translations read the pl. חֲסָדָיו according to the K'ri, but the sing. number is the reading of the LXX., Vulg., and Arab.

BOOK V, Psalms CVII–CL.

PSALM CVII.

This Psalm, which is introduced into our Forms of Prayer to be used at Sea, as a thanksgiving after a storm, contains an exhortation to praise God for His goodness in watching over His creatures, and delivering them from manifold dangers. The liturgical formula (ver. 1) is found in Jer. xxxiii. 11. Verse 40 is a quotation from Job xii. 21, 24.

Verse 2. גְּאוּלֵי יְהֹוָה (the) redeemed-of-the-Lord, i. e. those who had returned from the Babylonish Captivity.

Verse 3. וּמִיָּם and-from-(the) South, or from the sea; the word is often put for the Mediterranean, which, being west of Judea, came to signify generally *the West*, when it expresses one of the cardinal points. That evidently cannot be the meaning here, where another word is used for *West*. It may perhaps signify the Red Sea, which, being to the south of Judea, might denote the south point. Bishop Hare and Dr. Kennicott read מִיָּמִין instead of וּמִיָּם.

Verse 4. The Syr. renders the word בִּישִׁימוֹן as a prop. name, 'in the desert of Assimon.'

Verse 5. רְעֵבִים Hungry, pl. of רָעֵב verb. adj. m. from רָעֵב to be hungry.

צְמֵאִים thirsty, pl. of צָמֵא verb. adj. m. from צָמֵא to be thirsty.

Verse 8. We must understand עַל before חַסְדּוֹ.

Verse 9. שֹׁקֵקָה longing, prob. (according to Gesenius) Kal pres. part. f. s. from שָׁקַק to run up and down, to seek after anything eagerly, to be greedy; although the root, according to Kimchi, is שׁוּק to desire, which in Piel doubles the last radical. He considers it an adjective, and quotes Gen. iii. 16 as an authority for rendering it 'longing.' In Mendelssohn's Beor it is stated that שָׁקְקָה comprehends the meaning of *desiring* and that of *drinking*, as if it were referable to the root שָׁקָה as well as to שׁוּק. The meaning of *watering* is certainly found in this word in Ps. lxv. 9.

Verse 11. Observe the paronomasia between הִמְרוּ and אִמְרֵי, and between עֲצַת and נָאָצוּ.

Verse 16. נְחֹשֶׁת brass, subst. com. gen. R. perhaps נָחַשׁ to shine.

וּבְרִיחֵי and-(the) bars-of, pl. constr. of בְּרִיחַ subst. m., a crossbeam, a bar, a defence to a door, with ו cop. i. 1; sometimes used metaphorically for a prince, inasmuch as he defends a state. R. בָּרַח iii. 1.

Verse 17. אֱוִלִים Fools, pl. of אֱוִיל subst. m. R. אוּל xxxviii. 6.

Verse 20. We must understand אֹתָם after the verb וַיְמַלֵּט.

מִשְּׁחִיתוֹתָם from-their-grave-pits, or pitfalls, subst. f. pl. with pr. מ ii. 3 and suff. 3 m. pl. R. שָׁחָה v. 8. The word occurs elsewhere only in Lam. iv. 20.

Verse 27. יָחוֹגּוּ They-reel-to-and-fro, or spin round and round, Kal 3 m. pl. fut. from חָגַג xlii. 5.

כַּשִּׁכּוֹר like-the-drunkard, verb. n. m. with pr. כ i. 3, from שָׁכַר lxix. 13.

Verse 29. לִדְמָמָה to-a-gentle-breeze, verb. n. f. from דָּמַם iv. 5 with pr. ל iv. 3. The only other places where the word occurs are 1 Kings xix. 12 and Job iv. 16. Comp. St. Matt. viii. 26.

For גַּלֵּיהֶם (the) waves-thereof, the Syr., Bishop Hare, and Houbigant read גַּלֵּי הַיָּם 'the waves of the sea.'

Verse 30. יִשְׁתֹּקוּ they-be-quiet, Kal 3 m. pl. fut. from שָׁתַק, found elsewhere only in Prov. xxvi. 20 and Jonah i. 11, 12.

מָחוֹז (the) haven-of, constr. of מָחוֹז subst. m., only found here. R. חוז, unused in Heb., to enclose, to surround.

Verse 33. לְצִמָּאוֹן into-dry-ground, verb. n. m. with pr. לְ ii. 1, from צָמֵא to be thirsty.

Verse 34. לִמְלֵחָה into-a-salt-marsh, (like the land around Sodom and Gomorrah,) subst. f. with pr. לְ iv. 3. R. מָלַח lx. 2.

Verse 35. לַאֲגַם־ into-a-pool-of, subst. m. with pr. לְ x. 18. R. אָגַם, according to Gesenius, to be corrupt, to be stagnant (of water); according to Fürst, to collect together.

Verse 37. כְּרָמִים vineyards, pl. of כֶּרֶם subst. f. (masc. only in Is. xxvii. 2). R. כָּרַם, unused in Heb., to be noble.

תְּבוּאָה increase, subst. f., prop. what comes in as produce, gain, increase, fruit. R. בּוֹא v. 8.

Verse 38. וּבְהֶמְתָּם and-their-cattle, abs. form sing. (used collect.) of בַּהֲמוֹת viii. 8 with ו cop. i. 1 and suff. 3 m. pl.

Verse 39. מֵעֹצֶר through-oppression, verb. n. m. from עָצַר cvii. 30 with pr. מ iii. 5.

Verse 40. בְּתֹהוּ in-(the) wilderness, or void place, subst. m. with pr. ב i. 1, desolateness, wasteness, emptiness. R. תָּהָה, unused in Heb., to be waste, desolate.

Verse 41. מֵעוֹנִי from-affliction, or after affliction, xviii. 24.

Verse 43. For וְיִתְבּוֹנְנוּ the LXX. has the sing., which is also the case in our translation of the parallel passages, Jer. ix. 12 and Hos. xiv. 9.

PSALM CVIII.

Psalm cviii is a compilation from two other Psalms, lvii. 7-11 and lx. 5-12, with a few variations to suit its immediate occasion. It is one of the Proper Psalms for Ascension Day.

Verse 2. The LXX., Vulg., Arab., and Syr. repeat the words 'my heart is fixed,' as in Ps. lvii.

כְּבוֹדִי (with) my-glory, i. e. my soul. The Syr. reads כִּנּוֹרִי for כְּבוֹדִי.

Verse 4. In Ps. lvii we find אֲדֹנָי instead of יְהוָֹה.

Verse 5. For מֵעַל the LXX. reads עַד.

Verse 7. For וַעֲנֵנוּ (to be read וַעֲנֵנוּ) the K'ri has וַעֲנֵנִי.

Verse 10. The Syr. has 'I will cry' or 'make a noise.'

Verse 12. After הֲלֹא the LXX., Syr., and some MSS. read אַתָּה, as in Ps. lx.

Verse 13. עֶזְרָת help, i. q. עֶזְרָה xxii. 20.

PSALM CIX.

In this, the last of the Psalms of imprecation, (perhaps composed by David on the occasion of his sufferings from the persecution of Saul,) the Psalmist complains of his slanderous enemies, and devotes them to destruction. It should be regarded as a Messianic Psalm, the predictions contained in it being applied by St. Peter (Acts i. 20) to the betrayers and murderers of Christ.

Verse 4. אַהֲבָתִי my-love, verb. n. f. from אָהַב to love, with suff. 1 s.

וַאֲנִי תְפִלָּה but-I-(am) prayer, i. e. give myself to prayer.

Verse 6. וְשָׂטָן and-Satan, or an adversary, verb. n. m. from שָׂטַן xxxviii. 21.

Verse 7. יֵצֵא רָשָׁע let-him-go-forth-guilty, or wicked; the Chal. has 'he shall return condemned;' the Syr. has the plur. 'and when they are judged they shall go forth condemned.'

Verse 8. פְּקֻדָּתוֹ his-office, or charge, verb. n. f. from פָּקַד viii. 5 with suff. 3 m. s. Comp. Acts i. 20.

Verse 10. We find in the LXX. ἐκβληθήτωσαν ἐκ τῶν οἰκοπέδων αὐτῶν, 'let them be cast out of their ruinous dwellings,' probably reading גֹּרְשׁוּ for דָּרְשׁוּ.

Verse 11. The LXX. has ἐξερευνησάτω, 'let him search,' as if the reading were יְבַקֵּשׁ instead of יְנַקֵּשׁ.

נוֹשֶׁה (the) extortioner, or usurer, Kal pres. part. m. s. from נָשָׁה lv. 16.

Verse 13. אַחֲרִיתוֹ his-posterity, or his latter end; the LXX. and Vulg. have 'his children;' the Syr. reads the word with the pl. suffix.

For אַחֵר the LXX., Vulg., and Arab. read אֶחָד.

For שְׁמָם the LXX., Syr., Vulg., and Arab. read שְׁמוֹ.

Verse 16. יַעַן Because, prop. a subst., purpose, intent, from the root עָנָה to purpose, to signify, but used either as a prep. on account of, or as a conj. because.

וְנִכְאֵה even-(the) broken-in, Niph. pres. part. m. s. from כָּאָה, unused in Kal, to reprove, to rebuke, to be fainthearted, to be sad.

Verse 17. קְלָלָה cursing, verb. n. f. from קָלַל xxxvii. 22.

Verse 18. כְּמַדּוֹ as-his-garment, subst. m. (with pr. כ i. 3 and suff. 3 m. s.), a garment, so called from being spread out. R. מָדַד lx. 8.

Verse 19. We must understand אֲשֶׁר before יַעְטֶה and יַחְגְּרֶהָ.

וּלְמֵזַח and-for-a-girdle, subst. m. with ו cop. i. 1 and pr. ל ii. 1. R. according to Gesenius מָזַח; according to Fürst זָחַח, unused in Heb., to bind, to tie.

Verse 20. פְּעֻלַּת (the) reward-of, or the doing of; פְּעֻלָּה signifies both *work* and *the reward* of work.

Verse 21. We must understand some such word as חֶסֶד after the verb עֲשֵׂה.

Verse 23. נֶהֱלָכְתִּי I-am-gone, more literally, am made to go hence, Niph. 1 s. pret. from הָלַךְ. The Niph. form only occurs here.

נִנְעַרְתִּי I-have-been-driven-away, Niph. 1 s. pret. from נָעַר to move to and fro, to shake; Pi. to thrust or drive out.

Verse 24. בִּרְכַּי My-knees, subst. f. dual with suff. 1 s., in the sing. found only in Is. xlv. 23. R. בָּרַךְ iii. 9.

Verse 29. כַמְעִיל as-a-mantle, subst. m., a cloak, an upper garment, with pr. כ i. 3, and the art., the Dagesh being omitted exceptionally. R. מָעַל, perhaps originally meaning to cover, hence metaph. to act covertly, to be faithless.

Verse 31. מִשֹּׁפְטֵי נַפְשׁוֹ from-those-that-judge-his-soul; the LXX. and Vulg. have 'from those that pursue *my* soul.'

PSALM CX.

In this, the most prominent of the Messianic class of Psalms, which has been appointed by the Church to be read on Christmas Day, David predicts the exaltation in heaven and the everlasting priesthood of the Messiah. This Psalm is frequently referred to in the New Testament; see St. Matt. xxii. 42–45, Acts ii. 34, 35, Heb. i. 13, &c.

Verse 1. *My Lord* is understood here to mean the Messiah.

Verse 2. מַטֵּה עֻזְּךָ (the) rod-of-Thy-strength, i. e. thy powerful rod or sceptre.

Verse 3. נְדָבֹת freenesses, or readinesses, or freewill offerings, i. e. Thy people give (devote) themselves a willing sacrifice.

בְּיוֹם חֵילֶךָ in-(the)day-of-Thy-power, or perhaps, in the day of Thy host, i. e. in the day Thou musterest Thy host to the battle.

For בְּהַדְרֵי we find in some MSS. בְּהַרְרֵי in (the) mountains of, by which we are to understand the mountains of Jerusalem.

מֵרֶחֶם more-than-(the)womb-of, or from (the) womb of.

מִשְׁחָר (the)morning, or the dawn, subst. m. (i. q. שַׁחַר), only found here.

טַל (the)dew-of, subst. m. R. טָלַל, unused in Heb., to pour down gently, to moisten.

יַלְדֻתֶךָ Thy-youth, in a collective sense = thy young men, subst. f. with suff. 2 m. s. R. יָלַד to bring forth, to beget. The Syr. has 'In the splendour of holiness have I begotten Thee as a child (son) from the womb of old.'

Verse 4. דִּבְרָתִי (the)order-of, subst. f., i. q. דָּבָר vii. 1 with Chirek-compaginis, xviii. 32.

מַלְכִּי־צֶדֶק Melchizedek, (king of righteousness, compounded of the old construct form of מֶלֶךְ ii. 2 and צֶדֶק iv. 2,) prop. name of a king of Salem (Jerusalem) and priest of Jehovah.

Verse 5. The Chal. has 'the majesty of the Lord upon Thy right hand.'

Verse 6. מָלֵא He-hath-filled-with, Kal 3 m. s. pret. The Chal. supplies 'the earth.' Some consider it as an adjective governing גְוִיּוֹת, and translate '(it, i. e. the field of battle, or the land, is) full of corpses.'

גְוִיּוֹת (the)dead-bodies, pl. of גְּוִיָּה subst. f., body, prop. belly, from the unused root גָּוָה, of the same sense as גָּבַב to be elevated, to rise up like a lump.

רֹאשׁ is sing. but used apparently in a collective sense for the Jewish nation. The LXX. and both our translations have the word in the plur.

All the ancient interpreters, except St. Jerome, seem to have read רַבִּים in the plur. Luther has über große Lande.

Verse 7. יָרוּם is the reading of six MSS. and of the Syriac.

PSALM CXI.

The Psalmist here praises God for all the great and glorious works which He had done for His people. It is an acrostic or alphabetical Psalm; but, unlike the twenty-fifth and others of the same class, the alphabetical arrangement is preserved entire. It is one of the Proper Psalms for Easter Day. See Introduction to Ps. ix.

Verse 5. טֶרֶף food, lit. prey, the spoil of the Egyptians.

Verse 9. פְּדוּת redemption, verb. n. f. from פָּדָה to redeem.

Verse 10. שֵׂכֶל understanding, or success, verb. n. m. from שָׂכַל ii. 10.

PSALM CXII.

In this Psalm, which, like the last, is alphabetical, the Psalmist describes the blessedness of the man who feareth the Lord, and the envy of the wicked on beholding the happiness of the righteous. See Introduction to Ps. ix.

Verse 1. Before יָרֵא we must understand the pron. אֲשֶׁר, as well as before חָפֵץ.

Verse 4. This verse contains an allusion to what happened in Egypt, when the Israelites had *light* in their dwellings, while the land was wrapt in darkness.

Verse 5. טוֹב־אִישׁ חוֹנֵן A-good-man-sheweth-favour, or perhaps, 'Happy (is) the man who,' &c.

דְּבָרָיו his-affairs; Luther has ſeine Sachen, but the LXX. and our Prayer-Book Version have 'his words.'

Verse 7. מִשְּׁמוּעָה Because-of-tidings, verb. n. f. from שָׁמַע to hear, with pr. מ ii. 3.

PSALM CXIII.

This Psalm, (which has been appointed by the Church as one of the Proper Psalms for Easter Day,) contains an exhortation to praise God for His greatness and for His goodness and condescension to mankind. Psalms cxiii–cxviii are called 'the Hallel,' which was sung at the greater Jewish Feasts, especially the

Passover and the Feast of Tabernacles. It is commonly supposed that a portion of the Hallel was 'the hymn' which our Lord and His apostles sang (St. Matt. xxvi. 30, St. Mark xiv. 26) after His last Passover. Verses 7 and 8 are almost word for word from the Song of Hannah (1 Sam. ii. 6, 8).

Verse 5. הַמַּגְבִּיהִי who-exalteth (himself), Hiph. pres. part. m. s. (poet.) from גָּבַהּ x. 4 with Chirek-compaginis and ה prefixed as the relat. A repetition, without example elsewhere, of the so-called Chirek-compaginis is peculiar to this Psalm; see xviii. 32.

Verse 6. הַמַּשְׁפִּילִי Who-stoopeth-down, Hiph. pres. part. m. s. (poet.) from שָׁפֵל xviii. 28 with Chirek-compaginis and ה prefixed as the relat.

Verse 7. מֵאַשְׁפֹּת from-(the) dunghill, subst. m. with pr. מ viii. 6. R. perhaps שָׁפַת lxviii. 14. The sing. of the word is not found in the Old Testament, but it occurs in the Mishna.

Verse 8. The LXX., Vulg., Syr., and Arab. read לְהוֹשִׁיבוֹ.

Verse 9. עֲקֶרֶת (the) barren-woman, verb. adj. f. from עָקַר to root out, to pluck up, to be barren.

PSALM CXIV.

This Psalm commemorates the Exodus from Egypt, and refers in joyful terms to the many wonderful works which were then wrought on behalf of God's chosen people. It was one of the Psalms used by the Jews in their service of the Feast of the Passover, and is appointed by the Church to be read on Easter Day. The LXX., Vulg., Arab., Syr., and Æth. put Psalms cxiv and cxv into one, and then divide Psalm cxvi into two.

Verse 1. לֹעֵז speaking-strangely, Kal pres. part. m. s. from לָעַז to speak barbarously, in a foreign tongue; not met with elsewhere in the Old Testament, though of frequent occurrence in Rabbinical works. The LXX. has λαοῦ βαρβάρου.

Verse 2. *Judah* is here *fem.* in accordance with the general principle that *lands* and *nations* are fem.

Verse 3. יִסֹּב was-turned, Kal (Gesenius), Niph. (Fürst) 3 m. s. fut. from סָבַב.

Verse 4. הֶהָרִים The-mountains, i. e. Sinai and the adjoining hills.

Verse 5. The art. used here and prefixed to the following nouns indicates the vocative.

Verse 8. חַלָּמִישׁ (the)flint, subst. m. R. prob. חָלַם to be hard, to be firm.

In לְמַעְיְנוֹ we have a genuine instance of the old termination of the stat. constr. This final Cholem-compaginis, however, is by no means so widely used as the final Chirek. With the exception of this place and Num. xxiv. 3, 15, בְּנוֹ בְעֹר, it is found only in the phrase חַיְתוֹ אֶרֶץ (or הַשָּׂדֶה), which first occurs in Gen. i. 24.

PSALM CXV.

This Psalm, which in all the ancient versions, except the Chaldee, is united with the preceding, is by some thought to have been composed by Jehoshaphat. It contains an exhortation to confidence in God because He is truly glorious, and idols are but vanity. Verse 2 is a quotation from Ps. lxxix. 10.

Verse 1. וְעַל is the reading of several MSS. and of all the ancient versions.

Verse 7. יְמִישׁוּן they-handle, Hiph. 3 m. pl. fut. with ן parag. from מוּשׁ i. q. מָשַׁשׁ to touch, to feel. Comp. Gr. μάσσω.

Verse 9. The LXX., Syr., Vulg., and Arab. read בֵּית יִשְׂרָאֵל. For the imperatives בְּטַח and בִּטְחוּ all the ancient interpreters have the preterites בָּטַח and בָּטְחוּ both in this and the two following verses.

Verse 10. בֵּית אַהֲרֹן O-house-of-Aaron, i.e. the Priests and Levites.

The verb בָּטְחוּ is plur. because בַּיִת is a collective noun.

PSALM CXVI.

In this Psalm, perhaps composed upon Hezekiah's recovery, the Psalmist professes his love and duty to God for his deliverance, and studies to be thankful. The Aramaisms in verses 7, 12, 19 are evidences of its belonging to a late period of Hebrew history. The LXX. and Vulg. divide this Psalm into two, Pss. cxiv and cxv according to their division, of which Ps. cxv begins with what we reckon ver. 10 of Ps. cxvi.

Verse 1. The LXX., Vulg., Syr., and Arab. omit the suff. of קוֹלִי.

Verse 2. The word אֵלָיו is to be understood after אֶקְרָא.

Verse 3. וּמְצָרֵי and-(the)pains-of, pl. constr. of מֵצַר verb. n. m. from צָרַר iii. 2. The word occurs elsewhere only in Ps. cxviii. 5 and Lam. i. 3.

Verse 4. אָנָּה I-beseech-Thee, interj. of entreaty, compounded of אָה and נָא vii. 10. The word is written thus, with ה instead of א, in five other places. Before אָנָּה we must understand לֵאמֹר.

Verse 6. יְהוֹשִׁיעַ, unusual form for יֹשִׁיעַ.

Verse 7. לִמְנוּחָיְכִי unto-thy-rest, subst. m. pl., i. q. מְנוּחָה xxiii. 2, (found only here,) with pr. לְ iv. 3 and Aramaic form of suff. 2 f. s.

Verse 8. For חִלַּצְתָּ 2nd pers. the LXX. gives the verb in the 3rd pers.

Verse 12. תַּגְמוּלוֹהִי His-benefits, subst. m. pl. (i.q. גְּמוּל) with suff. 3 m. s. R. גָּמַל vii. 5. This Aramaic pl. suff. occurs only here in Biblical Hebrew.

Verse 16. The pr. לְ instead of the acc. after the trans. verb פִּתַּחְתָּ is an Aramaic construction, and one of the signs of the later date of the Psalm.

PSALM CXVII.

This very short Psalm, which is in many MSS. connected with the following, and which somewhat resembles Ps. c, was perhaps designed to be a chorus or doxology to a longer ode. It contains an exhortation to praise God for His mercy and truth. Many think it was used at the close of the public services of the Temple.

Verse 1. הָאֻמִּים ye-peoples, pl. of אֻמָּה subst. f. (with the art. i. 1), found only, besides this passage, in Gen. xxv. 16 and Num. xxv. 15, where the form תֹ instead of יִ is used. R. אָמַם iii. 7.

PSALM CXVIII.

This Psalm, probably composed for the opening of the Second Temple (Ezra vi. 15, 16), is entirely one of thanksgiving. It has been appointed by the Church as one of the Proper Psalms for Easter Day, and was the favourite Psalm of Luther. The twenty-second verse is frequently quoted in the New Testament; see St. Matthew xxi. 42, St. Mark xii. 10, Ephes. ii. 20. Verse 1 is literally from Ps. cvi. 1, and ver. 14 (like Is. xii. 2) is taken from Ex. xv. 2.

Verse 2. The LXX. and Arab. have 'house of Israel.'

The LXX. and Arab. repeat in this and the two following verses the words 'that He is good.'

Verse 7. The ב of בְּעֹזְרָי is the so-called *Beth essentiae;* see xxxiv. 5.

Verse 12. כִּדְבֹרִים like-bees, pl. of דְּבוֹרָה subst. f. with pr. כ ii. 9. R. perhaps דָּבַר ii. 5.

דֹּעֲכוּ they-were-extinguished, Pu. 3 pl. pret. from דָּעַךְ to be extinguished; though most of the ancient versions render the verb in the sense of *to burn.* Luther has ſie bämpfen.

קוֹצִים thorns, pl. of קוֹץ subst. m., so called from the idea of cutting and wounding. R. קוץ i. q. קצץ to cut.

Verse 14. וְזִמְרָת and-song, poet. form for זִמְרָה lxxxi. 3; or perhaps for זִמְרָתִי, as possibly the vowel Kamets under ר shews that the suff. is understood.

Verse 16. רוֹמֵמָה is-exalted. Gesenius and Fürst consider this as Kal part. f. from רָמַם, though it may possibly be either Palel 3 f. s. pret. or Palel part. from רום with loss of the מ. The LXX., Vulg., Syr., and Arab. have 'hath exalted me.'

Verse 22. פִּנָּה (the) corner, subst. f. R. פָּנָה ii. 12.

Verse 25. We must understand לֵאמֹר before אָנָּה.

There is no doubt that this is the passage from whence the joyful exclamation was taken, which was shouted by the multitude who accompanied our Lord on His journey to Jerusalem (St. Matt. xxi. 9). The word 'Ωσαννά is a contraction of the two Hebrew terms נָא and הוֹשִׁיעָה.

Verse 27. The LXX. has συστήσασθε ἑορτὴν ἐν τοῖς πυκάζουσιν; Luther has Schmücket das Feſt mit Maien, u. ſ. w.

PSALM CXIX.

This Psalm is the most extended alphabetical poem in the Bible. It consists of one hundred and seventy-six verses, and is divided into twenty-two portions, which are severally headed in the English Bible by the successive letters of the Hebrew alphabet; and each part comprises eight verses, all beginning with the

Hebrew letter which forms the heading. In Lam. iii a similar arrangement is adopted, but there the stanzas consist only of three verses, each beginning with the same letter. In every verse but one—ver. 122—there is direct reference to the Law under some one of the ten names: *word, saying, testimony, way, judgment, precepts, commandment, law, statutes,* and *faithfulness* (or, according to another reading, *righteousness*). The first clause of ver. 136 is from Lam. iii. 48. See Introduction to Ps. ix.

Verse 3. At the commencement of the verse we must understand אַשְׁרֵי as well as the pron. אֲשֶׁר before לֹא.

Verse 5. אַחֲלַי O-that, a particle of entreaty, compounded of אָח and לִי=לוֹ, found only here and in 2 Kings v. 3.

Verse 9. For כִּדְבָרְךָ many MSS. have the plur., which is the case also in verses 16, 17, 25, 28, 42, and 101.

Verse 11. For אִמְרָתֶךָ the LXX., Vulg., and Syr. have the plur. here and in verses 103, 148, and 162.

Verse 14. For כְּעַל Kennicott, with the Syr., reads מֵעַל 'more than in.'

Verse 18. גַּל Open-Thou, or reveal, Pi. 2 m. s. imp. apoc. for גַּלֵּה from גָּלָה.

Verse 20. גָּרְסָה breaketh, Kal 3 f. s. pret. from גָּרַס to break in pieces, to crush, to be broken. The word occurs elsewhere only in Lam. iii. 16.

לְתַאֲבָה for-(the) longing, subst. f. with pr. לְ ii. 1, found only here instead of תַאֲוָה. R. תָּאַב (i. q. אָוָה x. 3), found only in Ps. cxix. 40, 174.

Verse 22. גַּל Remove; Dr. Perowne, Hupfeld, and Delitzsch consider this word the same as in ver. 18, from גָּלָה; though, according to Dr. Phillips, Gesenius, Hengstenberg, and Fürst, it is Kal 2 m. s. imp. from גָּלַל.

Verse 24. שַׁעֲשֻׁעָי my-delight, subst. m. pl. with suff. 1 s. R. שָׁעַע xciv. 19.

Verse 28. דָּלְפָה melteth, or droppeth, Kal 3 f. s. pret. from דָּלַף, found only here, Job xvi. 20, and Eccles. x. 18.

מִתּוּגָה for-heaviness, verb. n. f. from יָגָה xiii. 3 with pr. מ ii. 3.

Verse 30. After שִׁוִּיתִי there is an ellipsis of some such word as לְנֶגְדִּי, which is supplied in Ps. xvi. 8.

Verse 38. אֲשֶׁר לְיִרְאָתֶךָ who-(is devoted)to-Thy-fear; or perhaps, 'which (promise) is for Thy fear,' i. e. either is given to them that fear Thee, or which has the fear of Thee for its aim and object.

Verse 39. יָגֹרְתִּי I-fear, Kal 1 s. pret. from יָגֹר i. q. גּוּר.

Verse 41. The LXX. renders this verse καὶ ἔλθοι ἐπ' ἐμὲ τὸ ἔλεός σου, sing.; but the Targum and Jerome rightly (comp. ver. 77 and Is. lxiii. 7) have the plur. חֲסָדֶיךָ.

Verse 43. לְמִשְׁפָּטֶיךָ is the reading of the LXX., Syr., Chal., and Vulg.

Verse 45. בָרְחָבָה at-liberty, or at large, i. e. tranquilly and without anxiety, lit. in a wide place.

Verse 50. נֶחָמָתִי my-comfort, verb. n. f. from נָחַם xxiii. 4 with suff. 1 s. Comp. Job vi. 10, the only other place where the word occurs.

Verse 53. זַלְעָפָה Burning indignation; the LXX. has ἀθυμία, 'deep dejection,' Vulg. *defectio*.

Verse 56. Kennicott would read with the LXX. and Bishop Hare זֹאת הָיְתָה־לִּי נֶחָמָה 'This was my comfort.'

Verse 60. הִתְמַהְמָהְתִּי delayed, Hithp. 1 s. pret. from מָהַהּ or מָהְמָהּ, prob. to deny, to refuse, found only in Hithp. to delay, to linger.

Verse 62. חֲצוֹת־ (At)halves-of, Kal inf. constr. (used as a subst.) from חָצָה to separate, to divide.

Verse 67. שֹׁגֵג went-astray, or was ignorant, Kal pres. part. m. s. from שָׁגַג to wander, to go astray, to err, to be ignorant.

Verse 68. The LXX. and Syr. insert the word יְהוָה after אַתָּה.

Verse 69. טָפְלוּ have-forged, Kal 3 pl. pret. from טָפַל, (not often found,) to patch, to sew together, fig. to frame (lies). שֶׁקֶר a-lie, i. e. a false accusation.

Verse 70. טָפַשׁ Is-fat, Kal 3 m. s. pret., only found in this passage, to be fat, to be stupid. The LXX., Syr., Arab., and Vulg. have 'is made cheese like milk.'

Verse 78. עִוְּתוּנִי they-have-perverted-me, Pi. 3 pl. pret. with suff. 1 s. from עָוַת, not used in Kal, to be bent; Pi. to bend, to pervert, to falsify.

Verse 79. The K'thiv is וְיֵדְעוּ (to be read וְיֵדְעוּ), and the K'ri וִידְעֵי.

Verse 83. בְּקִיטוֹר in-(the)smoke, subst. m. with pr. בְ i. 1. R. קָטַר lxvi. 15. For בְּקִיטוֹר the LXX. and Vulg. have 'in the frost.' The skin bottles of the East (see Josh. ix. 4) are often hung up near the roof, where they become blackened with smoke, and sometimes shrivelled with heat; hence they well represent one whom affliction has made an object of pity rather than of attraction.

Verse 85. שִׂיחוֹת, instead of שִׂיחוֹת, is apparently the reading of the LXX.

Verse 91. There is an ellipsis of some such particle as עַד before הַיּוֹם.

Verse 96. תִּכְלָה perfection, verb. n. f. from כָּלָה ii. 9. The word occurs nowhere else.

Verse 97. שִׂיחָתִי my-meditation, verb. n. f. from שִׂיחַ with suff. 1 s.

Verse 98. תְּחַכְּמֵנִי make-me-wise; prob. 3 pers. f. s. and not 2 pers. m. s. fut. from חָכַם to be wise. A fem. sing. of the verb with a plur. noun gives a collective idea to the noun.

Verse 103. נִמְלְצוּ sweet-are, Niph. 3 pl. pret. from מָלַץ to be smooth, to be sweet, only found here. For Dagesh euphonic see Gesenius' Grammar, Sect. 20.

לְחִכִּי unto-my-taste, or my palate, subst. m. with pr. לְ ii. 1 and suff. 1 s. R. חָנַךְ to be narrow.

אִמְרָתֶךָ the sing. to be taken in a collective sense for אִמְרָתֶיךָ.

Verse 106. Some such noun as שְׁבוּעָתִי is to be understood after וָאֲקַיֵּמָה.

Verse 109. The LXX., Syr., Vulg., and Luther have 'in my hands,' instead of 'in my hand.'

Verse 111. הֵמָּה inexactly for הֵנָּה.

Verse 113. סֵעֲפִים (vain) thoughts, or perhaps divided persons, i.e. of a divided mind, doubters, sceptics, plur. of סָעֵף verb. adj. from סָעַף to divide.

Verse 116. מִשִּׂבְרִי of-my-hope, verb. n. m. from שָׂבַר civ. 27 with pr. מ ii. 3 and suff. 1 s.

Verse 118. סָלִיתָ Thou-hast-made-light-of, Kal 2 m. s. pret. from סָלָה to lift up, to weigh, to despise; in Kal found only here, in Pi. in Lam. i. 15, and in Pu. in Job xxviii. 16, 19.

תַּרְמִיתָם their-deceit, subst. f. with suff. 3 m. pl. R. רָמָה v. 7.

Verse 119. סִיגִים dross, pl. of סִיג subst. m., prop. what is separated from or removed, hence the refuse of metal, scoria, dross. R. סוּג xxxv. 4. The reading of the LXX. was probably שׁוֹגִים 'those that err.'

For הִשְׁבַּתָּ Kennicott, with Bishop Hare and Houbigant, would read חָשַׁבְתָּ 'Thou esteemest.' The LXX., Vulg., and Arab. have the 1st pers. חָשַׁבְתִּי.

Verse 120. סָמַר trembleth, or has stood up, Kal 3 m. s. pret., to stand on end, used of the hair, hence used of a man seized with terror.

Verse 128. Possibly the reading should be פִּקּוּדֶיךָ.

The second כֹּל is wanting in the LXX., Vulg., Syr., Arab., and Æth.

Verse 130. פֵּתַח־ (The) unfolding-of, or opening, or revelation, verb. n. m. from פָּתַח v. 10.

Verse 131. פָּעַרְתִּי I-opened, Kal 1 s. pret. from פָּעַר. The phrase *to open the mouth* is an expression denoting longing desire, as in Job xxix. 23.

יָאָבְתִּי I-longed, Kal 1 s. pret. from יָאַב, not found elsewhere.

Verse 137. וְיָשָׁר מִשְׁפָּטֶיךָ and-upright-(are) Thy-judgments; a sing. predicate prefixed when the noun is in the plur.; or perhaps, 'and upright (in) Thy judgments.'

Verse 143. וּמָצוֹק and-anguish, verb. n. m. with ו cop. i. 1, from צוּק to be narrow, compressed.

Verse 147. בַּנֶּשֶׁף in-the-dawning-of-the-morning, subst. m. with pr. בּ i. 1; the evening or morning twilight when a colder gale blows. R. נָשַׁף to blow.

For לִדְבָרֶיךָ the K'ri, Targum, Syr., and Jerome substitute the sing. as in verses 74, 81, 114.

Verse 149. כְּמִשְׁפָּטֶךָ defective plur. as in ver. 43.

Verse 155. רָחוֹק ... יְשׁוּעָה a masc. predicate prefixed, the noun being fem.

Verse 160. רֹאשׁ־דְּבָרְךָ (The) beginning-of, or *the sum* of; Luther has 'Thy Word is nothing but truth.'

The LXX., Syr., Vulg., Chal., and Arab. have מִשְׁפְּטֵי.

Verse 161. K'thiv מִדְּבָרֶיךָ (to be read מִדְּבָרֶיךָ), K'ri מדברך.

Verse 165. מִכְשׁוֹל a-stumbling-block, verb. n. m. from כָּשַׁל to fall, to stumble.

Verse 175. The LXX., Chal., Vulg., and Arab. read וּמִשְׁפָּטֶיךָ.

Verse 176. כְּשֶׂה like-a-sheep, subst. com. gen., used as the sing. of צֹאן viii. 8 with pr. כּ i. 3.

PSALM CXX.

This and the fourteen Psalms which follow it are entitled *Songs of Degrees*, or *of goings up*, and are by some persons supposed to have been sung either by the Jews as they went up to Jerusalem at the three great annual festivals, or by the pilgrims who were returning from Babylon to the Holy Land. Others imagine the word מַעֲלוֹת to denote particular musical tones, *elevated* or *loud tones*, and that these Psalms were to be sung in a loud or grand chorus; and others again that the word signifies *excellence*, and that they are so called to denote the excellence of their composition.

Verse 1. הַמַּעֲלוֹת the-goings-up, pl. of מַעֲלָה verb. n. f. from עָלָה i. 3. Luther has 'A Song in high chorus.'

Verse 2. וּמִלָּשׁוֹן is the reading of ten MSS., the LXX., Syr., Vulg., and Arab. (The abs. is here used for the constr.)

Verse 3. What shall He give unto thee, and what shall He add unto thee, O tongue of deceit? Or, What shall the deceitful tongue give unto thee? or, What shall it profit thee?

Verse 4. The particle עִם is sometimes one of similitude, as in Ps. cvi. 6, 'We have sinned *like* as our fathers.'

רְתָמִים broom, not, as in the English Version, (following Jerome,) juniper, pl. of רֹתֶם subst. com. gen. (fem. only in 1 Kings xix. 4); *Genista monosperma*, a shrub growing in the deserts of Arabia with yellowish flowers and a bitter root. The wood has the power of retaining heat a long time. R. רָתַם to bind. Hupfeld would read אָהֳלֵי instead of נַחֲלֵי, and would either understand רְתָמִים as the name of a tribe, or a locality in which the broom was plentiful (as Rithmah, Num. xxxiii. 18, 19), or else that by *tents of broom* are meant poor wretched hovels made of broom.

Verse 5. אוֹיָה Woe-is, an interj. of lamentation, only found here, with the termination הָ.

מֶשֶׁךְ Meshech, a barbarous people inhabiting the Moschian mountains between Iberia, Armenia, and Colchis. The LXX. and several ancient versions render the word not as a proper name, but (as if from the verb מָשַׁךְ to draw out) *for a length of time.*

קֵדָר Kedar, (black skin, black skinned man; R. קָדַר to be of a dirty blackish colour,) prop. name of a son of Ishmael, (see Gen. xxv. 13,) and of an Arabian tribe sprung from him.

Verse 6. The pron. לֹה is pleonastic.
The LXX., Vulg., Syr., and Arab. read the pl. שֹׂנְאַי.

Verse 7. There is an ellipsis of the noun אִישׁ after אֲנִי.

PSALM CXXI.

In this Psalm, which has been adopted into our Service for the Thanksgiving of Women after Childbirth, the Psalmist describes the safety of the godly who put their trust in the protection of the Almighty. In the third verse a new speaker is introduced, who addresses to the previous one the remainder of the Psalm. This is the only one of the Songs of Degrees that is inscribed שִׁיר לַמַּעֲלוֹת and not שִׁיר הַמַּעֲלוֹת.

Verse 1. I will lift up mine eyes unto the mountains (i.e. the mountain group of Zion) from whence cometh my help. Or, Shall I lift up mine eyes to the mountains? Whence should my help come?

Verse 3. רַגְלֶיךָ is the reading of several MSS. and of the Arab.

וְאַל is the reading of several MSS. and of all the ancient versions except the Chal.

Verse 7. Luther understands this verse and the next as expressive of *desire* instead of *assurance.*

PSALM CXXII.

The Psalmist here expresses his joy at the opportunity afforded him of going to the house of God; he then proceeds to describe the glory of Jerusalem, and to offer up a prayer for her peace and welfare. In ver. 3 there occurs the first abbreviation of אֲשֶׁר into שֶׁ.

Verse 1. The words *of David* are omitted in the LXX., Syr., Vulg., and Arab.

Verse 3. Here, and in the following verses, the praises of Jerusalem are sung.

For הַבְּנוּיָה Luther has Jerusalem ist gebauet.

שֶׁחֻבְּרָה־ which-(is) joined, Pu. 3 f. s. pret. from חָבַר xxxviii. 6 with the relat. pron. שֶׁ=אֲשֶׁר prefixed.

The reflexive pron. לָהּ is used emphatically, as in Ps. cxx. 6.

Verse 5. יָשְׁבוּ are-set, lit. do sit; the Chal. has 'were placed.'

Verse 6. יִשְׁלָיוּ they-shall-prosper, poet. for יִשְׁלוּ Kal 3 m. pl. fut. from שָׁלָה or שָׁלוּ to be safe, secure. Comp. Lat. *salv-us, salus.* Note the play of words on שָׁלוֹם, יִשְׁלוּ, and in the next verse שַׁלְוָה, perhaps also with an allusion to the name of Jerusalem.

Verse 7. בְּחֵילֵךְ within-thy-rampart, subst. m. with pr. בּ i. 1 and suff. 2 f. s. R. חוּל x. 5.

שַׁלְוָה prosperity, subst. f. R. שָׁלָה cxxii. 6.

Verse 8. The part. נָא is redundant.

PSALM CXXIII.

We have here an expression of confidence in God, with a prayer for the deliverance of the godly from the insolence of their adversaries.

Verse 2. שִׁפְחָה a-maiden, subst. f. R. prob. שָׁפַח to be attached to, to be associated with.

גְּבִרְתָּהּ her-mistress, subst. f. with suff. 3 f. s.; abs. form גְּבֶרֶת. R. גָּבַר xii. 5.

Verse 4. הַשַּׁאֲנַנִּים those-that-are-at-ease, i. e. those whom affluence had made careless and insolent; the LXX. has τοῖς εὐθηνοῦσι; pl. of שַׁאֲנָן verb. adj. m. from שָׁאַן to be quiet, not used in Kal.

לִגְאֵיוֹנִים of-(the)proud, (i. e. the Assyrian); pl., according to the K'thiv, of גְּאֶיוֹן adj. m. with pr. לְ iv. 3. R. גָּאָה x. 2. The K'ri reads לִגְאֵי יוֹנִים 'the proud ones of the oppressors.'

PSALM CXXIV.

In this Psalm, which in the LXX., Syr., Vulg., and Arab. is anonymous, the Church blesses God for a miraculous deliverance from her enemies.

Verse 2. אָדָם men, used collectively.

Verse 3. אֲזַי Then, adv. demonstr., i. q. אָז ii. 5, compounded of זַי=זֶה and אָ. It occurs nowhere but in this and the two following verses of this Psalm.

Verse 5. הַזֵּידוֹנִים the-proudly-swelling, pl. of זֵידוֹן verb. adj. m. from זוּד xix. 14 with art. prefixed. The word is an ἅπαξ λεγόμενον.

PSALM CXXV.

The Psalmist here speaks of the safety of such as trust in God, and concludes by a prayer for the godly and against the wicked.

Verse 1. Before לֹא־יִמּוֹט the pron. אֲשֶׁר must be understood; the antecedent to which is either הַר־צִיּוֹן, or הַבֹּטְחִים taken distributively.

The LXX. and Vulg. have 'They that trust in the Lord are as Mount Zion; He that inhabiteth Jerusalem shall not be moved for ever,' as if they considered the first word of the next verse to belong to this, and reading יוֹשֵׁב for יֵשֵׁב. Luther has Die auf den Herrn hoffen, die werden nicht fallen, sondern ewiglich bleiben, wie der Berg Zion.

Verse 3. יָנוּחַ shall-rest, i. e. lie heavy, so as to oppress.

שֵׁבֶט (the) rod-of, i. e. the power of.

גּוֹרַל הַצַּדִּיקִים (the) lot-(or country) of-the-righteous, i. e. the Holy Land itself.

בְּעַוְלָתָה unto-iniquity, poet. for עַוְלָה xxxvii. 1.

Verse 5. עֲקַלְקַלּוֹתָם their-crooked (ways), verb. adj. fem. pl. with suff. 3 m. pl.) from עָקַל, not used in Kal, to twist, to pervert. The word occurs, besides this place, only in Judges v. 6.

PSALM CXXVI.

This Psalm, (by some supposed to have been written by Ezra,) contains an acknowledgment of God's mercy in the restoration of many of the captives to their native land, concluding with a prayer for the safe return of the remainder of the exiles. The first part of ver. 3 is from Joel ii. 21.

Verse 1. שִׁיבַת (the) captivity-of, constr. of שִׁיבָה subst. f., i. q. שְׁבוּת, which is found in some MSS.; i. e. those who were led away captive from Zion. The abstract noun is put for the concrete. R. שׁוּב vi. 5. (Or, 'When returned the returning of Zion.')

כְּחֹלְמִים like-them-that-dream, i. e. we could scarcely believe it.

Verse 2. שְׂחוֹק laughter, verb. n. m. from שָׂחַק to laugh.

הִגְדִּיל hath-magnified, used adverbially when followed by another verb in the infinitive.

Verse 4. We have here a prayer for the return of those Jews who still remained in captivity.

The K'thiv is שְׁבוּתֵנוּ (to be read שְׁבִיתֵנוּ), and the K'ri שביתנו.

בַּנֶּגֶב in-the-south, subst. m. (with pr. ב i. 1), a dry, parched quarter, the south, so called from its dryness and heat. R. נָגַב, unused in Heb., to be dried up.

Verse 6. מֶשֶׁךְ־ a-handful-of, or a drawing out of, or a scattering of, verb. n. m. from מָשַׁךְ to draw. The word occurs only here and in Job xxviii. 18.

אֲלֻמֹּתָיו his-sheaves, pl. of אֲלֻמָּה subst. f. with suff. 3 m. s. R. אָלַם xxxi. 19.

PSALM CXXVII.

In this Psalm, (which is used in our Service for the Thanksgiving of Women after Childbirth,) the Psalmist declares that without God's blessing all human efforts and precautions are in vain. This and the seventy-second are the only two Psalms ascribed to Solomon; in the LXX. it is anonymous; in the Syr. it is said to have been spoken by David concerning Solomon.

Verse 2. מַשְׁכִּימֵי being-early-of, Hiph. pres. part. m. pl. (constr.) from שָׁכַם, only used in Hiph., virtually an adv. *early* when joined to another verb.

הָעֲצָבִים the-sorrows, pl. of עֶצֶב or עָצָב verb. n. m. from עָצַב xvi. 4 with the art. (see i. 1).

For כֵּן the LXX. and Vulg. read כִּי.

For יְדִידוֹ (sing.) the LXX., Vulg., Syr., and Arab. have the plur.

שֵׁנָא in-sleep, (an adverbial accusative like עֶרֶב, לַיְלָה, בֹּקֶר,) lxxvi. 6 with Aramaic termination for שֵׁנָה. Luther has denn seinen Freunden giebt er es schlafend.

Verse 3. שָׂכָר reward, verb. n. m. from שָׂכַר to hire. We should understand יְהוָה after שָׂכָר.

Verse 4. בְּנֵי הַנְּעוּרִים sons-of the-youth, i. e. children in the vigour of youth.

Verse 5. אַשְׁפָּתוֹ his-quiver, subst. f. (with suff. 3 m. s.), perhaps so called from the idea of hiding. R. אָשַׁף, unused in Heb., which appears to have had originally the meaning of covering, hiding, and laying up.

יְדַבְּרוּ they-shall-subdue, or destroy, or shall speak with, pl. of יְדַבֵּר ii. 5.

PSALM CXXVIII.

In this Psalm, which is used in our Marriage Service, the Psalmist describes the manifold blessings of those who fear God.

Verse 3. In אֶשְׁתְּךָ we find Seghol under א, the usual punctuation being אִשְׁתְּךָ.

פֹּרִיָּה fruitful, for פָּרָה Kal pres. part. f. s. from פָּרָה i. 3.

כִּשְׁתִלֵי like-shoots-of, pl. constr. of שָׁתִיל verb. n. m. from שָׁתַל i. 3 with pr. כ ii. 9.

Verse 5. וּרְאֵה and-thou-shalt-see, or, and see thou; by a sudden change the imperat. is put for the fut.

PSALM CXXIX.

This Psalm, which somewhat resembles Ps. cxxiv, contains an exhortation to praise God for deliverance from many afflictions, and concludes by a curse upon the haters of the Church.

Verse 1. The Chal. and Syr. have 'Many have been my adversaries.'

Israel is here mentioned as an individual.

Verse 3. גַּבִּי my-back, subst. m. with suff. 1 s. R. גָּבַב to be curved, to be hollow like an arch or vault. Comp. Lat. *gibbus;* Ger. Giebel, Gipfel; and Eng. *gable.*

לְמַעֲנוֹתָם (to be read לְמַעֲנוֹתָם) their-furrows, pl. of מַעֲנָה, subst. f. with pr. לְ ii. 1 and suff. 3 m. pl. R. עָנָה ix. 13. The word only occurs here and in the sing. in 1 Sam. xiv. 14. The K'ri is למעניתם.

Verse 6. שֶׁקַּדְמַת that-afore, constr. of קִדְמָה subst. f., beginning, origin, with the relat. pron. שֶׁ i.q. אֲשֶׁר prefixed; in the constr. state it becomes a prep. R. קָדַם xvii. 13.

שָׁלַף it-groweth-up, Kal 3 m. s. pret., lit. ere it has unsheathed; the LXX. has πρὸ τοῦ ἐκσπασθῆναι, 'before it is drawn out of its sheath.'

Verse 7. וְחִצְנוֹ and-his-bosom, or, according to some, 'his arm,' subst. m. with suff. 3 m. s. R. חָצַן, unused in Heb., according to Gesenius, to be strong; according to Fürst, to enclose, to surround.

מְעַמֵּר he-that-bindeth-sheaves, Pi. pres. part. m. s. from עָמַר, unused in Kal, to bind closely together.

PSALM CXXX.

This Psalm is a cry to God for the forgiveness of sin; it is the sixth of the penitential Psalms (see Psalm vi), and is appointed to be used in the Service on Ash-Wednesday. It is by some persons thought to have been composed by David on the occasion of his repentance for his sin with Bathsheba, though others suppose it to have been written by Ezra. In verses 1–6 the Psalmist speaks *in the name of* Israel, in verses 7, 8 *to* Israel.

Verse 1. Deep waters are used in Scripture as an emblem of affliction both of body and mind.

Verse 2. קַשֻּׁבוֹת attentive, fem. pl. of קַשֻּׁב verb. adj. from קָשַׁב v. 3. The word occurs elsewhere only in 2 Chron. vi. 40 and vii. 15.

Verse 4. הַסְּלִיחָה forgiveness, verb. n. f. from סָלַח xxv. 11. This word occurs besides only in Neh. ix. 17 and Dan. ix. 9.

The LXX. seems to have read שִׁמְךָ, the Vulg. תּוֹרָה, and the Chal. תֵּרָאֶה for תִּוָּרֵא.

Verse 6. Luther has ' from one morning watch to another.'

PSALM CXXXI.

This Psalm contains a profession of humility, and an exhortation to Israel to trust in God.

PSALM CXXXII.

This Psalm, which has been appointed as one of the Proper Psalms for Christmas Day, and which was perhaps composed by Solomon on the occasion of the dedication of the Temple, contains a prayer that God would remember His promises to David and to his seed. Verses 8–10 form a part of the prayer which Solomon offered at the dedication of the Temple. See 2 Chron. vi. 41, 42.

Verse 1. עֻנּוֹתוֹ his-being-afflicted, Pu. inf. constr. (used as a noun), from עָנָה ix. 13 with suff. 3 m. s. The LXX., Vulg., and Syr. seem to have read עַנְוָתוֹ ' his meekness;' the Chal. however translates the word ' affliction.'

Verse 2. The expression ' the mighty God of Jacob' occurs besides only in four passages, viz. Gen. xlix. 24, Is. i. 24 (Mighty One of Israel), xlix. 26, and lx. 16.

Verse 3. Into (the) tent of my house, i. e. the tent which is my house; as in the next clause, the couch which is my bed.

Verse 4. תְּנוּמָה slumber, verb. n. f. from נוּם to slumber.

We find in the LXX. the words καὶ ἀνάπαυσιν τοῖς κροτάφοις μου added at the end of this verse, and this is followed by the Vulg. and the Prayer-Book Version.

Verse 5. מִשְׁכָּנוֹת an-habitation, lit. habitations or tabernacles; the plur. put by enallage for the sing.

Verse 6. שְׁמַעֲנוּהָ we-heard-of-it; the suff. 3 f. s. is probably an indefinite neuter, though some consider that it refers to the Ark.

בְּאֶפְרָתָה at-Ephrathah; the older and more solemn name for Bethlehem, a town in the tribe of Judah, (with pr. בּ i. 1 and ה local.) It here signifies *the South*, as *the forest* of Lebanon, the great forest of Canaan (called here, as in Is. xxii. 8, xxix. 17, simply *the forest*), signifies *the North*. So the whole connection is, 'and this vow (verses 2, 5) was not in vain; for we, His people, heard from North to South the joyous invitation to come to the Temple at Zion.'

בִּשְׂדֵי־יָעַר in-(the)fields-of-(the)forest, or in the fields of Jaar, Jaar being a shortened form of Kirjath-Jearim, 'the city of woods,' in which place the Ark remained for twenty years. See 1 Sam. vi. 21, vii. 1, 2. Comp. Eng. *Wootton* or *Forest-town*.

Verse 8. וַאֲרוֹן and-(the)Ark-of, constr. of אָרוֹן subst. com. gen. (masc. only in 2 Sam. vi. sqq., 2 Chron. viii. 11), ark, chest, into which things are collected to be kept, (with ו cop. ii. 6.) R. אָרָה to collect, to gather. 'The ark of Thy strength,' i. e. the symbol of Thy power and majesty. This designation of the Ark occurs only here and in 2 Chron. vi. 41.

Verse 11. There is an ellipsis of some such word as שְׁבוּעַת before אֱמֶת.

Verse 12. וְעֵדֹתִי and-My-testimony; either sing. for עֵדוּתִי xix. 8 with suff. 1 s., like תַּחְנֹתִי for תַּחֲנוּתִי 2 Kings vi. 8, or else plur. (see xxv. 10) with suff. of the sing., as, for instance, Deut. xxviii. 59, where we find מַכּוֹתְךָ for מַכּוֹתֶיךָ. The LXX., Vulg., Chal., and Arab. have the plur.

זוֹ which, i. q. זֶה.

Verse 14. פֹּה here, adv. of place, perhaps contracted from פֵּהוּ, בָּהוּ in this, or that, sc. place, like בֹּה for כָּהוּ.

Verse 15. צֵידָהּ Her-provision, masc. of צֵידָה lxxviii. 25 with suff. 3 f. s. The LXX. has θήραν, but another reading of the Greek Version is τὴν χήραν αὐτῆς, which has been followed by the Vulg., Arab., and Æth., the rendering of the Vulg. being *viduam ejus*.

Verse 17. There will I make a horn to shoot forth for David, i. e. the power and prosperity of his kingdom shall be great.

PSALM CXXXIII.

In this Psalm, (probably composed by David on the occasion of the assembling of the tribes of Israel to make him king,) is described the benefit of the Communion of Saints.

Verse 1. לְדָוִד is omitted by the Chal., LXX., and the Targum.

Verse 2. הַזָּקָן the-beard, subst. com. gen.

Aaron is used here for the Priests generally.

מִדּוֹתָיו his-garments, pl. of מִדָּה xxxix. 5 with suff. 3 m. s.; the fem. form of this noun, signifying *garments*, occurs nowhere else. In all other cases it denotes *measures*.

PSALM CXXXIV.

This short Psalm—the last of the Songs of Degrees—contains an exhortation to bless God; it was probably sung by the Levites at the closing of the gates of the Temple.

Verse 1. The LXX. and Vulg. carry on בַּלֵּילוֹת to the next verse.

Verse 2. יְדְכֶם is an incorrect form for יְדֵיכֶם, which is found in forty-three MSS.

The LXX. reading is לְקֹדֶשׁ.

PSALM CXXXV.

This Psalm, entitled *a Hallelujah* in the LXX., contains an exhortation to praise God for His mercy, His power, and His judgments. The beginning is taken from Ps. cxxxiv. 1; ver. 4 from Deut. vii. 6; ver. 7 occurs almost word for word in Jer. x. 13 and li. 16; ver. 14 is a quotation from Deut. xxxii. 36. From the fifteenth verse to the end (which, with a few verbal differences, is the same as a portion of Ps. cxv), it describes the vanity of idols, and concludes by an exhortation to bless God. This Psalm was perhaps sung by the Levites at the opening of the gates of the Temple.

Verse 4. Jacob is here used for the posterity of Jacob.

לִסְגֻלָּתוֹ for-His-treasure, verb. n. f. with pr. לְ iv. 3 and suff. 3 m. s. from סָגַל, unused in Heb., to enclose, to acquire.

Verse 7. נְשִׂאִים (the) vapours, subst. m. pl., vapours which ascend from the earth. R. נָשָׂא to lift up.

מוֹצֵא He-sendeth-forth, perhaps incorrect for מוֹצִיא Hiph. pres. part. m. s. from יָצָא xvii. 2, or else for וַיּוֹצֵא, which is found in the parallel passages in Jer. x. 13, li. 16.

Verse 9. בְּפַרְעֹה upon-Pharaoh, a common title of the ancient kings of Egypt, with pr. בְּ i. 1.

Verse 11. לְסִיחוֹן Sihon, (sweeping away, i. e. a leader carrying everything before him; R. סוּחַ to sweep away); prop. name, with pr. לְ ii. 1, (which is here the sign of the accusative,) of a king of the Amorites reigning in Heshbon.

הָאֱמֹרִי the-Amorite, (prop. mountaineer, from the unused אָמֹר); prop. name of a Canaanitish nation who inhabited the mountainous parts of Judæa, (with the art. i. 1.)

וּלְעוֹג and-Og, (long-necked, gigantic); prop. name (with ו cop. i. 1 and pr. לְ ii. 1) of a king of Bashan, celebrated for his great stature.

Verse 17. אַף also, xvi. 6, though some persons, instead of taking it as an adverb, consider that it has the signification of *nose*, as in the corresponding passage in Ps. cxv. 6.

Verse 18. וְכֹל is the reading of several MSS., LXX., Vulg., Syr., and Arab.

Verse 20. הַלֵּוִי Levi, (adhesion, R. לָוָה xxxvii. 21); prop. name of the third son of Jacob by Leah, the ancestor of the tribe of Levi, which was set apart for the service of the sanctuary, and of which was the family of Aaron, to whom the priesthood was appropriated.

PSALM CXXXVI.

This Psalm of praise and thanksgiving, which was entitled *a Hallelujah* in the LXX., and which was probably sung on the great festivals, is by some persons thought to be a continuation of the preceding one. In the Jewish Liturgy it was called *the Great Hallel*, and it is in great part taken from the Book of Deuteronomy. The words כִּי לְעוֹלָם חַסְדּוֹ were probably sung as a chorus in the Temple by the whole congregation. Verses 17–22 are nearly identical with Ps. cxxxv. 10–12.

Verse 4. The pr. לְ being prefixed to the first word of this and the following verses, shews that הוֹדוּ is understood before it in each instance.

Verse 13. לִגְזָרִים into-parts, pl. of גֶּזֶר verb. n. m. with pr. לְ iv. 3, from גָּזַר to divide.

Verse 15. וְחֵילוֹ and-his-host, or his strength.

Verse 23. שֶׁבְּשִׁפְלֵנוּ Who-in-our-low-estate, verb. n. m. from שָׁפֵל xviii. 28 with שֶׁ prefixed as the relat. pron., pr. בְ i. 1, and suff. 1 pl.

PSALM CXXXVII.

In this Psalm, (which in the LXX. is ascribed to Jeremiah,) is described the trouble and oppression which the Jews had experienced in captivity. The last three verses contain a curse upon Edom and Babylon.

Verse 2. עֲרָבִים (the) willows, subst. m. pl. (sing. unused). R. עָרַב, perhaps to be white.

Verse 3. שׁוֹבֵינוּ those-that-led-us-away-captive, Kal pres. part. m. pl. with suff. 1 pl. from שָׁבָה.

וְתוֹלָלֵינוּ and-they-that-spoiled-us, or laid us on heaps, subst. m. pl. with suff. 1 pl. Some suppose that the word, (which is only found here,) is derived from תָּלַל, perhaps to rob, to plunder; though others consider it as an Aramaism for שׁוֹלְלֵינוּ or שׁוֹלָלֵינוּ.

The ancient versions have 'of the songs of.'

Verse 5. The Chal. has 'May I forget my right hand;' the Syr. 'May my right hand forget me;' the LXX. ἐπιλησθείη, as if the reading were תִּשָּׁכַח. Luther has ſo werde meiner Rechten vergeſſen.

Verse 6. If I bring not up Jerusalem above (the) head of my gladness, i. e. If I do not make Jerusalem the subject of my chiefest joy.

Verse 9. עֹלָלַיִךְ thy-little-ones, lit. thy sucklings, pl. of עוֹלָל i. q. עוֹלֵל (viii. 3) with suff. 2 f. s.

PSALM CXXXVIII.

The Psalmist here praises God for the truth of His word, prophesies that the kings of the earth shall praise Him, and professes his own confidence in Him. In the LXX. this Psalm is ascribed to Haggai and Zechariah.

Verse 1. After אוֹדְךָ the LXX., Chal., Vulg., Arab., and Syr. insert the word יְהוָה.

אֱלֹהִים (the)gods, perhaps meaning 'the angels,' according to the LXX. and Vulg.; or possibly 'the false gods' of the heathen.

Verse 2. Luther has 'for Thou hast made Thy name glorious above all through Thy Word.'

Verse 3. There is an ellipsis of אֲשֶׁר after יוֹם.
Luther has 'When I call upon Thee, do Thou hear me.'
The LXX., Vulg., Syr., Chal., and Arab. seem to read תַּרְחִיבֵנִי or תַּרְחֲבֵנִי instead of תַּרְהִבֵנִי.

Verse 6. וְשָׁפָל yet-(the)lowly, verb. adj. m. from שָׁפֵל xviii. 28.

יֵידָע He-knoweth, unusual form for יֵדַע.

Verse 7. וְתוֹשִׁיעֵנִי יְמִינֶךָ and-Thy-right-hand shall-save-me, or perhaps (as Luther translates) 'Thou shalt save me (with) Thy right hand,' as the verb *may* be 2 *pers. m. s.* instead of 3 *pers. f. s.*

PSALM CXXXIX.

The Psalmist here describes the omnipresence and omniscience of God, praises Him for His infinite mercies, and concludes by expressing his abhorrence of the wicked. By the LXX. this Psalm is ascribed to David; though in some copies it is said to be a Psalm of Zechariah in the dispersion. From the many Aramaisms found in it, it is more probable that it was written *after* the Exile than *before*.

Verse 1. The suffix of the preceding clause is to be supplied after the verb וַתֵּדָע.

Verse 2. לְרֵעִי my-thought, or will, subst. m. (only found here and in ver. 17), with pr. לְ ii. 1 and suff. 1 s. R. רָעָה, Chal. to will.

Verse 3. וְרִבְעִי and-my-lying-down, (Chal. form for רִבְצִי,) verb. n. m. from רָבַע to lie down, i. q. רָבַץ with suff. 1 s.

זֵרִיתָ Thou-hast-searched, or winnowed, or sifted; Luther has ſo biſt Du um mich.

הִסְכַּנְתָּה art-acquainted-with, Hiph. 2 m. s. pret. from סָכַן to inhabit, to dwell, to associate with (any one); Hiph. to form acquaintance with, hence to know.

Verse 5. צַרְתָּנִי Thou-hast-beset-me, Kal 2 m. s. pret. from צוּר xlix. 15 with suff. 1 s. The LXX., Vulg., and Syr. have 'Thou hast formed me,' and our Prayer-Book Version 'Thou hast fashioned me,' as if it were from יָצַר.

Verse 6. The K'thiv is פְּלִאָיה (to be read פְּלִאָיָה) fem. of פְּלָאִי; the K'ri is פליאה fem. of the form פְּלִיא; verb. adj. from פָּלָא ix. 17.

לֹא־אוּכַל לָהּ I-cannot-(reach) it, lit. I shall not be able unto it; the expression is elliptical, as in Pss. xxi. 12 and ci. 5.

Verse 8. אֶסַּק I-ascend, Kal 1 s. fut. from נָסַק, (only found in this passage,) a Chal. word = the Hebrew עָלָה.

Verse 9. We must supply the particle אִם before the verb אֶשָּׂא.

אַחֲרִית יָם (the) extremity-of-(the) sea, i. e. the furthest west.

Verse 11. יְשׁוּפֵנִי let-cover-me, Kal 3 m. s. fut. with suff. 1 s. from שׁוּף, prob. to gape upon, to lie in wait for, to attack, to overwhelm, only found besides in two other passages, i. e. Gen. iii. 15 and Job ix. 17.

בַּעֲדֵנִי about-me, poet. for בַּעֲדִי iii. 4.

Verse 12. כַּחֲשֵׁיכָה as-(is) the-darkness, i. q. חֲשֵׁכָה xviii. 12 with pr. כ xxxiii. 22.

כָּאוֹרָה so-(is) the-light, fem. of אוֹר iv. 7 with pr. כ xviii. 34. The fem. only occurs here and in Esther viii. 16. The repeated כ has the signification of as .... so.

Verse 13. קָנִיתָ hast-possessed, or formed.
The LXX., Vulg., Syr., and Arab. read מִבֶּטֶן.

Verse 14. After נוֹרָאוֹת we must supply some such word as עֲלִילוֹת.
For נִפְלֵיתִי I have been made wonderful, the LXX., Syr., Vulg., and Jerome have the 2nd pers.

Verse 15. עָצְמִי my-bone, or strength, or body, subst. m., i. q. עֶצֶם vi. 3 with suff. 1 s.

Verse 16. גָּלְמִי My-unformed-substance, subst. m. with suff. 1 s., prop. something rolled together, hence rude and unformed matter. The word occurs nowhere else in the Old Testament, but is frequently found in the Rabbinical writings. R. גָּלַם to roll together.

יָמִים יֻצָּרוּ (as to the) days (when) they-were-fashioned, or what days they were fashioned.

Instead of the K'thiv וְלֹא (which is followed by the LXX., Vulg., Targum, and Syr.) the K'ri has ולו, referring to גָּלְמִי.

Verse 20. יֹאמְרוּךָ for יְאַמְּרוּךָ they-will-speak-of-Thee. The א is here omitted, as in Ps. civ. 29, תֹּסֵף for תֶּאֱסֹף. Or possibly the correct reading may be יַמְרוּךָ will provoke Thee, or rebel against Thee, from מָרָה. The LXX. and Vulg. read תאמרו.

נָשֻׂא perhaps an anomalous form for נָשְׂאוּ; some persons consider it as a pass. part., שְׁמֶךָ being understood.

עָרֶיךָ Thine-enemies, pl. of עָר subst. m. with suff. 2 m. s. R. עִיר ix. 7. For עָרֶיךָ Dr. Perowne would read עָלֶיךָ; several MSS. have עָרֶיךָ. The LXX., Syr., and Vulg. take the word to mean 'Thy cities.'

s

Verse 21. וּבִתְקוֹמְמֶיךָ and-with-those-that-rise-up-against-Thee, for וּבִמְתְקוֹמְמֶיךָ. This is the only instance of an apoc. Hithp. part.

Verse 22. תַּכְלִית Perfection-of, verb. n. f. from כָּלָה ii. 9.

Verse 24. עֹצֶב pain, or grief, or perhaps image, verb. n. m. from עָצַב xvi. 4.

PSALM CXL.

This Psalm, probably composed by David when persecuted by Saul and Doeg, contains a prayer for protection against the violence and malice of his enemies. We find in it several words which do not occur elsewhere.

Verse 2. The נ in תִּנְצְרֵנִי is retained (as in Ps. lxi. 8, lxxviii. 7, and Prov. v. 2), though it is usually elided.

Verse 4. עַכְשׁוּב an-adder, subst. m., only found in this passage. R. עָבַשׁ to be rolled together.

Verse 8. נָשֶׁק battle, or armour, subst. m. (in pause); abs. form נֶשֶׁק or נֵשֶׁק. R. נָשַׁק ii. 12.

Verse 9. מַאֲוַיֵּי (the) desires-of, subst. m. pl., only found here. R. אָוָה x. 3.

זְמָמוֹ his-wicked-device, subst. m. (with suff. 3 m. s.), a counsel or purpose in a bad sense; the word is an ἅπαξ λεγόμενον. R. זָמַם x. 2.

תָּפֵק further, Hiph. 2 m. s. fut. from פּוּק to go out; Hiph. to give out, to finish, to bring to an end, to let succeed.

Verse 10. The K'thiv is יַכַּסּוּמוֹ (to be read יְכַסּוּמוֹ), and the K'ri יכסימו.

As the word ראש also signifies *poison*, the verse may perhaps be rendered 'May the poison of those surrounding me, may the mischief of their lips cover them.'

Verse 11. יַפִּלוּ (to be read יָמִיטוּ) let-(men) cast; the K'thiv is Hiph., but the K'ri ימוטו let fall, or be cast, is Niph.

בְּמַהֲמֹרוֹת into-floods-of-waters, or whirlpools, subst. f. pl. with pr. בְּ i. 1. The word is an ἅπαξ λεγόμενον. R. הָמַר, unused in Heb., to flow in a rapid stream (of water). Comp. Gr. ὄμβρος; Lat. *imber*.

Verse 12. אִישׁ לָשׁוֹן (The) man-of (the) tongue, i. e. of *evil* tongue, a slanderer or detractor.

לְמַדְחֵפֹת for-overthrowing, or hastily, urgently, subst. f. pl. with pr. לְ ii. 1; the word is an ἅπαξ λεγόμενον. R. דָּחַף to thrust, to push. Or, an evil speaker, a wicked man of violence, be established in the earth; let him be hunted to (his) overthrow.

Verse 13. יָדַעְתָּ for יָדַעְתִּי, which is found in the K'ri; see xvi. 2.

PSALM CXLI.

This Psalm, perhaps composed by David after sparing Saul's life in the Cave at Engedi, contains a petition for deliverance from the hands of cruel adversaries, as well as a prayer that he may not be led away by the temptations of the wicked.

Verse 2. מַשְׂאַת (the) lifting-up-of, or perhaps the offering, the gift of, constr. of מַשְׂאֵת (contracted from מַשְׂאֶת), verb. n. f. from נָשָׂא to lift up.

Verse 3. שָׁמְרָה a-watch, prob. verb. n. f. from שָׁמַר. The word is found nowhere else. Some persons consider it as an imperat. with ה parag.

דַּל (the) door-of, verb. n. m. from דָּלָה xxx. 2. The masc. form of the word occurs nowhere else.

Verse 4. בְּמַנְעַמֵּיהֶם of-their-dainties, subst. m. pl. with pr. בְּ i. 1 and suff. 3 m. pl. The word occurs nowhere else. R. נָעֵם to be pleasant, to be lovely.

Verse 5. שֶׁמֶן רֹאשׁ אַל־יָנִי רֹאשִׁי (it shall be) an-oil-of (the) head-(which) shall-not-break my-head; or let not (their) precious oil break my head, &c., or rather let not my head refuse (it), i. e. the chastisement which the righteous man will inflict.

For רֹאשׁ the LXX. and Syr. read רָשָׁע.

Several MSS. read more fully יָנִיא for יָנִי.

Verse 6. נִשְׁמְטוּ have-been-hurled-down, Niph. 3 pl. pret. from שָׁמַט to smite, to throw down. Comp. Ger. schmeißen, to strike; A. Sax. *smitan;* Eng. *to smite.*

Verse 7. It is hardly necessary to supply the word *wood* after 'cleaveth,' as the verse may be very well rendered 'as one furroweth and cleaveth the earth,' i. e. with the plough.

Verse 8. תְּעַר pour-out, or make bare, for תְּעַר Pi. 2 m. s. fut. from עָרָה xxxvii. 35, or perhaps for תַּעַר, which would be the Hiph. form.

Verse 9. The pl. form מֹקְשׁוֹת, instead of מֹקְשִׁים, is only found here.

Verse 10. בְּמַכְמֹרָיו into-their-own-nets, subst. m. pl. with pr. בְּ i. 1 and suff. 3 m. s., used distributively, each one of them into his own net. R. כָּמַר, not used in Kal, i. q. כָּבַר to plait, to braid. Luther has Die Gottlosen müssen in ihr eigen Netz fallen mit einander.

PSALM CXLII.

In this, the last of the eight Psalms which, according to their Inscriptions, are to be referred to David's persecution by Saul, the Psalmist declares that in his trouble all his comfort was in prayer to God. See Introduction to Ps. xviii.

Verse 5. For הַבֵּיט, a hybrid form of הַבֵּט and הַבִּיט, the 2nd pers. s. *imp.*, the ancient versions have mostly the 1st pers. *pret.*

אֵין דּוֹרֵשׁ לְנַפְשִׁי there-is-none seeking-for my-soul, or no man seeks after my soul, (i. e. to preserve it or avenge it); comp. Gen. xlii. 22.

Verse 8. מִמַּסְגֵּר out-of-prison, verb. n. m. from סָגַר to shut up, with pr. מ ii. 3.

יַכְתִּרוּ shall-compass-about; the LXX. and Syr. have 'shall *wait* for me;' others (considering the word as a denom. from כֶּתֶר) translate it 'shall adorn themselves as with crowns,' i. e. shall triumph.

PSALM CXLIII.

This Psalm is the last of the seven penitential Psalms (see Ps. vi), and is one of those appointed for Ash-Wednesday. It is said in some copies of the LXX. to be 'A Psalm of David when he was pursued by his son Absalom.' In *the first* part the Psalmist complains of his misfortunes, and in *the second* prays for grace, for deliverance, and for the destruction of his enemies.

Verse 3. דִּכָּא for דָּכָא.

Verse 5. The LXX., Chal., Vulg., Luther, and the Welsh Version have 'on (the) works of.'

Verse 9. Before אֵלֶיךָ the LXX. and Arab. insert the word כִּי. The LXX., Vulg., and Arab. seem to have read חָסִיתִי for כִּסִּיתִי. The Syr. omits the last two words of the verse.

Verse 10. תַּנְחֵנִי let-lead-me; this may be either 2 *pers. m. s.* or 3 *pers. f. s.* fut. from נָחָה.

PSALM CXLIV.

The Psalmist here praises God for having given him the victory, and prays for deliverance from his enemies and for the prosperity of his people. In some copies of the LXX. it is said to have been composed by David after the victory over Goliath. Verse 9 is the only passage in the last two Books of the Psalter in which the word אֱלֹהִים occurs, with the exception of Ps. cviii. Verse 11 is the same, (excepting the omission of מַיִם רַבִּים,) as the latter part of the seventh, and the whole of the eighth verse.

PSALM CXLIV. vv. 2, 3, 5, 7, 10, 12, 13.

Verse 2. The pron. לִי is pleonastic.

For עַמִּי some MSS., Chal., Syr., Arab., and Roman Vulg. read עַמִּים, as in the parallel passages in Ps. xviii. 48 and 2 Sam. xxii. 48. The Masora has enumerated Ps. cxliv. 2, 2 Sam. xxii. 44, and Lam. iii. 14 as the three passages in which עַמִּי is written, although rendered as if it were עַמִּים by the Targum, Syr., and Jerome.

Verse 3. וּבֶן is the reading of several MSS., LXX., Vulg., Syr., and Arab.

Verse 5. The verbs in this and the next three verses are found in the imp., whilst in the corresponding passage in Ps. xviii they are in the pret. tense.

Verse 7. Many MSS. read the sing. יָדְךָ as in Ps. cxxxviii. 7, and this is followed by the LXX.

Verse 10. The Syr. reads לַמֶּלֶךְ in the sing.

Instead of עַבְדּוֹ the Syr., Vulg., and Luther read עַבְדְּךָ, and this is followed by our Prayer-Book Version.

Verse 12. כִּנְטִעִים as-plants, subst. m. pl., (only found here,) with pr. כ ii. 9. R. נָטַע to plant.

כְזָוִיֹת as-corner-pillars, subst. f. pl. from the unused sing. זָוִיָה or זָוִית, with pr. כ i. 3. The only other place where the word occurs is Zech. ix. 15. R. זָוָה, unused in Heb., according to Gesenius, to hide, to conceal, to hide oneself, to betake oneself to a corner; according to Fürst, to shine, to glitter, to appear afar off (of a projecting corner).

Verse 13. מְזָוֵינוּ Our-garners, pl. of מָזוּ (for מָזוֶה), subst. m., (only found here,) with suff. 1 pl. R. either זָוָה, unused in Heb., prob. to hide, to conceal, to lay up, to preserve, or else מָזָה to gather in.

מִזַּן from-kind, subst. m., kind, species, (with pr. מ ii. 3,) an Aramaic word found besides only in 2 Chron. xvi. 14. R. perhaps זָנַן, unused in Heb., to form, to put into shape.

בְּחוּצוֹתֵינוּ in-our-fields, or pastures. The word is rendered *fields* (not *streets*) in Job v. 10 and Prov. viii. 26.

Verse 14. אַלּוּפֵינוּ Our-oxen, subst. epicene (with suff. 1 pl.), i. q. אֶלֶף viii. 8.

מְסֻבָּלִים laden, or able to bear burdens, or laden with flesh, and so *strong*, or perhaps with young, hence *pregnant;* Pu. part. m. pl. from סָבַל to bear, to carry.

יוֹצֵאת going-out, Kal pres. part. f. s. from יָצָא xvii. 2, used substantively and as a neuter.

צְוָחָה outcry, subst. f., sometimes used as a shout of joy and sometimes as a cry of sorrow. R. צָוַח to cry out.

The Hebrew word אַלּוּף does not anywhere else mean an ox, but a guide, friend, leader, captain, prince, as in Prov. ii. 17, xvi. 28, Jer. xiii. 21, Zech. xii. 5, 6. The verse may therefore be rendered 'that our captains may be strong, that there be no breaking in (of the enemy), and no going out (of the people) into captivity.'

Verse 15. שֶׁכָּכָה which-(is)thus, adv. contr. from כָּה כָּה so and so, i. q. כֹּה כֹּה with שֶׁ prefixed as the relat.

שֶׁיהוָֹה (to)which-Jehovah (is); this is the only instance of the שֶׁ being prefixed to יְהוָֹה.

PSALM CXLV.

This is the last of the eight alphabetical Psalms, (reckoning the ninth and tenth as forming one); it is deficient in the נ stanza. The LXX., Syr., Vulg., and Arab. supply the deficiency by intercalating a verse after the thirteenth, נֶאֱמָן יְהוָֹה בְּכָל־דְּבָרָיו וְחָסִיד בְּכָל־מַעֲשָׂיו. See Introduction to Ps. ix. It has been appointed to be used in the Service of the Church on Whit-Sunday; and, like the other Psalms to the end of the Psalter, celebrates in the most beautiful manner the majesty, the righteousness, and particularly the goodness of God. It is the only Psalm that bears the title תְּהִלָּה, whose plur. תְּהִלּוֹת is become the collective name of the Psalms.

Verse 1. The LXX., Vulg., and Arab. have '*my* King.'

Verse 3. חֵקֶר a-searching, verb. n. m. from חָקַר, i. e. His greatness is infinite.

Verse 5. וְדִבְרֵי and-(the)things-of, or the words of; the LXX., Vulg., and Syr. read יְדַבְּרוּ.

The LXX. and Vulg. substitute 3 *pers. pl.* for 1 *pers. sing.* here (for אָשִׂיחָה), and in the next verse (for אֲסַפְּרֶנָּה).

Verse 6. The K'thiv has the pl. וּגְדֻלּוֹתֶיךָ (to be read וּגְדֻלָּתֶיךָ), but in the K'ri it has been corrected to the sing. וגדולתך.

Verse 7. The adj. רַב is here placed *before* the subst., though some take it as a subst. for רֹב.

Verse 8. The K'thiv is וּגְדָיל (to be read וּגְדוֹל), and the K'ri וגדל.

Verse 9. The LXX., followed by the Æth., has τοῖς ὑπομένουσι, but the Hebrew is supported by the Chal., Vulg., and Arab.; the Syr. has omitted the word לַכֹּל altogether.

Verse 12. The LXX. and Luther have *Thy* mighty acts for *His*, and *Thy* kingdom for *His* kingdom in the next sentence.

Verse 14. וְזוֹקֵף and-raiseth-up, Kal pres. part. m. s. from זָקַף. The only other place where the word occurs is Ps. cxlvi. 8.

Verse 15. The Vulg. reads יְהוָֹה after יְשַׂבֵּרוּ.

Verse 17. וְחָסִיד and-holy, or merciful, or bountiful; the only other place where the word is used of God is Jer. iii. 12.

PSALM CXLVI.

This begins another series of Hallelujah Psalms, which continues to the end of the Book. It contains an exhortation not to trust in man but in God alone. It has been ascribed in the LXX., Vulg., and Syr. to Haggai and Zechariah, as is the case also with the two following Psalms.

Verse 4. עַשְׁתֹּנֹתָיו his-thoughts, lit. smooth thoughts, all his sleek and polished plans, subst. f. pl. (only found here), with suff. 3 m. s. R. עָשַׁת to shine, to form, (Chal. to think, to purpose); only used in Kal in Jer. v. 28, and in Hithp. to bethink oneself, to recollect, in Jonah i. 6.

Verse 5. The ב of בְּעֶזְרוֹ is the *Beth essentiae* (see xxxiv. 5).

Verse 8. פֹּקֵחַ openeth (the eyes of), Kal pres. part. m. s. from פָּקַח used of eyes, as פָּתַח is of doors.

עִוְרִים (the) blind, pl. of עִוֵּר verb. adj. m. from עָוַר, not used in Kal, to be blind.

PSALM CXLVII.

This Psalm was doubtless written to commemorate the goodness of God in bringing back His people from their captivity, and rebuilding the walls of Jerusalem. In the LXX. it is divided into two parts, a new Psalm beginning at ver. 12.

Verse 1. זַמְּרָה to-sing-praise-unto; perhaps Pi. inf. constr. with ה parag. from זָמַר iii. 1, though some persons consider it as Pi. 2 m. s. imp., whilst others would read either זַמְּרוּ or אֲזַמְּרָה.

Verse 4. מוֹנֶה telling, or counting, Kal pres. part. m. s. from מָנָה i. q. מָנָע ii. 3.

Verse 8. הַמַּצְמִיחַ הָרִים חָצִיר Who-maketh-(the) mountains-to-bring-forth-grass; the LXX. and Vulg. have added from Ps. civ. 14, 'and herb for the use of men,' whence it has found its way into our Prayer-Book Version. This addition is also found in the Æth. and Arab.

Verse 9. עֹרֵב (the) raven, subst. m. (pl. עֹרְבִים), perhaps so called from its black colour. R. עָרַב xxx. 6.

The words 'unto God' are added in Job xxxviii. 41; the LXX. has τοῖς ἐπικαλουμένοις αὐτόν, and this is followed by the Vulg., Luther, and our Prayer-Book Version.

Verse 10. בְּשׁוֹקֵי in-(the)legs-of, pl. constr. of שׁוֹק subst. f. with pr. בּ i. 1. R. שׁוּק lxv. 10.

Verse 16. כַּצֶּמֶר like-the-wool, subst. m. with pr. כּ i. 3, perhaps so called from its being shorn off; (see ii. 8.) R. צָמַר, unused in Heb., perhaps i. q. זָמַר to cut off.

כְּפוֹר (the) hoarfrost, subst. m., perhaps so called because it *covers* the ground. R. כָּפַר xvii. 12.

Verse 17. קַרְחוֹ His-ice, subst. m. (with suff. 3 m. s.), so called from its *smoothness*. R. קָרַח xlii. 1.

כְפִתִּים like-morsels, pl. of פַּת verb. n. f. from פָּתַת to break, with pr. כּ i. 3.

קָרָתוֹ His-cold, verb. n. f. with suff. 3 m. s. from קָרַר, unused in Heb., to be cold.

Verse 18. יַשֵּׁב He-causeth-to-blow, Hiph. 3 m. s. fut. from נָשַׁב to blow; Hiph. to cause to blow, to drive away by blowing.

Verse 19. The K'thiv דְּבָרוֹ (to be read דְּבָרוֹ) sing., is followed by the LXX. and Vulg., whilst the K'ri דבריו is plur.

PSALM CXLVIII.

In this glorious Hymn of Praise the Psalmist exhorts the whole creation to praise God.

Verse 2. The K'thiv צְבָאָיו (to be read צְבָאוֹ) is sing., but the K'ri צבאיו is plur. as in ciii. 21.

Verse 4. Ye heavens of heavens, i.e. the highest heavens; Luther has 'ye heavens everywhere.'

Verse 5. After נִבְרָאוּ the LXX. and Vulg. add from the parallel passage, Ps. xxxiii. 9, the other clause, 'He spake, and it was done,' or as they render 'and they were made.'

Verse 6. וְלֹא יַעֲבוֹר (which) shall-not-pass, is the rendering of the LXX., Jerome, and Syr. Perhaps it may signify 'and not one transgresseth it,' the verb in the sing. being used distributively.

Verse 13. This order of the words, *'earth and heaven,'* occurs only here and in Gen. ii. 4. In the Prayer-Book Version we find 'heaven and earth.'

Verse 14. For 'the praise of all His saints,' Luther and our Prayer-Book Version have 'all His saints shall praise Him.' קְרֹבוֹ near-unto-Him, i. q. קָרוֹב לוֹ.

PSALM CXLIX.

We have here another Hymn of Praise to celebrate the benefits which God had bestowed on the children of Israel. It is uncertain at what period the Psalm was composed.

Verse 3. בְמָחוֹל in-(the) dance, or with the pipe. Some consider the word as=חָלִיל a flute, a pipe, from חָלַל v. 1, though others think that it is derived from חוּל x. 5.

Verse 5. עַל־מִשְׁכְּבוֹתָם upon-their-beds, i. e. at night.

Verse 6. פִּיפִיּוֹת two-edged, subst. f. pl. Comp. 2 Macc. xv. 27.

Verse 7. תּוֹכָחוֹת punishments, pl. of תּוֹכֵחָה i. q. תּוֹכַחַת, see xxxviii. 15.

Verse 8. בְּזִקִּים with-chains, subst. m. pl. with pr. בְ i. 1. R. זָקַק, perhaps to tie fast, to bind.

PSALM CL.

In this great closing Hallelujah, or Doxology of the Psalter, is an exhortation to everything that hath breath to praise the power and majesty of God upon all kinds of musical instruments.

Verse 3. בְּתֵקַע with-(the)sound-of, verb. n. m. from תָּקַע xlvii. 2 with pr. בּ i. 1; the word occurs nowhere else.

Verse 4. בְּמִנִּים with-stringed-instruments; probably the same word as in Ps. xlv. 9 (with pr. בּ i. 1), with the exception of which passage the word occurs nowhere else.

וְעֻגָב and-pipe, subst. m., an ancient musical instrument, the inventor of which was Jubal, see Gen. iv. 21. R. עָגַב, prob. to breathe, to blow. The only other places where the word occurs are Job xxi. 12 and xxx. 31.

Verse 5. בְּצִלְצְלֵי־ with-(the)cymbals-of, pl. constr. of צְלָצַל subst. m., a tingling, a clinking, a tinkling instrument, a cymbal. R. צָלַל to tingle.

By '*the cymbals of hearing*' we may probably understand smaller instruments, which had *a clear, high* sound, and by '*the cymbals of shouting*' larger ones, with *a deep, loud* sound.

INDEX.

א

אָב Psalm iii. verse 1.
אָבַד i. 6.
אֲבַדּוֹן lxxxviii. 12.
אָבָה, אֶבְיוֹן ix. 19.
אֲבִימֶלֶךְ xxxiv. 1.
אָבַר, אַבִּיר xxii. 13.
אֲבִירָם cvi. 17.
אָבֵל xxxv. 14.
אֶבֶן, אָבַן xci. 12.
אֵבֶר lv. 7.
אַבְרָהָם xlvii. 10.
אַבְשָׁלוֹם iii. 1.
אֶנַם, אָנַם cvii. 35.
אֱדוֹם lx. 2.
אֲדוֹמִי lii. 2.
אֲדֹנָי, אָדוֹן ii. 4.
אָדַר, אַדִּיר viii. 2.
אָדָם viii. 5.
אֲדָמָה xlix. 12.
אָהַב iv. 3.
אֹהֶל xv. 1.
אֹהָלוֹת xlv. 9.

אַהֲרֹן lxxvii. 21.
אוֹד xviii. 19.
אָוָה x. 3.
אוֹיֵב iii. 8.
אוֹיָה cxx. 5.
אֱוִיל cvii. 17.
אָוֶל xxxviii. 6.
אוּל v. 5.
אִוֶּלֶת xxxviii. 6.
אוֹן iii. 3.
אָוֶן v. 6.
אוֹן lxxviii. 51.
אוֹפִיר xlv. 10.
אוֹצָר xxxiii. 7.
אוֹר iv. 7.
אוֹרָה cxxxix. 12.
אוֹת lxv. 9.
אוֹתָם ix. 13.
אוֹתְךָ xxv. 5.
אָז ii. 5.
אֵזוֹב li. 9.
אֲזַי cxxiv. 3.
אָזַן v. 2, lxii. 10.

אֹזֶן x. 17.
אֵזָר lxv. 7.
אֶזְרָח xxxvii. 35.
אֶזְרָחִי lxxxviii. 1.
אָח xxii. 23.
אֶחָד xiv. 3.
אָחַר, אָחוֹר ix. 4.
אֲחֻזָּה, אָחַז ii. 8.
אֲחִימֶלֶךְ lii. 2.
אַחֲלַי cxix. 5.
אַחֵר xvi. 4.
אַחֲרוֹן xlviii. 14.
אַחֲרִית xxxvii. 37.
אָטָד, אָטַר lviii. 10.
אָטַר lxix. 16.
אֵיד xviii. 19.
אַיֵּה xlii. 4.
אִיִּים lxxii. 10.
אֵיךְ xi. 1.
אַיָּל xlii. 2.
אֵיל lxxxviii. 5.
אַיָּלָה xviii. 34.
אַיָּלוּת xxii. 20.

INDEX.

אַיֶּלֶת xxii. 1.
אֵימָה, אָיֹם lv. 5.
אֵימִים lxxxviii. 16.
אַיִן, אֵין iii. 3.
אִישׁ i. 1.
אִישׁוֹן xvii. 8.
אֵיתָן lxxiv. 15, lxxxix. 1.
אַךְ xxiii. 6.
אֹכֶל lxxviii. 18.
אֶבֶן xxxi. 23.
אָלַל, אַל iv. 5.
אַל v. 5.
אֶל ii. 1.
אָלָה x. 7.
אֵלֶּה xv. 5.
אֱלֹהִים iii. 3.
אַלּוּף lv. 14, cxliv. 14.
אָלַח xiv. 3.
אֱלִיל xcvi. 5.
אֵלִימוֹ ii. 5.
אָלַם xxxi. 19.
אֶלֶם lviii. 2.
אֻלָּם xxxviii. 14.
אַלֻּמָּה cxxvi. 6.
אַלְמָנָה lxviii. 6.
אֶלֶף, אָלַף viii. 8.
אֶלֶף l. 10.
אַל־תַּשְׁחֵת lvii. 1.
אִם xxii. 10.
אִם i. 2.
אָמָה lxxxvi. 16.
אַמָּה cxvii. 1.

אֱמוּנָה xxxiii. 4.
אָמַן, אֱמוּנִים xii. 2.
אָמַל vi. 3.
אָמֵן xli. 14.
אָמְנָם lviii. 2.
אָמֵץ xviii. 18.
אָמַר ii. 7.
אֹמֶר v. 2.
אֹמֶר xix. 3.
אִמְרָה xii. 7.
אֱמֹרִי cxxxv. 11.
אֲמָרְתְּ xvi. 2.
אֱמֶת xv. 2.
אָנָה xii. 3, xiii. 2.
אָנָּה cxvi. 4.
אֱנוֹשׁ viii. 5.
אָנַח, אֲנָחָה vi. 7.
אֲנִי ii. 6.
אֳנִיָּה xlviii. 8.
אַף ii. 5.
אָנַק, אֲנָקָה xii. 6.
אָסִיר lxviii. 7.
אָסַף l. 1.
אַף ii. 5, xvi. 6.
אָפָה xvi. 6.
אָפַק, אָפִיק xviii. 16.
אֹפֶל, אָפֵל xi. 2.
אֶפֶס, אָפַס ii. 8.
אָפַף xviii. 5.
אָפָר, אֵפֶר cii. 10.
אֶפְרֹחַ lxxxiv. 4.
אֶפְרַיִם lx. 9.

אֶפְרָתָה cxxxii. 6.
אֶצְבַּע viii. 4.
אָרַב x. 8.
אַרְבֶּה lxxviii. 46.
אַרְבָּעִים xcv. 10.
אָרָה vii. 3.
אָרוֹן cxxxii. 8.
אֶרֶז, אָרַז xxix. 5.
אֹרַח viii. 9.
אַרְיֵה vii. 3.
אֲרַם נַהֲרַיִם lx. 2.
אֲרַם צוֹבָה lx. 2.
אַרְמוֹן xlviii. 4.
אֶרֶץ ii. 2.
אָרַשׁ, אֲרֶשֶׁת xxi. 3.
אֵשׁ xi. 6.
אַשּׁוּר xvii. 5.
אַשּׁוּר lxxxiii. 9.
אֶשְׁכָּר lxxii. 10.
אָשָׁם v. 11.
אָשָׁם lxviii. 22.
אַשְׁמֻרָה lxiii. 7.
אַשְׁפָּה, אֶצֶף cxxvii. 5.
אַשְׁפֹּת cxiii. 7.
אָשֵׁר, אֲשֶׁר i. 1.
אַשְׁרֵי i. 1.
אֵשֶׁת lviii. 9.
אֵת ii. 3, xii. 3.
אָתָא vi. 4.
אָתָה lxviii. 32.
אַתָּה ii. 7.
אֶתְמוֹל xc. 4.

INDEX. 271

ב

בְּאֵר vii. 16.
בְּאֵר lv. 24.
בָּאַשׁ xxxviii. 6.
בָּבֶל lxxxvii. 4.
בֶּגֶד, בָּגַד xxii. 19.
בָּרַד, בָּדָד iv. 9.
בַּהַל ii. 5.
בֶּהָלָה lxxviii. 33.
בְּהֵמָה, בַּהַם viii. 8.
בּוֹא v. 8.
בּוּז xxxi. 19.
בּוּם xviii. 34.
בּוּם xliv. 6.
בּוֹר vii. 16.
בּוּשׁ vi. 11.
בּוּשָׁה lxxxix. 46.
בּוּת v. 8.
בָּזָה xv. 4.
בָּחוּר lxxviii. 31.
בָּחִיר lxxxix. 4.
בָּטָא cvi. 33.
בֶּטַח, בָּטַח iv. 9.
בֶּטֶן, בָּטָן xvii. 14.
בֵּין lxviii. 14.
בֵּין v. 2.
בַּיִת v. 8.
בָּכָא lxxxiv. 7.
בְּכִי, בָּכָה vi. 9.
בָּכַר, בְּכוֹר lxxviii. 51.
בָּלָה, בַּל x. 4.
בָּלַג xxxix. 14.

בַּלָהוֹת, בַּלָּהָה lxxiii. 19.
בְּלִי lxiii. 2.
בְּלִיַּעַל xviii. 5.
בְּלַל lxxxvii. 4.
בָּלַם xxxii. 9.
בָּלַע lii. 6.
בַּלְעֲדֵי xviii. 32.
בָּמָה xviii. 34.
בֵּן ii. 7.
בֶּן יְמִינִי vii. 1.
בַּעֲדִי iii. 4.
בְּעִיר lxxviii. 48.
בַּעַל פְּעוֹר cvi. 28.
בָּעַר ii. 12, lxxviii. 48.
בַּעַר xlix. 11.
בָּעַת xviii. 5.
בְּעָתִים lxxxviii. 17.
בָּצַע x. 3.
בֶּצַע xxx. 10.
בָּצַר lxxvi. 13.
בִּקְעָה civ. 8.
בֹּקֶר, בָּקַר v. 4.
בָּקַר lxvi. 15.
בָּקַשׁ iv. 3.
בַּר ii. 12, xix. 9.
בַּר lxv. 14.
בֹּר xviii. 21.
בָּרָא ii. 12, lxxiii. 4.
בָּרָד, בָּרַד xviii. 13.
בְּרוֹשׁ civ. 17.
בָּרוֹת lxix. 22.
בַּרְזֶל ii. 9.

בָּרַח iii. 1.
בְּרִיא lxxiii. 4.
בְּרִיחַ cvii. 16.
בְּרִית xxv. 10.
בְּרָכָה, בָּרַךְ iii. 9.
בִּרְכַּיִם cix. 24.
בָּרָק, בָּרַק xviii. 15.
בָּרַר xviii. 21.
בָּרַשׁ civ. 17.
בָּשָׂר, בָּשַׂר xvi. 9.
בָּשָׁן xxii. 13.
בֹּשֶׁת xxxv. 26.
בַּת ix. 15.
בְּתוּלָה, בָּתַל xlv. 15.

ג

גָּאָה x. 2.
גֵּאָה xciv. 2.
גַּאֲוָה x. 2.
גָּאוֹן xlvii. 5.
גֵּאוּת xvii. 10.
גֵּאָיוֹן cxxiii. 4.
נָבַב, גַּב cxxix. 3.
גָּבַהּ, גָּבֹהַּ x. 4.
גֹּבַהּ ci. 5.
גִּבְלָה civ. 18.
גְּבוּל lxxviii. 54.
גְּבוּלָה lxxiv. 17.
גִּבּוֹר xix. 6.
גְּבוּרָה xx. 7.
גָּבַל lxxiv. 17.
גְּבָל lxxxiii. 8.

INDEX.

גִּבְנֻנִּים, גַּבְנֹן lxviii. 16.
גִּבְעָה, גֶּבַע lxv. 13.
גָּבַר xii. 5.
גֶּבֶר xxxiv. 9.
גֶּבֶר xviii. 26.
גְּבֶרֶת cxxiii. 2.
גַּג cii. 8.
גָּדַד xviii. 30, lxv. 11.
גְּדוּד xviii. 30, lxv. 11.
גָּדוֹל xii. 4.
גְּדוּלָה lxxi. 21.
גּוֹרָל lxxix. 11.
גָּדַע lxxv. 11.
גָּדַף xliv. 17.
גֶּדֶר, גָּדַר lxii. 4.
גְּדֵרָה lxxxix. 41.
גֵּוָה ii. 1, cx. 6.
גּוּז xc. 10.
גּוּחַ xxii. 10.
גּוִי ii. 1.
גְּוִיָּה cx. 6.
גּוּר v. 5, xxii. 24.
גּוֹרָל xvi. 5.
גֵּז, גָּזַז lxxii. 6.
גֵּוָה lxxi. 6.
גָּזַל, גֵּזֶל lxii. 11.
גֶּזֶר cxxxvi. 13.
גַּחֶלֶת xviii. 9.
גַּיְא, גַּיָה xxiii. 4.
גִּיחַ xxii. 10.
פִּיל ii. 11, xliii. 4.
גַּל xxii. 9.

גַּל xlii. 8, cxix. 22.
גַּלְגַּל lxxvii. 19.
גֻּלָּה xviii. 16.
גֹּלֶם, גָּלַם cxxxix. 16.
גִּלְעָד lx. 9.
גַּם viii. 8.
גָּמוּל xxviii. 4.
גָּמַל vii. 5.
גָּמַר vii. 10.
גַּנָּב, גָּנַב l. 18.
גְּעָרָה, גָּעַר xviii. 16.
גָּעַשׁ xviii. 8.
גֶּפֶן, גָּפַן lxxviii. 47.
גָּפְרִית, גֹּפֶר xi. 6.
גֵּר xxxix. 13.
גָּרוֹן, גֵּרָה v. 10.
גֶּרֶן xxxi. 23.
גָּרַל xvi. 5.
גֶּרֶס cxix. 20.
פָּשָׁם, גֶּשֶׁם lxviii. 10.
גַּת lvi. 1.
גִּתִּית viii. 1.

ד

דָּאַב lxxxviii. 10.
דָּאַג xxxviii. 19.
דֹּאַג lii. 2.
דָּאָה xviii. 11.
דָּבַב, דִּבָּה xxxi. 14.
דְּבוֹרָה cxviii. 12.
דְּבִיר xxviii. 2.
דָּבַק xxii. 16.

דָּבַר ii. 5.
דָּבָר vii. 1.
דֶּבֶר lxxviii. 50.
דִּבְרָה cx. 4.
דְּבַשׁ, דָּבַשׁ xix. 11.
דָּג, דָּגָה viii. 9.
דָּגַל xx. 6.
דָּגָן iv. 8.
דָּדָה xlii. 5.
דּוּד, דָּוִד iii. 1.
דּוּד lxxxi. 7.
דְּוַי, דָּוָה xli. 4.
דּוּמָה xciv. 17.
דּוּמִיָּה xxii. 3.
דּוֹנַג xxii. 15.
דּוֹר, דּוּר x. 6.
דָּחָה xxxv. 5.
דְּחִי lvi. 14.
דִּין vii. 9, ix. 5.
דַּיָּן lxviii. 6.
דַּךְ ix. 10.
דַּכָּא xxxiv. 19, xc. 3.
דָּכָה x. 10.
דָּכִי xciii. 3.
דָּכַךְ ix. 10.
דַּל xli. 2, cxli. 3.
דָּלַג xviii. 30.
דָּלָה xxx. 2.
דָּלַל xli. 2.
דָּלַף cxix. 28.
דָּלַק vii. 14.
דֶּלֶת lxxviii. 23.

INDEX.

דָּם v. 7.
דָּמָה xvii. 12.
דְּמוּת lviii. 5.
דְּמִי lxxxiii. 2.
דִּמְיוֹן xvii. 12.
דָּמַם iv. 5.
דְּמָמָה cvii. 29.
דֹּמֶן, דָּמֶן lxxxiii. 11.
דִּמְעָה, דָּמַע vi. 7.
דָּנַג xxii. 15.
דֵּעָה lxiii. 11.
דֵּעַ cxviii. 12.
דַּעַת xix. 3.
דֳפִי, דָּפָה l. 20.
דָּבַר, דְּרוֹר lxxxiv. 4.
דֶּרֶךְ, דָּרַךְ i. 1.
דָּרַשׁ ix. 11.
דֶּשֶׁא, דָּשָׁא xxiii. 2.
דָּשֵׁן xx. 4, xxii. 30.
דֶּשֶׁן xxxvi. 9.
דָּתָו cvi. 17.

ה

הָבוּ xxix. 1.
הֶבֶל, הָבַל xxxi. 7.
הָגָג v. 2.
הָגָה i. 2.
הָגָה xc. 9.
הָגוּת xlix. 4.
הָגִיג v. 2.
הִגָּיוֹן ix. 17.
הַגָּרִים, הגר lxxxiii. 7.

הָדַם, הָדַר xcix. 5.
הָדַר viii. 6.
הֲדָרָה xxix. 2.
הוֹד viii. 2.
הַוָּה, הֹוָה v. 10.
הוּם xxxiii. 7.
הֹן, הוֹן xliv. 13.
הוּת lxii. 4.
הַזְכִּיר xxxviii. 1.
הֵיכָל, הָכָל v. 8.
הֵימָן lxxxviii. 1.
הֲלִיכוֹת lxviii. 25.
הָלַךְ i. 1.
הָלַל v. 6.
הָלַם lxxiii. 10.
הָמוֹן, הָמָה xxxvii. 16.
הָמָם xviii. 15.
הִנְדֹּף lxviii. 3.
הִנֵּה vii. 15.
הַר ii. 6.
הָרִים lxxv. 7.
הָרַע xv. 4.
הָרַס xi. 3.
הָתַת lxii. 4.

ו

וְדֻפְקָה x. 10.
וִיהִי ix. 10.

ז

זְאֵב, זָאַב lxxxiii. 12.
זָבַל, זְבוּל xlix. 15.

זֶבַח, זָבַח iv. 6.
זֶבַח lxxxiii. 12.
זְבֻלוּן lxviii. 28.
זֵד xix. 14.
זָהָב, זָהַב xix. 11.
זָחָה lii. 10.
זָהַר xix. 12.
זוּ cxxxii. 12.
זוּ ix. 16.
זִיד, זוּד xix. 14.
זָוִיּוֹת, זָוָה cxliv. 12.
זוּן l. 11.
זוּלָתִי xviii. 32.
זוּף liv. 2.
זוּר xliv. 21.
זוּת lii. 10.
זֵידוֹן cxxiv. 5.
זִיו l. 11.
זִיפִים, זִיף liv. 2.
זַיִת lii. 10.
זָכָה li. 6.
זָלַל, זְלָלוּת xii. 9.
זַלְעָפָה xi. 6.
זִמָּה xxvi. 10.
זְמִירָה, זָמִיר xcv. 2.
זָמַם x. 2.
זָמַם cxl. 9.
זָמַר iii. 1.
זִמְרָה lxxxi. 3.
זִמְרָת cxviii. 14.
זֵן, זָן cxliv. 13.
זָנַח xliii. 2.

T

INDEX.

זָעַם vii. 12.
זַעַם xxxviii. 4.
זְקִים cxlix. 8.
זָקֵן cxxxiii. 2.
זָקֵן cv. 22.
זִקְנָה lxxi. 9.
זָקוּף cxlv. 14.
זָקַק xii. 7.
זָרָה xliv. 12.
זְרוֹעַ x. 15.
זָרַף, זַרְזִיף lxxii. 6.
זָרַם lxxvii. 18.
זֶרַע, זָרַע xviii. 51.

ח

חָבַר, חֲבוּרָה xxxviii. 6.
חָבַל vii. 15.
חֶבֶל xvi. 6.
חָבֵר xlv. 8.
חָבֵר lviii. 6.
חַג lxxxi. 4.
חָגַג xlii. 5.
חָגַר lxxvi. 11.
חָדַד, חַד lvii. 5.
חָדָה xxi. 7.
חָדֵל, חָדַל xxxix. 5.
חֶדֶר cv. 30.
חָדָשׁ, חָדַשׁ xxxiii. 3.
חֹדֶשׁ lxxxi. 4.
חוּד xlix. 5.
חָוָה xix. 3.
חוּל x. 5.

חוֹל lxxviii. 27.
חוֹמָה li. 20.
חוּם lxxii. 13.
חוּץ xviii. 43.
חוּג xxxv. 13.
חוּשׁ xc. 10.
חַוָּה xi. 4.
חָזוֹן lxxxix. 20.
חָזַר, חֲזִיר lxxx. 14.
חָזַק, חָזָק xviii. 2.
חָזָק xxxv. 10.
חָטָא, חַטָּא i. 1.
חֵטְא li. 7.
חֲטָאָה xxxii. 1.
חַטָּאת xxv. 7.
חִטָּה lxxxi. 17.
חַי xviii. 47.
חִידָה xlix. 5.
חַיִּים, חָיָה vii. 6.
חַיִל xviii. 33.
חֵיל cxxii. 7.
חִיל x. 5, xlviii. 7.
חֵילָה xlviii. 14.
חֵיק, חִיק xxxv. 13.
חִישׁ xc. 10.
חִיתוֹ l. 10.
חֵךְ cxix. 103.
חָכָה xxxiii. 20.
חָכָם xix. 8.
חָכָם xlix. 11.
חָכְמָה xxxvii. 30.
חֵלֶב, חָלָב xvii. 10.

חֶלֶד xvii. 14.
חַלָּה xxxv. 13.
חֲלוֹם lxxiii. 20.
חֲלוֹתִי lxxvii. 11.
חֳלִי xli. 4.
חֲלִיפָה lv. 20.
חֶלְכָה x. 8.
חָלַל v. 1.
חָלָל lxix. 27.
חַלָּמִישׁ cxiv. 8.
חָלַף lv. 20.
חָלַץ vi. 5.
חָלַק v. 10.
חֵלֶק xvi. 5.
חֶלְקָה xii. 3.
חֲלַקְלַקּוֹת xxxv. 6.
חָם lxxviii. 51.
חֵמָא lv. 22.
חָמַד xix. 11.
חֶמְדָּה cvi. 24.
חַמָּה xix. 7.
חֵמָה li. 20.
חֵמָה vi. 2.
חָמַם xix. 7.
חָמַם, חָמַם vii. 17.
חֹמֶץ, חָמֵץ lxix. 22.
חָמַר xlvi. 4.
חָנָה xxvii. 3.
חַנּוּן lxxxvi. 15.
חַנּוֹת lxxvii. 10.
חָנַט lxxxi. 17.
חֲנִית xxxv. 3.

INDEX.

חֲנֻכָּה xxx. 1.	חֵקֶר cxlv. 3.	טוֹבָה xvi. 2.
חִנָּם xxxv. 7.	חֶרֶב, חָרַב vii. 13.	טָחוֹת, טוּחַ li. 8.
חֲנָמָל, חָנַם lxxviii. 47.	חֹרֶב cvi. 19.	טוּל xxxvii. 24.
חָנַן iv. 2.	חָרְבָּה ix. 7.	טִירָה, טוּר lxix. 26.
חָנְנֵנִי ix. 14.	חַרְבֹּן xxxii. 4.	טִיט xviii. 43.
חָנֵף xxxv. 16.	חָרַג xviii. 46.	טָלַל, טַל cx. 3.
חֶסֶד v. 8.	חָרָה, חָרוֹן ii. 5.	טָמֵא lxxix. 1.
חָסִיד, חָסַד iv. 4.	חָרוּץ lxviii. 14.	טַעַם, טָעַם xxxiv. 1.
חָסָה ii. 12.	חֶרְמוֹן, חָרַם xlii. 7.	טָפַח, טֶפַח xxxix. 6.
חֲסִידָה civ. 17.	חֶרְפָּה, חָרַף xv. 3.	טָפֵל cxix. 69.
חָסְיָה lvii. 2.	חֹרֶף lxxiv. 17.	טָפַשׁ cxix. 70.
חָסָל, חָסִיל lxxviii. 46.	חֶרֶץ lxviii. 14.	טֶרֶם, טָרַם xxxix. 14.
חָסֹן, חֲסִין lxxxix. 9.	חַרְצֻבּוֹת, חִרְצָב lxxiii. 4.	טֶרֶף lxxvi. 5.
חָסֵר viii. 6.	חָרַק xxxv. 16.	
חָפַף, חֻפָּה xix. 6.	חָרַשׁ, חֶרֶשׁ xxii. 16.	י
חָפַז xxxi. 23.	חָרַשׁ xxviii. 1.	יָאַב cxix. 131.
חֵפֶץ, חָפֵץ i. 2.	חֶרֶשׁ xxxviii. 14.	יְאֹר lxxviii. 44.
חֵפֶשׂ, חָפַשׂ lxiv. 7.	חָשַׂף xxix. 9.	יְבוּל lxvii. 7.
חָפְשִׁי, חָפַשׁ lxxxviii. 6.	חֲשֵׁיכָה cxxxix. 12.	יָבָל ix. 9.
חֵץ vii. 14.	חֲשֵׁכָה, חָשְׁכָה xviii. 12.	יָבִין lxxxiii. 10.
חָצַב xxix. 7.	חַשְׁמַנִּים, חָשַׁם lxviii. 32.	יַבָּשָׁה lxvi. 6.
חָצָה lv. 24.	חָשַׁק xci. 14.	יַבֶּשֶׁת xcv. 5.
חֲצוֹת cxix. 62.	חָתַן, חָתָן xix. 6.	יָגוֹן, יָגָה xiii. 3.
חֲצִי cii. 25.	חָתַת lxxxix. 41.	יָגַע, יָגִיעַ lxxviii. 46.
חָצִיר xxxvii. 2.		יָגֹר cxix. 39.
חֹצֶן cxxix. 7.	ט	יָד viii. 7.
חָצַץ vii. 14.	טִבְחָה xliv. 23.	יָדָה vi. 6.
חָצָץ lxxvii. 18.	טָבַע ix. 16.	יְדוּתוּן xxxix. 1.
חֲצֹצְרָה xcviii. 6.	טָהֵר, טָהוֹר xii. 7.	יָדִיד xlv. 1.
חָצֵר, חָצַר x. 8.	טָהַר lxxxix. 45.	יָדַע i. 6.
חָקַק, חֹק ii. 7.	טוֹב iv. 7.	יָדַעַת cxl. 13.
חֻקָּה xviii. 23.	טוּב xxv. 7.	יָהּ lxviii. 5.

T 2

INDEX.

יָהַב xxix. 1.	יָסַף x. 18.	יָרַד, יֵרֵד xlv. 4.
יְהָב lv. 23.	יָסַר ii. 10.	יְרֵכָה, יַרְכָּה xlviii. 3.
יְהוּדָה xlviii. 12.	יָעַד i. 5.	יָרַע civ. 2.
יְהֹוָה i. 2.	יָעַל xviii. 5.	יָרָק, יֶרֶק xxxvii. 2.
יוֹאָב lx. 2.	יָעֵל civ. 18.	יְרַקְרַק lxviii. 14.
יוֹם i. 2.	יַעַן cix. 16.	יָרֵשׁ iv. 8.
יָחֵן, יָנוּ xl. 3.	יָעַץ i. 1.	יְרֻשָּׁה lxi. 6.
יוֹנָה lv. 7.	יַעֲקֹב xiv. 7.	יִשְׂחָק cv. 9.
יוֹנַת אֵלֶם רְחֹקִים lvi. 1.	יַעַר, יָעַר xxix. 9.	יִשְׂרָאֵל xiv. 7.
יוֹנֶקֶת lxxx. 12.	יָפָה xlv. 3.	יֵשׁ, יָשָׁה vii. 4.
יוֹסֵף lxxvii. 16.	יָפָה xlviii. 3.	יָשַׁב i. 1.
יַחַד ii. 2.	יָפֵחַ, יָפַח xxvii. 12.	יְשׁוּעָתָה iii. 3.
יְחִידָה xxii. 21.	יֳפִי xlv. 12.	יִשַׁי lxxii. 20.
יָחַל xxxi. 25.	יָפַע l. 2.	יְשִׁימוֹת lv. 16.
יָחַם vi. 2.	יָצָא xvii. 2.	יְשִׁימוֹן, יָשַׁם lxviii. 8.
יָטַב xxxiii. 3.	יָצַב ii. 2.	יִשְׁמְעֵאלִים lxxxiii. 7.
יֵדַע cxxxviii. 6.	יָצַע, יָצוּעַ lxiii. 7.	יָשֵׁן, יָשַׁן iii. 6.
יַיִן lx. 5.	יָצַק xli. 9.	יָשֵׁן lxxviii. 65.
יָבַח vi. 2.	יֵצֶר ciii. 14.	יָשַׁע iii. 3.
יָכֹל xiii. 5.	יָקוּשׁ xci. 3.	יֶשַׁע xii. 6.
יָלַד ii. 7.	יָקַץ lxxviii. 65.	יָשָׁר v. 9.
יַלְדוּת cx. 3.	יָקָר, יָקַר xxxvi. 8.	יָשָׁר vii. 11.
יֶלֶק, יָלַק cv. 34.	יָקַר xlix. 13.	יֹשֶׁר xxv. 21.
יָמַם, יָם viii. 9.	יִרְאָה ii. 11.	יָתַם, יָתוֹם x. 14.
יָמִין xvi. 8.	יָרַד vii. 17.	יָתַן lxxiv. 15.
יִמְרוּךְ cxxxix. 20.	יַרְדֵּן xlii. 7.	יֶתֶר, יָתַר xi. 2.
יָנָה lxxiv. 8.	יָרַדֹף vii. 6.	
יְנִי cxli. 5.	יָרָה i. 2.	כ
יָצִין lxxii. 17.	יְרוּשָׁלַיִם li. 20.	כָּאַב xxxii. 10.
יָנְקִים viii. 3.	יָרֵחַ viii. 4.	כָּאֵב xxxix. 3.
יָסַד ii. 2.	יָרִיב xxxv. 1.	כָּאָה cix. 16.
יְסוּדָה lxxxvii. 1.	יְרִיעָה civ. 2.	כְּאָרִי xxii. 17.

INDEX.

כָּבַב viii. 4.
כָּבֵד iii. 4.
כָּבֹד iii. 4, xxxviii. 5.
כָּבוֹד iii. 4.
כְּבוּדָּה xlv. 14.
כֶּבֶל, בָּבֶל cv. 18.
כָּבַס li. 4.
בֹּהַן, כָּהַן lxxviii. 64.
כּוֹכָב viii. 4.
כּוּל lv. 23.
כּוּן i. 4.
כּוּס xi. 6, cii. 7.
כּוּשׁ vii. 1, lxviii. 32.
כּוֹשָׁרוֹת lxviii. 7.
כָּזָב, כָּזַב iv. 3.
כָּחַח, בַּח xxii. 16.
כָּחַד xl. 11.
כָּחַשׁ xviii. 45.
כַּחַשׁ lix. 13.
כִּי i. 2.
כִּילָפוֹת lxxiv. 6.
בַּל i. 3.
כָּל־ ii. 12.
כָּלָא xl. 10.
כֶּלֶב xxii. 17.
כָּלָה ii. 9.
כְּלָיוֹת vii. 10.
כָּלִיל li. 21.
כָּלַל i. 3.
כָּלְמָה, כָּלַם iv. 3.
כָּלַף lxxiv. 6.
כָּמַהּ lxiii. 2.

כָּמַר cxli. 10.
בֵּן i. 4, cv. 31.
כַּנָּה lxxx. 16.
כִּנּוֹר xxxiii. 2.
כָּנַס xxxiii. 7.
כָּנַע lxxxi. 15.
כְּנַעַן cv. 11.
כָּנָף, כָּנַף xvii. 8.
כַּנֵּר xxxiii. 2.
כִּסֵּא, כָּסָא ix. 5.
כֵּסֶה, כָּסָא lxxxi. 4.
כָּסָה xxxii. 1.
כְּסִיל xlix. 11.
כֶּסֶל, כָּסַל xxxviii. 8.
כִּסְלָה lxxxv. 9.
כָּסַם lxxx. 14.
כֶּסֶף, כָּסַף xii. 7.
כַּעַס vi. 8.
כָּפַף, כַּף vii. 4.
כְּפוֹר cxlvii. 16.
כָּפָר, כְּפִיר xvii. 12.
כֹּפֶר xlix. 8.
כַּר xxxvii. 20.
כָּרָה vii. 16.
כְּרוּב xviii. 11.
כֶּרֶם, כָּרַם cvii. 37.
כִּרְסֵם lxxx. 14.
כָּרַע xvii. 13.
כָּרַר xxxvii. 20.
כָּרַת xii. 4.
כַּשִּׂיל lxxiv. 6.
כָּשַׁל ix. 4.

כָּשַׁר lxviii. 7.
כֶּתֶם, כָּתַם xlv. 10.
כָּתַר xxii. 13.

ל

לֹא i. 1.
לֵאָה lxviii. 10.
לָאַד xxxiv. 8.
לְאֹם, לָאַם ii. 1.
לֵאמֹר lxxi. 11.
לֵב iv. 8.
לְבָאִם, לָבָא lvii. 5.
לֵבָב, לָבַב iv. 5.
לִבָּה vii. 10.
לָבַשׁ, לְבוּשׁ xxii. 19.
לָבָן li. 9.
לְבָנוֹן xxix. 5.
לֶהָבָה, לָהַב xxix. 7.
לָהַט lvii. 5.
לוֹ lxxxi. 14.
לוּחַ xxxvii. 21, lxxiv. 14.
לוֹט, לוּט lxxxiii. 9.
לֵוִי cxxxv. 20.
לִוְיָתָן lxxiv. 14.
לוּלְיָא xxvii. 13.
לוּן xxv. 13.
לוּץ i. 1.
לֶחִי, לָחַח iii. 8.
לָחַד lxxii. 9.
לֶחֶם, לָחַם xiv. 4.
לַחַץ, לָחַץ xlii. 10.

INDEX.

לָחַשׁ xli. 8.	מְגִלָּה xl. 8.	מוּעָקָה lxvi. 11.
לָטַשׁ vii. 13.	מָגֵן iii. 4.	מוֹפֵת lxxi. 7.
לַיִל i. 2.	מַגֵּפָה cvi. 29.	מוֹץ, מֹץ i. 4.
לִין xxv. 13.	מָנַר lxxxix. 45.	מוֹצָא xix. 7.
לָמַד xviii. 35.	מַד cix. 18.	מוּק lxxiii. 8.
לָמָּה ii. 1.	מִדְבָּר xxix. 8.	מוֹקֵד cii. 4.
לָמוֹ ii. 4.	מִדָּה, מָדַד xxxix. 5.	מוֹקֵשׁ xviii. 6.
לַעַג ii. 4.	מָדוֹן lxxx. 7.	מוּר xv. 4.
לָעַג xliv. 14.	מִדּוֹת cxxxiii. 2.	מוֹרָא lxxvi. 12.
לָעַג xxxv. 16.	מַרְחֵפוֹת cxl. 12.	מוֹרָה ix. 21.
לָעֵז cxiv. 1.	מִדְיָן lxxxiii. 10.	מוֹרֶה lxxxiv. 7.
לָקַח vi. 10.	מָה iii. 2.	מוּשׁ lv. 12, cxv. 7.
לָשַׁד, לְשַׁד xxxii. 4.	מַהֲמַה, מָהַהּ cxix. 60.	מוֹשָׁב i. 1.
לָשׁוֹן, לָשׁוֹן v. 10.	מָהִיר xlv. 2.	מוֹשָׁעוֹת lxviii. 21.
לָתַע lviii. 7.	מַהֲמֹרוֹת cxl. 11.	מָוֶת, מוּת vi. 6.
	מָהַר xvi. 4.	מוּת לַבֵּן ix. 1.
מ	מָהַר lxix. 18.	מִזְבֵּחַ xxvi. 6.
מְאֹד vi. 4.	מְהֵרָה xxxi. 3.	מֵזֶו cxliv. 13.
מַאֲוַיִּים cxl. 9.	מוֹ xi. 2.	מֵזַח cix. 19.
מָאוֹר lxxiv. 16.	מוֹא i. 3.	מְזִמָּה x. 2.
מֹאזְנַיִם lxii. 10.	מוֹאָב lx. 10.	מִזְמוֹר iii. 1.
מַאֲכָל xliv. 12.	מוּג xlvi. 7.	מִזְרָח l. 1.
מָאַן lxxvii. 3.	מוֹד xvi. 8.	מֵחַ lxvi. 15.
מָאַס xv. 4, lviii. 8.	מוּזָר lxix. 9.	מָחָא xcviii. 8.
מַאֲרָב x. 8.	מוֹט x. 6, lxvi. 9.	מָחָה ix. 6.
מָבוֹא l. 1.	מוּל xxxvii. 2.	מָחוֹז cvii. 30.
מַבּוּל xxix. 10.	מֻן xvii. 15.	מָחוֹל xxx. 12.
מִבְטָח xl. 5.	מוֹסָדוֹת xviii. 8.	מָחַח lxvi. 15.
מִבְצָר lxxxix. 41.	מוּסָר l. 17.	מְחִיר xliv. 13.
מִגְדָּל xlviii. 13.	מוֹסְרוֹת ii. 3.	מַחֲלַת liii. 1.
מָנוֹר xxxi. 14.	מוֹעֵד lxxiv. 4.	מַחֲלַת לְעַנּוֹת lxxxv.
מְגֹרָה xxxiv. 5.	מוֹעֵצוֹת v. 11.	מַחֲמָאוֹת lv. 22.

INDEX. 279

מַחֲנֶה xxvii. 3.
מַחְסֶה xiv. 6.
מַחְסוֹם xxxix. 2.
מַחְסוֹר xxxiv. 10.
מָחָר xliv. 13.
מָחַץ xviii. 39.
מֶחְקָר xcv. 4.
מַחֲשָׁבָה xxxiii. 10.
מַחְשָׁךְ lxxiv. 20.
מְחִתָּה lxxxix. 41.
מַטֶּה cv. 16.
מִטָּה vi. 7.
מָטָר xi. 6.
מָטָר lxxii. 6.
מִי iv. 7.
מַיִם i. 3.
מִין xvii. 15.
מִישׁוֹר xxvi. 12.
מֵישָׁרִים ix. 9.
מֵיתָרִים xxi. 13.
מַכְאוֹב xxxii. 10.
מַכָּה lxiv. 8.
מָכוֹן xxxiii. 14.
מָכַךְ cvi. 43.
מִכְלָה l. 9.
מִכְלָל l. 2.
מַכְמֹרִים cxli. 10.
מִכְשׁוֹל cxix. 165.
מִכְתָּם xvi. 1.
מָלֵא lxxiii. 10.
מִלֵּא xxiv. 1.
מַלְאָךְ xxxiv. 8.

מְלָאכָה lxxiii. 28.
מִלָּה xix. 5.
מִלּוֹשְׁנִי ci. 5.
מֶלַח, מָלַח lx. 2.
מִלְחָה cvii. 34.
מִלְחָמָה xviii. 35.
מָלַט xxii. 6.
מֶלֶךְ, מָלַךְ ii. 2.
מַלְכוּת xlv. 7.
מַלְכִּי־צֶדֶק cx. 4.
מָלַל xix. 5.
מָלַץ cxix. 103.
מַלְקוֹחַ xxii. 16.
מַלְתָּעוֹת lviii. 7.
מַמְלָכָה xlvi. 7.
מִמֶּנּוּ ii. 3.
מֶמְשָׁלָה ciii. 22.
מַן lxi. 8.
מָן lxxviii. 24.
מִנְּהוּ lxviii. 24.
מָנוֹד xliv. 15.
מְנוּחָה xxiii. 2.
מְנוּחִים cxvi. 7.
מָנוֹס lix. 17.
מִנְחָה xx. 4.
מֶנִּי xviii. 23.
מִנִּי xliv. 11, xlv. 9.
מִנִּים cl. 4.
מָנָה ii. 3.
מַנְעַפִּים cxli. 4.
מְנַשֶּׁה lx. 9.
מְנָת xi. 6.

מַסְגֵּר cxlii. 8.
מִסְגְּרוֹת xviii. 46.
מָסָה vi. 7.
מַסָּה xcv. 8.
מֶסֶךְ, מָסַךְ lxxv. 9.
מָסָךְ cv. 39.
מַסֵּכָה cvi. 19.
מְסִלָּה lxxxiv. 6.
מָסַס xxii. 15.
מִסְפֵּד xxx. 12.
מִסְפָּר xl. 13.
מִסְתָּר x. 8.
מַעֲלָה xvii. 5.
מָעַד xviii. 37.
מָעָה xxii. 15.
מָעוֹג xxxv. 16.
מָעוֹז xxvii. 1.
מָעוֹן xxvi. 8.
מְעַט, מָעַט ii. 12.
מָעַל, מְעִיל cix. 29.
מֵעִים xxii. 15.
מַעְיָן lxxiv. 15.
מַעֲלָה lxxiv. 5.
מַעֲלוֹת cxx. 1.
מַעֲלָלִים xxviii. 4.
מָעֳמָד lxix. 3.
מַעֲמַקִּים lxix. 3.
מַעַן v. 9.
מַעֲנִית, מַעֲנֶה cxxix. 3.
מַעֲרָב lxxv. 7.
מְעָרָה lvii. 1.
מַעֲשֶׂה viii. 4.

INDEX.

מִפְלָט lv. 9.
מִפְעָלָה xlvi. 9.
מָצָה lxxiii. 10.
מְצוּדָה xviii. 3.
מִצְוָה xix. 9.
מְצוֹלָה lxxxviii. 7.
מְצוּלָה lxviii. 23.
מָצוֹק cxix. 143.
מְצוּקָה xxv. 17.
מָצוֹר xxxi. 22.
מִצְעָד xxxvii. 23.
מִצְעָר xlii. 7.
מֵצַר cxvi. 3.
מִצְרַיִם lxviii. 32.
מִקְדָּשׁ lxviii. 36.
מַקְהֵלִים xxvi. 12.
מָקוֹם xxiv. 3.
מָקוֹר xxxvi. 10.
מִקְנֶה lxxviii. 48.
מָקַק xxxviii. 6.
מַר lxiv. 4.
מֹר xlv. 9.
מָרָה v. 11.
מָרוֹם vii. 8.
מֶרְחָב xviii. 20.
מְרִיבָה lxxxi. 8.
מִרְמָה v. 7.
מַרְעִית lxxiv. 1.
מָרַר xlv. 9.
מַשָּׂא xxxviii. 5.
מַשְׂאֵת cxli. 2.
מְשׂוּגָב ix. 10.

מָשׂוֹשׂ xlviii. 3.
מַשְׂכִּיל xiv. 2, xxxii. 1.
מַשְׂכִּית lxxiii. 7.
מִשְׂאָלָה xx. 6.
מִשְׁבְּצוֹת xlv. 14.
מִשְׁבָּרִים xlii. 8.
מֹשֶׁה xviii. 17.
מֹשֶׁה lxxvii. 21.
מַשּׁוּאוֹת lxxiii. 18.
מָשַׁח, מָשִׁיחַ ii. 2.
מִשְׁחָר cx. 3.
מָשַׁךְ xxxvi. 11.
מֶשֶׁךְ cxx. 5.
מֶשֶׁךְ cxxvi. 6.
מִשְׁכָּב iv. 5.
מִשְׁכָּן xxvi. 8.
מָשָׁל viii. 7.
מָשָׁל xliv. 15.
מִשְׁלַחַת lxxviii. 49.
מִשְׁמָן lxxviii. 31.
מִשְׁעָן xviii. 19.
מִשְׁעֶנֶת xxiii. 4.
מִשְׁפָּחָה xxii. 28.
מִשְׁפָּט i. 5.
מֶתֶג, מָתַג xxxii. 9.
מָתַי, מָתָה vi. 4.
מָתוֹק xix. 11.
מְתִים xvii. 14.
מְתֹם xxxviii. 4.
מָתְנַיִם, מָתַן lxvi. 11.
מַתָּנָה lxviii. 19.
מִתְנַקֵּם viii. 3.

מָתַק xix. 11.
מִתְרוֹנֵן lxxviii. 65.

נ

נָא vii. 10.
נֹאד lvi. 9.
נָאָה xxiii. 2.
נָאוָה xxxiii. 1.
נָאוֹת xxiii. 2.
נְאֻם xxxvi. 2.
נָאַף l. 18.
נָאַץ x. 3.
נָאַר lxxxix. 40.
נָבָא li. 2.
נִבְזֶה xv. 4.
נָבַט x. 14.
נָבִיא li. 2.
נָבֵל i. 3.
נָבָל xiv. 1.
נֵבֶל xxxiii. 2.
נְבֵלָה lxxix. 2.
נָבַע xix. 3.
נָבַר xviii. 27.
נֶגֶב, נָגַב cxxvi. 4.
נֶגֶד, נָגַד v. 6.
נֹגַהּ, נָגַהּ xviii. 13.
נָגַח xliv. 6.
נָגִיד lxxvi. 13.
נָנוֹן, נְגִינָה iv. 1.
נֶגַע xxxviii. 12.
נֵר lxiii. 11.
נֵר xxxiii. 7.

INDEX. 281

נָדַב xlvii. 10.
נְדָבָה liv. 8.
נָדַד xxxi. 12.
נָדַח v. 11.
נָדִיב xlvii. 10.
נֶדֶר, נָדַר xxii. 26.
נָהַג xlviii. 15.
נָהַל xxiii. 2.
נְהָמָה, נָהַם xxxviii. 9.
נָהָר, נָהַר xxiv. 2.
נוֹא xxxiii. 10.
נוּד xi. 1, xxxiii. 7.
נוֹד lvi. 9.
נָוֶה lxviii. 13.
נָוֶה lxxix. 7.
נוֹזְלִים lxxviii. 16.
נוּחַ xvii. 14.
נוּט xcix. 1.
נוּם lxxvi. 6.
נוּן lxxii. 17.
נוּס lx. 6.
נוּף xix. 11.
נוֹף xlviii. 3.
נוּר xviii. 29, xxi. 10.
נוּשׁ lxix. 21.
נֵזֶר, נָזַר lxxxix. 40.
נָחָה v. 9.
נְחוּשָׁה xviii. 35.
נְחִילָה v. 1.
נַחַל, נָחַל xviii. 5.
נַחֲלָה, נָחַל ii. 8.
נַחֲלַת xvi. 6.

נָחַם xxiii. 4.
נֶחָמָה cxix. 50.
נָחָשׁ xviii. 35.
נָחָשׁ, נָחַשׁ lviii. 5.
נְחֹשֶׁת cvii. 16.
נָחַת xviii. 35.
נָטָה vi. 7.
נָטַע xliv. 3.
נְטָעִים cxliv. 12.
נָטַר ciii. 9.
נִיא xxxiii. 10.
נִינָם lxxiv. 8.
נָכָה iii. 8.
נְכוֹנָה v. 10.
נְכִים xxxv. 15.
נָבָל cv. 25.
נֵכָר, נָכַר xviii. 45.
נָכְרִי lxix. 9.
נִמְאָס xv. 4.
נֵס lx. 6.
נָסָה iv. 7.
נָסָה xxvi. 2.
נָסִיךְ lxxxiii. 12.
נָסַךְ ii. 6.
נֶסֶךְ xvi. 4.
נָסַס lx. 6.
נָסַע lxxviii. 26.
נֶסֶק cxxxix. 8.
נְעוּרִים xxv. 7.
נָעַם, נָעִים xvi. 6.
נַעַל, נָעַל lx. 10.
נַעֲלָמִים xxvi. 4.

נֹעַם xxvii. 4.
נַעַר cix. 23.
נַעַר xxv. 7.
נֹעַר lxxxviii. 16.
נָפַל v. 11.
נֵפֶל lviii. 9.
נִפְלָאוֹת ix. 2.
נָפַץ ii. 9.
נֶפֶשׁ, נָפַשׁ iii. 3.
נֹפֶת xix. 11.
נַפְתָּלִי lxviii. 28.
נָצַב xxxix. 6.
נָצַח iv. 1.
נֶצַח ix. 7.
נָצַל vii. 2.
נָקִי, נָקָה x. 8.
נִקָּיוֹן xxvi. 6.
נִקְלֶה xxxviii. 8.
נָקַם lviii. 11.
נְקָמָה xviii. 48.
נָקַשׁ ix. 17.
נֵר xviii. 29.
נָשַׂג vii. 6.
נְשִׂיאִים cxxxv. 7.
נָשַׁק lxxviii. 21.
נָשָׂא lv. 16, lxxxix. 23.
נָשַׁב cxlvii. 18.
נָשָׁה lv. 16.
נְשִׁיָּה lxxxviii. 13.
נֶשֶׁךְ, נָשַׁךְ xv. 5.
נְשָׁמָה, נָשַׁם xviii. 16.
נֶשֶׁף, נָשַׁף cxix. 147.

U

INDEX.

נָשַׁק ii. 12.
נֶשֶׁק, גֶּשֶׁק cxl. 8.
נָשַׁר, גֶּשֶׁר ciii. 5.
נָתַב, נָתִיב lxxviii. 50.
נָתַן iv. 8.
נָתַן li. 2.
נָתַק ii. 3.
נָתַר cv. 20.

ס

סָבָא lxxii. 10.
סָבִיב, סָבַב iii. 7.
סְבָךְ lxxiv. 5.
סֶבֶל, סָבַל lxxxi. 7.
סְגֻלָּה, סָגַל cxxxv. 4.
סָגַר xxxv. 3.
סוּג, סוֹג xxxv. 4.
סוֹד xxv. 14.
סוּחַ cxxxv. 11.
סוּט ci. 3.
סוּס xx. 8.
סוּף lxxiii. 19, cvi. 7.
סוּפָה lxxxiii. 16.
סוּר vi. 9.
סוֹרְרִים lxvi. 7.
סָחַר xxxviii. 11.
סֹחֵרָה xci. 4.
סֵטִים ci. 3.
סִיג cxix. 119.
סִיחוֹן cxxxv. 11.
סִינַי lxviii. 9.
סִיסְרָא lxxxiii. 10.

סִיר lviii. 10.
סָךְ xlii. 5.
סָבַח x. 9.
סֻכּוֹת lx. 8.
סָכַךְ v. 12.
סָכַן cxxxix. 3.
סָכַר lxiii. 12.
סָלָה, סֶלָה iii. 3.
סָלָה cxix. 118.
סָלַח xxv. 11.
סַלַּח lxxxvi. 5.
סְלִיחָה cxxx. 4.
סָלַל lxviii. 5.
סֶלַע, סָלַע xviii. 3.
סָמַר cxix. 120.
סָעַד xviii. 36.
סֹעָה, סָעָה lv. 9.
סְעִף, סָעַף cxix. 113.
סַעַר, סָעַר lv. 9.
סַף lxxxiv. 11.
סָפַר ii. 7.
סֵפֶר xl. 8.
סִפְרָה lvi. 9.
כַּפֹּרֶת lxxi. 15.
סָרַר lxvi. 7.
סָתַר x. 8.
סֵתֶר xviii. 12.

ע

עָב xviii. 12.
עֶבֶד xviii. 1.
עֲבֹדָה civ. 14.

עָבוּר cv. 45.
עֶבְרָה, עָבַר vii. 7.
עָבַת, עֲבֹת ii. 3.
עֲנָב cl. 4.
עָנַל xvii. 5.
עֵגֶל xxix. 6.
עֲגָלָה xlvi. 10.
עַד iv. 3.
עַד xxvii. 12.
עֵדָה i. 3.
עֵדָה i. 5, xxv. 10.
עֵדוּת xix. 8.
עֲדִי xxxii. 9.
עֶרֶן, עָדַן xxxvi. 9.
עֵדֶר, עָדַר lxxviii. 52.
עוֹב xviii. 12.
עוּג xxxv. 16.
עוֹג cxxxv. 11.
עוּגָב cl. 4.
עוֹד, עוּד x. 18.
עָוָה xviii. 24.
עוּט xlv. 2.
עֹל, עָוַל vii. 4.
עָוִיל, עוּל lxxviii. 71.
עוֹלָה xxxvii. 1.
עוֹלָה xx. 4.
עוֹלֵל viii. 3.
עוֹלֵל cxxxvii. 9.
עוֹלָם v. 12.
עֲוָלָתָה cxxv. 3.
עָוֺן xviii. 24.
עוּף xi. 4.

INDEX.

עוֹף l. 11.
עוּק lv. 4.
עוּר vii. 7, lvii. 1.
עִוֵּר cxlvi. 8.
עֲוֺת cxix. 78.
עַז xviii. 18.
עֹז, עַז viii. 3.
עִזּוּז xxiv. 8.
עָזוּז lxxviii. 4.
עֵזֶר xx. 3.
עֶזְרָה xxii. 20.
עֶזְרָת cviii. 13.
עֵט xlv. 2.
עָטָה lxxi. 13.
עָטוּף lxi. 3.
עָטַר v. 13.
עֲטָרָה xxi. 4.
עִי lxxix. 1.
עַיִן v. 6.
עֵין־דֹּאר lxxxiii. 11.
עָיֵף lxiii. 2.
עִיר ix. 7.
עָכַר xxxix. 3.
עָכָשׁוּב, עֲכָב cxl. 4.
עַל, עָלָה i. 3.
עָלָה i. 3.
עֲלוּמִים lxxxix. 46.
עֲלִיָּה civ. 3.
עֶלְיוֹן vii. 18.
עֲלִיל xii. 7.
עָלַל, עֲלִילָה ix. 12.
עָלַם v. 12.

עַלְמָה xlvi. 1.
עַל־מוּת ix. 1, xlviii. 15.
עָלַץ v. 12.
עָלְתָה xcii. 16.
עַם iii. 7.
עַם xviii. 24.
עָמַד i. 1.
עִמָּדִי xxiii. 4.
עַמּוּד lxxv. 4.
עַמּוֹן lxxxiii. 8.
עָמָל, עָמֵל vii. 15.
עֲמָלֵק lxxxiii. 8.
עָמַם iii. 7.
עָמַם lxviii. 20.
עָמֹק lxiv. 7.
עֵמֶק lx. 8.
עֹמֶר cxxix. 7.
עָנַג xxxvii. 4.
עָנָה iii. 5, ix. 13.
עָנוּ ix. 13.
עֲנָוָה xviii. 36.
עֱנוּת xxii. 25.
עָנִי ix. 13.
עָנִי ix. 14.
עָנָן, עָנַן lxxviii. 14.
עָנָף, עָנֵף lxxx. 11.
עָנָק lxxiii. 6.
עֳפִי, עָפָה civ. 12.
עַפְעַפִּים xi. 4.
עָפָר, עָפַר vii. 6.
עֵץ i. 3.
עָצַב xvi. 4.

עֶצֶב cxxvii. 2.
עֹצֶב cxxxix. 24.
עֲצַבִּים cvi. 36.
עֶצֶבֶת xvi. 4.
עֵצָה i. 3.
עֵצָה i. 1.
עָצוּם x. 10.
עֶצֶם, עָצַם vi. 3.
עֹצֶם cxxxix. 15.
עֶצֶר cvi. 30.
עֹצֶר cvii. 39.
עָקֵב xiv. 7.
עָקֵב xli. 10.
עָקֵב xix. 12.
עָקָה lv. 4.
עֲקַלְקַל, עָקַל cxxv. 5.
עֲקֶרֶת cxiii. 9.
עָקֵשׁ, עִקֵּשׁ xviii. 27.
עָר ix. 7, cxxxix. 20.
עָרַב, עֶרֶב xxx. 6.
עֶרֶב cvi. 35.
עָרֹב lxxviii. 45.
עֹרֵב lxxxiii.12, cxlvii.9.
עֲרָבָה lxviii. 5.
עֲרָבִים cxxxvii. 2.
עָרָה xxxvii. 35.
עָרִיץ xxxvii. 35.
עָרַךְ v. 4.
עֵרֶךְ lv. 14.
עָרַם lxxxiii. 4.
עַרְעָר cii. 18.
עֹרֶף xviii. 41.

INDEX.

עֲרָפֶל xviii. 10.
עָרַץ x. 18.
עָרָר cii. 18.
עָרֵשׂ vi. 7.
עֵשֶׂב ,עָשַׂב lxxii. 16.
עָשׂוֹר xxxiii. 2.
עָשָׁר lx. 2.
עָשׁ xxxix. 12.
עָשִׁיר ,עָשַׁר xlv. 13.
עָשָׁן ,עָשֵׁן xviii. 9.
עֹשֶׁק lxii. 11.
עֵשֶׂר xlix. 7.
עָשַׁשׁ vi. 8.
עֶשְׁתֹּנוֹת cxlvi. 4.
עֵת i. 3.
עַתּוּד ,עָתַד l. 9.
עַתָּה ii. 10.
עָתַק vi. 8.
עָתָק xxxi. 19.

פ

פָּאַר lxxi. 8.
פָּנַשׁ lxxxv. 11.
פֵּרוּת cxi. 9.
פִּדְיוֹן xlix. 9.
פֶּה v. 10.
פֹּה cxxxii. 14.
פּוּג xxxviii. 9.
פַּח lxxxviii. 16.
פּוּץ xviii. 15.
פּוּק cxl. 9.
פּוּר xxxiii. 10.

פָּז ,פַּז xix. 11.
פָּזַר liii. 6.
פָּתַח ,פַּח xi. 6.
פַּחַד ,פָּחַד xiv. 5.
פָּטַר xxii. 8.
פִּיָּה v. 10.
פִּינְחָס cvi. 30.
פִּימִיּוֹת cxlix. 6.
פֶּלֶא ix. 2.
פֶּלֶא lxxvii. 12.
פְּלָאיָה cxxxix. 6.
פֶּלֶג ,פָּלַג i. 3.
פָּלָה iv. 4.
פָּלַט xvii. 13.
פָּלֵט xxxii. 7.
פָּלַל iv. 2.
פֶּלֶס lvi. 8.
פַּלָּצוּת ,פָּלַץ lv. 6.
פְּלִשְׁתִּים ,פְּלֶשֶׁת ,פָּלַשׁ lvi. 1.
פָּנָה ,פֵּן ii. 12.
פִּנָּה cxviii. 22.
פָּנִים iii. 1.
פְּנִימָה xlv. 14.
פָּסַג xlviii. 14.
פֶּסַח lxxii. 16.
פֶּסֶל ,פְּסִילִים lxxviii. 58.
פֶּסֶל xcvii. 7.
פָּסַס xii. 2.
פָּעַל v. 6.
פֹּעַל ix. 17.

פְּעֻלָּה xvii. 4.
פַּעַם ,פָּעַם xvii. 5.
פָּעַר cxix. 131.
פָּצַח xcviii. 4.
פָּצַם lx. 4.
פָּקַד viii. 5.
פְּקֻדָּה cix. 8.
פְּקוּדִים xix. 9.
פָּקַח cxlvi. 8.
פַּר xxii. 13.
פֶּרֶא civ. 11.
פֶּרֶד xxii. 15.
פֶּרֶד xxxii. 9.
פְּרִי ,פָּרָה i. 3.
פָּרַח lxxii. 7.
פָּרִיץ xvii. 4.
פָּרַס lxix. 32.
פַּרְעֹה cxxxv. 9.
פֶּרֶץ cvi. 23.
פָּרַק vii. 3.
פָּרַר lxxiv. 13.
פָּרַשׁ xliv. 21.
פֶּשַׁע ,פָּשַׁע v. 11.
פַּת cxlvii. 17.
פִּתְאֹם lxiv. 5.
פָּתָה lxxviii. 36.
פִּתּוּחַ lxxiv. 6.
פָּתַח v. 10.
פֶּתַח xxiv. 7.
פֶּתַח cxix. 130.
פֶּתִי xix. 8.
פְּתִיחָה lv. 22.

INDEX.

פָּתַל xviii. 27.
פֶּתֶן, פָּתַן lviii. 5.

צ

צָבָא xxiv. 10.
צָדַד, צַד xci. 7.
צָדַק, צַדִּיק i. 5.
צֶדֶק iv. 2.
צָהֳרַיִם xxxvii. 6.
צַוָּאר lxxv. 6.
צוֹבָה, צוֹב lx. 2.
צוּד xviii. 3.
צָוָה vii. 7.
צְוָחָה cxliv. 14.
צוֹם, צוּם xxxv. 13.
צוּף xix. 11.
צוּץ lxxii. 16.
צוּר xviii. 3, xlix. 15.
צְחִיחָה, צָחַח lxviii. 7.
צַיִד cxxxii. 15.
צֵידָה lxxviii. 25.
צִיָּה, צִיָּה lxiii. 2.
צִיּוֹן ii. 6.
צִיִּים lxxii. 9.
צִיץ ciii. 15.
צִיר xlix. 15.
צֵל, צָלַל xvii. 8.
צֶלַח i. 3.
צֶלֶם, צָלַם xxxix. 7.
צַלְמוֹן lxviii. 15.
צַלְמָוֶת xxiii. 4.
צִלְצֵעַ lxxxiii. 12.

צֶלַע, צָלַע xxxv. 15.
צִלְצָל cl. 5.
צִמָּא lxix. 22, cvii. 5.
צִמָּאוֹן cvii. 33.
צָמַד l. 19.
צָמַח lxv. 11.
צֶמֶר, צָמַר cxlvii. 16.
צָמַת xviii. 41.
צִנָּה viii. 8.
צִנָּה v. 13.
צִנּוֹר xlii. 8.
צָנַן v. 13.
צָנַר xlii. 8.
צַעַד, צָעַד xviii. 37.
צָעִיר lxviii. 28.
צֹעַן lxxviii. 12.
צְעָקָה, צָעַק ix. 13.
צָפָה v. 4.
צָפוֹן xlviii. 3.
צָפַר, צִפּוֹר viii. 9.
צְפִינֶךָ xvii. 14.
צְפַרְדֵּעַ lxxviii. 45.
צַר iii. 2..
צַר xlv. 13.
צָרָה ix. 10.
צָרַף xii. 7.
צָרַר iii. 2.

ק

קָאַת, קָאָה cii. 7.
קָבַר v. 10.
קָדַד vii. 17.

קָדוֹשׁ xvi. 3.
קָדִים xlviii. 8.
קָדַם xvii. 13.
קֶדֶם xliv. 2.
קַדְמָה cxxix. 6.
קָדְקֹד vii. 17.
קָדַר, קֵדָר cxx. 5.
קֹדֶשׁ, קָדַשׁ ii. 6.
קָדַשׁ xxix. 8.
קָהָל, קָהַל xxii. 23.
קָו xix. 5.
קָוָה ix. 19.
קוּט xcv. 10.
קוֹל iii. 5.
קוּם i. 5.
קוּף xix. 7.
קוּץ iii. 6.
קוֹץ cxviii. 12.
קוֹשׁ vii. 13.
קֶטֶב, קָטַב xci. 6.
קָטָן, קָטֹן civ. 25.
קְטֹרֶת, קָטַר lxvi. 15.
קִיטוֹר cxix. 83.
קַיִץ xxxii. 4.
קִיר lxii. 4.
קִישׁוֹן lxxxiii. 10.
קָלָה xxxviii. 8.
קָלוֹן, קָלָה lxxiii. 17.
קָלַל xxxvii. 22.
קְלָלָה cix. 17.
קָלָם, קֶלֶס xliv. 14.
קַן lxxxiv. 4.

INDEX.

קָנָא xxxvii. 1.	ר	רוֹמֵמָה cxviii. 16.
קִנְאָה lxix. 10.	רָאָה iv. 7.	רוּעַ xxvii. 6.
קָנָה, קָנֹה lxviii. 31.	רֹאשׁ iii. 4, lxix. 22.	רוּץ xviii. 30.
קִנְיָן civ. 24.	רִאשׁוֹן lxxix. 8.	רוּק ii. 1.
קֵץ xxxix. 5.	רֵאשִׁית lxxviii. 51.	רוּשׁ xxxiv. 11.
קָצָה xix. 7.	רֹב v. 8.	רָוָח, רָוָה cvi. 15.
קָצֶה xix. 5.	רַב xviii. 15.	רָוַז ii. 2.
מִקְצוֹעַ xlviii. 11.	רָבַב iii. 2.	רָחַב iv. 2.
קֶצַע קְצִיעוֹת xlv. 9.	רְבָבָה iii. 7.	רָחָב ci. 5.
קָצַר, קָצִיר lxxx. 12.	רָבָה xvi. 4.	רְחוֹב lv. 12.
קֶצֶף, קָצַף xxxviii. 2.	רְבוֹתַיִם lxviii. 18.	רַחוּם lxxviii. 38.
קָרָא iii. 5, xxxv. 3.	רְבִיבִים lxv. 11.	רָחוֹק x. 1.
קָרַב xv. 3.	רֶבַע, רָבַע cxxxix. 3.	רָחַם xviii. 2.
קֶרֶב lv. 19.	רָנַן iv. 5.	רֶחֶם xxii. 11.
קֶרֶב v. 10.	רָגַל xv. 3.	רַחֲמִים xxv. 6.
קֻרְבָּה lxxiii. 28.	רֶגֶל viii. 7.	רָחַץ xxvi. 6.
קַרְדֹּם lxxiv. 5.	רָגַם, רִגְמָה lxviii. 28.	רַחַץ lx. 10.
קָרָה xlviii. 3, cxlvii. 17.	רָגַע, רֶגַע vi. 11.	רָחַק x. 1.
קָרוֹב xv. 3.	רֶגֶז xxxv. 20.	רָחֵק lxxiii. 27.
קָרַח, קֹרַח xlii. 1.	רָגַשׁ ii. 1.	רָחַשׁ xlv. 2.
קֵרֵחַ cxlvii. 17.	רֶגֶשׁ lv. 15.	רִיב xviii. 44.
קִרְיָה xlviii. 3.	רִגְשָׁה lxiv. 3.	רִיק ii. 1.
קֶרֶן xviii. 3.	רָדַם lxxvi. 7.	רֵיקָם vii. 5.
קַרְסֻלַּיִם, קָרֵס xviii. 37.	רָתַב lxxxvii. 4.	רֶכֶב xx. 8.
קָרַר cxlvii. 17.	רֹחַב xc. 10.	רְכוּב civ. 3.
קַשׁ lxxxiii. 14.	רְחָבִים xl. 5.	לִכֶס, רָכַס xxxi. 21.
קֶשֶׁב v. 3.	רָחָם xlvii. 10.	רֵם xxii. 22.
קַשָּׁב cxxx. 2.	רוּד lv. 3.	רָמָה v. 7.
קָשָׁה lx. 5.	רְוָיָה, רָוָה xxiii. 5.	רְמִיָּה xxxii. 2.
קָשַׁט, קֹשֶׁט lx. 6.	רוּחַ i. 4.	רֶמֶשׂ civ. 25.
קַשָּׁשׁ lxxxiii. 14.	רוּם iii. 4.	רָנָה xvii. 1.
קֶשֶׁת vii. 13.	רוֹמָם lxvi. 17.	רַנֵּן xxxii. 7.

INDEX. 287

רָנַן v. 12.
רְנָנָה lxiii. 6.
רֶסֶן, רָסַן xxxii. 9.
רַע v. 5.
רֵעַ xii. 3, cxxxix. 2.
לֹעַ xxviii. 4.
רָעָב xxxiii. 19.
רָעֵב cvii. 5.
רְעָדָה, רָעַד ii. 11.
רָעָה xii. 3.
רָעַל lx. 5.
רַעַם xviii. 14.
רַעַם lxxvii. 19.
רַעֲנָן, רָעֵן xxxvii. 35.
רָעַע ii. 9.
רָפָא vi. 3.
רְפָאִים lxxxviii. 11.
רָפָה xxxvii. 8.
רָפַס lxviii. 31.
רָץ, רוּץ lxviii. 31.
רָצָד lxviii. 17.
רָצָה, רָצוֹן v. 13.
רֶצַח, רָצַח xlii. 11.
רַק xxxii. 6.
רָקַד xxix. 6.
רָקִיעַ xix. 2.
רִקְמָה, רָקַם xlv. 15.
רָקַע xix. 2.
רָקַק xxxii. 6.
רֶשַׁע, רָשָׁע i. 1.
רֶשַׁע v. 5.
רֶשֶׁף, רָשַׁף lxxvi. 4.

רֶשֶׁת ix. 16.
רָתַם, רֹתֶם cxx. 4.

שׁ

שְׂאֵת lxii. 5.
שֹׂבַע xvi. 11.
שֶׁבֶר civ. 27.
שֵׂבֶר cxix. 116.
שָׂגַב ix. 10.
שָׂנֶה lxxiii. 12.
שְׂדֵרָה lxxviii. 12.
שָׂדֶה, שָׂדַי viii. 8.
שֶׂה cxix. 176.
שׂוֹט xl. 5.
שָׂחָה vi. 7.
שְׂחוֹק cxxvi. 2.
שָׂחַק ii. 4.
שָׂטַם lv. 4.
שָׂטַן xxxviii. 21.
שָׂטָן cix. 6.
שֵׂיבָה, שִׂיב lxxi. 18.
שִׂיחָה cxix. 97.
שָׂכָה lxxiii. 7.
שָׂכַל ii. 10.
שֵׂכֶל cxi. 10.
שָׂכָר, שָׂכַר cxxvii. 3.
שָׂלָה, שָׂלוּ cv. 40.
שַׂלְמָה civ. 2.
שָׂמֵחַ xxxv. 26.
שִׂמְחָה iv. 8.
שָׂנֵא v. 6.
שִׂנְאָה xxv. 19.

שָׁעַף xciv. 19.
שַׁעַר lxviii. 22.
שַׁעַר, שַׂעֲרָה xl. 13.
שָׂפָה xii. 3.
שַׂק, שָׁקַק xxx. 12.
שַׂר, שָׂרַר xlv. 17.
שַׂרְעַפִּים xciv. 19.
שָׂשׂוֹן, שָׂשָׂה xlv. 8.
שָׁאַג, שְׁאָגָה xxii. 2.
שָׁאוֹן, שָׁאָה xl. 3.
שְׁאוֹל vi. 6.
שָׁאוּל xviii. 1.
שָׁאַל ii. 8.
שְׁאֵלָה cvi. 15.
שָׁאַן, שַׁאֲנָן cxxiii. 4.
שָׁאַף lvi. 2.
שְׁאָר, שָׁאַר lxxiii. 26.
שְׁאֵרִית, שָׁאַר lxxvi. 11.
שִׁבָה xiv. 7.
שְׁבוּעָה cv. 9.
שְׁבוּת xiv. 7.
שָׁבַח lxiii. 4.
שֵׁבֶט, שָׁבַט ii. 9.
שְׁבִי lxviii. 19.
שְׁבִיל lxxvii. 20.
שַׁבְלוּל, שָׁבָל lviii. 9.
שִׁבֹּלֶת lxix. 3.
שָׂבַע xv. 4.
שִׁבְעִים xc. 10.
שִׁבְעָתַיִם xii. 7.
שָׁבַר iii. 8.
שֶׁבֶר, שָׁבַר lx. 4.

שָׁבַת viii. 3.	שָׁחַח x. 10.	שָׁלֵם iii. 1.
שַׁבָּת xcii. 1.	שְׁחִיחוֹת cvii. 20.	שָׁלֵם lxxvi. 3.
שָׁבַתִּי xxiii. 6.	שַׁחַל, שָׁחַל xci. 13.	שְׁלֹמֹה lxxii. 1.
שָׁגַג cxix. 67.	שָׁחַק xviii. 43.	שְׁלֹמָה xci. 8.
שָׁנָה vii. 1.	שְׁחָקִים xviii. 12.	שָׁלַף cxxix. 6.
שָׁנַח xxxiii. 14.	שַׁחַר, שָׁחַר xxii. 1.	שָׁם xiv. 5.
שְׁנִיאָה xix. 13.	שָׁחַת xiv. 1.	שֵׁם v. 12.
שִׁנָּיוֹן vii. 1.	שַׁחַת vii. 16, xvi. 10.	שַׁמָּה xlvi. 9.
שָׁגַל, שֵׁגַל xlv. 10.	שָׁטַח lxxxviii. 10.	שְׁמוּאֵל xcix. 6.
שָׂדַד, שֹׂד xii. 6.	שֶׁטֶף, שָׁטַף xxxii. 6.	שְׁמוּעָה cxii. 7.
שָׂדֶה, שַׂר xxii. 10.	שַׁי, שָׁיא lxviii. 30.	שָׁמַט cxli. 6.
שַׁדַּי lxviii. 15.	שִׁיבָה cxxvi. 1.	שָׁמַיִם ii. 4.
שֵׁדִים cvi. 37.	שִׂיחָה lvii. 7.	שְׁמִינִית vi. 1.
שׁוֹא xxxv. 17.	שִׁיר vii. 1, xxviii. 7.	שָׁמֵן, שֶׁמֶן xxiii. 5.
שָׁוְא, שׁוֹא xii. 3.	שִׁירָה xviii. 1.	שְׁמָנִים xc. 10.
שׁוֹאָה xxxv. 8.	שִׁית iii. 7, lxxiii. 6.	שֵׁמַע xviii. 45.
שׁוּב vi. 5.	שְׁכוֹל xxxv. 12.	שְׁמֻרָה lxxvii. 5.
שׁוּד xci. 6.	שִׁכּוֹר cvii. 27.	שָׁמְרָה cxli. 3.
שָׁוָה xvi. 8.	שְׁכֶם xxi. 13, lx. 8.	שִׁמֻרִים lxxv. 9.
שׁוּחַ vii. 16.	שָׁכַן xxxi. 12.	שֶׁמֶשׁ xix. 5.
שׁוּעַ, שֵׁוַע v. 3.	שֶׁכֶר, שָׁכַר lxix. 13.	שֵׁן iii. 8.
שָׁעַל lxiii. 11.	שֶׁלֶג, שָׁלַג li. 9.	שָׂנֵא cxxvii. 2.
שׁוֹף cxxxix. 11.	שָׁלוּ, שָׁלֵו xxx. 7.	שִׁנְאָן lxviii. 18.
שׁוֹפָר xlvii. 6.	שְׁלֵו lxxiii. 12.	שָׁנָה xxxi. 11.
שׁוּק lxv. 10.	שִׁלּוֹ lxxviii. 60.	שָׁנָה lxxvi. 6.
שׁוֹק cxlvii. 10.	שַׁלְוָה cxxii. 7.	שְׁנַיִם עָשָׂר lx. 2.
שׁוֹר, שׁוֹר lxix. 32.	שָׁלוֹם iii. 1.	שָׁנֵן xlv. 6.
שׁוּר xviii. 30, xcii. 12.	שָׁלַח xviii. 15.	שְׁנָת cxxxii. 4.
שׁוּשׁ, שׂוֹשׂ xlv. 1.	שֻׁלְחָן xxiii. 5.	שָׁסַס lxxxix. 42.
שׁוּשַׁן עֵדוּת lx. 1.	שָׁלִישׁ lxxx. 6.	שָׁעַל lxiii. 11.
שָׁחַד, שֹׁחַד xv. 5.	שָׁלַךְ ii. 3.	שָׁעַע xciv. 19.
שָׁחָה v. 8.	שָׁלָל, שָׁלַל lxviii. 13.	שַׁעַר, שָׁעַר ix. 14.

שַׁעֲשֻׁעִים cxix. 24.	תְּבוּאָה cvii. 37.	תֵּימָן lxxviii. 26.
שֶׁפַח xxii. 28.	תְּבוּנָה xlix. 4.	תִּירוֹשׁ iv. 8.
שִׁפְחָה cxxiii. 2.	תָּבוֹר lxxxix. 13.	תָּכַךְ, תֹּךְ x. 7.
שָׁפֵל xviii. 28.	תֵּבֵל ix. 9.	תִּכְלָה cxix. 96.
שָׁפָל cxxxviii. 6.	תַּבְנִית cvi. 20.	תַּכְלִית cxxxix. 22.
שָׁפָל cxxxvi. 23.	תָּבַר lxxxix. 13.	תָּכַן lxxv. 4.
שָׁפָן civ. 18.	תַּגְמוּלִים cxvi. 12.	חֶלֶם, תָּלַם lxv. 11.
שָׁפַר xvi. 6.	תִּגְרָה xxxix. 11.	תָּלַע xxii. 7.
שָׂפַת, שְׂפָתַיִם lxviii. 14.	תֹּהוּ, תָּהָה cvii. 40.	תָּם xxxvii. 37.
שִׁקּוּיִם cii. 10.	תְּהוֹם xxxiii. 7.	תֹּם vii. 9.
שִׁקְמוֹת lxxviii. 47.	תְּהִלָּה ix. 15.	תְּמוּנָה xvii. 15.
שָׁקַף xiv. 2.	תּוּגָה cxix. 28.	תְּמוּתָה lxxix. 11.
שֶׁקֶץ xxii. 25.	תּוֹדָה xxvi. 7.	תָּמִיד xvi. 8.
שְׁקָקָה cvii. 9.	תָּוָה lxxviii. 41.	תָּמִים xv. 2.
שֶׁקֶר, שָׁקַר vii. 15.	תּוֹחֶלֶת xxxix. 8.	תָּמַם vii. 9.
שִׁרְיוֹן xxix. 6.	תָּוֶךְ xxii. 15.	תֶּמֶס lviii. 9.
שָׂרִים lxviii. 26.	תּוֹכֵחָה cxlix. 7.	תָּמָר, תָּמַר xcii. 13.
שְׁרִירוּת lxxxi. 13.	תּוֹכַחַת xxxviii. 15.	תָּנָה viii. 2.
שָׁרַר v. 9.	תּוֹלָל cxxxvii. 3.	תְּנוּמָה cxxxii. 4.
שֹׁרֶשׁ lii. 7.	תּוֹלַעַת xxii. 7.	תַּנּוּר xxi. 10.
שֵׁרֵשׁ lxxx. 10.	תּוֹמִיךְ xvi. 5.	תַּנְחוּמִים xciv. 19.
שָׁרַת ci. 6.	תּוֹעֵבָה lxxxviii. 9.	תַּגִּים xliv. 20.
שֵׂתוּ xlix. 15.	תּוֹעָפוֹת xcv. 4.	תַּנִּין lxxiv. 13.
שָׁתוּל i. 3.	תּוֹצָאוֹת lxviii. 21.	תָּנַן xxi. 10, xliv. 20.
שָׁחוֹת xi. 3.	תּוֹר lxxiv. 19.	תָּעַב v. 7.
שָׁתִיל cxxviii. 3.	תּוֹרָה i. 2.	תַּעֲלֻמָה xliv. 22.
שָׁתַק cvii. 30.	תּוֹשָׁב xxxix. 13.	תַּעֲצֻמוֹת lxviii. 36.
	תַּחֲלוּאִים ciii. 3.	תַּעַר, תָּעַר lii. 3.
ת	תַּחֲנוּנוֹת lxxxvi. 6.	תֹּף lxxxi. 3.
תָּאֵב, תָּאַב cxix. 20.	תַּחֲנוּנִים xxviii. 2.	תִּפְאֶרֶת lxxi. 8.
תַּאֲוָה x. 3.	תַּחַת viii. 7.	תְּפִלָּה iv. 2.
תְּאֵנָה cv. 33.	תַּחְתִּיּוֹת lxiii. 10.	תֹּפֶף lxviii. 26.

x

תִּקְוָה ix. 19. | תֶּקַע cl. 3. | תַּרְעֵלָה lx. 5.
תְּקוּפָה xix. 7. | תְּרוּעָה xxvii. 6. | תַּרְשִׁישׁ xlviii. 8.
תָּקַע xlvii. 2. | תַּרְמִית cxix. 118. | תְּשׁוּעָה xxxiii. 17.

ADDITIONS AND CORRECTIONS.

Page 1, line 4, *for* Psalms i–xvi. *read* Psalms i–xli.
Ps. i. 2, *for* תוֹרָה *read* תּוֹרָה
 ,, ii. 4, *for* in-(the)heavens *read* in-the-heavens
 ,, iv. 1, *for* Musician or *read* Musician, or
 ,, v. 1, *for* Super ea *read* Pro ea
 ,, vii. 1, *for* דִּבְרֵי־ *read* דִּבְרֵי־
 ,, vii. 7, *for* צָוָה *read* צִוָּה
 ,, ix. 13, *for* i.q. צָעַד *read* i.q. זָעַף
 ,, xii. 9, *for* at-raising *read* at-(the)rising-of
 ,, xiv. 1, *for* מְזְמוֹר *read* מִזְמוֹר
 ,, xv. 3, *for* וְחֶרְפָּת *read*־וְחֶרְפָּה
 ,, xviii. 9, *for* אֲשֶׁן *read* עָשָׁן
 ,, xix. 5, (p. 69, l. 1,) *before* קַּוָּם *insert* Verse 5.
 ,, xxii. 28, *for* מְשִׁפְּחוֹת *read* מִשְׁפָּחוֹת
 ,, xxx. 7, *for* R. שָׁלוּ to be quiet, *read* R. שָׁלוּ or שָׁלָה to be quiet.
 ,, xlv. 12, *for* יָפִי *read* יָפְיֵ׃
 ,, li. 2, *for* נָבָא *read* נָבָא
 ,, lv. 7, *for* יָנַף *read* יָנַח or יֵחַן
 ,, lx. 2, *for* שְׁנֶם *read* שְׁנַיִם
 ,, lxix. 3, *for* שִׁבָּלִים *read* שִׁבֳּלִים
 ,, lxxiii. 7, *for* מַשְׁבִּית *read* מַשְׂכִּית
 ,, lxxiii. 12, *for* שָׁלוּ *read* שָׁלוּ
 ,, lxxiv. 5, *for* verb. n. f. from עָלָה i. 3 with pr. לְ ii. 1 *read* verb. n. m. from עָלָה i. 3 with pr. לְ ii. 1 and ה local.
 ,, lxxviii. 47, *for* נָפֶן *read* גֶּפֶן
 ,, lxxxiii. 2, *for* דָּמִי־ *read* דֳּמִי־
 ,, xciii. 3, *for* דָּכִי *read* דֳּכִי
 ,, xcv. 10, *for* אַרְבַּע *read* אַרְבַּע
 ,, ci. 5 and civ. 18, *for* נָבַהּ *read* גָּבַהּ

ADDITIONS AND CORRECTIONS.

Ps. cvi. 32, *for* רָעַע *read* רָעַע
„ cx. 3, *for* נְדָבֹת *read* נְדָבֹת
„ cxix. 160, *for* (The) beginning-of *read* (The) beginning-of Thy-word
„ cxlv. Introduction, *for* תְּהִלּוֹת *read* תְּהִלִּים
„ cxlvii. 8, *for* הָצִיר *read* חָצִיר
„ cxlvii. 10, *for* שׁוּק subst. f. *read* שׁוֹק subst. f.

A

SELECTION

FROM

THE PUBLICATIONS

OF

MESSRS. JAS. PARKER AND CO.,

BROAD-STREET, OXFORD,
AND 377, STRAND, LONDON.

OXFORD,
1873.

CONTENTS.

	PAGE
NEW Books	3
Scripture Commentaries	5
Ecclesiastical History	7
The Prayer-book	9
Doctrinal Theology	10
Parish Work	11
Devotional Works	12
Oxford Editions of Devotional Works	14
Biographies	15
The Christian Year	16
Church Poetry	17
Sermons	18
Historical Tales	20
Architecture and Archæology	21, 23
Architectural Topography	22
Archæology	24
Oxford Pocket Classics	25—29
Educational Works	30, 31
Daily Services	32

NEW BOOKS.

A Grammatical Analysis of the Hebrew Psalter;

Being an Explanatory Interpretation of Every Word contained in the Book of Psalms, intended chiefly for the Use of Beginners in the Study of Hebrew. By JOANA JULIA GRESWELL. Crown 8vo., price 6s.

The Bampton Lectures for 1873.

By the Rev. I. GREGORY SMITH, Prebendary of Hereford, and Vicar of Great Malvern.   [*In the Press.*

The Confirmation Class-book:

Notes for Lessons, with APPENDIX, containing Questions and Summaries for the Use of the Candidates. By EDWARD M. HOLMES, LL.B., Rector of Marsh Gibbon, Bucks, and Diocesan Inspector of Schools; Author of the "Catechist's Manual." Fcap. 8vo., limp cloth, 2s. 6d.

   Also, in wrapper, THE QUESTIONS AND SUMMARIES separate, 4 sets, 128 pp. in each, 1s. each.

Sermons preached before the University of Oxford

Between A.D. 1859 and 1872. By the Rev. E. B. PUSEY, D.D., Regius Professor of Hebrew, and Canon of Christ Church. 8vo., cloth, 6s.

The Last Twelve Verses of the Gospel according to S. Mark

Vindicated against Recent Critical Objectors and Established, by JOHN W. BURGON, B.D., Vicar of S. Mary-the-Virgin's, Fellow of Oriel College, and Gresham Lecturer in Divinity. With Facsimiles of Codex א and Codex L. 8vo., cloth, 12s.

Sermons preached before the University of Oxford:

Third Series, from MDCCCLXIII. to MDCCCLXX. By SAMUEL, Lord Bishop of Winchester, Prelate of the Most Noble Order of the Garter. 8vo., cloth, 7s. 6d.

Inventory of Furniture and Ornaments

Remaining in all the Parish Churches of Hertfordshire in the last year of the Reign of King Edward the Sixth: Transcribed from the Original Records, by JOHN EDWIN CUSSANS, F.R.Hist.S. Crown 8vo., limp cloth, 4s.

JAMES PARKER AND CO., OXFORD AND LONDON.

Sermons

On the Offices for the Visitation of the Sick, and the Burial of the Dead. By CHARLES JAMES BURTON, M.A., Chancellor of Carlisle, and Vicar of Lydd. Post 8vo., cloth, 3s. 6d.

Are we Better than our Fathers?

Or, A Comparative View of the Social Position of England at the Revolution of 1688, and at the Present Time. FOUR LECTURES delivered in St. Paul's Cathedral, November, 1871. By ROBERT GREGORY, M.A., Canon of St. Paul's. Crown 8vo., cloth, 2s. 6d.

Sermons on some Subjects of Recent Controversy.

Preached before the University of Oxford. 1. Outward Observances. 2. The Eucharistic Sacrifice. 3. The Better Covenant. 4. The Shiloh. 5. Summary View of the Christian Evidences. By CHARLES A. HEURTLEY, D.D., Margaret Professor of Divinity, and Canon of Christ Church. 8vo., cloth, 5s.

The Elements of Psychology,

On the Principles of BENEKE, Stated and Illustrated in a Simple and Popular Manner by DR. G. RAUE, Professor in the Medical College, Philadelphia; Fourth Edition, considerably Altered, Improved, and Enlarged, by JOHANN GOTTLIEB DRESSLER, late Director of the Normal School at Bautzen. Translated from the German. Post 8vo., cloth, 6s.

Christianity as Taught by S. Paul.

The BAMPTON LECTURES for the Year 1870. By WILLIAM J. IRONS, D.D., of Queen's College, Oxford; Prebendary of S. Paul's; and Rector of Wadingham. To which is added an Appendix of the CONTINUOUS SENSE of S. Paul's Epistles; with Notes and Metalegomena. 8vo., cloth, with Map, 14s.

The Works of S. Irenæus,

Translated by the late Rev. JOHN KEBLE (forming vol. 42 of the Series of the Library of the Fathers). 8vo., cloth, 14s.; to Subscribers, 10s. 6d.

Bibliotheca Patrum.

Vol. I.—S. AURELII AUGUSTINI CONFESSIONES, Post Editionem Parisiensem novissimam ad fidem Codicum Oxoniensium recognitæ, et post Editionem M. DUBOIS, ex ipso Augustino illustratæ. Editio Secunda. 8vo., cloth, 9s.; to Subscribers, 7s.

JAMES PARKER AND CO.,

The Minor Prophets;

With a Commentary Explanatory and Practical, and Introductions to the Several Books. By E. B. PUSEY, D.D., Regius Professor of Hebrew, and Canon of Christ Church. 4to., *sewed*, 5s. each Part.

Part I. contains HOSEA—JOEL, INTRODUCTION.
Part II. JOEL, INTRODUCTION—AMOS vi. 6.
Part III. AMOS vi. 6 to end—OBADIAH—JONAH—MICAH i. 12.
Part IV. MICAH i. 13 to NAHUM, end.
Part V. HABAKKUK, ZEPHANIAH, HAGGAI. [*In preparation.*

Daniel the Prophet.

Nine Lectures delivered in the Divinity School, Oxford. With a Short Preface in Answer to Dr. Rowland Williams. By E. B. PUSEY, D.D., Regius Professor of Hebrew, and Canon of Christ Church. *Sixth Thousand.* 8vo., 10s. 6d.

The Prophecies of Isaiah.

Their Authenticity and Messianic Interpretation Vindicated, in a Course of Sermons preached before the University of Oxford. By the Rev. R. PAYNE SMITH, D.D., Regius Professor of Divinity. 8vo., cloth, 10s. 6d.

A Plain Commentary on the Book of Psalms

(Prayer-book Version), chiefly grounded on the Fathers. For the Use of Families. 2 vols., Fcap. 8vo., cloth, 10s. 6d.

A Short Summary of the Evidences for the Bible.

By the Rev. T. S. ACKLAND, M.A., late Fellow of Clare Hall, Cambridge; Incumbent of Pollington cum Balne, Yorkshire. 24mo., cloth, 3s.

The Catena Aurea.

A Commentary on the Four Gospels, collected out of the Works of the Fathers by S. THOMAS AQUINAS. Uniform with the Library of the Fathers. A Re-issue, complete in 6 vols., cloth, £2 2s.

A Plain Commentary on the Four Holy Gospels,

Intended chiefly for Devotional Reading. By the Rev. J. W. BURGON, M.A., Vicar of St. Mary's, Oxford, and Gresham Lecturer in Divinity. New Edition. 5 vols., Fcap. 8vo., limp cloth, £1 1s.

The Psalter and the Gospel.

The Life, Sufferings, and Triumph of our Blessed Lord, revealed in the Book of Psalms. Fcap. 8vo., cloth, 2s.

A New Catena on St. Paul's Epistles to the Ephesians and Philippians.

A Practical and Exegetical Commentary. Edited by the late Rev. HENRY NEWLAND. 8vo., cloth, 7s. 6d.

EPHESIANS, separately, 8vo., 4s.; PHILIPPIANS, separately, 8vo., 3s. 6d.

Reflections in a Lent Reading of the Epistle to the Romans.

By the late Rev. C. MARRIOTT. Fcap. 8vo., cloth, 3s.

JAMES PARKER AND CO.,

A History of the Church,
From the Edict of Milan, A.D. 313, to the Council of Chalcedon, A.D. 451. By WILLIAM BRIGHT, D.D., Regius Professor of Ecclesiastical History, and Canon of Christ Church, Oxford. Second Edition. Post 8vo., 10s. 6d.

The Age of the Martyrs;
Or, The First Three Centuries of the Work of the Church of our Lord and Saviour Jesus Christ. By JOHN DAVID JENKINS, B.D., Fellow of Jesus College, Oxford; Canon of Pieter Maritzburg. Crown 8vo., cloth, 6s.

The Councils of the Church,
From the Council of Jerusalem, A.D. 51, to the Council of Constantinople, A.D. 381; chiefly as to their Constitution, but also as to their Objects and History. By E. B. PUSEY, D.D. 8vo., cloth, 10s. 6d.

The Ecclesiastical History of the First Three Centuries,
From the Crucifixion of Jesus Christ to the year 313. By the late Rev. Dr. BURTON. Fourth Edition. 8vo., cloth, 12s.

A Brief History of the Christian Church,
From the First Century to the Reformation. By the Rev. J. S. BARTLETT. Fcap. 8vo., cloth, 2s. 6d.

Ordinum Sacrorum in Ecclesia Anglicana Defensio,
Unacum Statutis, Documentis, et Testimoniis ordinum Anglicanorum valorem probantibus; et Registro Consecrationis Archiepiscopi Parkeri, in Bibliotheca Lambethæ Asservato, Photozincographice expresso. Editore T. J. BAILEY, B.A. Large Folio, cloth, £1 10s.

A Defence of Holy Orders in the Church of England,
Including the Statutes, Documents, and other Evidence attesting the Validity of Anglican Orders. Edited by the Rev. T. J. BAILEY, B.A., C.C. Coll., Cambridge. Crown 8vo., cloth, 6s.

History of the so-called Jansenist Church of Holland;

With a Sketch of its Earlier Annals, and some Account of the Brothers of the Common Life. By the late Rev. J. M. NEALE, Warden of Sackville College. 8vo., cloth, 5s.

A History of the English Church,

From its Foundation to the Reign of Queen Mary. Addressed to the Young. By M. C. S. Crown 8vo., cloth, 5s.

Bede's Ecclesiastical History of the English Nation.

A New Translation by the Rev. L. GIDLEY, M.A., Chaplain of St. Nicholas', Salisbury. Crown 8vo., cloth, 6s.

St. Paul in Britain;

Or, The Origin of British as Opposed to Papal Christianity. By the Rev. R. W. MORGAN. Crown 8vo., cloth, 3s.

Peter the Apostle never at Rome,

Shewn to be a Historical Fact: with a Dissertation of the Apostolic Authority of the Symbol (or Creed) of the Church. By J. H. BROWN, M.A., Rector of Middleton-in-Teesdale. Post 8vo., limp cloth, 2s. 6d.

Scotland and the Scottish Church.

By the Rev. H. CASWALL, M.A., Vicar of Figheldean, Wilts.; Author of "America and the American Church," &c. Fcap. 8vo., cloth, 2s. 6d.

The Sufferings of the Clergy during the Great Rebellion.

By the Rev. JOHN WALKER, M.A., sometime of Exeter College, Oxford. Epitomised by the Author of "The Annals of England." Fcap. 8vo., cloth, 5s.

JAMES PARKER AND CO.,

An Explanation of the Thirty-Nine Articles.

With an Epistle Dedicatory to the Rev. E. B. PUSEY, D.D. By A. P. FORBES, D.C.L., Bishop of Brechin. Second Edition, in one vol., Post 8vo., 12s.

The Principles of Divine Service;

Or, An Inquiry concerning the True Manner of Understanding and Using the Order for Morning and Evening Prayer, and for the Administration of the Holy Communion in the English Church. By the Rev. PHILIP FREEMAN, M.A., Vicar of Thorverton, and Archdeacon of Exeter, &c. *A Cheaper re-issue.* 2 vols. 8vo., cloth, 16s.

A History of the Book of Common Prayer,

And other Authorized Books, from the Reformation; and an Attempt to ascertain how the Rubrics, Canons, and Customs of the Church have been understood and observed from the same time; with an Account of the State of Religion in England from 1640 to 1660. By the Rev. THOMAS LATHBURY, M.A. Second Edition, with an Index. 8vo., cloth, 10s. 6d.

Catechetical Lessons on the Book of Common Prayer.

Designed to aid the Clergy in Public Catechising. By the Rev. Dr. FRANCIS HESSEY, Incumbent of St. Barnabas, Kensington, Author of "Catechetical Notes on the Parables and Miracles." Illustrating the Prayer-book, from its Title-page to the end of the Collects, Epistles, and Gospels. Fcap. 8vo., cloth, 6s.

A Short Explanation of the Nicene Creed,

For the Use of Persons beginning the Study of Theology. By A. P. FORBES, D.C.L., Bishop of Brechin. Second Edition, Crown 8vo., cloth, 6s.

FOR OXFORD EXAMINATIONS
UNDER THE NEW THEOLOGICAL STATUTE.

The Canons.
The Definitions of the Catholic Faith and Canons of Discipline of the First Four General Councils of the Universal Church. In Greek and English. Fcap. 8vo., cloth, 2s. 6d.

De Fide et Symbolo:
Documenta quædam nec non Aliquorum SS. Patrum Tractatus. Edidit CAROLUS A. HEURTLEY, S.T.P., Dom. Margaretæ Prælector, et Ædis Christi Canonicus. Fcap. 8vo., cloth, 4s. 6d.

Analecta Christiana,
In usum Tironum. Edidit et Annotationibus illustravit C. MARRIOTT, S.T.B. 8vo., 10s. 6d.

S. Aurelius Augustinus,
EPISCOPUS HIPPONENSIS,
De Catechizandis Rudibus, de Fide Rerum quæ non videntur, de Utilitate Credendi. In Usum Juniorum. Edidit C. MARRIOTT, S.T.B., olim Coll. Oriel. Socius. A New Edition, Fcap. 8vo., cloth, 3s. 6d.

Bede's Ecclesiastical History.
A new Translation by the Rev. L. GIDLEY. Crown 8vo., cloth, 6s.

Waterland on the Athanasian Creed.
A Critical History of the Athanasian Creed, by the Rev. DANIEL WATERLAND, D.D. Fcap. 8vo., cloth, 5s.

St. Cyril, Archbishop of Alexandria.
The Three Epistles (ad Nestorium, ii., iii., et ad Joan Antioch). A Revised Text, with an old Latin Version and an English Translation. Edited by P. E. PUSEY, M.A. 8vo., in wrapper, 3s.

Bishop Bull on the Nicene Creed.
Defensio Fidei Nicænæ. A Defence of the Nicene Creed out of the extant writings of the Catholic Doctors who flourished during the three first centuries of the Christian Church, in which also is incidentally vindicated the Creeds of Constantinople concerning the Holy Ghost. By GEORGE BULL, D.D., Lord Bishop of St. David's. A new Translation. 2 vols., 8vo., 10s.

Hooker's Fifth Book.
Of Divine Service. The Sacraments, &c., by Richard Hooker: being Selections from the Fifth Book of the Ecclesiastical Polity. Edited by the late Rev. J. KEBLE. 16mo., 1s. 6d.

Cur Deus Homo, or Why God was made Man;

By ST. ANSELM, sometime Archbishop of Canterbury. Translated into English, with an Introduction, &c. Second Edition, Fcap. 8vo., 2s. 6d.

On Eucharistical Adoration.

By the late Rev. JOHN KEBLE, M.A., Vicar of Hursley.—With Considerations suggested by a late Pastoral Letter (1858) on the Doctrine of the Most Holy Eucharist. 8vo., cloth, 6s. A Cheap Edition, 24mo., sewed, 2s.

The Administration of the Holy Spirit

IN THE BODY OF CHRIST. Eight Lectures preached before the University of Oxford in the Year 1868, on the Foundation of the late Rev. John Bampton, M.A., Canon of Salisbury. By the Right Rev. the LORD BISHOP OF SALISBURY. *Second Edition.* Crown 8vo., 7s. 6d.

JAMES PARKER AND CO.,

The Church's Work in our Large Towns.
By GEORGE HUNTINGTON, M.A., Rector of Tenby, and Domestic Chaplain of the Rt. Hon. the Earl of Crawford and Balcarres. Second Edit., revised and enlarged. Crown 8vo., cl. 6s.

The Church and School:
Or, Hints on Clerical Life. By H. W. BELLAIRS, M.A., One of Her Majesty's Inspectors of Schools. Crown 8vo., cloth, 5s.

A Manual of Pastoral Visitation,
Intended for the Use of the Clergy in their Visitation of the Sick and Afflicted. By A PARISH PRIEST. Dedicated, by permission, to His Grace the Archbishop of Dublin. Second Edition, Crown 8vo., limp cloth, 3s. 6d.; roan, 4s.

The Catechist's Manual;
With an Introduction by SAMUEL, LORD BISHOP OF OXFORD. Fifth Thousand. Crown 8vo., limp cloth, 5s.

Addresses to the Candidates for Ordination on the Questions in the Ordination Service.
By SAMUEL, LORD BISHOP OF OXFORD, Chancellor of the Most Noble Order of the Garter, and Lord High Almoner to Her Majesty the Queen. 5th Thousand. Cr. 8vo., cl., 6s.

The Cure of Souls.
By the Rev. G. ARDEN, M.A., Rector of Winterborne-Came, and Author of "Breviates from Holy Scripture," &c. Fcap. 8vo., cloth, 2s. 6d.

The Church Catechism Explained,
With a view to the Correction of Error in Religion and Viciousness in Life. By the Rev. EDWARD CHEERE, M.A., Perpetual Curate of Little Drayton, Salop. New Edition. Fcap. 8vo., cloth, 2s. 6d.

Questions on the Collects, Epistles, and Gospels,
Throughout the Year. Edited by the Rev. T. L. CLAUGHTON, Vicar of Kidderminster. For the Use of Teachers in Sunday Schools. Fifth Edition, 18mo., cl. In two Parts, *each* 2s. 6d.

Notes of Seven Years' Work in a Country Parish.
By R. F. WILSON, M.A., Vicar of Rownhams, Prebendary of Sarum, and Examining Chaplain to the Bishop of Salisbury. Fcap. 8vo., cloth, 4s.

OXFORD, AND 377, STRAND, LONDON.

DEVOTIONAL WORKS.

A GUIDE FOR PASSING ADVENT HOLILY,
By AVRILLON. Translated from the French, and adapted to the Use of the English Church. Fcap. 8vo., cloth, 5s.

ADVENT READINGS.
Advent Readings from the Fathers. Second Thousand. Fcap. 8vo., cloth, 3s. 6d.

A GUIDE FOR PASSING LENT HOLILY,
By AVRILLON. Translated from the French, and adapted to the Use of the English Church. Fourth Edition. Fcap. 8vo., cloth, 6s.

LENT READINGS FROM THE FATHERS.
Fcap. 8vo., cloth, 5s.

MEDITATIONS FOR THE FORTY DAYS OF LENT.
With a Prefatory Notice by the ARCHBISHOP OF DUBLIN. 18mo., cloth, 2s. 6d.

DAILY STEPS TOWARDS HEAVEN.
A small pocket volume containing a few PRACTICAL THOUGHTS on the GOSPEL HISTORY, with Texts for Every Day in the Year, commencing with Advent. Sixteenth Edition. Bound in roan, 2s. 6d.; morocco, 4s. 6d.
Large Type Edition, square Crown 8vo., cloth, 5s.

THE EVERY-DAY COMPANION.
By the Rev. W. H. RIDLEY, M.A., Rector of Hambleden, Bucks. Fcap. 8vo., cloth, 3s. Separately, Part I. ADVENT TO WHITSUNTIDE, 2s. Part II. WHITSUNTIDE TO ADVENT, 1s. 6d.

PRAYERS FOR MARRIED PERSONS.
From Various Sources, chiefly from the Ancient Liturgies. Selected and Edited by CHARLES WARD, M.A., Rector of Maulden. Second Edition, Revised. 24mo., cloth, 4s. 6d.

THOUGHTS DURING SICKNESS.
By ROBERT BRETT, Author of "The Doctrine of the Cross," &c. Fourth Edition, Fcap. 8vo., limp cloth, 1s. 6d.

OF THE IMITATION OF CHRIST.
Four Books. By THOMAS A KEMPIS. Small 4to., printed on thick toned paper, with red border-lines, mediæval title-pages, ornamental initials, &c. Third Thousand. Cloth, 12s.

TEACHINGS FROM THE CHURCH'S YEAR.
Post 8vo., on toned paper, cloth, 6s.

JAMES PARKER AND CO.,

The Clewer Manuals.
Edited by the Rev. T. T. CARTER, M.A., Rector of Clewer.

PART I. Daily Offices of Prayer and other Devotions. 18mo., 1s.
PART II. Hours of Prayer, Litanies, &c. 18mo., limp cloth, 1s.
PART III. Instructions and Devotions for Adult Baptism and Confirmation. 18mo., limp cloth, 1s.
PART IV. Repentance. 18mo., limp cloth, 1s. 6d.
PART V. No. 1. Instructions on the Holy Eucharist. 18mo., paper covers, 1s.
The second portion of this Part, containing Devotions for the Holy Communion, *is in preparation.*

Forms of Praise and Prayer,
In the Manner of Offices. For Private Use. Edited by the Hon. and Rev. W. H. LYTTELTON, M.A., Rector of Hagley. Crown 8vo., toned paper, limp cloth, 3s. 6d.; roan, 4s.

Earl Nelson's Family Prayers,
With Responsions and Variations for the Different Seasons, for General Use. Sewed, 3d. each; with Psalter, cloth, 9d.

The Calendar of Lessons; for Private or Family Use. Cloth, 6d.

Family Prayers, with the Psalter and a Calendar of Lessons, for the Use of the Master. Cloth, 1s. Fourth revised Edition.

Liturgia Domestica:
Services for every Morning and Evening in the Week. Third Edition. 18mo., 2s. Or in two Parts, 1s. each.

For the Lord's Supper.

DEVOTIONS BEFORE AND AFTER HOLY COMMUNION. Second Edition, in red and black, on toned paper, 32mo., cloth, 2s. With the Service, cloth, 2s. 6d.

THE OLD WEEK'S PREPARATION. Cloth, 2s.

SPIRITUAL COMMUNION, (From PATRICK and WILSON). 4d.

LAKE'S OFFICIUM EUCHARISTICUM. New Edition. Cloth, red edges, 1s. 6d.

BP. WILSON ON THE LORD'S SUPPER. Cloth, 1s.; sewed, 6d. An Edition with Rubrics, &c. cloth, 2s.

DEVOTIONS FOR HOLY COMMUNION FROM HORST. 18mo., 1s.

Oxford Editions of Devotional Works.

Fcap. 8vo., chiefly printed in Red and Black, on Toned Paper.

Andrewes' Devotions.
DEVOTIONS. By the Right Rev. LANCELOT ANDREWES. Translated from the Greek and Latin, and arranged anew. Cloth, 5s.

The Imitation of Christ.
FOUR BOOKS. By THOMAS À KEMPIS. A new Edition, revised. Cloth, 4s.

Laud's Devotions.
THE PRIVATE DEVOTIONS of Dr. WILLIAM LAUD, Archbishop of Canterbury, and Martyr. Antique cloth, 5s.

Spinckes' Devotions.
TRUE CHURCH OF ENGLAND MAN'S COMPANION IN THE CLOSET. By NATHANIEL SPINCKES. Floriated borders, antique cloth, 4s.

Sutton's Meditations.
GODLY MEDITATIONS UPON THE MOST HOLY SACRAMENT OF THE LORD'S SUPPER. By CHRISTOPHER SUTTON, D.D., late Prebend of Westminster. A new Edition. Antique cloth, 5s.

Taylor's Golden Grove.
THE GOLDEN GROVE: A Choice Manual, containing what is to be Believed, Practised, and Desired or Prayed for. By BISHOP JEREMY TAYLOR. Antique cloth, 3s. 6d.

Taylor's Holy Living.
THE RULE AND EXERCISES OF HOLY LIVING. By BISHOP JEREMY TAYLOR. Ant. cloth, 4s.

Taylor's Holy Dying.
THE RULE AND EXERCISES OF HOLY DYING. By BISHOP JEREMY TAYLOR. Ant. cloth, 4s.

Wilson's Sacra Privata.
THE PRIVATE MEDITATIONS, DEVOTIONS, and PRAYERS of the Right Rev. T. WILSON, D.D., Lord Bishop of Sodor and Man. Now first printed entire. Cloth, 4s.

Ancient Collects.
ANCIENT COLLECTS AND OTHER PRAYERS, Selected for Devotional Use from various Rituals, with an Appendix on the Collects in the Prayer-book. By WILLIAM BRIGHT, D.D. Fourth Edition. Antique cloth, 5s.

Devout Communicant.
THE DEVOUT COMMUNICANT, exemplified in his Behaviour before, at, and after the Sacrament of the Lord's Supper: Practically suited to all the Parts of that Solemn Ordinance. 7th Edition, revised. Edited by Rev. G. MOULTRIE. Fcap. 8vo., toned paper, red lines, ant.cl., 4s.

ΕΙΚΩΝ ΒΑΣΙΛΙΚΗ.
THE PORTRAITURE OF HIS SACRED MAJESTY KING CHARLES I. in his Solitudes and Sufferings. Cloth, 5s.

JAMES PARKER AND CO.,

A Memoir of the Rev. John Keble, M.A.,
Late Vicar of Hursley. By the Right Hon. Sir J. T. COLERIDGE, D.C.L. Third Edition, with Corrections and Additions. Post 8vo., on toned paper, in cloth, 10s. 6d.

Letters of Spiritual Counsel and Guidance.
By the late Rev. J. KEBLE, M.A., Vicar of Hursley. Second Edition. Post 8vo., cloth, 6s.

The Life of the Right Reverend Father in God, Thomas Wilson, D.D.,
Lord Bishop of Sodor and Man. Compiled, chiefly from Original Documents, by the late Rev. JOHN KEBLE, M.A., Vicar of Hursley. In Two Parts, 8vo., cloth, 21s.

Memoir of Joshua Watson,
Edited by EDWARD CHURTON, Archdeacon of Cleveland. New Edition, Crown 8vo., cloth, 7s. 6d.

Life of John Armstrong, D.D.,
Late Lord Bishop of Grahamstown. By the Rev. T. T. CARTER, M.A., Rector of Clewer. With an Introduction by the present LORD BISHOP OF WINCHESTER. Third Edition. Fcap. 8vo., with Portrait, cloth, 7s. 6d.

The Life and Contemporaneous Church History of Antonio de Dominis,
Archbishop of Spalatro, which included the Kingdoms of Dalmatia and Croatia; afterwards Dean of Windsor, Master of the Savoy, and Rector of West Ilsley in the Church of England, in the reign of James I. By the late HENRY NEWLAND, D.D., Dean of Ferns. 8vo., cloth, 7s.

Calixtus, Abbot of Konigslutter.
The Life and Correspondence of George Calixtus, Lutheran Abbot of Königslutter. By the Rev. W. C. DOWDING, M.A. Post 8vo., cloth, 8s. 6d.

Footprints on the Sands of Time.
Biographies for Young People. Dedicated to her Nephews and Nieces by L. E. B. Fcap., cloth, 2s. 6d.

OXFORD, AND 377, STRAND, LONDON.

THE AUTHORIZED EDITIONS OF
THE CHRISTIAN YEAR,
With the Author's latest Corrections and Additions.

SMALL 4to. EDITION.

Handsomely printed on toned paper, with red border lines and initial letters.

		s.	d.
Cloth extra	. .	0 10	6
Calf antique	. .	1 0	0
Morocco antique	. .	1 8	0

FOOLSCAP 8VO. EDITION.

		s.	d.
Cloth	. . .	3	6
Morocco, plain	. .	8	0
Morocco, best plain	. .	10	6
Morocco antique	. .	14	0
Calf antique	. .	10	0
Vellum	. . .	10	0

24mo. EDITION.

		s.	d.
Cloth	. . .	2	0
Morocco, plain	. .	6	0
Morocco, best plain	. .	7	6
Morocco antique	. .	10	0
Calf antique	. .	8	0
Vellum	. . .	8	0

32mo. EDITION.

		s.	d.
Cloth, limp	. .	1	0
Cloth boards, gilt edges	.	1	6
Morocco, plain	. .	3	0
Morocco, best plain	. .	7	0
Morocco antique	. .	8	0
Calf antique	. .	6	6
Vellum	. . .	6	6

48mo. EDITION.

		s.	d.
Cloth, limp	. .	0	6
Cloth boards	. .	0	9
Roan	. . .	1	6

FACSIMILE OF THE 1ST EDITION, with a list of the variations from the Original Text which the Author made in later Editions.
2 vols., 12mo., boards . 7 6

AN ILLUSTRATED EDITION will shortly be issued under the direction of the Author's representatives.

NOTICE.—Messrs. PARKER are the sole Publishers of the Editions of the "Christian Year" issued with the sanction and under the direction of the Author's representatives. All Editions without their imprint are unauthorized.

By the same Author.

LYRA INNOCENTIUM. Thoughts in Verse on Christian Children. *Twelfth Edition.* Fcap. 8vo., cloth, 5s.
——— 48mo. edition, limp cloth, 6d.; cloth boards, 1s.

MISCELLANEOUS POEMS BY THE REV. JOHN KEBLE, M.A., Vicar of Hursley. [With Preface by G. M.] *Third Edition.* Fcap., cloth, 6s.

THE PSALTER, OR PSALMS OF DAVID: In English Verse. *Fourth Edition.* Fcap., cloth, 6s.

The above may also be had in various bindings.

A CONCORDANCE TO THE "CHRISTIAN YEAR." Fcap. 8vo., toned paper, cloth, 7s. 6d.

MUSINGS ON THE "CHRISTIAN YEAR;" WITH GLEANINGS FROM THIRTY YEARS' INTERCOURSE WITH THE LATE REV. J. KEBLE, by CHARLOTTE M. YONGE: to which are added Recollections of Hursley, by FRANCES M. WILBRAHAM. *Second Edit.* Fcap. 8vo., cloth, 7s. 6d.

JAMES PARKER AND CO.,

The Child's Christian Year.
Hymns for every Sunday and Holyday throughout the Year. Cheap Edition, 18mo., cloth, 1s.

Hymns on the Imitation of Christ.
THE INNER LIFE. HYMNS on the "Imitation of Christ" by THOMAS A'KEMPIS; designed especially for Use at Holy Communion. By the Author of "Thoughts from a Girl's Life," "Light at Eventide," &c. Fcap. 8vo., cloth, 3s.

The Cross, and Verses of Many Years.
By the Rev. CHARLES NEVILE, M.A., Prebendary of Lincoln, and Rector of Fledborough; and MARIA NEVILE. Fcap. 8vo., cloth, 7s. 6d.

The Mother of Jesus, and other Poems.
By ALAN BRODRICK, M.A., Ex. Coll., Oxon., Vicar of Whittlebury. Second Edition. Limp cloth, 3s.

Poems
By the late Rev. SAMUEL RICKARDS, M.A., Rector of Stowlangtoft. Fcap. 8vo., toned paper, cloth, 3s. 6d.

Poems and Translations.
By E. H. HOUGHTON, M.A. Crown 8vo., limp cloth, 4s.

Hymns on the Litany.
By A. C. Fcap. 8vo., on toned paper, cloth extra, 3s.

The Cleveland Psalter.
The Book of Psalms in English Verse. By E. CHURTON, M.A., Archdeacon of Cleveland. Fcap. 8vo., cloth, 7s. 6d.

By the late Rev. ISAAC WILLIAMS.

THE CATHEDRAL. 32mo., with Engravings, 4s. 6d.; Fcap. 8vo., 7s. 6d.

THOUGHTS IN PAST YEARS. 32mo., cloth, 4s. 6d.

THE BAPTISTERY; or, The Way of Eternal Life. With Thirty-four Plates. A new Edition, 2 vols., Fcap. 8vo., cloth, 14s. Cheap Edition, without Plates, 32mo., cloth, 3s. 6d.

THE CHRISTIAN SCHOLAR. Fcap. 8vo., 10s. 6d.; 32mo., cloth, 4s. 6d.

THE SEVEN DAYS; or, The Old and New Creation. Fcap. 8vo., cloth, 7s. 6d.

OXFORD, AND 377, STRAND, LONDON.

RT. REV. THE LORD BISHOP OF OXFORD.

SERMONS preached before the University of Oxford: Second Series, from 1847 to 1862. By SAMUEL, LORD BISHOP OF OXFORD, Lord High Almoner to the Queen, Chancellor of the Most Noble Order of the Garter. 8vo., cloth, 10s. 6d.

———— THIRD SERIES, from 1863 to 1870. 8vo., cloth, 7s. 6d.

REV. E. B. PUSEY, D.D.

PAROCHIAL SERMONS. Vol. I. From Advent to Whitsuntide. Seventh Edition. 8vo., cloth, 6s.

PAROCHIAL SERMONS. Vol. II. Sixth Edition. 8vo., cloth, 6s.

PAROCHIAL SERMONS preached and printed on Various Occasions. 8vo., cloth, 6s.

NINE SERMONS, preached before the University of Oxford, A.D. 1843—1855. 8vo., cloth. [*Reprinting.*

SERMONS preached before the University of Oxford, between A.D. 1859 and 1872. 8vo., cloth, 6s.

ELEVEN SHORT ADDRESSES during a Retreat of the Companions of the Love of Jesus, engaged in Perpetual Intercession for the Conversion of Sinners. 8vo., cloth, 3s. 6d.

RT. REV. THE LORD BISHOP OF SALISBURY.

SERMONS ON THE BEATITUDES, with others mostly preached before the University of Oxford; to which is added a Preface relating to the recent volume of "Essays and Reviews." New Edition. Crown 8vo., cloth, 7s. 6d.

REV. J. KEBLE.

VILLAGE SERMONS ON THE BAPTISMAL SERVICE. 8vo., cloth, 5s.

SERMONS, OCCASIONAL AND PAROCHIAL. 8vo., cloth, 12s.

REV. R. H. CAVE, M.A.

CHRISTIANITY AND MODERN THOUGHT. Four Advent Sermons, preached (in substance) in the Church of S. Thomas, Stamford Hill, in December, 1871. By ROBERT HAYNES CAVE, M.A. Fcap. 8vo., cloth, 2s. 6d.

Rev. E. Monro.

ILLUSTRATIONS OF FAITH. Eight Plain Sermons:—Abel; Enoch; Noah; Abraham; Isaac, Jacob, and Joseph; Moses; The Walls of Jericho; Conclusions. Fcap. 8vo., cloth, 2s. 6d.

Plain Sermons on the Book of Common Prayer. Fcap. 8vo., cloth, 5s.

Historical and Practical Sermons on the Sufferings and Resurrection of our Lord. 2 vols., Fcap. 8vo., cloth, 10s.

Sermons on New Testament Characters. Fcap. 8vo., 4s.

Lenten Sermons at Oxford.

The Series for 1859. Fcap. 8vo., cloth, 5s.

The Series for 1863. 8vo., cloth, 7s. 6d.

The Series for 1865. 8vo., cloth, 7s. 6d.

The Series for 1866. 8vo., cloth, 7s. 6d.

The Series for 1867. 8vo., cloth, 7s. 6d.

The Series for 1868. 8vo., cloth, 5s.

The Series for 1869. 8vo., cloth, 7s. 6d.

The Series for 1870-71, *in the Press.*

Short Sermons for Family Reading,

Following the Course of the Christian Seasons. First Series. By the Rev. J. W. BURGON, M.A., Vicar of St. Mary-the-Virgin's, Oxford. 2 vols., Fcap. 8vo., cloth, 8s.

SECOND SERIES. 2 vols., Fcap. 8vo., cloth, 8s.

Rt. Rev. J. Armstrong, D.D.

PAROCHIAL SERMONS. By the late Lord Bishop of Grahamstown. Fifth Edition. Fcap. 8vo., cloth, 5s.

SERMONS on the Fasts and Festivals. Third Edition. Fcap. 8vo., cloth, 5s.

Sermons for the Christian Seasons.

SERMONS FOR THE CHRISTIAN SEASONS. First Series. Edited by JOHN ARMSTRONG, D.D., late Lord Bishop of Grahamstown. 4 vols., Fcap. 8vo., cloth, 16s.

———————————— Second Series. Edited by the Rev. JOHN BARROW, D.D., late Principal of St. Edmund Hall, Oxford. 4 vols., Fcap. 8vo., cloth, 16s.

A SERIES OF
TALES ILLUSTRATING CHURCH HISTORY.
Each of the following separately. Price One Shilling.

    I. The CAVE in the HILLS; or, Cæcilius Viriāthus.
   II. The EXILES of the CEBENNA.
  III. The CHIEF'S DAUGHTER.
  IV. The LILY of TIFLIS.
    V. WILD SCENES AMONGST THE CELTS.
  VI. The LAZAR-HOUSE of LEROS.
 VII. The RIVALS: a Tale of the Anglo-Saxon Church.
VIII. The CONVERT of MASSACHUSETTS.
  IX. The QUAY of the DIOSCURI: a Tale of Nicene Times.
    X. The BLACK DANES.
  XI. The CONVERSION of ST. VLADIMIR.
 XII. The SEA-TIGERS: a Tale of Mediæval Nestorianism.
XIII. The CROSS in SWEDEN.
XIV. The ALLELUIA BATTLE; or, Pelagianism in Britain.
 XV. The BRIDE of RAMCUTTAH.
XVI. ALICE of FOBBING.
XVII. The NORTHERN LIGHT.
XVIII. AUBREY DE L'ORNE; or, The Times of St. Anselm.
XIX. LUCIA'S MARRIAGE.
XX. WOLFINGHAM.
XXI. THE FORSAKEN; or, The Times of St. Dunstan.
XXII. THE DOVE OF TABENNA; and THE RESCUE.
XXIII. LARACHE: a Tale of the Portuguese Church.
XXIV. WALTER THE ARMOURER; or, The Interdict.
XXV. THE CATECHUMENS of the COROMANDEL COAST.
XXVI. THE DAUGHTERS OF POLA.
XXVII. AGNES MARTIN; or, The Fall of Wolsey.
XXVIII. ROSE AND MINNIE; or, The Loyalists.
XXIX. DORES DE GUALDIM; a Tale of the Portuguese Revolution of 1640.

Or in Volumes, cloth, lettered, 5s. each.

Vol. I. ENGLAND, vol. i. contains Nos. 1, 5, 7, 10 and 14.
Vol. II. ENGLAND, vol. ii. contains Nos. 16, 18, 21, 24 and 27.
Vol. III. AMERICA AND OUR COLONIES, contains Nos. 3, 8, 20, 25 and 28.
Vol. IV. FRANCE AND SPAIN, contains Nos. 2, 22, 23 and 29.
Vol. V. EASTERN AND NORTHERN EUROPE, contains Nos. 6, 11, 13, 17 and 26.
Vol. VI. ASIA AND AFRICA, contains Nos. 4, 9, 12, 15 and 19.

JAMES PARKER AND CO.,

The Glossary of Architecture Abridged.
A CONCISE GLOSSARY OF TERMS USED IN GRECIAN, ROMAN, ITALIAN, AND GOTHIC ARCHITECTURE.
By JOHN HENRY PARKER, M.A., F.S.A.
A New Edition, revised. Fcap. 8vo., with 470 Illustrations, in ornamental cloth, price 7s. 6d.

Rickman's Gothic Architecture.
AN ATTEMPT TO DISCRIMINATE THE STYLES OF ARCHITECTURE IN ENGLAND, FROM THE CONQUEST TO THE REFORMATION: with a Sketch of the Grecian and Roman Orders. By the late THOMAS RICKMAN, F.S.A. Seventh Edition, with considerable Additions, chiefly Historical, by JOHN HENRY PARKER, M.A., F.S.A., and numerous Illustrations. Medium 8vo., cloth. [*Reprinting.*

Architectural Manual.
AN INTRODUCTION TO THE STUDY OF GOTHIC ARCHITECTURE.
By JOHN HENRY PARKER, M.A., F.S.A.
Fourth Edition, Revised and Enlarged, with 180 Illustrations, and a Glossarial Index. Fcap. 8vo., in ornamental cloth.
[*Reprinting.*

Architectural Topography.
OR, AN ARCHITECTURAL ACCOUNT OF EVERY CHURCH IN

BEDFORDSHIRE, 2s. 6d.
BERKSHIRE, 2s. 6d.
BUCKINGHAMSHIRE, 2s. 6d.
CAMBRIDGESHIRE, 4s.
HUNTINGDONSHIRE, 2s. 6d.
OXFORDSHIRE, 2s. 6d.
SUFFOLK, *with Engravings*, 7s. 6d.

Its Dedication.—Supposed date of Erection or Alteration.—Objects of Interest in or near.—Notices of Fonts.—Glass, Furniture, —and other details.—Also Lists of Dated Examples, Works relating to the County, &c.

OXFORD, AND 377, STRAND, LONDON.

ENGLISH CATHEDRALS.

THE ARCHITECTURAL HISTORY OF CANTERBURY CATHEDRAL. By Professor WILLIS, M.A., F.R.S., &c. With Woodcuts and Plans. 8vo., cloth, 10s. 6d.

THE ARCHITECTURAL HISTORY OF YORK CATHEDRAL. By Professor WILLIS, M.A., F.R.S., &c. With Woodcuts and Plans. 8vo., 2s. 6d.

WESTMINSTER ABBEY.

GLEANINGS FROM WESTMINSTER ABBEY. By GEORGE GILBERT SCOTT, R.A., F.S.A. With Appendices supplying Further Particulars, and completing the History of the Abbey Buildings, by Several Writers. *Second Edition, enlarged.* Medium 8vo., cloth, gilt top, 15s.

CHESTER.

THE MEDIÆVAL ARCHITECTURE OF CHESTER. By JOHN HENRY PARKER, M.A., F.S.A. With an Historical Introduction by the Rev. FRANCIS GROSVENOR. Illustrated by Engravings. 8vo., cloth, 5s.

DOVER.

THE CHURCH AND FORTRESS OF DOVER CASTLE. By the Rev. JOHN PUCKLE, M.A., Vicar of St. Mary's, Dover. With Illustrations from the Author's Drawings. Medium 8vo., cloth, 7s. 6d.

NORTHAMPTON.

ARCHITECTURAL NOTICES of the CHURCHES in the ARCHDEACONRY of NORTHAMPTON. With numerous Illustrations on Wood and Steel. Royal 8vo., cloth, £1 1s.

IFFLEY.

A HISTORY OF THE TOWNSHIP OF IFFLEY, OXFORDSHIRE. By EDWARD MARSHALL, M.A., formerly Fellow of C.C.C. Crown 8vo., cloth, 4s.

JAMES PARKER AND CO.,

MEDIÆVAL GLASS PAINTING.

AN INQUIRY INTO THE DIFFERENCE OF STYLE OBSERVABLE IN ANCIENT GLASS PAINTINGS, especially in England, with Hints on Glass Painting, by the late CHARLES WINSTON. With Corrections and Additions by the Author. *A New Edition.* 2 vols., Medium 8vo., with numerous coloured Engravings, cloth, £1 11s. 6d.

MEDIÆVAL BRASSES.

A MANUAL OF MONUMENTAL BRASSES. Comprising an Introduction to the Study of these Memorials, and a List of those remaining in the British Isles. With Two Hundred Illustrations. By the Rev. HERBERT HAINES, M.A., of Exeter College, Oxford. 2 vols., 8vo., 21s.

MEDIÆVAL IRONWORK.

SERRURERIE DU MOYEN-AGE,

Par RAYMOND BORDEAUX.

Forty Lithographic Plates, by G. Bouet, and numerous Woodcuts.

Small 4to., cloth, 20s.

MEDIÆVAL ARMOUR.

ANCIENT ARMOUR AND WEAPONS IN EUROPE. By JOHN HEWITT, Member of the Archæological Institute of Great Britain. The work complete, from the Iron Period of the Northern Nations to the Seventeenth Century. 3 vols., 8vo., £2 10s.

MEDIÆVAL CASTLES.

THE MILITARY ARCHITECTURE OF THE MIDDLE AGES. From the French of M. VIOLLET-LE-DUC, by M. MACDERMOTT, Esq., Architect. With 151 original French Engravings. Medium 8vo., 21s.

MEDIÆVAL MANNERS AND CUSTOMS.

OUR ENGLISH HOME: Its Early History and Progress. With Notes on the Introduction of Domestic Inventions. *Third Edition.* Crown 8vo., 5s.

OXFORD, AND 377, STRAND, LONDON.

The Prayer-book Calendar.

THE CALENDAR OF THE PRAYER-BOOK ILLUSTRATED. (Comprising the first portion of the "Calendar of the Anglican Church," with additional Illustrations, &c.) With Two Hundred Engravings from Medieval Works of Art. *Sixth Thousand.* Fcap. 8vo., cloth, 6s.

Archæological Handbook.

THE ENGLISH ARCHÆOLOGIST'S HANDBOOK. By HENRY GODWIN, F.S.A. A Summary of the Materials available for Investigation of the Monuments of this Country, from the earliest times to the fifteenth century,—with Tables of Dates, Kings, &c., List of Coins, Cathedrals, Castles, Monasteries, &c. Crown 8vo., cloth, 7s. 6d.

Mediæval Sculpture.

A SERIES OF MANUALS OF GOTHIC ORNAMENT. No. 1. STONE CARVING; 2. MOULDINGS; 3. SURFACE ORNAMENT. 16mo., 1s. each.

Mediæval Sketch-Book.

FACSIMILE OF THE SKETCH-BOOK OF WILARS DE HONECORT, AN ARCHITECT OF THE THIRTEENTH CENTURY. With Commentaries and Descriptions by MM. LASSUS and QUICHERAT. Translated and Edited, with many additional Articles and Notes, by the Rev. ROBERT WILLIS, M.A., F.R.S., Jacksonian Professor at Cambridge, &c. With 64 Facsimiles, 10 Illustrative Plates, and 43 Woodcuts. Royal 4to., cloth, £2 10s. *The English letterpress separate, for the purchasers of the French edition,* 4to., 15s.

The Archæology of Rome.

THE ARCHÆOLOGY OF ROME. By JOHN HENRY PARKER, C.B., M.A., F.S.A. Medium 8vo. Illustrated by Plans, Wood Engravings, &c. [*Nearly ready.*

Christ's Hospital, Abingdon.

"A MONUMENT OF CHRISTIAN MUNIFICENCE;" or, AN ACCOUNT OF THE BROTHERHOOD OF THE HOLY CROSS, AND OF THE HOSPITAL OF CHRIST IN ABINGDON, by FRANCIS LITTLE. 1627. Edited, with an Introduction and Appendix, for the Governors of the Hospital, from a MS. in their possession, by CLAUDE DELAVAL COBHAM, B.C.L., M.A. Fcap. 8vo., cloth, 4s.

A SERIES OF GREEK AND LATIN CLASSICS
FOR THE USE OF SCHOOLS.

GREEK POETS.

	Cloth.	
	s.	d.
Æschylus	3	0
Aristophanes. 2 vols.	6	0
Euripides. 3 vols.	6	6
———— Tragœdiæ Sex	3	6
Sophocles	3	0
Homeri Ilias	3	6
———— Odyssea	3	0

GREEK PROSE WRITERS.

	s.	d.
Æschines in Ctesiphontem, et Demosthenes de Corona	2	0
Aristotelis Ethica	2	0
Herodotus. 2 vols.	6	0
Thucydides. 2 vols.	5	0
Xenophontis Memorabilia	1	4
———— Anabasis	2	0

OXFORD, AND 377, STRAND, LONDON.

LATIN POETS.

	Cloth.
	s. d.
Horatius	2 0
Juvenalis et Persius	1 6
Lucanus	2 6
Lucretius	2 0
Phædrus	1 4
Virgilius	2 6

LATIN PROSE WRITERS.

	s. d.
Cæsaris Commentarii, cum Supplementis Auli Hirtii et aliorum	2 6
——— Commentarii de Bello Gallico	1 6
Cicero de Officiis, de Senectute, et de Amicitia	2 0
Ciceronis Tusc. Disp. Lib. V.	2 0
——— Orationes Selectæ	3 6
Cornelius Nepos	1 4
Livius. 4 vols.	6 0
Sallustius	2 0
Tacitus. 2 vols.	5 0

JAMES PARKER AND CO.,

TEXTS WITH SHORT NOTES.

Uniform with the Series of "Oxford Pocket Classics."

GREEK WRITERS. TEXTS AND NOTES.

SOPHOCLES.

	Sewed.	
	s.	d.
Ajax (*Text and Notes*)	1	0
Electra ,, ...	1	0
Œdipus Rex ,, ...	1	0
Œdipus Coloneus ,, ...	1	0
Antigone ,, ...	1	0
Philoctetes ,, ...	1	0
Trachiniæ ,, ...	1	0

The Notes only, in one vol., cloth, 3s.

ÆSCHYLUS.

Persæ (*Text and Notes*)	1	0
Prometheus Vinctus ,, ...	1	0
Septem Contra Thebas ,, ...	1	0
Agamemnon ,, ...	1	0
Choephoræ ,, ...	1	0
Eumenides ,, ...	1	0
Supplices ,, ...	1	0

The Notes only, in one vol., cloth, 3s. 6d.

OXFORD, AND 377, STRAND, LONDON.

EURIPIDES.

	Sewed.
	s. d.
Hecuba (*Text and Notes*)	1 0
Medea　　　,,	1 0
Orestes　　,,	1 0
Hippolytus　,,	1 0
Phœnissæ　,,	1 0
Alcestis　　,,	1 0

The above Notes only, in one vol., cloth, 3s.

Bacchæ　　,,	1 0

ARISTOPHANES.

The Knights (*Text and Notes*)	1 0
Acharnians　　,,	1 0
The Birds　　　,,	1 6

The Frogs, *in preparation*.

HOMERUS.

Ilias, Lib. I.—VI. (*Text and Notes*)	2 0

DEMOSTHENES.

De Corona (*Text and Notes*)	2 0
Olynthiac Orations　,,	1 0

Philippic Orations, *in the Press*.

ÆSCHINES.

In Ctesiphontem (*Text and Notes*)	2 0

JAMES PARKER AND CO.,

LATIN WRITERS. TEXTS AND NOTES.

VIRGILIUS.

	Sewed.
	s. d.
Bucolica (*Text and Notes*)	1 0
Georgica ,, ...	2 0
Æneidos, Lib. I.—III. ,, ...	1 0

HORATIUS.

Carmina, &c. (*Text and Notes*) . . .	2 0
Satiræ ,, . . .	1 0
Epistolæ et Ars Poetica ,, . . .	1 0

The Notes only, in one vol., cloth, 2s.

PHÆDRUS.

Fabulæ (*Text and Notes*)	1 0

LIVIUS.

Lib. XXI.—XXIV. (*Text and Notes*) cloth, 4s. 6d. ;	4 0

TACITUS.

The Annals (*Notes only*), 2 vols., cloth . .	7 0

CÆSAR.

Lib. I.—III. (*Text and Notes*) . . .	1 0

SALLUSTIUS.

Jugurtha (*Text and Notes*)	1 6
Catilina ,, ...	1 0

M. T. CICERO.

In Q. Cæcilium—Divinatio (*Text and Notes*) .	1 0
In Verrem Actio Prima ,, .	1 0
Pro Lege Manilia, and Pro Archia ,, .	1 0
In Catilinam ,, .	1 0
Pro Plancio ,, .	1 6
Pro Milone ,, .	1 0
Orationes Philippicæ ,, .	1 6

The above Notes only, in one vol., cloth, 3s. 6d.

De Senectute and De Amicitia ,, .	1 0
Epistolæ Selectæ ,, .	1 6

CORNELIUS NEPOS.

Lives (*Text and Notes*)	1 6

Other portions of several of the above-named Authors are in preparation.

EDUCATIONAL WORKS.

JELF'S GREEK GRAMMAR.—A Grammar of the Greek Language, chiefly from the text of Raphael Kühner. By WM. EDW. JELF, B.D., late Student and Censor of Ch. Ch. Fourth Edition, with Additions and Corrections. 2 vols., 8vo., £1 10s.

This Grammar is in general use at Oxford, Cambridge, Dublin, and Durham; at Eton, King's College, London, and most other public schools.

MADVIG'S LATIN GRAMMAR.—A Latin Grammar for the Use of Schools. By PROFESSOR MADVIG, with Additions by the Author. Translated by the Rev. G. WOODS, M.A. A New Edition, with an Index of Authors. 8vo., cloth, 12s.

Competent authorities pronounce this work to be the very best Latin Grammar yet published in England. This new Edition contains an Index to the Authors quoted.

LAWS OF THE GREEK ACCENTS. By JOHN GRIFFITHS, M.A. Fifteenth Edition. 16mo., 6d.

TWELVE RUDIMENTARY RULES for Latin Prose Composition. By EDWARD MOORE, B.D. Second Edition. 16mo., 6d.

RUDIMENTARY RULES, with Examples, for the Use of Beginners in Greek Prose Composition. By JOHN MITCHINSON, D.C.L., Fellow of Pembroke College, Oxford; Head Master of the King's School, and Hon. Canon, Canterbury. 16mo., sewed, 1s.

SYLLABUS OF LATIN PRONUNCIATION. Drawn up at the request of Head-Masters of Schools. 8vo., 3d.

POETARUM SCENICORUM GRÆCORUM, Æschyli, Sophoclis, Euripidis, et Aristophanis, Fabulæ, Superstites, et Perditarum Fragmenta. Ex recognitione GUIL. DINDORFII. Editio quinta. One Vol., Royal 8vo., cloth, 21s.

THUCYDIDES, with Notes, chiefly Historical and Geographical. By the late T. ARNOLD, D.D. With Indices by the Rev. R. P. G. TIDDEMAN. Seventh Edition. 3 vols., 8vo., cloth lettered, £1 16s.

JAMES PARKER AND CO.,

Uniform with the Series of the "Oxford Pocket Classics."
THE LIVES OF THE MOST EMINENT ENGLISH POETS: WITH CRITICAL OBSERVATIONS ON THEIR WORKS. By SAMUEL JOHNSON. 3 vols., 24mo., cloth, 2s. 6d. each.

CHOICE EXTRACTS FROM MODERN FRENCH AUTHORS, for the Use of Schools. 24mo., cloth, 3s.

ANNALS OF ENGLAND. An Epitome of English History. From Cotemporary Writers, the Rolls of Parliament, and other Public Records. 3 vols., Fcap. 8vo., with Illustrations, cloth, 15s. *Recommended by the Examiners in the School of Modern History at Oxford.*
 Vol. I. *From the Roman Era to the Death of Richard II.*
 Vol. II. *From the Accession of the House of Lancaster to Charles I.*
 Vol. III. *From the Commonwealth to the Death of Queen Anne.*
 The Volumes separately, 5s. each.

A LIBRARY EDITION, Revised and Enlarged, with additional Woodcuts, in one volume, 8vo., *in the Press.*

THE NEW SCHOOL-HISTORY OF ENGLAND. By the Author of "The Annals of England." Sixth Thousand. Crown 8vo., with Four Maps, limp cloth, 5s.

ERASMI COLLOQUIA SELECTA: Arranged for Translation and Re-translation; adapted for the Use of Boys who have begun the Latin Syntax. By EDWARD C. LOWE, D.D., Head Master of S. John's Middle School, Hurstpierpoint. Fcap. 8vo., strong binding, 3s.

PORTA LATINA: A Selection from Latin Authors, for Translation and Re-translation; arranged in a Progressive Course, as an Introduction to the Latin Tongue. By EDWARD C. LOWE, D.D., Head Master of Hurstpierpoint School; Editor of Erasmus' "Colloquies." Fcap. 8vo., strongly bound, 3s.

Η ΚΑΙΝΗ ΔΙΑΘΗΚΗ. The Greek Testament with English Notes. By the Rev. EDWARD BURTON, D.D., sometime Regius Professor of Divinity in the University of Oxford. Sixth Edition, with Index. 8vo., cloth, 10s. 6d.

OXFORD, AND 377, STRAND, LONDON.

Crown 8vo., in roan binding, 12s.; calf limp, or calf antique, 16s.; best morocco, or limp morocco, 18s.

THE SERVICE-BOOK OF THE CHURCH OF ENGLAND,

BEING A NEW EDITION OF "THE DAILY SERVICES OF THE UNITED CHURCH OF ENGLAND AND IRELAND,"
ARRANGED ACCORDING TO THE NEW TABLE OF LESSONS.

THE PUBLISHERS' PREFATORY NOTE.

IN 1849, the revival of Daily Service in many of our parish churches suggested the publication of a volume containing those portions of the Bible which were appointed for the First and Second Lessons printed together with so much of the Prayer-book as was required in the Daily Service of the Church.

In 1856, a new edition being required, several improvements were adopted, and references given, by which the Daily Lessons were rendered available for use in reading the Sunday Lessons also.

The new "Prayer-book (Table of Lessons) Act, 1871," has necessitated reprinting nearly the whole book, and opportunity has been taken of still further adding to the improvements.

The Lessons appointed for the Immoveable Festivals are printed entire in the course of the Daily Lessons where they occur. For the Sundays and Moveable Festivals, and for the days dependent on them, a table containing fuller references, with the initial words and ample directions where the Lesson may be found, is given. Where the Lesson for the Moveable Feast is not included entire amongst the Daily Lessons, it is printed in full in its proper place. Also in the part containing Daily Lessons, greater facilities have been provided for verifying the references.

There are also many modifications in the arrangement, wherein this Service-book differs from the Prayer-book: the Order for the Administration of the Holy Communion is printed as a distinct service, with the Collects, Epistles, and Gospels, which belong to the same: the Psalms immediately follow Daily Morning and Evening Prayer: the Morning and Evening Lessons also are by this arrangement brought nearer to the Service to which they belong, while the Occasional Offices are transferred to the end of the book. This plan of arrangement will shew the aim and object of the work, viz. to provide a convenient and portable volume for those persons who have the privilege of attending the appointed Daily Service in the Church or read it in their own houses.

JAMES PARKER AND CO., OXFORD AND LONDON.

www.ingramcontent.com/pod-product-compliance
Lightning Source LLC
Chambersburg PA
CBHW021150230426
43667CB00006B/333